CLIMBING
THE TREE...

AND
FALLING

A MEMOIR
BY M. A. WAJED

SKYSCRAPER

SKYSCRAPER PUBLICATIONS

Climbing the Tree ... and Falling

First published 2018 by Skyscraper Publications
20 Crab Tree Close, Bloxham, Oxon OX15 4SE, U.K.
www.skyscraperpublications.com

First published 2018

A CIP catalogue record for this book is available
from the British Library.

ISBN-13: 978-1-911072-28-7

Cover concept, design and typesetting
by chandlerbookdesign.com

Printed by CPI Group (UK) Ltd, Croydon CR0 4YY

Dedication

*This book is dedicated to my deceased parents,
who are buried side by side in a village graveyard
in Bangladesh where I was born. It was their total
sacrifice in life made me of what I am today.*

C O N T E N T S

PART III TOWARDS THE FALL

PART IV AFTER THE FALL

Foreword

I have had the pleasure of knowing Dr Wajed since 1957 when we were medical students together at Chittagong Medical College. He was very studious and his favourite subject was medicine and I recall he used to carry a copy of 'Davidson's Book of Medicine' with him at all times.

One thing that I have always admired about him was his habitual diary writing. Not only was it consistent but he used to write in highly poetic way when documenting all his doing of the day. Once, the topic arose and somehow he forced me also to write a daily diary. Now, since 1963, I too write daily.

This memoir has a vividness and an immediacy precisely because he has kept his diaries in which he recorded over the decades a series of events that range from high humour to deep tragedy, all told accurately and movingly.

He is an unassuming man of 5 feet 10 inches, medium build, modestly dressed, wearing glasses for his myopic eye sight, yet endowed with a clear memory of the past and a vision of the future. But beyond his physicality, he is a man laden with humility despite an unmatchable record of professional and academic achievements. He is enthusiastic and inquisitive like a young child, cheerful and evoking happy responses by his unique style of humour; interacting with patients, colleagues, juniors and seniors with equal interest and cheerfulness; dynamic in pursuit of his goals.

When Dr Wajed asked me to write this foreword, I hesitated to try to capture his character and his good qualities in a few sentences. I am still unable to fully express the beauty of his character that I have had the privilege to become acquainted with. I can only say that I'm sure his words, and this book will do him more justice than my simple comments.

In friendship

Brig (R) M. Salim SI(M)
MBBS, FCPS, FRCA, D.Sc PhD,
Professor Emeritus Anaesthesiology & MSc Pain Medicine
Riphah International University, Islamabad

Prologue

" **Y**outh is a blunder, manhood a struggle and old age is a repentance" – I read these words somewhere in my youth and they have remained with me. But for me life had been a struggle since the day I was born. This was the struggle to survive in the hostile world, in the face of disease, deprivation, lack of human empathy and many other factors.

This manuscript was completed about 20 years ago, at a time when I was caused to think deeply about my life, following a catastrophic event.

'Climbing the Tree and Falling ...' as title says, has similarities with my life.

I was born in a remote village, Dharmadaha, in the Province of Bengal, then under British rule. My village became part of Pakistan (East Pakistan) on the Partition of India in 1947, and after the 1971 Liberation Struggle it is now the People's Republic of Bangladesh.

The village had no motorable road, no electricity, the nearest railway station was 20 miles away and the nearest hospital was 36 miles away. The only transport was bicycles for those who could afford them, otherwise bullock carts.

There were about a thousand families in the village, divided equally between Hindus and Muslims. Both communities lived happily for many generations without any conflict, but after Partition, all the Hindus migrated to India.

In Dharmadaha, everyone was known to each other. All the elders knew whose son I was. There was a group of six to eight boys of various ages, between ten and sixteen, who would roam the orchards belonging to the villagers. It was a kind of adventure to nick fruits from other people's trees. This ritual act was accepted and tolerated by everybody, with a certain amount of scolding when caught.

Every generation of children enjoyed the poem called 'Lichu Chor' (Lycee Thief) by the national poet of Bangladesh, Kazi Nazrul Islam (1899–1976), written about a hundred years ago, describing how a group of boys climbed a lychee tree, and as one of them was trying to pick the ripe ones, the branch broke and the boy fell on to the shoulder of the gardener who was having his midday nap. The gardener chased him, but the boy got away.

So in my childhood I was in the company of a wild group of boys, who would steal fruit, mainly mangoes, blackberries, jack fruit and lychees. These fruits are seasonal, and ripen in the rainy season. We knew that in the morning after heavy rain, the fruit would be ripe for picking. The trees are often big with wide trunks and slippery with rain. It was not possible to get up the tree in the usual way. Sometimes one of us would climb on the shoulder of a strong boy, then try to get higher in the tree. On other occasions, we would pull down a branch, and then cling upside down on all fours like a monkey and get to the top branch to get the ripe fruit. Some boys would be on the lookout for the owner, while others would collect the fruit being dropped from the top. Usually this process worked well, but accidents did happen, where a branch snapped and a boy fell, breaking a limb.

Once we targeted a palm tree. Young palms have a tender soft, juicy interior, which is extremely delicious. In Bangladesh it is called 'Taal Sanch'. One boy, named Ala, was particularly good at climbing the branchless palm tree. He started climbing, holding a knife in his teeth. From the top of the tree, he released a few bunches, which fell to the ground with huge thuds. The owner was nearby and came running towards us. All the boys ran away, except me, and Ala at the top of the tree. The owner whom we knew was very surprised to see me in the company of such a wild group. He said: "If you wanted some of it, why didn't you ask me? I could have taken it to your house". What could I say? I apologised profusely and begged him not to tell my father. He didn't.

On another occasion, a boy from our group, named Benu, fell from the tree and broke his left arm. He was in severe pain but there was no medical help. Village charlatans put a bamboo stake on either side of the broken arm and bandaged it with old clothes. He survived. After I went to medical school, I used to see him in the village, with his broken left arm which was a few inches shorter than the right but he was able to do manual work to make a living.

In some ways, I feel that the progress of my life has some resemblance to those incidents:

I managed to climb to the top of my tree of life with great difficulty, standing on the shoulders of my parents and elder brothers. Against all the odds, which included poverty, deprivation, disease, and the lack of understanding in those around me, I managed to become a doctor, which was totally unexpected. And to come to the UK and become a Consultant Physician was like a dream.

I had a happy marriage, with three healthy children at various stages of education, in the best university of the land. I thought I had succeeded in life, and reached the top of the tree to pick the desired fruit.

Then a branch snapped. I fell from the top of the tree with a totally unexpected family tragedy and now I feel as if I have broken a limb and am continuing to limp towards the end.

This book is primarily written to express myself and in doing so, if any character, alive or dead, or their descendants find any comments uncomfortable, it could not be helped, for I had to tell the truth as it happened. Suppressing some of the facts or omitting it altogether would not have served the purpose of the memoir.

Perhaps this book will encourage children from under-privileged backgrounds to believe that no matter how adverse the circumstances, and whatever the obstacles, – financial, social, racial – if one has the burning desire to succeed in life and has high ambition, it is possible to achieve it.

I end this Prologue by quoting a few lines from a Bengali poet, K. C. Mazumder (1837–1907). The rough translation is "O traveller, why do you tire seeing the long road ahead? Who can succeed without enthusiasm? Why do you stop seeing a thorn while plucking a flower? Can you enjoy the pleasure without going through the pain?"

Map of British India, 1937

Childhood

do not know precisely how old I am. I don't know my exact birthday. People in the Western world will probably laugh at this statement, but this is the fact. Even now in rural Bangladesh or India people do not have any system of recording their births. There are no birth certificates for most of the children born in rural areas, who constitute 80% of the population, because childbirth takes place at home. It is only at the time of the census every ten years or so that a head count is done in every household. Though my father was literate, he never recorded the date of my birth anywhere. My mother was illiterate and used to say I was born in winter on a Saturday. So I actually don't know when or which day I was born. Knowing your birthdate is not necessary until taking the GCSE, or Matriculation Examination as it was called in those days. When my time came to sit the Matriculation Examinations a date had to be invented and mine was the 18th July, 1937. In fact, I had the opportunity to confirm the approximate date when I later learnt that there had been an attempt on the life of my father when I was three months old. That incident happened in 1937.

When I was born at home, no doctor or midwife attended and, in fact, there was no help of any kind. Accidents could happen and I saw two or three deaths in the village, some of them our close relatives. Sometimes both mother and child died. I am also certain that my umbilical cord was severed with a "bamboo split", a natural knife made from the bark of a thick bamboo cane. I know this because my mother told me that my umbilicus was infected and took a long time to heal. When my eldest brother's eldest son was born in the mid-forties his umbilical cord was severed with a bamboo split and the result was that he died within a few days from tetanus, a common cause of death in rural areas in those days. The first symptom is muscle spasm of the mouth which means that babies cannot suck their mother's milk and they die of starvation. Village folk used to believe that the child had been possessed by an evil spirit, and tried various useless remedies.

The family in which I was born used to be called "middle-class" by Bengal standards, but to all intents and purposes we were born poor. We were called middle-class because we could afford two square meals a day, whereas the vast majority of the villagers did not. Many of them had only one meal a day or even less food than that.

The village in which I was born was remote. The nearest railway station was 20 miles away. There were no vehicular roads, no clinics, no electricity – virtually nothing. In 1937, the village population would have been around a thousand people. Fifty per cent were Hindu, and the rest were Muslim. Our house was at the end of the Muslim section. Most of the houses in the village were mud huts with straw thatched roofs. Only our house had a corrugated tin roof, which gave our family a bit more respectability than the rest, and enhanced our prestige. There were hardly any brick-built houses in the village, perhaps no more than three or four. Both communities lived in peace and harmony. The Hindus were slightly better off, literate and a little sophisticated, whereas the Muslims were mainly labourers, landowning peasants who lived on the products of the land. Although only 8-10% of people on average were literate, illiteracy was more acute amongst the Muslims. As far as I know, my grandfather, who may have been born in the early part of the nineteenth century, had been the only literate Muslim in the village. My grandfather married twice. In his first marriage, there were three sons, of which my father was the youngest.

My grandmother died when my father was a few months old, so he was brought up by my maternal great-grandmother, who died at a very great age, virtually blind and immobile. Everybody used to call her *"Karta"* - the elder. My grandfather married again, and there were two sons and a daughter. My step grandmother survived a long time, so I knew her, beautiful and elegant even in her old age.

Among my uncles, my father was the only one who went to school. He went to the village primary school and was probably the only Muslim student, with his teacher and all the students being Hindus. After he finished his primary education, it would have been expected for him to go to the secondary school, just across the river in Shikarpore. But he never continued his studies because the family was poor and he had to look after himself as my grandfather was busy with his young family. Like me, my father never knew his birthday but he used to say that "he was seven years old the year when there was a big earthquake". Later I found out that the earthquake was in 1897, when there were many casualties, particularly in nearby Assam, now a Province of India.

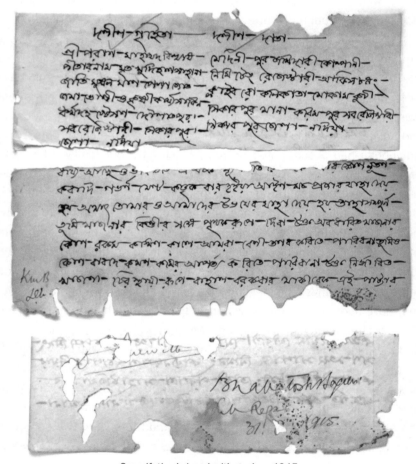

Grandfather's handwriting, circa 1915

As a memento of my grandfather's literacy, I have a sample of his writing written with a quill pen on old fashioned paper. Those who knew how to read and write used to be called "Biswas" and hence our family name was "Biswas", a name which was abandoned after the creation of Pakistan in 1947, as it was closely linked with the Hindu religion.

I had five siblings, two brothers and three sisters. I was the youngest by far. I must have been born when my father was in his late forties or early fifties, after my eldest brother had already married. Because I was the youngest child, I was over-protected by everyone. My mother used to say that she had asked for another boy – "who would tend the cattle and goats", because the servants used to be erratic and leave without any notice, causing immense trouble within the household.

When I was no more than three or four months old, a terrible disaster befell our family. This was such a calamity that in later years, my mother, brother and sisters used to talk about it in choking voices and with tears in their eyes. The family survived the ordeal but it left a deep scar both physically and mentally. The incident must have happened sometime in 1937, and concerned a plot of land my father bought to build a house, for his family, including his six children. The land was purchased legitimately, but, as I learnt later, the man from whom the land was bought was illiterate and aggressive. He was misled by a group of villagers who did not see eye to eye with my father and told the previous owner that when the land was sold to my father, a small pond at the end of the plot was not included and that therefore my father was not allowed to fish there. Of course, the truth was that the pond was included in the land and our family was horrified to be told that they could not fish there.

Apparently, one morning while my father was going to the pond to catch fish, the aggressive man who had sold the land attacked my father from behind and stabbed him in the back of the neck, in the chest and other places. with a sharp scythe-like instrument.

I saw the scar in my father's neck as a boy and later as a medical student. It was a 6- to 8-inch slash at the nape of the neck. It must have cut the skin, muscles and maybe some vertebrae. If it had been at the side, crucial blood vessels such as jugular veins or carotid arteries would have been severed.

Villagers knew that he might be attacked, but none warned him. My father lay unconscious on the ground, and my uncle, my father's eldest brother, came running and got my father in his arms. My eldest brother, a young man of about 25, was told about the attack while he was tilling the land in a nearby field, and he went berserk. Instead of helping with my injured father, he was hell-bent on killing the man who inflicted the injury and had to be restrained by villagers.

My father was taken to a hospital where he was given stitches and looked after, and he survived, making a full recovery. The assailant was prosecuted for attempted murder and jailed. When he was released, he left the village with his family and we heard later that he died pitifully, blind and helpless, while my father led a very successful life and lived until the age of 97.

The incident happened eighty years ago and we are still living on the same plot of land containing the same pond which still has abundant fish in it.

My eldest brother must have been born around 1914 or 1915. He was very handsome in his youth and went to primary school and on to the nearby high secondary school, where my father had wanted to study but could not afford it. My mother told me that my brother was not keen on study and would rather play cards or football during school hours. I never heard him regret not doing well at school. Being the eldest son of the family, he had tremendous responsibilities and soon found himself looking after the land and growing crops for the family. He managed whatever land my father had with the help of one or two servants. There was poverty, but it was a happy family, before the tragedy of the attempted murder of my father.

My second brother was six years younger than the eldest. In the village, he was known to be a hard-working and intelligent boy, going to the village primary school and on to the prestigious secondary school. In fact, when I later looked at his performance and the results, he was below average. But he managed to pass the Matriculation Examination in 1941 in the third division, which was an achievement for a Muslim boy. Indeed, he was one of the very few Muslims in our area who completed a secondary education, and was entitled to go on to study at college or university.

Though my brother was ready to continue his education and my father did find some money to send him to a prestigious college, fate intervened and my sister fell ill. It was 1941, when World War II was raging, Japan was on the borders of Bengal, and Bengal itself was in the grip of a terrible famine. My father's savings were exhausted and my brother never made it to university.

No one escaped the terrible scourge of the Bengal famine of 1942/43, but we were less affected than many because, living in an agrarian society, we always had food available at home. It may not have been wholesome, but at least it kept us going. The people who suffered most were people like weavers, labourers and other trades who had to depend on their technical skills rather than the produce of the land.

Because of the war effort, there were jobs available in 1941-42. My brother got a job in Calcutta, which was the capital of Bengal. People from the village thronged the city in search of work and food. Calcutta was on the frontline of the war with Japan and there was hardly any food or civil administration. Whatever food was there was hoarded by corrupt businessmen to get higher prices. The result was death – the deaths of people in their thousands. My brother and others who were in Calcutta at that time would come and tell us that at night there was usually a blackout for Japanese bombers. As you walked the dark streets you were as likely to trip on a dead body as on rubble or some other obstacle.

I was barely four or five years old so I don't know if anybody died of starvation in our village. The available food was rationed and never enough for any family. I saw people walking who looked like skeletons. There were thefts almost every night – fruit from a jackfruit tree or crops from the fields.

The main effects of the famine on our family were due to lack of cash. There were essential items we needed that could only be bought in the village shop, but most of them weren't available, apart from cooking salt, so we had to make do in other ways.

There was no soap, for example, either for washing clothes or for personal use. For washing clothes, we had to burn old and withered banana leaves, which were in plentiful supply, into fine ashes which were then kept in an earthen jar. A few spoonfuls would be used in boiling water along with the dirty clothes. After boiling for about half an hour or more, the clothes would be taken to the nearest water source, usually the river, and thoroughly battered over a wooden platform. This would clean them nicely and then they could dry quickly in the scorching sunshine. Heavily soiled clothes would be boiled in a similar way but with a different ash called *khar*, from other types of burnt vegetation.

During the war, I saw in the shops a ball of washing soap which would be sold by cutting pieces off it, with the price depending on the weight. Only the well-to-do with some cash would be able to afford it.

Another scarce item for our family was paper. As 95% of people were illiterate, most people had no need for paper. It was only in our household that we used it, for writing letters and keeping household accounts. These were written by my father on coarse, buff-coloured paper. Those who had a connection with the nearby European settlement at Shikarpore used to get relatively good quality paper. One of my cousins worked for them and I remember he brought some A4 sized white paper which I cherished.

Our main day-to-day work for school was written on palm leaves. Palm leaves grow everywhere and young leaves were harvested and then separated from the stocks. The leaves are naturally green, but they had to be decomposed under the water for four weeks and then sun-dried, after which they had to be cut into equal-sized pieces and each leaf would be used as one page. So as primary school pupils we would take a dozen or so leaves to school and the teacher would mark our writing and correct the sums. Once a leaf had been used it could be washed and re-used again.

The only ink available to buy was in the form of a tablet. One or even half a tablet would be dissolved in an inkpot and we would use a pen with a detachable nib to write with it. You could buy the handle and the nib separately. But this was not the ink we used in the primary school. We used ink produced locally at home. This was done by burning barley until it became black. It then had to be ground with a pestle and mortar and water added to it. It would make lovely water-soluble black ink, which we stored in a big bottle and then transferred to ink pots, for daily use.

We also made the pens at home, rather than buying them, either from branches of bamboo shoot called *kanchi* or from cane, or sometimes from duck feathers. My father would make a lovely pen with a sharp knife and we would write with our homemade ink of burnt barley on the palm leaves. This was life at the village school for me and the other children.

I did hear a rumour that there were pens where you did not have to dip the nib in the ink every time you wrote a word or sentence. But I never saw a fountain pen until much later.

The clothes we wore were very basic. Almost 99% of people went barefoot and the only clothes they wore were to cover the bare essentials in the form of a loin cloth. In most cases these were woven by the local weavers who were craftspeople and their techniques passed on from father to son. These people used to buy cheap thread in bulk and then gradually and patiently unravel them and in their makeshift workshops they would make clothes. They were part of the community but lived in their own areas, and normally their children would only marry within their community, either from the same village or villages nearby. So there was no intermingling at the social level with the rest of the population. Although they were Muslims, they used to be regarded as slightly inferior socially to the farming community.

As schoolchildren at the village school we would only wear shorts with, perhaps, a short-sleeved shirt or vest. Virtually all the children and even the teachers went barefoot most of the year.

But in the winter, footwear became more necessary. The men would wear homemade wooden sandals called *kharam*, and farmers would wear roughly made footwear called *panai* made from cowhide. Also, there was a community of people, usually lower class Hindus, who would make shoes. These people were called *Chamars*, one of the castes known as 'untouchables'. They would take measurements and make a bespoke shoe for you. Not everybody could afford these shoes, but I remember wearing one or two pairs as a child through the winter season. I was proud to show off my new shoes with socks to others.

These *Chamars* used to live in an area outside the village where they had no contact with upper-class Hindus or the Muslims. There was another group of people living nearby called *Moochi*. Their job was to collect hide and skin from dead animals, process them very crudely and then sell them. When these people used to visit our house for any reason they would not sit on a bench, but lower down on the ground.

With the partition of India in 1947, all these Hindu groups suddenly disappeared. They crossed over the border into India and are no doubt still living the same sort of segregated existence.

There were hardly any families in our village who could afford two square meals of rice a day. Even in our household, which was supposed to be 'rich', we had rice with vegetable curry at night, and some crude chapati made from grain or lentils for midday meals. Breakfast was leftover rice from the previous night.

The majority of people were undernourished and would perhaps have only one meal a day. This was the situation during the early and mid-1940s but it improved after the end of the War and particularly after Independence.

There was no running water. Most of the people used river water, which was heavily polluted and carried various diseases, including cholera.

In a few houses, including our own, there was a well, but even here the water was impure but a little bit better than the river water.

There were no means of sewage disposal. People simply went into the bush to relieve themselves. Much later, I managed to build a lavatory for our household.

The only form of wheeled transport in our local area was by bullock cart, usually the property of the well-to-do, and there were no motorable roads, only mud tracks. Moving crops, people and other commodities would be by bullock carts, but the poorer people would just carry goods on their heads.

(2)

Growing Up

I was probably about five years old in 1942 so my memories of life in the village are sometimes vague. The Muslims were poor, mainly an agrarian society, eking out an existence by tilling the land, which was mainly owned by the Hindus. Among the Hindus, there was a caste system and the children of higher caste used to go to school, well dressed and expected to go to higher education. The children of the lower caste Hindus were very much like Muslims, earning their livelihood from the land. I remember that Muslim labourers would work for the Hindus and eat and drink in their houses, but never the other way round. Muslims were regarded as lower class and treated in the same way as lower class untouchable Hindus.

Our house was at the end of the Muslim area, where the Hindu area started. One of the Hindu men used to own a grocery shop, a family business. Often, my mother would send me to buy something from the shop, perhaps common salt or washing soda. These would be wrapped in paper and left in place and I would collect it. When handing over the money I would have to drop it from a height of eight to ten inches into the shopkeeper's hand. The whole purpose was to avoid the shopkeeper touching me, a mere boy of five or six. This happened with all the Muslims. It was accepted by everyone as a social custom, because Muslims were regarded as "untouchables".

One day a Hindu from another village needed drinking water. Because he did not know the village well, he came to our house. We were prepared to give him water, but when he learned that we were Muslim he insisted on getting the water himself from our well, which is inside the house. My brother refused to do that and off the man went without water.

When elderly Hindus and Muslims got together for recreation and conversation they would usually smoke a water pipe called a *hookah*. But the Hindus wanted to avoid smoking from the same pipe as a Muslim so it would be wrapped in mango leaves.

The conversation in our society in 1942 was mainly about the war. The older people would be always talking about the British and the Germans and the Japanese, and saying the names of Hitler and Churchill. When I listened I thought they were single individuals fighting one another.

My earliest recollection of war was of flights of aeroplanes flying ten to twelve in a group. I didn't know how to count, but at the sound of the aeroplanes, village folk would come out and count them 1-2-3-4. I also remember one plane connected by a rope to another. Village folk used to say that the one being towed had "broken down" as if it was one car towing another. Many years later I realised they were gliders, for transporting troops behind the enemy lines in Burma.

There was an enormous effort from the British Government to recruit people to join the war. Even from our own village about ten young men joined up, including my brother-in-law and my elder brother. My brother-in-law was the eldest son of his family, from a village about ten miles further north. He was a gentleman, educated at village standard but was totally disliked by his father who had a second wife, and would not give any property or land to the children of his previous marriage. When the opportunity came, he joined the British army and left his wife, my sister, and his 3-year-old son with us in our house. He was posted to the Middle East, to Iraq.

My elder brother was very young. He sat his GCSE in 1941, but his results were not good and my father did not have the resources to send him on to higher education, so he joined up and was sent to Calcutta. He trained as an air raid warden, to see that people stayed indoors when the air raid sirens sounded.

In rural Bengal in 1942 there was no radio, no newspaper, and little means of communication with the wider world, but the news of the war in Europe and in the Far East filtered through, and elders discussed such events as the fall of Rangoon and bombing of Calcutta. The lives of ordinary people were devastated by the effects of the war and famine, and epidemics of cholera, malaria, dysentery and other parasitic diseases. The life expectancy of the population at that time was barely more than 40 years.

Our village was struck by an epidemic of cholera in 1942. Cholera is caused by water-borne bacilli, and the faeces and vomit of a sufferer are contaminated with it. The village people did not know the causes and village after village was wiped out, particularly when the rainy season was just over and dry season had not yet started. Both Hindus and Muslims believed that it was a curse or an evil spirit that causes such devastation and death. Elders used to discuss with great fear that cholera had arrived in an adjacent village and could strike our village at any time. People were frightened to go out at night in case the evil spirit attacked them. There were no lights, no roads, the fields were still muddy, mosquitoes were everywhere, frogs called, crickets chirruped, and people huddled inside their houses, terrified of cholera. No one knew that it was a waterborne disease and so no one took any precautions.

There was no government-sponsored publicity campaign, and of course no question of vaccination. The Government of India was too busy with the war and how to prevent the fall of India to a Japanese invasion.

So cholera arrived in our village. I did not know much about it or that it could cause death. At the age of five, I was not even frightened of death as I had little experience of it.

My eldest sister at that time was in her late twenties, very healthy and beautiful. She had a three-year-old son. I, two years older, did not get on well with him. His father was away in the Middle East in the British Army. Very often I was asked to look after him when my mother and sisters were busy with housework. Early one morning in 1942 when I woke up, I found my sister lying on the veranda of the house virtually unconscious. My mother and other womenfolk were clustered around her and they were wailing loudly. It turned out that she had been struck by cholera at the dead of night and by the daybreak she was exhausted and virtually unconscious. In fact, she died soon afterwards. I remember her lying flat, as if in a deep sleep and the whole family crying loudly, particularly my mother who was uncontrollable, wailing over her daughter's body while other womenfolk tried to comfort her. Meanwhile, my sister's small son did not know what was going on and thought his mother was asleep and so he started sucking her breast. When I think about that today, I feel what a pathetic and heart-rendering sight that was.

Meanwhile, there were other families who also been affected in the nearby houses and there had been many other deaths. According to Muslim and village customs, the dead have to be buried as soon as possible. All the arrangements, mainly digging a grave, washing the body, and clothing it in a white shroud, are carried out by close relatives and the extended village family. While the arrangements were under way for the burial of my sister, it became apparent that my eldest brother had also been infected. He kept going to the toilet and by the time my sister was buried, he was seriously ill.

After the burial, the relatives and village folk left and there were only my parents and a few servants around to cope with the new emergency, my brother's infection, and all they could do was sit around my eldest brother's bed and pray to Allah. There was no medicine, no saline drip and no doctor of any kind. Night fell and there was no food in the house. My uncle's family (my father's elder brother) invited us to eat with them. I do not remember who else was at that meal, but I do remember that I didn't like the food and I could not eat.

I came home, which was virtually next door. It was dark, the ground was soft, and I had an eerie feeling. I had witnessed one death in the family, and my brother was seriously ill and might die at any moment. Although it was early in the night, everything seemed ominous in the dark. There was the howling of jackals from the nearby forest and it was pitch dark everywhere, interrupted only by the brief flashes of fireflies.

I soon felt unwell myself, wanting to go often to the toilet but only producing pure water, and when I told my mother this, they immediately knew that I too have been attacked by cholera. I remember going to the toilet once more and then nothing. When I regained consciousness, my legs and arms were racked with painful cramps and my father was trying to massage them with warm mustard oil and trying to keep the limbs straight. All the time he was uttering a verse from the Holy Quran, the phrase "there is no god but Allah and the Prophet Mohammed, praise be upon him, is his messenger"

What a night that was for my parents. One daughter already dead and two of their sons seriously ill and at death's door. In that situation, there was no medical help, and not even any moral or emotional support, for people were frightened to visit the stricken family in case the evil spirit afflicted them.

A few days passed, of which I have no memory as I remained unconscious. When I finally opened my eyes, I saw a few oranges in a bowl on a nearby table. I started to stand up but my mother rushed to stop me. My legs were weak and jelly-like and there were ulcers behind my elbows and buttocks. As a doctor, I now know they were bedsores, so I must have been lying in unconscious in one position for many hours. It took long time for those ulcers to heal.

Those oranges and few other things had been brought for me by my brother from Calcutta. He was sent a telegram only saying "younger brother seriously ill". I saw him and my eyes glittered. Somehow the danger passed and I survived,

I recovered slowly and was able to stand and take few steps. I found out that my eldest brother had survived, but while I was unconscious my sister's three-year-old son had become infected and died. Also, when I fully recovered I found most of my village playmates had succumbed and there was hardly anyone I could play with.

During the epidemic, I remember no one would come to visit except one or two close relations, and a friend of my brother's who was educated and defied his family to come and visit us. He would keep my brother in Calcutta informed about the family. Also, I remember at night a 'fakir' would travel from house to house, chanting a few lines from the Quran. Those chants would give quite a lot of moral support to the ordinary village folk.

Cholera also broke out among the Hindus, whose custom was either to burn the bodies, or just dump them in the river, causing more pollution and creating a vicious circle of infection. Fish ate the bodies in the river, and so did turtles, alerted to the bodies being dropped in the water by the chanting of a 'mantra'. As a boy with my playmates we used to go to the riverbank and would chant the 'mantra' in unison. The turtles would surface, thinking that a dead body had arrived, and we would laugh and count how many of them had appeared. Later in medical school,

I learned this was a conditioned reflex, as they connected our chanting with the possibility of food.

So cholera and famine took its toll of the population, although cholera never returned with such ferocity after that epidemic.

The season changed and people went back to their usual occupation, which was mainly to cultivate the land for the next crop. In our family, my eldest brother recovered enough to look after the land with the help of two servants. My father maintained his position as head of the family and in overall charge, and my mother was always crying for my deceased sister. I never saw her without tears in her eyes.

At this time, there was a debate within the family as to whether my brother-in-law should be told of the death of his wife and son. He wrote letters home every two months addressed to my father, since my sister was illiterate. I remember that the letters had been opened by censors.

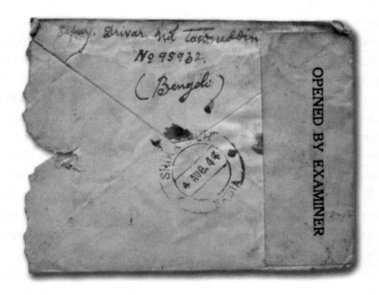

The family decided – rightly or wrongly – that my brother-in-law should not be told of these deaths. So my father must have written to say that everything was okay. No one in the village had a camera so there was no question of him asking for a photograph of his wife and son.

Sometime in 1943, while the war in Europe and Far East was still raging, my brother-in-law got leave to come home. This was his first homecoming since he had gone to war. So there was a dilemma about how to break the news to him. There was no fixed date or time for his return, but he gave an approximate day. I was six years old and was instructed by everybody that if I happened to see him coming, on no account must I tell him the bad news. Eventually he came home and before he entered the village he was told by the news by someone he encountered. How he felt God only knows, but I remember him entering our house in full military uniform and insisting on finding their graves. He wanted to dig up the corpses and meet his beloved wife and darling son of whom he must have dreamt while he was away fighting in the desert. I remember four or five people trying to restrain him and how during the struggle his uniform got torn. Then I remember him fainting and I saw his relatives sponging his brow with cold water.

Over the following days, he calmed down and was consoled by village folks, some of whom were also in the Army and on home leave. They had something in common to talk about. He had two months leave and mainly stayed in our house, though occasionally he visited his father some miles away.

My mother was very fond of her son-in-law though her daughter had gone. It happened that there was a girl about the same age as my sister. Apparently she used to play with my sister as a young girl. She had been widowed after a short marriage – perhaps her husband was also a cholera victim. My mother proposed that this widowed girl would be "adopted" as her daughter and that my widower brother-in-law should marry her. This was accepted by all concerned and the wedding was carried out. By this time his leave of two months was over, so off he went to his post in the Middle East while his wife, now our "sister", stayed with us in our family. That must have given some consolation to my mother.

By this time, I had started going to the village school which was about half a mile from our home. I walked there in bare feet, in shorts and a tee-shirt, carrying a book and a slate to write on.

From the very beginning I was good at my studies and carried out whatever task I was given. There were two teachers: one Hindu, the headmaster, and the other a Muslim; we used to call him the second master.

The work was primitive but at the end of the year there would be exams. In each exam, I used to get top marks and sometimes I was given the task of teaching the boys of the lower classes. Needless to say, that there were no girls in the whole school of nearly seventy pupils, because girls' education in the village at that time was unheard of.

The years passed and I remember one day in 1946 I saw a man riding a bicycle near the school. He seemed to be an educated man and stopped to talk to the two teachers. We overheard something about an 'Atom Bomb' – by that time Hiroshima had been bombed, on 6th August 1946 – and the man also said that the war was coming to an end. I think he must have worked at nearby European settlement and heard the news there. People in the village were relieved that the war was over and that, after all, Japan would not be invading our village.

Though the war had ended, there was new unrest, and a new problem brewing, which would be much more serious and would affect the lives of the village people more than the cholera epidemic and the Second World War. This was the Partition of India, the creation of Pakistan, the migration of populations and Hindu-Muslim riots, which I will deal with in the next chapter.

My primary education was not compulsory. Perhaps only ten percent of the inhabitants of the village used to send their boys to the primary school, mainly to learn to read and write. There was no provision for the girls. Those who completed their education at the primary school were regarded as literate and, by this criterion, at that time only 8-10% of the population were literate. So this vast population depended on the ten percent of the literate population when it came to sell or buy any property. Those who were illiterate had to put their left thumbprint where a signature would be required.

I finished primary school at the end of 1946. I was the only boy expected to go on to secondary education in my class of twenty, and it was a big step, for there would be an examination held in a different centre some six miles away from home and papers would be marked independently. I was taken by my headmaster along with other boys from our village and nearby villages as well. Most of the boys taking the exam were Hindus as was my head teacher. At that stage, I never felt any difference between the religions. I was treated exactly the same as the others.

Secondary schools

The nearest secondary school was about two miles away, across the Mathabhanga river. The site of the school was a renowned one, a town called Shikarpore where there was a small European settlement. It was the headquarters of the Midnapore Zamindary Company, which owned much land in Bengal and was run by Europeans. The General Manager used to live there in great style and the school, post office, and bazaars were built around this settlement. The ordinary people were under the impression that this 'sahib' was the direct representative of the king who lived in England. Many people used to work for him and he was often asked to rule on complaints between neighbours or other villagers. So I was destined to go to Shikarpore School – where my brother had completed his matriculation six years earlier.

I went to Shikarpore High School in 1947, a memorable year in the history of the Indian sub-continent when the British left India after ruling for nearly 200 years and the sub-continent was partitioned into India and Pakistan.

I arrived at the school with a good primary school report and I was expected to do well. A few of the teachers recognized me from my likeness to my brother who had been there few years earlier. Some of them asked me where he was and what job he was doing.

Shikarpur H. E. School.

1136

Received from *md. W. Ali*
of Class *V* Sec. *B* Roll No. *4*

	Rs.	As.	P.
Tuition fee for......*march*......	2	~	~
Advance / Arrear fees for..................			
Admission or Transfer fee ...			
Examination fee			
Game fee			
Fine for		*1*	~
Library fee			
Poor fund			
Total ...	**2**	*1*	~

Dated *25 3 194 7*. Receiving Officer.

N.B.—The School fee is payable on or before the 15th of each mo

I found myself among nearly sixty boys, some my age and height and others older and bigger. The bigger boys had entered secondary education after failing a few times in primary school. To go on to secondary education was a big achievement for them. They were not so good at their studies and some of them spent their time smoking and talking about girls, of which there were four in the class. From the beginning, I worked hard, doing my homework and attending classes regularly. But no matter how hard I tried, I couldn't beat some of the boys who were so good at all the subjects. The students were over 95% Hindus and I was one of the few Muslims. But there was one Muslim boy who was so good that he came first in every exam and in every subject. He showed great promise but I don't remember his name —we used to call him Unto. He was even good at sports. Every one of us dreamt of becoming like Unto.

At the age of ten we were unaware of the political undercurrents of the time, but I guessed that change was on the way, from hearing of the many processions and demonstrations in the surrounding villages about plans for Indian independence. Basically the Muslims under the leadership of the Muslim League wanted India to be partitioned so that they could be part of a Muslim homeland to be called Pakistan, incorporating the initials of Punjab, Kashmir and Sindh.

But the Hindu leaders, under the influence of the Indian Congress party, wanted to leave India united. The political atmosphere became very bitter, with serious friction between Hindus and Muslims. There were daily discussions among the village elders about the future, but the Muslims, being overwhelming illiterate, were not really aware of what exactly was going on and they were brainwashed into supporting partition. A few names – Jinnah, Gandhi, Nehru and Patel – would come up in the discussion time and time again.

At school, I noticed disagreements between the older boys. They would argue about Pakistan and often fighting would start. The white walls of the school building were littered with graffiti, some welcoming Pakistan and others condemning it. Still young, I was not very bothered about it and just I kept at my studies. There was not much political discussion at home, either. And then the Partition of India happened, on 14th August 1947.

There had been Hindu/Muslim riots in many parts of Bengal. Calcutta, being the capital of Bengal, was engulfed in racial violence and terrible massacres on the both sides. There was a pall of gloom in our household, because my brother was still in Calcutta. However, he survived, having been sheltered by one of his Hindu friends. When he came home, he told of how he took shelter in a house with a group of friends consisting of both Hindus and Muslims. So when someone knocked at the door, if it was a Hindu whoever answered said that there were only Hindus in the house, and vice versa if the caller was a Muslim. There were also serious Hindu/Muslim riots in Bihar, where Muslim peasants were slaughtered by their Hindu landlords. Then, a few days later, Muslims took revenge in Noakhali, a mainly Muslim area, and slaughtered Hindus. Although the physical appearance of Hindus and Muslims was more or less the same, Hindus wore slightly different clothes from Muslims. Also, married

Hindu women wore a vermilion dot on the forehead. The main difference between Hindu and Muslim men is that Muslims are circumcised, so during the riots, if someone claimed to be Muslim and was then found to be uncircumcised he became a target, and vice versa for Muslims in Hindu dominated areas.

I remember during the riots the Hindu leader Mahatma Gandhi said he would fast unto death unless Hindus and Muslims, whom he saw as brothers, did not stop fighting, and his threat helped to bring the situation under control, temporarily.

14th August 1947, the date fixed for independence, arrived and nobody knew exactly how India would be divided, apart from that Muslim majority areas would be Pakistan and the Hindu majority areas would be India. On this basis, the whole of Bengal, including Calcutta, would have been in Pakistan but the last Viceroy of India, Lord Mountbatten, and his Surveyor Cyril Radcliffe decided otherwise. Under immense pressure from the Congress Party and perhaps connected to the personal friendship between Lady Mountbatten and Pandit Nehru, the partition of India was carried out in such a way that it favoured India overwhelmingly. Bengal was divided and Shikarpore, where my school was, would become part of India whereas our village would be in Pakistan. But this was not confirmed until a few months after Independence Day.

I remember that day very well. There was wide anticipation in the whole village that something was going to happen but ordinary village folk did not quite know what. All the Muslim population of the village were jubilant, thinking that the whole of Bengal would be in Pakistan. I found that my Hindu friends and their parents were slightly apprehensive.

The day was clear, with scorching sunshine, and the midday sun was so strong that no one went out without an umbrella to protect them from the heat of the sun. (This type of climate led to Rudyard Kipling's well-known line "Only mad dogs and Englishmen go out in the midday sun.")

In the morning, village folk including my father put on their best clothes and proceeded to the nearby township of Shikarpore, where my secondary school was situated. Along with a few of the village boys I accompanied the village elders. We had to cross a small river which was swollen at that time of the year and we had to go by ferry. About twenty or thirty of us crossed the river and walked towards my school where some sort of ceremony would take place. On our way to the school we had to pass the white settlement. A few of the village elders glanced surreptitiously to see if there were any white people around. Some of them closed their umbrellas as a mark of respect, as was the custom.

We reached the school at around ten o'clock, where there were lots of other people already gathered. Then we waited for the ceremony, due to begin at midday.

I saw three men all dressed in smart clothes climb onto the flat roof of the school building where a flagpole had been erected. There was one Muslim, one Hindu and one Englishman, the General Manager of the local estate. All three raised the flag of Pakistan to up the flagpole by pulling a cord. The flag was huge and consisted of a third white, and two-thirds green with a crescent and star in the middle. While the flag fluttered from the top of the flagpole, the people chanted "Pakistan Zindabad", "long live Pakistan". It was a wonderful moment – everybody seemed happy.

My father decided to return home. I myself was very proud of the fact that the whole thing had happened in my own school and I showed off to other boys from my village who accompanied us, knowing that I was a cut above them, since I had made it to the famous Shikarpore High School.

We returned to the village and we had to pass through the Hindu area before we could reach our house. As we were going down the road, a man whose son went to the village primary school and was known to my father asked him what had happened. My father replied "it is now Pakistan – the British rule has ended." The man asked "What does that mean?" My father replied, "It will be like the days of Nawab Serajodola, when everything was cheaper and people were free and happy". He was referring to the last of the Mughal Emperors in Bengal who was defeated by Clive of India in 1757 in the infamous battle of Plassey, marking the beginning of the British Empire in India.

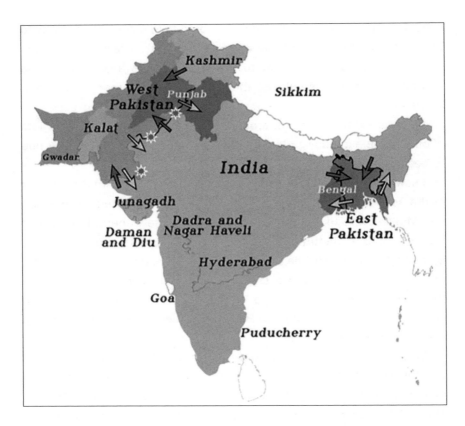

So the village people settled back into their everyday lives, and the Muslims were happy in the knowledge that they had won independence and now everything would be fine and rosy. But the truth was different and we didn't know it. Even the Muslim leaders didn't know what was really happening, let alone the village folks who had no radio, no newspapers and no method of communication. The only news that filtered through was by word of mouth.

But the white settlement in Shikarpore knew what was happening and some people working over there used to bring third- and fourth-hand news to the village.

What actually happened was as follows: on 14th August 1947, independence was declared and Pakistan was born, supposedly a homeland for Indian Muslims, but among the ordinary citizens no one knew how the Indian sub-continent was going to be divided. News began to filter through that Bengal too would be divided along the lines of its

Hindu/Muslim majorities. After the celebration at my school, I had been attending school regularly, and everywhere there was palpable tension, leading to occasional fights between Hindu and Muslim boys. As a young boy in a very junior class I felt uncomfortable.

Two to three months passed and people were still not sure how partition be achieved. If the Muslim majority areas became Pakistan, then a district known as Murshidabad should be Pakistan, for not only was it the capital of free Bengal until 1757 but also 80% of the people were Muslim. Then the rumour came that our small river was going to be the international boundary, with Pakistan on our side and on the other side would be India. There was small sigh of relief with this news but we were worried about losing my school in Shikarpore.

But many people did not agree with any of this and thought that British Raj was the best regime and should continue.

While the political tension continued, I carried on going to school at Shikarpore. Nobody seemed too worried, the teachers were the same and I continued as if nothing happened.

Then one day when I went school, I found uniformed soldiers occupying the school buildings. They were Indian soldiers, although the Pakistani flag was still flying from the flagpole on the roof of our school. I told my father and the village folks about the arrival of the Indian soldiers and from then on they gradually accepted the idea of partition and that our small river, the Mathabhanga, was indeed going to be the international boundary.

In the summer of 1947, as every summer, school was held in the mornings to avoid the scorching mid-day sun. One day, I and my schoolmates, mainly Hindus, arrived at school to see soldiers were marching and doing general drills. For the first time I saw what a rifle looks like and also a bayonet. Some of the soldiers were Ghurkhas with their knives dazzling in the morning sunshine. The other boys were laughing and cheering them, but I felt bad. I thought these were not my soldiers. Indeed, they were my "enemies". During the parade a soldier noticed a small Pakistani flag still fluttering on an iron fence nearby, left over from the Independence Day celebrations. I saw him leave his place in the parade, take the flag, tread on it and rip it apart. I was horrified. It cast a deep shadow on my mind, and I began to resent my fellow students who seemed to be enjoying this desecration of my flag – the flag of Pakistan.

Once again, I told my father and elder brother and others in the village about this. I did not get any answer from them. What could they say? A few days later, I saw the big Pakistani flag on the roof of my school building being ripped apart and burned, and the Indian flag raised in its place.

Now, nearly six months after Independence Day, it was clear that Shikarpore was in another state, another country. So what would be my fate with regards to school? There must have been discussion among the teaching staff and I was told that I should continue to come to school as before. The Muslim boys from senior classes had already stopped going. Instead they started at schools on our side of the border, though these were few and far between and not of good quality. My father insisted that I stay at the Shikarpore school.

The time came for the examination to determine whether I got promoted to the next class. I was in class V and hoped to get into class VI. My results were good, but I didn't secure any of the top three places though I may have been in the top ten. It did not worry me, but my father and brother felt I should have done better. People in the village also had very high hopes for me and they too were disappointed at the result. The boy who was secured top marks in every subject was the Muslim boy called Unto. He came from Shikarpore and so his house was in what was now India.

So in 1948 I was in the second year of the secondary school. The situation in the village was unsettling and volatile. People generally accepted that the partition of India, and Bengal for that matter, had taken place and the international boundary was on their doorstep. There was not much mixing between the Hindus and Muslims and each community was fearful about what the future held. Muslims were aggrieved and upset that the township and facilities of Shikarpore were lost and that even the capital of Bengal, Calcutta, would not be in Pakistan. In many people's views, without Calcutta and its port facilities the fledgling East Pakistan would not survive economically. The Hindus in our village, on the other hand, were very worried about their fate. They could not reconcile themselves to the idea of staying in the village as a minority under Muslim rule.

In 1948 on our side of the border some border militias were in evidence. To my child's eye they were not as well-dressed or as well-armed as the soldiers on the Indian side I saw every day when I went to school. I continued my school normally. Neither the Indian soldiers nor the Pakistani militias raised any objection to me crossing the border. Indeed, ordinary people still crossed the border in the same way as before Partition.

One day at school in 1948, I noticed that everyone, from the teachers to the students, was sombre and sad. We were told that the great leader Mahatma Gandhi had been shot. It turned out that the culprit was a Hindu Nationalist. If it had been a Muslim, the outcome would have been very different, with unimaginable bloodshed throughout India and Pakistan. Everybody in the school was crying openly. Someone had got a radio and commentary was being broadcast from Delhi. The reception wasn't very good, the broadcast was in English and there might have been a hundred people trying to listen to it. The teachers and the students of the upper class were clustered close to the radio and we the juniors were at the periphery. I could only hear a grunting noise, and could not understand any of the words apart from the name Mahatma Gandhi and his assassin, Nathuram Godse. Both the teachers and the students were saying through their tears that the father of the nation was gone.

The school remained closed for three or four days, and there were various condolence meetings both at school and outside, organised by public and political bodies. The Muslim population back in our village was also sad and subdued. My mother was particularly upset because she liked the humble way Gandhi used to live, or at least the public perception of the simple life, with minimal clothes and attending only to basic needs.

Another event that I remember from 1948 was the invasion of the princely state of Hyderabad in South India. When India was partitioned, there were many princely states and their rulers were given the option to join India or Pakistan. Most of the states joined India but problems arose with Kashmir in the north-east, and Hyderabad in the Deccan. The Kashmir situation still remains unresolved. It was a state where the population was overwhelmingly Muslim but the ruler, Hari Singh, was Hindu. India laid claim to Kashmir because the Maharaja chose to join India. This situation has still not been accepted by Pakistan and the result has been at least two wars between the two countries with the problem still being unresolved more than seventy years after the partition.

The question of Hyderabad was settled. The situation was the opposite to Kashmir. The majority of the population were Hindus whereas the ruler, the Nizam of Hyderabad, was Muslim, and apparently the richest man in the world at that time. The Nizam announced that he wanted Hyderabad, buried deep in the territory of India, to remain independent of either India or Pakistan, but India invaded Hyderabad in 1948, and simply overran the state. Although there was no fighting, the Indian Press portrayed it as a great victory and at school there was a special meeting in the main hall where the teachers gave exuberant talks and showed pictures of the head of the Army and Air force who had been in charge of that campaign. The Hindu boys were jubilant and proud of the achievement but, like other Muslims, I felt unhappy and somewhat humiliated. Outside school, there were arguments and fistfights with some of the boys and the tension between the Hindu and Muslim boys continued to increase.

At home I explained this to my father and brothers but, again, they made no comment on the day's events. But I knew that my days at the Shikarpore school were numbered.

In the later part of 1948, an official came to the school and told us that the school pupils would be divided into four "Houses". He invited us to suggest names for these Houses. Three names came very easily – Gandhi, Nehru, and Subhash Bose, a nationalist and campaigner for the independence of India through revolution. He collaborated with Germany and Japan to try to drive the British out of India. Bose was a Bengali, and both Hindus and Muslims were proud of him. Though he died in his early forties in a plane crash, the Hindus believed that he was alive and would come back any day. So three names were settled. In the oldest class there was a Muslim boy who was entrusted with the fourth name and he would be the captain of that house. All the Muslims encouraged him to suggest the name of a prominent Muslim politician. All the Muslim boys from junior classes expected him to name the house "Jinnah" after the Muslim leader and founder of Pakistan. But he was mature, intelligent and had foresight, and he named the house "Stalin". So I became a member of "Stalin" House.

It was the end of 1948, and the exams came and went. I don't remember my grades, but all I know is that I passed. There was some tension in the air, both in the minds of the teachers and the students. In fact, the whole population on both sides of the border were tense, unsettled and apprehensive.

At this time, I was aware of unease among the Hindu population on our side of the border. Some of them were keen to sell their properties and approached my father, and others were looking for Muslims on the other side of the border to exchange with. Every morning when I got home from school I would notice Hindus from the interior of the country crossing the river to India.

By early 1949, the school children from our side of the border dwindled. Muslim boys stopped going to Shikarpore and Hindu families were desperate to find some place to live on the Indian side. But I and one of my relations, a cousin, continued going to the school in Shikarpore. My father was approached by the border militia and some other elders and told not to send me to school on the other side, but he could not comprehend the fact that our beloved Shikarpore school was now in another country.

But one episode changed the situation and I stopped going there sometime in early 1949. One afternoon some boys and I were coming home from school and we had to walk a mile along the bank of the river till the crossing point. It was winter and the river was dry so we usually crossed over a makeshift bamboo bridge. As we approached the crossing I noticed from a distance that there was a crowd of about a hundred people near a banyan tree. When we got closer they wanted us to stop, but I didn't know why, so, as I was one of the youngest and quite small, I carried on walking and no none stopped me. I got to the bridge and crossed the river to our side but when I looked back I found none of the others were following me and in fact they had been detained. On our side of the border there was a similar crowd and some of the elders asked if I had been manhandled. I came home and found out that one of the so-called head men from Shikarpore had come to our village as they often have done and this time was detained for no apparent reason.

In retaliation, the schoolchildren were detained. They were eventually allowed home but I never went to Shikarpore again.

So I left school unexpectedly without saying goodbye to anyone. I missed it a lot and I missed my friends and for a long time afterwards I used to dream of returning there but the opportunity never arose. Some of my friends went back during the Bangladesh war in 1971, twenty-five years later, and found that school and the surroundings were not as beautiful as they remembered them.

I was now fourteen and at a vital stage in my education, and it was time to prepare for the matriculation examination, or "Matric".

The nearest suitable school was about six miles north of our village. It was not as renowned as Shikarpore school, but was still a secondary school. My schoolfellows gave up studying and just hung around the village shop. Some of them joined a paramilitary group called "Ansar Bahini" whose main function was to steal goods from fleeing refugees to India, of which there was a steady stream and our village was the last staging post.

In my situation, giving up studying was unthinkable, but I was tempted to follow the example of my friends in the village and I began to keep bad company. I started smoking hand-rolled cigarettes and generally abandoned my books and became intrigued by what is happening at the border, though I never joined the groups who were plundering goods from the fleeing population. My parents had dinned into me that I should never take advantage of any human suffering. But on one occasion I was with a group who were dividing up looted goods from the fleeing Hindus, mainly copper utensils. As they were sharing them out I arrived on the scene, younger than the others. Because I had turned up, they offered me a brass utensil which was really good and I was pleased with it, but when I took it home I was scolded by my parents and brother who compelled me to take it back to the leader of the gang.

I overheard people started talking about me, suggesting that I should abandon my studies and go back to the fields to help plough the land. Even at that stage, that comment hurt me and I decided that I must make up my mind to do something worthwhile, though I didn't know what.

My father decided that I should go to the secondary school six miles from our house. The road was bad and there was virtually no communication to speak off between the two places. The only method of transport was a bicycle, and I didn't have one. We actually had a bicycle at home, a present to my brother at his wedding in 1946. Since he was not at home – after Partition he came back to East Pakistan to look for jobs – that bicycle would have been ideal for me, but it was kept under lock and key and I was warned not to touch it.

So I had to walk six miles to the Khas-Mothurapur secondary school, sometimes alone, sometimes in the company of other boys from our village. Those six miles involved crossing green fields, walking along the river bank past the border security force, and along roads which are used mainly by bullock carts. I would wear only shorts and a tee-shirt with an umbrella to protect me from summer sun and monsoon rain. By the time I reached school I was usually late, for my family had neither clock not watches. Going to Shikarpore school. which was only two miles from home, I would use the shadow of a house like a sundial. But there was no such shadow on the six-mile trek to the Mothurapur school.

The head teacher of the school was a Muslim and very strict. He knew my father and was pleased that his school had been chosen for me. But he was not pleased with my attendance. I just could not go to school every day because of the sheer exhaustion it caused. The school itself was not properly run, for although the Headmaster was there and taught classes regularly, because of the turmoil in the country most of the Hindu teachers had either migrated or were about to do so, and there was an enormous vacuum. So I could see that my studies were suffering because I couldn't attend the school regularly from such a distance. I somehow managed during the summer season but it became impossible in the rainy season.

So it was decided that I should stay with my sister in a village about two miles from the school. She was married to a farmer in an agrarian community so they were poor and somehow eking out an existence. My presence there was an additional burden to them. Although my parents agreed to pay for my board, pocket money and clothing, the atmosphere in their home made it very difficult to study. They had a small house and a big family and at night when I tried to study under a hurricane lamp, the farmers and their workers would talk about they had done during the day and what was planned for the following day. They would laugh, joke and smoke, and occasionally someone would bring a handmade cigarette to me. This was the drawback of staying at my sister's house but at least the distance I had to cover to reach the school was manageable. I would stay with her from Sunday to Thursday and come home for the weekend, which was Friday and Saturday. I used to count the hours and days till Thursday when I would be at home.

The rainy season arrived and the monsoon caused flooding. My sister's house was on land which must have been a river bed many years ago, and so during the rainy season, on the road from my sister's house to the school there was only water as far as the eye could see. There was no visible road, only the trees marking the boundary and we boys used to wade through knee-deep and sometimes chest-deep water.

What we usually did was to tie our books with a dry cloth, usually a lungi or waist cloth, and tee-shirt. I would wear a small loin cloth, hold the books wrapped in dry cloth over my head and wade through. Near the school the water got deeper. It had been a proper river, now dried up, but during the rainy season it came to life with rain from above and water from the swollen Ganges not far away. So about for about two to three hundred yards where the water was deeper and the current flowing fast, we had to swim. It was a difficult task, protecting the books and dry cloths with one hand and swimming with my feet and one free hand. But that was the situation and everybody from our village who went to that school had to do it.

After reaching the dry land, we would wipe ourselves dry, put on the dry waistcloth and shirt and off we went to school. The same procedure had to be repeated after school was over and every day during the rainy season, which lasted maybe three months.

Once again, my journey to school became too much for me. It was apparent to my father and brother that they had to make some other arrangements for me to be able to study.

The rainy season was over and the winter was approaching, the time when I had to prepare for the examinations. The only solution was for me to board, living within the school compound.

The boarding house was run by the students, about ten to fifteen pupils from various classes. It was not easy to get a place there and paying for food and rent was expensive. The boys who boarded were from far away and usually from well-to-do families.

But I managed to get a place with the idea of staying for two to three months until the exams were over.

At the boarding house I was the youngest, having just reached puberty. I began to notice the changes in my body which had already happened to other boys who were in senior classes and some of them shaved regularly.

I settled in well and in fact it was the best time since I had left Shikarpore School. I was happy, free, enjoying playing volleyball in the afternoon in the school compound. I developed friendships with a few other boys. It was wonderful time. Although the quality of food was mixed, there were plenty other things to occupy me.

But I was aware that my parents were spending their hard-earned money and I did not neglect my studies. I hoped to do well in the exams and this was the first time I had a proper environment for study. There were other boys preparing for their "matric" exam, behind their books all the time, and this stimulated me to study harder. I gained a reputation in the class as "well-behaved and intelligent", so I was very pleased.

I would go home maybe once a fortnight or even once a month, and during one of those trips I encountered an endless human procession of Hindu refugees going to India and Muslims coming from India. In one night, about fifty people took shelter in our house and all of them all had stories of atrocities perpetrated by the Hindus. They stayed overnight and moved on to the interior on the following day.

During this time the village was virtually cleared of Hindus and their place taken over by Muslims. It was a time of tremendous upheaval and difficult for me to grasp fully at that age.

My mother was a kind-hearted woman and kept repeating 'What has happened to the world? Why have the people with whom we have lived in friendly terms for centuries had to leave? What is this 'independence'? The British Raj was so much better."

My father was bitter too. He was angry at the way the division had taken place with the loss of Shikarpore School and so much disruption to my studies, and the local situation.

I remember that some of my father's Hindu friends left some valuables for safekeeping, mainly brass and copper plates, some jute and other crops, and some money. In the climate of the time, such goods would never get returned to their owners. Indeed, there had been many Muslims who became well off by plundering the possessions of the fleeing Hindu population, but not in our household.

I remember my father sending my elder brother with some of the Hindu goods, money and other articles to the border, taking a considerable risk with the border militias but he managed to get them to the border and hand them over to the owner on the other side of the river.

So while I was still at the boarding house and preparing for the exams, the migration of the population was completed. In my school I met three boys from Shikarpore School whose parents migrated to the village nearby. I was pleased to see them and became very friendly very quickly. I asked them about Unto, the Muslim boy, who was extremely good at studies and all the sports but they knew nothing about him. He too must have migrated but no one knew where.

The exams came and went. I did very well, coming first in three subjects and in overall third position in the whole class. So I was promoted to the next class, class IX, and a new chapter of my life began.

New life in Kushtia

I t became apparent to all concerned that I had to move to a better school than the current one. I was now fifteen and the all-important matriculation examination was only two years away. A move to another school was vital for my further education.

The obvious choice was move to Kushtia, the district headquarters and a town rather than a village. I had so far been a village boy with plenty of friends, open air, green fields, a river full of fish and other attractions. Not for a single moment in any season was I bored. Even in the rainy season when the fields were full of water, the river was swollen and everywhere was a quagmire, life was good for me. I would go out with my trusted friends, pick wild berries, eat mangoes and jackfruit, and catch fish in the river. We were never short of food at home because all sorts of crops were grown on our own land. Except, perhaps, for cooking salt and soap powder everything was home produced.

The plan was that I should move to Kushtia for the next stage of my education and stay with one of my brothers and his wife.

To remind you, I had six siblings. I was the youngest and must have been born when my father was in his late forties or early fifties. The age difference between my eldest brother and myself is nearly thirty years. In fact, my eldest brother was married even before I was born. The next sibling was my second brother, who was perhaps more than twenty years older than me. He was known among the village folk to be "intelligent" and indeed he passed his matriculation examination from Shikarpore School, though he got a third-class grade, but in 1941 that was a great achievement, particularly for Muslim boys. In 1951, when it was decided that I should move, the plan was that I should live with him. By this time, he had been married for six years and had a daughter. Tradition at that time demanded that the women stayed at home and looked after the children while the men earned a livelihood. My brother was a clerk in a local government office, not well paid, and living in rented accommodation with his wife and daughter. My sister-in-law was poorly educated and was the daughter of local village chief. It was an arranged marriage, as was the custom. Initially my brother was not happy in the marriage, but later on they settled down.

When it was decided that I would stay with them, my father contributed to the costs. The distance from our village to Kushtia was 36 miles, with very poor communications.

When I moved to Kushtia in 1951, I found that in addition to accommodating me, their tiny home was expected to house my brother, his wife and daughter, and my sister-in-law's brother. He was two years younger than me, and he too intended to study while living in his sister's house. Neither my father nor I knew of these arrangements, but by the time we found out nothing could be done.

The house had three rooms, with a corrugated tin roof and wall, and a cement floor. The middle room, slightly larger than the rest, was occupied by my brother and his family and a room on the east side was used as dining area and also had a bed for my sister-in law's brother. I was given the remaining room on the west side, usually used for guests.

I was to stay in that house for six years, until I went to medical school, and those six years were among the worst years of my life. I still feel both physically and mentally crippled by living there. I lost all my self-confidence in those tormenting years and in fact have never recovered. Nobody in my village believed the stories I told of those years, apart from my parents, but they were helpless to do anything as they were worried about what people would say. How could we explain it if I did go back to the old school?

My parents were not well enough off to pay for me to go to another school in another town. They would not be able to afford for me to stay in a hostel or mess, so I just stayed put and suffered in silence. Seventy years later these memories are still painful.

I started my new life in Kushtia about the beginning of the school term, in September or October of 1951.

The new school was only about five hundred yards from my brother's house, so it was very convenient. There were five secondary schools in the town, one exclusively for girls, while the other three were co-educational, but with boys outnumbering girls. My school was entirely for Muslim boys and at the time it was the best school. I was admitted there without any entry exam.

Because it was a Muslim school the dress code was strict: long-sleeved shirt, trousers or white pyjama bottoms, and a cap and black shoes. My immediate problem was: who was going to pay for these? My parents felt that because I was now in my brother's care my expenses should be borne by him. It was also the case that money was short at home. My brother was a lower division clerk and his salary was quite low, so it was quite a burden for him. However, my brother did manage to get one set of required clothing, although I should really have had two sets so that one could be washed while I wore the other. However, I was thankful that I did have at least one set.

I noticed distinctly the hostile attitude of my sister-in-law towards me. She did not like the idea that so much money – or indeed any money – should be spent on me. She did not speak to me about this directly but I sensed that she was unhappy. On the other hand, her brother was well off and all their clothes were bought by his father. So from the very beginning I was marked by my sister-in-law as someone who was an unnecessary burden and this view could not be easily shaken. I could feel the difference in the way she spoke to me and to her brother David. Her body language towards me was totally different.

The next step was buying the things I needed for class. I needed new books, notebooks, textbook, paper, pencils and so on. Once again money was needed but I did not have the nerve to ask my brother. But when my father came to visit and I told him about the books he managed to buy me what I needed.

I started my class in the new school and for the first time since I left Shikarpore I felt that I was somewhere which was comparable to – even better than – Shikarpore School. Before the day's classes, we had to stand in the playground lined up in our respective "houses". A teacher would stand in front of each "house" and the proceedings start by a recitation from the Holy Quran by one of the pupils. Then the national anthem would be sung by another and the national flag would be raised the flagpole. After that we would go to the classes. The flag would be lowered by a student at the end of the day.

In my class there must have been about fifty students, of various age groups, from fifteen up to eighteen. The older ones must have failed to do well in their lower classes. There were some very talented boys in the class, some of them the children of local higher officials, such as senior police officials or local administrators. They were well dressed and smart, wearing different clothes on different days, whereas I would wear the same clothes day in, day out. Some of the boys were so rich that a servant would come at midday with a packed lunch. One or two of them used to arrive in a Government car. At that time there were no private vehicles in Kushtia, apart from one Volkswagen Beetle belonging to a local mill owner.

As a village boy in simple clothes and speaking a slightly different dialect, I felt inferior to the town boys. I could not have conversations with them because I knew they would tease me for my dialect, so I was more or less isolated. The only person I could speak to freely was David, two years younger than me. There were lots of sports, such as cricket, volleyball, badminton and football, but I could not join any of them because I did not have proper sportswear.

My awkwardness at the time was aggravated by the abnormal behaviour of my sister-in-law. These were my adolescent years and I was self-conscious about everything, including body image. Also, I did not have enough food, not because there was no food, but because my sister-in-law did not like me and deliberately starved me, so I was always hungry.

I was a carefree village boy suddenly thrown into surroundings which were hostile both at home and at school. As a result I was not gaining weight, felt weak, and was terribly worried that no girl would ever glance at me.

I had a slim constitution, but lack of proper food and nutrition made me even thinner. When I went home, my mother noticed the change in my state and I when I told her why she was horrified and started crying.

My father and eldest brother listened carefully but didn't comment. While I was home for the holidays, perhaps for two months, I regained my strength and colour but dreaded returning to Kushtia. However, my father told me that I had to put up with it and I went back to continue my studies.

My life in Kushtia in my brother's house was like being a house servant, for that was exactly my role, although servants are sometimes treated far better than I was. When I write these words I am not exaggerating a single fact, and my contemporaries in the village and old friends from past schools were well aware that I was far from happy with my brother and his wife. Many of them predicted that I would stop my studies before the matriculation examination. So in later years when I became a doctor, there was astonishment as to how it had happened. Looking back, I myself sometimes think that getting to medical school was a miracle.

This is how my days unfolded in Kushtia: I would wake up in the morning – and there would be no breakfast. It just wasn't on offer. My brother would go out with his shopping basket to do the daily marketing for vegetable, fish or meat. His wife would eat some left-over rice from the previous night and maybe her brother would share some with her. My brother would have his breakfast of tea and biscuits in a restaurant outside. That left me at home with nothing to eat, although I think breakfast is one of the most important meals of the day. Sometimes I would eat rice snacks, a little like rice crispies, which had been sent by my mother from the village. Everyone would share this while it lasted, but when it was finished they would go their own way and I would be without any breakfast at all.

My daily duty, come rain or shine, summer or winter, was to collect drinking water from the well situated about five hundred yards from the house. After bringing the water I had to make "wood chips" with an axe so that the fire could be started for cooking. I would light the fire and get the stove ready for cooking. After doing these two tasks I would try to concentrate on my studies.

In my room there was a bed but no table or chair, though my father did send me a table and chair a year or two later. Until then I would keep my books on the floor and sit on a mat to read them.

My brother would come from shopping with vegetables and condiments and his wife and a part-time maid would cook the food which had to be ready for my brother before he went to the office at about ten. He would have a bath, eat his meal and leave for the office.

I would then have my bath and eat, very often the first meal of the day. The food was boiled rice with vegetable curry, or maybe some fish or meat curry. The food would be steaming hot just as it was time to go to school and I would try to eat, but I couldn't always eat enough.

By the time I returned home from school at around four-thirty I was once again terribly hungry and dying for food. Usually at that time I just had to go hungry. If I was lucky and if my brother's wife was in a better mood she would say "Eat some leftover rice with a bit of curry". When that happened I would be cock-a-hoop. But most days there wasn't any food for me. As my wife's brother was well off, he would go out and buy something delicious from a restaurant but for me there was nothing. Sometimes if I had one anna (less than a penny) I would buy some fried peanuts and eat them, accompanied by enough water from a nearby well to fill my belly.

My classmates would go home, change their clothes, have something to eat and then play some games, but I had neither the facility nor the physical or mental strength to play in any sports. A boy in my class, a son of the police superintendent, used to play tennis with other officers behind an iron mesh fence. I would watch him from a distance as he played, wearing white shorts, a tee- shirt and matching trainers and say to myself – 'What a difference there is between him and me...'

After school, I would roam aimlessly for a while, but I had to return home before dark, because my evening job was to clean the glass of the hurricane lamps, put oil in them and light them, one for each room. Those were the days before houses had electricity. Then I would wash up and start reading for next day's lessons.

My brother would come home just after five and after changing out of his office clothes he would go out again to spend the evening with his office friends. I would be hungry, since I had had virtually no food since my first meal around ten in the morning, but there was no way I could ask for any food. If I did, I would be told 'no'.

My brother would return by eight p.m. and have his evening meal and at last I would be called to eat. I would have some rice with vegetable or meat curry and some dal. On many occasions I still felt hungry but would not be offered a second helping. I used to discuss this with my friends and they said that if the bowl of rice was put in front of me I could take as much as I wanted. But this never happened.

After meals, I used to feel tired and sleepy. But my brother would shout at me and ask why I wanted to sleep so early when I should be studying. So I would carry on somehow, perhaps till eleven p.m. without really being able to concentrate.

The following morning the cycle would start all over again. This was my routine. Because of the way I was treated, I had no self-respect. It seemed that nobody considered me as a human being and I was just a necessary evil and would one day wither away.

There were occasional breaks in the routine. The grandparents-in-law of my brother were old and often visited, mainly to have health check-ups and consult doctors for their various ailments. When they came to stay with us I was required to extend my servant role to them. Sometime I had to accompany them to the doctors; sometimes I had to buy food or drink for them in the market. I was never paid for these extra services, though they were well off financially. Of course, I was handed compliments like "what a hard-working lad!" and so on, but you can't eat compliments, and although there was more food around during their stay I had to endure my usual meagre portions. What's more, I even had to sleep on the floor because they were given my bed.

One other task which broke the routine was a monthly trip to the husking mill. I had to take wheat and rapeseed for making into flour and oil. I usually welcomed this trip because it gave me the opportunity to embezzle a few pence. This is how I did it: I would be given some money to pay for the processing of the wheat and rapeseed, say 10 annas (5 pence) for the wheat and 5 annas for the rapeseed. Then the rickshaw fare would be added So what I did was to walk to the mill, thus saving the rickshaw fare, and then I would bargain with the mill clerk and save some money there. So all in all, every month or so I could save as much as half a rupee (eight annas) which was quite a lot of money. I desperately needed a fountain pen, which would cost me several rupees, and it was my goal to save that much somehow.

That is how life went on in Kushtia. At school I tried to do as well as I could under the circumstances. The town boys were well dressed and spoke nicely and I was verbally bullied by them as soon as I opened my mouth. One day, our class tutor wanted us to write a page about what would be our ambition when we grew up. This was in English, which was compulsory for everyone. My essay was highly appreciated by the teacher who read it aloud to the class. From then onwards I did have a little respect from fellow students.

In 1951 we were told at school that the Prime Minister of Pakistan would visit the town and we would have to line the road holding Pakistani flags to welcome him. The visit was at a weekend, when I had to wash and clean my school clothes and make them ready for school. The clothes were wet, so what should I wear? I would have to go to school for the teacher to escort us to our fixed places. I was in a dilemma. Then I was told that I could wear my brother's shirt and pyjamas. They were far too big for me, but I had no option. I put them on and looked silly, but went and stood along with other boys. God knows what they thought when they saw me, and my self-respect was severely dented.

The year 1951 passed, the exams came and went and I was promoted to the next, all-important, class. This was Class X, the top class, where all of us were preparing for our matriculation exam which we would take early in 1953.

In 1952 two remarkable things happened which I remember vividly. In that year there were demonstrations by the students of Dacca University demanding that Bengali should be made one of the state languages, because the Central Government based in Karachi in West Pakistan wanted to impose Urdu as the only state language. There were great upheavals in Dacca, both among the general public under the leadership of Sheikh Mujibur Rahman, and among the students.

In one of these peaceful demonstrations on 21st February, 1952, the police opened fire on the students and there were number of fatalities. If I remember correctly three students died as well as a few members of the public. This news spread like wildfire throughout the country. A few students from Dacca came to our school and wanted us to boycott classes and demonstrate in front of Government offices. This was the first time I experienced such a boycott. Like other boys, we left classes in the middle of lessons. The teachers desperately wanted us to stay but nobody took any notice. We left school and most of the boys processed to the town centre shouting anti-Government slogans. I went straight home because I did not have that fighting spirit. My immediate worry was food, clothing and some money. My brother wanted to know why I did not join the procession, and because I could not give him a reason he said I was "good for nothing". These types of boycotts and demonstrations went on for quite a long time. There were many public meetings, with some arrests among the students, enhancing their prestige among the fellow students. When they returned after spending few days in custody, they were treated like heroes.

At one of these meetings my brother heard a boy from my class, Refaul, give a speech and he hinted that I should do the same. But he knew little about my physical and mental state. I was a misfit everywhere, both at home and outside. My young, independent mind was slowly but surely being throttled at home. Little did he realise that my mental condition made me entirely unlike any of the boys at school.

The other memorable episode was a theft in our house. At night I used to close the doors. Then one morning I noticed that the door to my room was wide open, though I remember closing it at night. In my room there was nothing valuable, only books and a small suitcase full of letters. The letters were mainly writings by me to myself since I used to write from time to time about what was happening to me, giving an account of my life.. The thief must have been very disappointed for he came away with virtually nothing.

I had saved some money to buy a fountain pen and it was in one of the envelopes. In the morning, when I told my brother that a theft had occurred he was relieved that it was not his room because the family had some cash and jewellery. He asked me to go to a nearby deserted spot where the thief might have abandoned my suitcase. I went to the place, which was usually used as dumping ground for night soil, and found my suitcase. The lock was broken but the letters and envelope were still inside. I gathered up the letters along with the envelope which had the six or seven rupees intact. I was so pleased that I had not lost the letters, which would have been very helpful in writing this account, but unfortunately they were stolen again, in 1971 during the Bangladesh war. My father-in-law had been looking after them but during the civil war the whole house was looted.

In early 1953 it was time for the matriculation examination. It was a big occasion in my life. I remember there were fifty-three of us who were to sit it. A group photograph was taken and as I was small in size I was asked to sit on the grass in front of the teachers. There were four of us who sat, including Refaul, the boy who had given a speech during the language demonstration a few months ago. Refaul was the best-dressed boy in the class and the son of a lawyer. He was good at his studies and his handwriting was superb. He would come to class early and sit in a particular place. One day he was late and I sat there instead. He pushed me and took the place and then I pushed him back and fighting started. I was stronger than him, and he could not win. Refaul complained to the teacher who did not listen to the whole story but instead punished me not only by giving away the seat, but also by making me stand during the lesson for nearly three-quarters of an hour. This was the first punishment of any sort I had received at school.

The examination came and I did my best. I remember that during the exam break other boys' parents, friends, and relations would come to meet them with coconut water, refreshments, tea and biscuits, and would encourage them to do well. But I had none of those things. It was just like any other day.

After the exam I went home to the village and waited for the results. It usually took three months before the results were out and one day somebody from Kushtia brought the news that I had passed, getting a second class grade. Ten boys got first class but I was pleased with my result. I knew that if I had received proper coaching and other help like other boys I would certainly have got a first class grade. Also, I was only sixteen.

I was at my village home when results arrived. There was some discussion among the family that I should pursue my higher education in Kushtia, which would mean going to the college nearby. The course there was equivalent to 'A' levels in the UK and took two years. You could choose Science or Humanities. I had no say in this myself. It was up to my brother and parents to decide, and they chose the Science course for me, physics, chemistry and biology. I was not very good at maths, so my choice would have been the Humanities.

However, I was thrilled that I would be going to college at all. At that time, nobody from my village had been to college, so I was something of a celebrity among my village friends.

A college education was expensive. It would cost tuition fees, along with the cost of using college facilities. I would need good quality clothes and of course money for buying books.

My good results and the fact that I was going to college gave me a bit of lift in my brother's household. I was also helped by the fact that my sister-in-law's brother, who was two years younger than me, failed to pass his class exam and wasn't promoted to the next class. My brother's in-laws decided to take their son back to their village because they thought the town education was not suitable for him.

I still had to do the same amount of housework but because of my success I was treated better and the food supply was bit more liberal.

But there was conflict over the money I needed for my education. Sometimes I heard loud arguments between my brother and his wife about it. I could hear every word from the adjacent room – but could do nothing.

The family managed to find money for tuition and a reasonable set of clothes, but the problem was the books. The ones I needed were all in English and from abroad. Many were expensive and nearest place one could buy them was in Calcutta – which was now in another country. Still, many boys bought their books from Calcutta.

The class started, but I did not have any books. I had to make do with a secondhand physics book which was much cheaper, and a biology book from one of my distant relations who already been to university. I did not have a chemistry book, but borrowed from other boys and made notes as much as possible.

College was really a different place. There were boys from various parts of the district and they were very intelligent. When I started the classes I felt as if I was swimming in an ocean. I was proud to be there but looking around me I felt entirely out of place. I didn't have the required books or notes and had difficulty understanding the lectures.

Just as at school, I felt inferior to the other boys, who had better clothes, seemed more intelligent and were much better at sports. But of course I continued to attend the college, which was barely five hundred yards from my brother's house.

Nearly a year passed and I went home for the summer. I needed to recuperate but I also had to study. The annual exam would take place after the vacation and we were expected to revise for it while we were at home, although in the village there was no atmosphere of study. Whenever I used to go home I would get in touch with my Hindu friends from Shikarpore School. Although Shikarpore was now in India and without easy access, we managed to meet somehow on the river bank and exchange ideas and find out who was doing what.

It was now summer, 1954. One day I felt unwell and was running a temperature. In the village community, when somebody was unwell with a high temperature it was usually taken to be because of sunstroke or an attack of malaria. People didn't have the means to pay for a doctor, and anyway, qualified medical practitioners were few and far between. Even now so many years after the events I am describing, there is no qualified medical practitioner in the village or within ten to twelve miles of it. People usually manage with herbal medicine, or various lotions or potions from charlatans.

I frequently became ill as a child, sometimes with severe malaria, on other occasions with acute attack of bacillary or amoebic dysentery, or a parasitic infestation. Like everybody else I usually managed to recover, not due to some so-called medicine from the village quack, but through my body developing resistance.

But this time it was different. My temperature did not settle down and after three days a village quack was asked to see me. He made the diagnosis of "acute constipation", and gave me some stuff to purge me. After the purging, I became weak, for in the village it was understood that if anybody got a fever he should not be given a proper diet of, say, rice or bread, till the temperature settled. (Similar to the expression in the west – 'feed a cold and starve a fever'.)

So I became bedbound and there was no sign of the temperature dropping. After several days, another "doctor" was called in and he diagnosed "remittent fever". He supplied further medicines of various colours which I was to take four times a day. I was instructed not to eat any solid food and only to take liquid food like green coconut water, glucose with water and some barley powder cooked like soup. The "doctor" would come to visit me every other day and would give me injections. By now, two weeks had passed and I was seriously ill. Everybody was increasingly concerned.

Now, my brother in Kushtia was told that my illness was serious. When he saw me, he was utterly shocked that I was so weak and dehydrated and looked like a skeleton. I was nearly at death's door. I was too ill to be transferred anywhere, not even to Kushtia, the district headquarters.

He returned to Kushtia to discuss the situation with the qualified doctors there and was advised that most probably I had enteric fever, a symptom of typhoid and it would help if a blood test could be done. My brother was taught how to sample a drop of blood from my finger tip on to a glass slide. I must give credit to my brother who rode his bike thirty-six miles to and from Kushtia almost every other day.

By now three weeks had passed. There was a belief among the village people that the fever would subside either on the seventh, fourteenth or twenty-first day. By the twenty-first day when my temperature did not go down, I was so weak that I was unable to get up from bed. There was a hole dug in the corner of the room for me to use as a lavatory, and my mother would clean it with her bare hands as and when required.

I was moribund. People gave up hope that I would survive. My father and eldest brother would pray loudly to Allah to spare my life.

Meanwhile the doctor from Kushtia suggested that I should be given a newly available antibiotic called chloramphenicol, commonly known as Chloromycetin. The drug had just come out and was expensive. My father found the money to buy these drugs and acquired four vials, each consisting of four capsules. He was cautioned that this was a "very strong drug" which might cause my heart to stop and so a few minutes before taking it, a few drops of another drug, called Coramine, had to be given to make my heart "stronger". I now know how futile this was.

One night my hands and feet got cold and my pulse could not be felt, and everybody was worried that the end was near.

However, I survived. My temperature went down after taking the third vial and I did not need the fourth one. I was unconscious most of the time, but there was a sigh of relief when I felt better. The fever finally stopped on the twenty-eighth day.

My food was now semi-solid with well-cooked fish and chicken. I was still not well enough to stand and needed help to sit up. I wanted to see my face and comb my hair, but my face was apparently so haggard that my mother did not allow me to look.

Gradually I got my strength back, my appetite increased, and I put on weight. But I now had abnormal fat around my face and trunk. All my hair fell out: whether this was due to the illness or the effect of the drugs or a combination of both, God knows, but I became totally bald.

Obviously, I could not return to the college. Indeed, I wasn't able to return to Kushtia for another three months, until I had grown stronger and my hair had started growing again. When I went back to my class, people didn't recognise me. The course had progressed and the annual exam was not far off.

Unfortunately, the way my family dealt with this situation was the worst thing they could have done. Instead of me staying in the same class for a year, so that I could catch up with what I had missed, my brother appealed to the principal to let me go up to the second year without sitting the examination, and he promised that I would cover what I had missed and still sit the final exam at the end of the second year. That was a bad decision.

In the light of my illness, the principal was sympathetic and I was moved up to the second year. It was a terrible mistake. After missing nearly six months of class, I could not understand what was being taught and couldn't cope. But who was going to listen?

There was a boy in the class from my nearby village, someone I had known at the Shikarpore School called Dider, who used to visit me at my brother's house. I tried to get some help from him, seeking his advice about how to progress. I found it impossible even to understand the simple abbreviations of chemistry, so my friend was a frequent visitor to me at my brother's house to help me out.

My brother's wife softened it a bit when I came back to Kushtia after nearly dying but soon she reverted to her old self. There is one example of her hostility to me which I cannot forget even after all these years.

One afternoon she was making some sweetmeats for herself, and maybe her husband, and I hoped I might get a taste at some point. Dider came to visit and we were discussing physics. In fact he was tutoring me. Since my friend was with me I felt he should have some of the sweets but did not have the nerve to ask my brother's wife to give him a portion, so I went to the kitchen and asked politely if she could give my portion to him. Her usual practice was to eat some first herself, then my brother would have some when he came from his office and then perhaps I would get a little of it. But when I asked for a portion before anybody had had any at all, she was furious. I had never seen before her in such a rage.

She put a portion on a plate and shrieked loudly "This is your portion! Give it to your friend!" She was shouting so loudly that Dider heard every word. When I took the food to him with a glass of water, I could see from his face that he was unhappy. He did not touch it, and it became cold and was clustered with flies, and stayed there all afternoon. My friend left after while and I took the fly-infested plate to her and said "Take your food – Dider wouldn't touch it." I don't remember her reaction, but after that my friend never came to my brother's house. Our friendship still continued but we carried on studying at his place, which was about two miles away from the college.

Such episodes were not rare. I remember the time my brother's wife's grandmother came on a regular visit for a medical checkup and was accompanied by few other grandchildren. As usual, I had to give up my bed, and my housework around the house obviously increased. One day my brother's wife noticed that a teacup was broken. She immediately suspected me and wanted an explanation. I told her I had nothing to do with it, but she never believed me and scolded me in front of the whole family, including her grandmother.

I continued my studies to the best of my ability but it was an uphill task and I knew I had little chance of passing the exam with good grades. I tried suggesting to my brother on number of occasions that it would be better to miss a year but he had no idea about college education and he thought it would be all right.

In the winter of 1955, I was under tremendous pressure to pass the approaching exam, which would be both theoretical and practical, in physics, chemistry and biology.

I did very badly in the first written exam, chemistry or biology, but the next examination was physics. I thought of cheating by copying some of the answers, using a method where questions which were likely to come up would be passed to someone outside who would write answers and return them to the candidate. The invigilators either overlooked these tricks or didn't know how to catch the culprits. This form of cheating was very common, particularly among boys who did not attend classes regularly, because they preferred to spend their time on sports.

I had never cheated in my life but out of desperation I thought I must try.

At the physics exam, I took my physics notes and left them as required on a table outside the entrance. Somebody took my notebook to the toilet and tore out the pages where I had written some of the answers to possible questions. One of the teachers found the book in the toilet and my name was written on it.

While we were busy trying to answer the questions in silence, a teacher came and tapped me on the shoulder and motioned to me to follow him to the principal's office. The whole class was looking at me aghast and saw that I was in some sort of trouble.

In the principal's room I was like a lamb to the slaughter. He showed me my book with the missing pages. I pleaded innocence and swore by the Quran that I did not do it. How could I tear the pages from my own book? But a teacher searched my pockets and found some of the answers I had prepared at home. I thought it was the end of the world. I could not speak – I had no excuse.

They asked me to sign a document that I had been found copying, and sent me back to the examination hall. I knew that was the end, but still continued with the rest of the examination, including the practical. I never revealed to anyone what happened in the principal's room.

Usually it takes three months before the results are out. But I knew that I had failed miserably, though my brother and parents still expected me too pass.

I was at home when the results came. Usually they were published in the national newspapers, but only the roll numbers were mentioned. When my brother was looking for my roll number he found the word "results withheld". He could not understand. If I had failed my roll number would not have been there, but instead it was "withheld". He went to see the principal, and found to his horror that I had not only failed miserably but had been expelled for cheating. I was also barred from sitting any exams for a year.

I came back to Kushtia thinking that this was the end of my education. My father came and was told of what had happened. Of course, everybody was sympathetic and accepted that it was not all my fault because I hardly had any time to prepare myself for the difficult exam. My class friends, including Dider, passed the exam with flying colours.

It was decided that I should continue with my studies but be readmitted to the first year and sit the exam in 1957. This was the best decision and a blessing in disguise. I am quite sure I would not have been where I am today, if this decision hadn't been taken. The major credit goes to my brother who had the main say, and I knew I had the ability if I was given the chance.

So I went back to the college as a first year student. Lot of things were in my favour. Firstly, my contemporaries had left. Those who had passed went on to university, and I was able to buy all the necessary books, notes, and biology dissections kit second-hand from them. Secondly, none of my new classmates knew me and I was two years older and more mature. Thirdly, by a stroke of good luck, all the teachers who had taught me earlier had left the college and been replaced by teachers who had just left university. They were all young and very enthusiastic about their first jobs.

On the home front, we changed accommodation and moved to a better house, brick-built, and I had a room of my own. My brother's wife had also matured and not as hostile to me as she had been over the previous four years, though I continued my housework in the same way as before. She developed more respect for me now that her brother had given up his studies and was looking after his father's business. Her father was a talented man, wealthy by village standards and affectionate towards me.

My course back in the first year began in earnest and I was determined to make an impression and vowed to get a first class grade in the exam in 1957.

I proved myself a good, hardworking and intelligent student. In the first term exam I got top marks in biology and chemistry, and also did well in physics. Fellow students began to respect me and the teachers were impressed with me. Some of them used to ask the students to consult me first if there was any difficulty. I began to like biology, and the dissection of frogs, cockroaches and earthworms. I even bribed the technician to allow me to take a dissection tray home, so that I could improve my skills, and produce very good biological drawings.

One day, a funny thing happened in the practical biology class. The subject of the lesson was the skeleton of a guinea pig. There was only skeleton of the guinea pig which we could see and touch it but had to leave it after studying it. The class was coming to an end and I suddenly had the idea that if I took just the hind leg of the skeleton home I could study it more closely. So I put it in my pocket. But when the teacher was tidying up, he suddenly noticed that one of the guinea pig's hind legs was missing. He was furious but thought that one of the less studious boys had taken it for fun. Little did he realise that his favourite pupil had got it in his pocket. He shouted at the class and was in a rage. How could I reveal that I was the culprit and had the best of intentions when I took it?

He announced that he would search everyone before we were allowed to leave the class, but he went on, "before I do that, I will turn the light off for one minute to allow whoever has taken the thigh bone to put it back." This saved my face, of course and I left it on the table. I never told the story to anyone in the class till I went to the medical school.

The first year went by, and once again I did very well in the annual examination. In the second year, the course got harder but for me it was no problem. I usually used to study the subject of each lesson the night before so when the teacher taught the following day I understood everything. I was now thoroughly enjoying my studies and college life. The principal who had expelled me had also left, so I was known by everybody, from the teachers to the students, as a brilliant student and expected to do well in the final exams.

I made two or three good friends who were also good at their studies. After the episode with Dider, I never asked any of my friends to my brother's house. I would normally go to them or they would knock on my door and we all go to the river bank, stroll around, smoke some cigarettes and talk. This was my life in early 1957.

In the next exams in mid-1957, the teachers and fellow students expected me to get a first class grade. I felt I had done well, but when the results came out I was disappointed that I missed the first class by only four marks. I needed 500 and I got 496. One of my classmates got first class as expected, as well as another boy who was not expected to do well. Both of them went to a prestigious engineering college, whereas I went to do medicine.

When the results were out, I was at my village home and the good results enhanced my prestige in the eyes of the village folk. One or two other people in the village had got as far as this in their education but opted for starting a job rather than continuing their studies, because a university education was expensive.

So when I passed my Intermediate exam, equivalent to A-level, there was some discussion as to whether I should continue my education or look for a job. Again, I have to credit my brother for maintaining that I must continue my studies.

In the societies of India, Pakistan and Bangladesh, decisions about higher education are largely decided by parents and guardians. If it had been up to me, perhaps I would not have gone in for medicine, but in the end I am glad I did.

Because I was good at biology and chemistry my family decided that I should study medicine. But the big question was: who was going to fund me? It was a very expensive affair, including tuition fees, living expenses in the capital city, books, equipment, clothes, and so on. It was a huge undertaking. Our home economy in the village was based entirely on agriculture produce, which was just about adequate to feed the family but it would be very difficult to produce extra cash, month after month. Apart from the initial expenses of admission fees, books, and accommodation, I would need a minimum of a hundred rupees a month. I could see no way this money would be forthcoming from the family's meagre resources. My brother was a lower division clerk at his local government office who himself had a large family by now and I could not expect him to bear the expense.

Nevertheless, it was decided that I should apply to the only medical college in the whole of East Pakistan, in Dacca, the capital.

So one summer day I set off for the capital to seek admission to the medical college.

Finding a medical school

I must say at that time, apart from one or two fellow students at the university, I did not have any friends, relations or acquaintances in the capital. The distance from Kushtia to Dacca was 175 miles and these days it is possible to make that journey in six to eight hours but in those days it was very difficult.

I had to take an afternoon train, which got me to the steamer station on the river Padma by ten p.m. We boarded the steamer which took the whole night at eight to ten knots to reach the suburb of the capital called Narayanganj. From there we had to take a coach to the middle of the city.

One of my brother's friends had a relation who was a professor in the medical college, and he gave me a letter to see whether the professor could help me get admitted as a student. When I reached the central coach station by midday on the following day I was tired and hungry, but I wanted to go straight to the professor's home to hand over the letter. In those days the only public transport was horse-drawn carriages so I hired one to the Professor's home, which was in an unimpressive part of the capital.

Carrying my suitcase and bedding, I knocked on the door. I was asked to come in by a servant, and was told that the professor was not yet home. I said that I would rather wait till he came home so that I could hand over the letter personally. I waited and waited, hungry, thirsty and sleepy, but I didn't care. I was used to this sort of thing at my brother's house in Kushtia.

Eventually the professor came home, at around four o'clock, and I handed the letter to him. He went in and shortly afterwards the servant brought a plate of rice and some curry. I needed a bath, but did not ask any favours and just ate the food. The professor asked me where I was going to stay. Seeing my suitcase and bedding, he immediately thought that I hoped to stay with him. But when I told him I would stay with a friend at the university hall of residence he was relieved and asked me to see him at the college. I left his house and went to the university hall of residence where I met the friend who was expecting me.

On the following day, I went to the medical college and the professor told me where to get the admission forms and apply for entry, which I could do myself. It turned out later that he had no authority or influence in the admission process.

Like other boys and girls, I submitted the admission form with the necessary fees and other requirements. I stayed in Dacca for two or three days and was severely affected by bacillary dysentery. When I got a bit better I decided to go back home and wait for the outcome of the application. Before I left Dacca, I saw the professor again in his office and he reassured me with the words: "You are a good boy with good results – you will get selected". I told my friends to contact me immediately either by letter or telegram when the list of names was put up on a notice board outside the principal's office, and I went home. When I had no news after a month I decided to return to Dacca to find out what was happening.

This time I stayed in a students' residence with a relation who was studying zoology at the university. The first night I was deep asleep, tired from the journey, and in the middle of the night there was sudden commotion with people running to and fro in the corridors of the residence hall. I woke up and found myself on the ground in front of the residence. It was a three-story building and I was on the first floor. There had been an earth tremor, which happens from time to time in the area. One boy broke his leg by jumping from the first floor but the rest of us were unharmed, though there was some damage to the building.

There were 120 places available at the medical college and we were told that a hundred would be taken in order of merit and the remaining twenty reserved for foreign graduates, some from ethnic minorities.

At the college, I saw a list of eighty successful applicants but my name was not on it. There were still another twenty names to follow but who could I approach to get favourable treatment? It was possible to solicit recommendations from family friends with influence, such as government ministers, and there were two boys on the list whose results were not any better than mine, so perhaps that's how they got in. I was desperate, but did not have anyone that I could approach, so one evening I phoned the professor and reminded him of my problem. He was busy and rather annoyed that I had phoned. Effectively, he told me that he had no influence in getting my name included in the remaining twenty candidates and hung up.

So that was the end of my dream of becoming a medical student and a doctor. What else could I do? Because I had wasted so much time concentrating on admission to medical school, places on other courses in the university were now filled, and I could see myself not getting admitted anywhere. It was very disappointing.

Having no relations or acquaintances in Dacca who could help, I was a small fish in a big pond. Then somebody suggested that I try to see the Member of Parliament for our area.

I went to see him one afternoon and introduced myself. He recognised the names of my father and brother and I explained my problem, but as he was an opposition MP he was not likely to be able to help. But there was another MP in the room, from Chittagong, a port city of East Pakistan (now Bangladesh). He asked why I didn't apply to the new medical college in Chittagong which was about to open? I had never heard of it, and Chittagong was very far from home.

But that night I thought about it quite a lot and spoke to one or two friends. Some of them encouraged me to try. So far as I was concerned I had no alternative for I was not going to be selected in Dacca, and the other university places had also gone.

The following day was a memorable day. It was 13th August, 1957. I opened up the national newspaper to find that applications for admission to the new medical college in Chittagong were closing that day. Chittagong was a day's journey and there was no way I could submit my application on that day. There were flights there but I would never be able to afford the airfare.

I suddenly thought of wiring the money with a message saying "Application follows".

I went to the main post office but there was a long queue, because the next day was a holiday, Independence Day. I realised that I might not reach the counter before closing time, so I jumped the queue and went straight to the counter clerk. There were protests from other customers but I shouted back that it was an urgent telegram, and I managed to send the fee and the message "Application follows".

In those days it was not possible to travel by train on Independence Day. Because the trains were free, everybody set off on a day out away from home at no cost. So I decided to travel to Chittagong on the 15th August, the day after Independence Day.

The distance from Dacca to Chittagong was more than 250 miles and it would take more than eight hours to get there. There were four classes on the trains and I could only afford the cheapest ticket, with wooden seats, no cushions, no facilities for food or drink and no toilet facilities.

I didn't think I had any friends or relations in Chittagong, which was very far from my village, though I found out that there was a distant relation who worked as a clerk in the railways and lived in the suburbs. I only knew his name and the area where he lived called Pahartali, about five miles from the centre of the town.

On the journey I passed railway stations with names that I had read in books and newspapers. While crossing the rural areas on the way I noticed two differences from my local countryside. One was that the soil was reddish in colour as opposed to greyish in our area. The other was that the cattle in the fields were multi-coloured, whereas in our area the cattle were either all white or all grey or all red – but not a mixture.

I arrived in Chittagong in the late afternoon and found that people were speaking in a language which I could not understand. It was neither Bengali, nor Urdu, nor English – the languages I could understand and speak. I was puzzled but kept quiet. Later I found that this was a colloquial language peculiar to the people of Chittagong and the nearby areas, and not spoken or understood anywhere else.

I didn't know where to stay that night. At the railway station, I hired a cycle rickshaw and the driver took me to a modest hotel near a park. I stayed there overnight and on the following day, I set off for the medical college, which was like a building site. There was lots of construction activity, with plasterers, carpenters and joiners all working away, but I managed to find my way through to the principal's office.

I checked that my fee had been received and handed in my application form, relieved that it was accepted.

At the college I saw boys milling around speaking the unfamiliar language and I asked one of them what it was. It turned out to be the Chittagonian language, a different dialect, related to Bengali but not intelligible to Bengali speakers.

I knew I couldn't afford to stay for long at the hotel so I decided to go to Pahartali to look for my distant relation. I had many concerns. I didn't know what he looked like, how he would behave towards me, or whether his wife would be as hostile as my brother's wife.

Pahartali is famous for two reasons. One is that it was the headquarters of Eastern Bengal Railways where all the high-ranking officials lived in beautiful houses. It was hilly and green with picturesque views. It was built by the British and after Independence the senior officials were mainly non-Bengalis from India, while the clerical posts were filled by Bengalis like my relative. The other reason Pahartali is famous is that in 1930 during British rule, there was a revolt against the British led by educated Hindus, who captured a police station and kept the area independent for two and a half days. The ringleaders were arrested and hanged, but after the creation of Bangladesh in 1971 they were regarded as heroes, with many roads and institutions named after them.

With only the name of my distant relation, I asked a few people whether they knew this man from Kushtia. After several inquiries, someone said that a man of that name ran a sweetmeat shop in the bazaar. I thought that it couldn't be him, because he worked for the railway company. Nevertheless, I went to the shop and found two or three people working there, making mouth-watering Indian sweets. I asked about the owner and, lo and behold, he was the man I was seeking, who turned out to work on the railways during the day and run the shop in the afternoon and at night to supplement his income. I was so pleased.

After about a quarter of an hour, he arrived. His name was Faiz, and I called him Faiz Bhai, "brother Faiz". He was tall and handsome and with a black beard. He asked one of his workers to give me some of the freshly-baked sweetmeats and a glass of water. When I finished he took me to his house, about half a mile from the shop. On the way we talked and he told me that because he only had a clerical job on the railways it was difficult to make ends meet and so the earnings from the sweetshop helped a lot

His home was in a row of terraced bungalow-type houses. There were many such terraces built for the lower classes of railway employees. The house consisted of a bedroom and a sitting room with a kitchen. In the sitting room there were two chairs, one table and one single bed. His wife never presented herself to me. Being very religious. she was maintaining purdah. There were several children, the oldest a girl of ten, and they were surprised to see their father home so early and asked questions about me.

Faiz Bhai said to me without hesitation, "This is your house, this is your bed, stay here as long as you want". Being an intelligent and religious man he realised he was helping a young man in his greatest hour of need.

So I was extremely pleased to have a roof over my head, and something to eat. Without Faiz Bhai's help, I would not have been able to stay in Chittagong, and might never have gone to medical school at all.

The college was about five miles from the house and some days I walked, other days I took a bus or borrowed Faiz's bicycle. I spent each day at the college, hanging around the office, mixing with other boys, and asking the clerical staff about when I would get an interview. In this way, nearly three weeks passed and then one day I was given an appointment for an interview.

At the interview I was asked a number of questions but they were most interested in why I had taken four years to pass my Intermediate (A-level) exam and I told them about my serious illness, from which I nearly died.

On the following day on the notice board I was thrilled to see my name among the successful candidates. At long last I was going to be a medical student. Since it was a new college, the student intake was limited to 75 as opposed to the 120 in Dacca.

Immediately, I sent a telegram to my brother to tell my family that I was selected

I was offered accommodation in a student hostel, a completely empty building with a few wooden beds and I reserved a place for myself with the best view.

Faiz Bhai was delighted with my success. The class was due to start at the end of September 1957, and I took my leave of him and set off on the journey home to bring money, clothes, bed sheets and so on.

My return journey home from Chittagong would take about a day. I had plenty of time on my own on that long journey and I thought long and hard. I had to confront the reality of the situation and my euphoria over getting a place in the medical college disappeared. I knew my family and our financial status and I could see no way that they could meet the expenses of a medical student for five long years or maybe more.

My immediate need was for more than 500 rupees for admission fees, tuition fees, books, hostel accommodation, subsistence, equipment and many other expenses. I could see no way in which my parents could pay for these.

When I reached home, my father and two elder brothers were there. Everyone was pleased at my success in getting into medical school, but I could read from their faces that they were worried about the massive financial undertaking.

Then, help came from an unexpected source. My brother's father-in-law was a successful businessman, financially well off, and was willing to bail us out in our hour of need. None of us suspected that he had an ulterior motive. He promised to give 200 rupees for the admission fees and he said he would contribute a monthly allowance. My father and brother agreed to pay the rest of the money and off I went, back to Chittagong College, a proud member of the first year's intake.

The hostel accommodation was superb. Three of us shared a room. My bed consisted of a homemade quilt, pillow and bed sheet, while the others had properly made mattresses and expensive bed covers, but I never felt bad about it.

I bought some second-hand textbooks, though my roommates had the latest editions. One of my roommates was a well-off non-Bengali from West Pakistan. I improved my English with him. He remained my roommate for six long years and I am still in touch with him.

He has recently retired as a Brigadier from the Pakistan Army and was an eminent anaesthetist in Pakistan.[1]

There were seventy-five entrants to the school, five of them girls. Boys and girls were segregated with their own common rooms. During the classes the girls sat on a separate bench in front, and when the class was over, the girls would leave first and then the boys.

In any medical school, one of the first the first experiences the students come across is the dissection of dead bodies. The first day was very difficult: apprehension, cutting up a human being, the smell of the formaldehyde, and so on. I didn't faint, but others did. Indeed, during the first week as many as ten boys must have dropped out. These were replaced by late admissions from West Pakistan. So when the class was in full swing, twenty percent of the students were from West Pakistan, thirty percent local Hindus, and the rest were local Muslims. I was the only one from a faraway district within East Pakistan.

Sometime in early October 1957, the college was officially opened by the Prime Minister of Pakistan, Mr H.S. Suhrawardy. I remember it very well because I was responsible, along with other boys, for arranging the welcoming ceremony, and putting a plaque on the building, which is still in place.

I was happy in my first year. Winter came and although I did not have any winter clothes, I somehow managed, by avoiding going out in the evening with other boys. One winter afternoon, for example, five of us decided to go to the beach. But when we gathered on the lawn in front of the hostel, I found I needed a jacket or sweater and I didn't have one, so I decided not to go. I had a good *chadder* or shawl, which was very good to keep warm indoors but it wasn't possible to wear it outside. The others were disappointed but never knew the reason.

While the other students were mainly taken up with their studies and how to do well in the next exam, my main worry was money. A hundred rupees a month was enough to live on although I knew some were getting 150 and even 200 rupees. But all I had was 70 rupees, or 80

[1.] This is Brig (R) M. Salim SI(M) MBBS, FCPS, FRCA, D.Sc PhD, who has written the foreword to this book.

if I was lucky. Fifty rupees would come from my father, a few more from my brother's father-in-law, and some from my brother's meagre salary. I had to manage with this amount, which meant no new clothes, and sometimes no refreshments in the afternoon. Luckily the hostel food included breakfast, lunch and evening meals.

This was the first time I found a lot of food on the table and could eat as much as I wanted, in contrast to my days in Kushtia. Though I was constantly short of cash, and didn't have proper clothes, I was very happy. I had many friends, and took up sport, which I never did in Kushtia. For the first time I held a cricket bat and ball in my hand, although my other friends had been cricketers from their school days. I played badminton and became good at it, and in later years I became proud to play with East Pakistan champions. I was also good at volleyball and in my final year I represented the college in a tour of the country.

But the study was hard, with thick anatomy, physiology and biochemistry books all in English by British authors. All of us found it quite difficult in the first six months, and I used to tell myself "You have no option, except to go forward." In fact, on my desk, I had in bold letters two lines of a poem by a famous Bengali poet, which said: "Either you succeed, or perish in the effort". Lot of boys were astounded at that statement and at my seriousness in studying.

The winter in Bangladesh is pleasant and mild. During the coldest weather, the temperature hardly goes below 10°C at night, and it lasts only two to three months. So the winter passed and it was 1958. The most important event in 1958 was the imposition of martial law in Pakistan, and General Ayub Khan took over as the Chief Martial Law Administrator. It did not really affect us in any way, though people felt it would help reduce corruption and other malpractices. I remember immediately after martial law, the price of clothes came down and lots of boys took advantage and bought clothes like jackets, trousers and shirts. But I was not able to buy any, for even if a 100-rupee jacket came down to 70 rupees, I still couldn't afford it.

Soon the summer holidays arrived and it was my first opportunity to go home after nearly nine months. I took the books and a human skeleton with me to study at home because the annual exam would be immediately after the summer holidays.

At home, in the eyes of the villagers, I was a hero, a famous person studying for the Bachelor of Medicine degree, the only one within a radius of twenty miles. My mother could see that I was happy and well-fed. But for all my happiness, I could not concentrate on my studies at home – there was no atmosphere for study. I felt rather complacent and didn't think much about the exams, which seemed so far away.

Then I discovered something that disturbed me a lot. My brother's father-in-law, who had been helping with my expenses, said that in order for the funds to continue I had to agree to marry his third daughter, my brother's wife's sister. It came as a shock to discover the ulterior motive behind his financial assistance. I and my brothers were very disturbed by this behaviour. I made it clear to everybody that no matter what happened I was not going to marry anyone, let alone his daughter. Everybody agreed with my decision but the question now was: who was now going to provide the necessary financial support?

The summer vacation was over and it was time to go back to Chittagong. On my way back I stopped at Kushtia, and found my brother's wife a different person, full of friendship, kindness and affection. On the day I departed for Chittagong she made special food for me to take on the day-long journey on the steamer. While I accepted her changed demeanour and the gestures she made, underneath I remained bitter and antagonistic towards her, both then and now half a century after the event.

Back at the medical college, I found everybody was serious about the forthcoming annual exams and I realised that I was unprepared. Still, I got on with revision to the best of my ability and because it was only an internal examination, I passed like everyone else and was promoted to the second year.

Meanwhile the new first year admissions started, so there were many other boys and few more girls at the college.

My second-year study was very intensive in all subjects. In anatomy, we had to dissect and learn about the brain, and in physiology there were also more complex areas to be covered. The examination between the second and third years would be a very tough one, and include both theory papers and practicals. There would be three outside examiners from places as far away as Karachi, Lahore and Peshawar, in the West Pakistan.

During my second year, I was extremely busy with my studies and my financial crises continued. I never received enough but managed somehow. Then one day I got a letter from my brother in Kushtia saying that it was becoming increasingly difficult for them to provide money every month. So it had been decided that I should marry the daughter of a businessman in a neighbouring town. The marriage had already been arranged and the parents and relations would travel to Chittagong to meet me on a specified date, four days from when I received the letter.

It was a bolt from the blue. What could I do? I was angry and frustrated that when others were preparing for the exam, I had to fight off a marriage. I had just managed to avoid an engagement in my first year and now I was confronted with another one. I did not want to be compelled to marry, but to be free like all the other students to build my career first.

I told a few of my friends about the letter, and some were sarcastic, others joked about the prospect of marriage, but one or two were sympathetic.

I decided that whatever happened I was not going to marry anyone for the time being. I booked a trunk call to my brother in Kushtia and told him in no uncertain terms that I was not prepared to marry. He believed me but advised me not to disrespect the girl's father who was already on his way to visit me in Chittagong.

The expected date came and the father and few other people arrived at my hostel, where my friends had arranged some refreshments for them. They asked me a few questions, had their tea and were about to leave. Then the father of the prospective bride, a dignified man and well dressed, offered me money, enough for a month's expenses. I was astounded. He explained: "From now on, I will be providing your expenses – this is just the beginning!" I told him and the accompanying guests that I was deeply "honoured" and that I would accept his money at some point but I was not prepared to do so when there was no legal marriage agreement. They were convinced and pleased with my reply and off they went.

After they left, I contemplated my future. If my father and brother were unable to provide my expenses and I was not prepared to marry anybody's daughter simply for money, what was the alternative? It looked as if it would not be possible for me to continue my studies in medicine.

One possibility was to enlist in the forces. There was an air force recruiting office within walking distance of the medical college, and I thought I could give up my studies and join the Pakistan Air Force. This was like any other branch of the armed forces and dominated by Punjabis and Pathans from West Pakistan. There were virtually no senior officers in the P.A.F from East Bengal (East Pakistan) though there may have been a few in the junior ranks.

Anyway, I made an appointment with the recruiting officer, and found that the person in charge was a Bengali. I told him my problem and the reason for trying to join the P.A.F. He listened very carefully and said that with my qualifications I could apply for commissioned officer rank but had no chance of being selected because of my background as East Pakistani. But I could join as a non-commissioned officer at any time if I wished.

I went back to the hostel but could not concentrate on my studies. I was at a crossroads having either to join the non-commissioned ranks of the P.A.F., or somehow continue to study.

A few days later, I received a lengthy letter from my brother. The family of the would-be bride had reported back to him. They had been very pleased to meet me and were impressed with my hospitality, but could not understand why I refused to accept their money. My brother explained that I was not going to marry anyone, let alone his daughter. He told me to "imagine it was all a bad dream", forget about it, concentrate on your studies and money will be found somehow.

With that reassurance, I felt tremendous relief and for the first time for many weeks, started concentrating on my studies for the forthcoming university exam, which everyone was dreading.

I managed to prepare myself to the best of my ability and the exam date was approaching fast. All the sixty-five students were on edge, for this would be a very tough examination with outside examiners. We would be examined in Anatomy, Physiology and Biochemistry. It was rumoured that one of the examiners in Anatomy had recently returned from doing his PhD in England, and his work was so renowned that his name appeared in the world-famous *Gray's Anatomy*, and indeed those who had the latest edition of the reference book found his name here. When he actually came to examine us, I found him very friendly and he asked the questions with the intention of helping us to pass.

Like other students, I sat all the examinations, both written and practical. There was no way to tell how I had done. To me it seemed that I did reasonably well, but I could not be certain about the outcome. While other students were confident that if they failed they would carry on regardless, for me failure would mean the end of my medical career.

So the examination was over and the summer vacation started. I packed my bags and went back to my village home, not knowing whether I would return to Chittagong to continue my studies. It would be nearly three months before the results would be out. When I left Chittagong I had left my address with a lady friend of mine to drop me a line to let me know the result.

In the village, everybody knew that I was "a doctor". Illiterate people did not know that I didn't have any clinical knowledge, and they would seek me out with their illnesses but I politely declined to see them. But there was one incident which I must mention. I was asked to see a patient, a boy of about seven or eight at his home, where I found there was already a "doctor", a village quack who had begged me to come.

The boy had climbed a tree to pick a guava. Guava trees are long and slender and as he was coming down, his shorts got caught in a dead branch. As he struggled to release himself, his shorts were torn and so was his scrotum. When I went to see him, I found that one testicle was quite open to the air, and his scrotum was missing, perhaps still hanging on the guava tree, and the boy was in a lot of pain.

I knew enough to decide that the open testicle had to be covered by suturing the adjoining skin. The boy screamed as I cut the ragged skin and asked the quack to suture the opposing sides. It was fixed. The boy got better and later as a young man he suffered no ill-effects.

I was waiting anxiously in my village home for the exam results and one day a letter arrived. To my great delight, I found that I had passed. The friend who had written to me had herself failed and out of sixty-five candidates, only thirteen had succeeded and I was one of them. I was so happy and so were my parents, and I thought to myself that there was now a chance that I would become a doctor.

6

Hopes dashed and raised

I returned to Chittagong in triumph. I was so happy and proud that despite all the difficulties in my pre-clinical years, and against all the odds, I had made it. At the students' hostel, my friends gave me a warm welcome.

The clinical classes started, covering medicine, surgery, gynaecology, pathology, pharmacology, public health and medical jurisprudence. These were vast subjects to contemplate as the academic year began.

In various ways, luck shone on me. Firstly, the financial aspect. I found a notice from the principal's office that some scholarships were available for the meritorious student, for which I applied without wasting any time. I explained my financial situation at home, and in the light of my good results I was given not only a monthly stipend but also, even more helpfully, the annulment of my tuition fee, which was a considerable amount of money and had to be paid twice a year. So with this financial assistance, I was able to buy text books which were needed immediately and also a couple of pairs of trousers, a white coat and a stethoscope. Also, our pathology teacher wanted us to wear a neck-tie, so with a white coat, a neck-tie, and a stethoscope in the pocket, I felt happy and proud and looked and felt like a budding doctor.

I found all the clinical subjects very interesting, from pathology to medical jurisprudence. The food was good at the hostel, and I continued to take part in the various indoor games, mainly badminton and volleyball.

By this time, other students had been admitted to the college, so the number of students also increased.

After three months into the clinical years, the pathology professor, a smart man from the Indian state of Hyderabad, decided to set an exam on what had been taught so far. He gave a week's notice. Pathology, which mainly deals with human organs when diseased, was one of my favourite subjects. I found it fascinating and thoroughly enjoyed it. The questions were easy and simple and I answered them to the best of my ability. A week later, as I was walking down a corridor in the college, I was asked by the professor to see him in his office. I wondered about the reason. Could it be that I had offended him by talking to girls in front of his office? I went into his office with tremendous apprehension. He asked me to sit and then asked how I thought I had done in the exam. I said that I hoped not too badly. Then he said "Will you swear that you did not copy from the book?" I was pleasantly surprised. I said "No, sir. You can ask me now and I could recite every word I have written." He was pleased and convinced and told me that I had secured the top mark. I was overjoyed. From that day onward, I was held in high esteem by my fellow students, and my name and fame spread to the other teachers. In classes or tutorials, the other students would be asked a question and when everybody failed to answer, it would be passed to me.

I was not only doing extremely well in my study, but also in sports, particularly volleyball where I was in the college team. At this point, there was another development. There were the Students Union elections. Since all the students had confidence in me, I was asked to stand for the President. I reluctantly agreed. My supporters were delighted. I was required to make a speech in front of the whole college explaining why they should vote for me. I had never spoken in the public before this. When I went to the dais, the fact that everybody was looking at me gave me a strange feeling. Never in my life had so many people looked at me at the same time. The election was held and I was elected as the president with an overwhelming majority.

This was the time of martial law and within the college I was seen as the first student. When any foreign dignitary or local ministers came to visit the college, I would represent the students and show them around.

At this time we were required to move to another hostel, which was bigger and multi-storied, and the current hostel would become a female students' hotel. The boys' new hostel was five hundred yards away behind a hill. I was asked by the principal to be 'Prefect' of the new hostel, which meant I would be responsible for the discipline of the hostel and looking after the welfare of the students.

So here I was, not only doing well in my studies, but also the Students' Union president and a prefect of the hostel. Our principal's son was admitted in his first year, and he mentioned to his friends that at the dining table the principal had been described me as the ideal student. I was flattered.

During my tenure as the Student Union president, we held the college sports for the first time, when a lot of civil and military dignitaries were invited and I had to receive them and introduce them to other members of the 'Cabinet'. I also took part in the sports and got a first prize in javelin throw – a shaving kit.

My third year in the medical school and first year in the clinical class passed very quickly. The fourth year arrived and I was able to concentrate more on my studies because my tenure as president of the Students' Union was coming to an end.

At this time, we were told that the President of Pakistan was coming to visit the college and would lay the foundation stone of the new hospital, which would have five hundred beds, and a heliport at the top to ferry patients from distant parts of the country. As the President of the Students Union I would have to meet and receive the country's President. But how? It was winter and I did not even have a jacket, but I would be required to wear a suit.

I was saved by my room-mate and close friend from West Pakistan. He had a suit and I tried it on and it actually fitted.

The president came and I was walking beside him as the photographers took their pictures. (I lost all of these photographs in the Bangladesh War of 1971). There were lots of foreign diplomats and other ministers, and as the Students' representation I sat in the front row.

In my fourth year, the college was full of students, many from West Pakistan, and some were very handsome and very good at cricket. A few were from the remote area of Pakistan call Swat. On the day of Eid –

the festival marking the end of Ramadan – various students from different parts of Pakistan would wear their national dress and it would look very colourful. Life was so smooth and enjoyable and many students looked to me as their role model. The number of girls also increased. There was a girl from Karachi, not particularly beautiful, but the way she walked, talked and dressed caught my eye. I said to myself that at this point in my student life when I have almost everything, it would be nice to find a girl that I could marry.

Religion and culture forbade free mixing and the only contact with the opposite sex was in the college corridors or in front of the girl students' hostel in the full view of others. I decided to express some interest in this girl, who must have been from a rich family, like most of the West Pakistanis. I sent a message through my own class friends who were staying in the ladies hostel. Some of them giggled, but nevertheless the message reached her. She responded and we met many times at the corridor and in front of the hostels and spoke about shared interests, our studies, hobbies and so on. By now everybody in the college, including the teachers, believed I was in love with this girl, but I was not sure. I was conscious of my background, my upbringing, and the tremendous financial burden now and when I qualified. The exams were getting nearer and so I concentrated on my studies.

The 2nd MBBS exam as it was called is another university exam. All the teachers and fellow students were confident that I would pass without any difficulty. The thirteen students who had passed the 1st MBBS exams were allowed to sit. We were the vanguard.

I did well in all the subjects and I was introduced to the examiners not only as a good student, but also the president of the Students' Union. After finishing the exam, we continued to study the remaining subjects of surgery, medicine and gynaecology. The final exam would be in another year's time, when I would qualify as a doctor, but would be the hardest exam of all.

While I was waiting for my results I was surprised one day when my cousin's brother, who worked in a police department in another district, knocked on my door at the hostel. I was in touch with his wife, writing letters, telling her about my life in the medical college, and she knew how hard up I was. But this was not a family visit. The man was in the Criminal Investigation Department (CID) and had come across my name in a police file, identifying me as one of the student leaders, and alleging that I was against the martial law regime. I first thought that he had come to Chittagong on an official visit and was paying a courtesy call to me, and would perhaps offer some financial help. However, it turned out that the sole purpose of his visit was to tell me to resign my post as the president of the Students' Union. I politely declined and he left.

But this man came to a sticky end in 1971. During the uprising, he wanted to prove to the Pakistanis that he was loyal to them, while the majority of the police force left for India and joined the war of liberation. But he was suspected of being a spy and was shot by the Pakistani army. His body lay on the road unclaimed for three days.

The results of the exam came out and, as expected, I passed easily, and began the final year of my medical studies. I was at the summit of my student life, with an immaculate academic record and the presidency of the Students' Union, which meant that I was the point of contact with the authorities over any student problem.

I remember one particular incident. A student from the first year failed three times to get into the clinical class. After three successive failures he should automatically have been removed from the course, and he came to me for help. I made a strong representation to the Military Administrator, explaining that he had some family problems and financial difficulties, and I argued that should be given another chance. He was allowed to stay and qualified as a doctor, and I later learnt that he became a high-earning oncologist in North America.

My financial situation was a bit better, with no tuition fees, the small allowance from home, and a small scholarship for maintenance.

Also at this time I was made the manager of the Students' Mess, which everybody has to do in turn. When my turn came, I would go to the market with a servant and do the shopping myself. There was always haggling. I would bargain with shopkeepers and buy the articles, but when it came to accounting I would put down the price that had been asked before I beat the tradesman down, as I did during my time in Kushtia. In this way, I saved a bit of money with which I would buy a pair of good quality trousers and a shirt.

With four years of intake, the medical school now had nearly 250 students, mainly boys but with a few girls. With my academic record and my social activities, I was at the peak of my success and had only a year to go before I qualified as a doctor. I was now in my final year and had to cover vast amounts of material in a short time.

But I had became complacent. I was one of the star students, and had done so well that I would surely easily pass the finals. I continued my studies but also spent time on my other pursuits, including being active in student politics.

But the biggest distraction from my work was taking part in a month-long college sports tour where we played other medical schools in East Pakistan. I was in the college volleyball team and was chosen to be leader of the whole group, including other sports. We were to visit three areas, Rajshahi, Dacca, and Sylhet. The tour would take about a month and would be financed by the Government. Although there would be a teacher in nominal charge, I was chosen to be the leader of the whole team, consisting of about fifty students. It was up to me whether I should accept this offer, and my self-confidence led me to think that I could easily manage a month away from my studies.

We were entertained lavishly in each of the places we visited, and being the leader, I was always occupying pride of place on any formal occasion.

When we reached Dacca and I met some of the students preparing for their final exam only months away, I realised what a mistake I had made in deciding to come on this trip. Dacca Medical College was the most prestigious medical school in East Pakistan, the one I failed to get into four years earlier. Everybody here was taking the exams very seriously and here was I ignoring my studies to tour the country. But there was nothing I could do, it was too late. After a month, we returned to Chittagong on a misty winter morning, and I found my fellow students glued to their books, which made me realise what a mountain I had to climb. I started revising in earnest.

One evening I was in a group of five students in a tutorial class at a patient's bedside. The professor of surgery asked me a question which I could not answer, but the other students could. He said in front of the other students and the patient: "if you can't answer this question, how do you expect to pass the exam in a few months' time?" I was shocked, horrified and humiliated. This was the first time in the last four and a half years that I had not been able to hold my head high in front of everybody. It dented my confidence and I realised how far behind I was.

The final exam was entirely different from earlier ones. Although there was a written paper, the most important part was the practical, where you are tested by being given a patient and have to make a diagnosis and answer questions from external examiners from Dacca and West Pakistan. The practical exam would consist of a long case, short cases and use of medical equipment. It was a lengthy and tedious process and would go on for several days. If you fail in one part, then that's it. You have to do equally well in all areas.

So the final exam date arrived. I did well in the written exam, but my main concern was the practicals. We had heard horror stories of candidates in Dacca Medical College where the pass rate was 10% and there were students who might take ten or twelve years to qualify.

During the practicals I held my nerve in the major subjects of medicine and surgery and became more hopeful. The last practical was gynaecology, an easy subject, I thought, so I devoted less energy to it. The practical exam seemed easy. I was given a case and did well, but there was one last question where I blundered. I gave totally the wrong answer. The examiners were visibly surprised and left the bedside. I then knew that I had failed.

I was disheartened and demoralised. The results would be out in two months' time and I had to hope against hope that I might pass. My fellow students and some of the teachers thought I would, but in my heart of hearts I knew there was no chance.

Meanwhile, a very close friend of mine who was a few years below me suggested that I visit a fakir or holy man whom he knew, for his blessings which might make me pass. When I arrived at his house, the fakir was on his own, a very old man with a white beard, with shaking head and hands. My friend explained to him why I had come. He was deaf, but after shouting he understood. He replied in an inaudible and Chittagonian accent that "I would be successful". He was sipping tea in a mug and handed over the half-finished mug of tea to me, and asked me to drink. I hesitated, but my friend looked at me and insisted I drink it. I did, and left.

I knew I would fail, so I decided that I would await the result in Dacca where no one could find me. The result would be declared at the Senate House of the university on an outside notice board.

That evening I walked past the Senate House. There were a number of students, all of them from Dacca Medical College and no one knew me. I went up to the notice board and scanned it. My fear and apprehension was confirmed – my name was not there. Only about five students had passed and I was not one of them – ironic in the light of the fact that, at one time it was anticipated that if there was one boy who would succeed it would be me.

I was thoroughly disappointed and did not know who to turn to. I told myself that those five students would be writing "Dr" before their name, whereas I – a star pupil – was still a student, with no money, and nowhere even to express myself.

I had written to my father that I had done badly in the exam, and the family graciously accepted it. They knew that in studying medicine, hardly anyone passes the first time. But my brother in Kushtia did not believe that I might not pass. In fact, with my past record he was so confident that he had already told his friends and some of my old friends that I had passed.

I stayed in Dacca for more than a week with a friend and relation, a university student. He was financially hard up like me, but at least he gave me shelter. We shared the same bed and ate food in his hostel. I did not feel like shaving, so I grew a thick, black beard. After a week or so I told myself, "You must pick yourself up and fight back". I had a portrait photograph taken in a studio and then shaved my beard.

I had only just enough money to return to Chittagong Railway Station. No money for food or drink and no rickshaw fare to go to the hostel which was about five miles from the railway station.

During the journey, I could not afford anything to eat or drink. The journey was about eight hours. When I reached Chittagong, I was tired and night was closing in. I had no option but to walk through the dark to my hostel.

My roommates were pleased to see me, welcomed me, comforted me and took me to the dining room for a meal and a cigarette. I felt happy to be back in my digs.

But I knew I was a failure. The high hopes with which my medical career started had evaporated. I was also conscious that I had already lost two years of study even before starting the medical course. I avoided all the senior students who had been with me for so long, particularly those who had passed. I felt inferior to them. Then of course, there was the question of financial support. How was I going to support myself? But I took comfort from the fact that I had only one subject to clear, one of the easiest subjects, and I would have no problem in passing the next examination which was only six months away.

I didn't receive any letter of consolation from my brother, but my father wrote a long letter from the village, giving me lots of help and courage. He asked me to have faith in God and continue studying, as if nothing had happened. He also wrote to me that the money would be provided from home since my brother who had contributed 20% of the required amount could not continue to do so, because he had decided to take early retirement from his clerical job. I knew this meant a further strain on my father and hardship to the family in Dharmadaha, but I had no option and hoped and prayed that six months should pass quickly.

But those six months turned into a year.

There had been a catastrophic cyclone in Chittagong which caused immense damage to the lives of people, their livestock and houses. The entire family of one of our teachers, including his parents and children, perished. They were all in their house celebrating a wedding when the cyclone and tidal waves struck. Also, the eldest sister of my roommate and close friend died, along with her entire family. Thousands of other people died too.

The exam was postponed and some of the students in clinical classes were drafted to go to the villages and islands to give vaccinations and inoculations to stricken people. I was the leader of a group of four volunteers and saw some awful sights of human suffering in the rural areas. There were dead and bloated bodies of cattle strewn everywhere and the atmosphere filled with a foetid smell. The army was mobilised and soldiers piled up the bodies, put petrol on them and set them alight. Survivors had no food, no shelter and nowhere to spend the night. It was a quagmire.

However, I returned to the students' dormitory and started concentrating on my studies. Martial law was in full swing, and there was student unrest countrywide, which meant I could not sit the exam, which kept on being postponed for one reason or another. I became impatient because I had nothing to do. My studies were not that laborious or difficult. I prayed for the exam finally to be held, but it kept on being postponed. My financial hardship worsened and in the end I started borrowing from friends, but kept a record of how much I borrowed and from whom. Also, I owed money to the college canteen and promised them to pay when I qualified. In this way, nearly a year passed and finally we were given the exam date of September, 1963.

As expected, the actual exam was not at all difficult. By this time, I was a veteran and had no problem in answering the theory or the practicals. After the exam, I knew I would pass and headed home immediately afterwards.

After a few months, the result was declared, once again from the Senate House in Dhaka University, and a friend of mine sent me a telegram addressed to "Dr Wajed". I should have been pleased but I had something else to think about.

While I was at home waiting for the result, I noticed that my urine had become unusually coloured and my stool rather grey. I checked my eyes and realised that I had jaundice. I felt generally unwell, and had gone off my food. While my parents and everybody at home and in the village rejoiced at the exam result, I could not share their happiness because of my health. I knew that I had infective hepatitis which could have serious repercussions, such as liver failure, but who could I share my worries with? Since I was now a doctor, everybody believed I was immune to all diseases, and even if I did have some ailment I should heal myself. At the village level, there was no medical care and no proper nutrition. However, I decided to increase my fluid intake, mainly with green coconut water and a glucose drink. I avoided eating any protein, such as meat.

In my honour on a Friday, my father slaughtered two goats, and invited my relations from far and wide and some village folk, and we had a good feast. Unfortunately, I could not eat any of this food, which my mother noticed and she begged me to eat and in turn I begged her not to insist. The poor woman was hurt and could not understand why. I tried to explain – but she was not convinced. Her view was that if I didn't have a temperature and was not bedridden nothing could be wrong.

Once the feast was over, I gradually got better and thought of trekking back to Chittagong for my house officer's job, the next stage in my training. Meanwhile, there was countrywide agitation by doctors for an increase in pay and salary which was much lower than our counterparts in West Pakistan and those who were in the army.

I got a letter from a friend in Chittagong who had also qualified, asking me to return to Chittagong immediately to provide leadership there and link up with our comrades in Dhaka. I wrote back that I was on my way and would be prepared to add fuel to the fire. But my real intention was rather different.

When I arrived back in Chittagong I was faced with a dilemma. It was clear that my fellow doctors and senior students wanted me to lead the movement for a countrywide strike but I was in no mood for such a struggle, purely for financial reasons. My family back at home was totally exhausted and I was in no position to ask for any more money from them to support me. I knew they would be relieved by this.

My roommate, Salim from West Pakistan, with whom I had shared a room for five years, had also passed the exam. He was non-political. He was jubilant that he passed and it did not matter to him if he just sat tight until the strike was settled one way or the other. But I was not prepared to do that.

I had heard that there was a private hospital in Mirzapore, nearly 200 miles north-west of Chittagong and about 100 miles from Dhaka, and they needed doctors. I told Salim that I would try my luck there, and he could accompany me if he so wished.

One night we packed our bags and left for the station. A few fellow students asked where we were going and I said that I was travelling to Dhaka in connection with the strike. They believed me. I headed straight for Mirzapore with Salim.

I may have betrayed the trust of my friends, but I had no option. I desperately needed to earn money to support myself. No matter what happened with the strike, revolts, doctors' pay and conditions, I could not care less. In fact, the strike did not last long. The government identified three or four ringleaders in Dhaka and bribed them to go to England, which was enough of an incentive for them to leave the country and the strike was over.

The doctor's life

The train left the platform of the Chittagong Railway Station for Dhaka. I had arrived six years earlier, a penniless youth, unsure of whether I would ever get into medicine, but six long years later, I was still penniless, but now a young doctor, full of hope and aspirations. Now I had to leave Chittagong at the dead of night and breaking the trust of so many fellow doctors and medical students who knew me as an ideal student and able leader.

My friend Salim was with me, which lessened the burden quite a bit, as he was a Punjabi from West Pakistan and not as emotional as us Bengalis. We were both travelling into the unknown, with the hope that we would get a job somewhere and earn enough money to support ourselves.

We were travelling to the capital Dhaka, and from there to the private hospital in Mirzapore. It was about a hundred miles from the capital and would take nearly half a day by ramshackle privately-owned buses. We arrived in Dhaka in the early morning and I avoided the Medical College and the university area in case I was seen by fellow doctors, who would wonder why we were in Dhaka instead of joining in the activism in Chittagong. The following morning we took a bus to Mirzapore and our final destination, Kumudini Hospital.

Mirzapore is in a district called Mymensingh. Before the partition of India and Bengal in 1947, Bengal had 28 administrative districts. The administrative head was called the District Magistrate and before independence this post was occupied by an Englishman. Of the 28 districts, Mymensingh was the largest. The vast majority of the population were Muslims, poor peasant folk who worked on the land owned by Hindu landlords or so-called *zamindars*. There were many such feudal lords who wielded enormous local powers and had total control over the people who worked for them. The Hindu *zamindars* were rich, educated, and had links with the English administration elite, whereas the vast majority of the Muslim population were illiterate, religious and eked out an existence from the Hindu-owned land.

So in spite of the Muslim majority, Mymensingh was under Hindu influence and our hospital in Mirzapore was no exception.

Kumudini Hospital was entirely private and financed by a Hindu businessman, Ranada Prasad Saha, who had been poor and uneducated in his youth. He was very old by the time I met him. The hospital was in the name of his mother who had died without any medical assistance. When Mr Saha made enough money in his jute business he decided to spend all his profits on building and equipping the hospital and on the day-to-day running. When I joined in the winter of 1963 or early 1964 it was a fully functioning hospital, with departments of surgery, medicine, and gynaecology with operating theatres and out-patient facilities. Treatment was totally free of charge. Although the medical, nursing and non-medical staff were overwhelmingly Hindu, the vast majority of the patients were Muslims. Mr Saha's intention was that his hospital should provide for people who were too poor to afford medical help. For this act of charity, Mr Saha was well known in political circles and had links with high officials. We were told that the President of Pakistan had visited the hospital a few years earlier. This influential and philanthropic man, along with his young son, was kidnapped by the Pakistan military during the Independence movement in 1971 and never heard from again.

I started my work at the Kumudini Hospital as a junior doctor in the medical ward. The consultant was a chest physician but had to deal with all sorts of medical problems which, in retrospect, he did not do well. I was recently qualified and put in charge of a ward of patients with various medical conditions, some of them really acute and complicated. There was no one to supervise my work and the consultant would do his round only once a day – so the day-to-day running of the ward was entirely up to me. If I made mistakes, patients could die. There was no accountability, and certainly I did not learn much there during my six months stay. There were two episodes which haunted me for a long time. One was that of a boy around 10 years of age, admitted with severe respiratory tract infection with uncontrollable cough. Along with other medication I gave him oral cough linctus but in an adult dose. It was my mistake and nobody queried it, not even the nurse who administered the drug. The nursing staff carried out the orders of the doctors without question. The boy's condition deteriorated, he had difficulty breathing, and died soon after. I know for a fact that this boy would not have died if there had been someone there to spot my mistake

The other episode involved a doctor. A local general practitioner of many years duration was admitted with shortness of breath and chest pain. I found him gasping for breath. There was no oxygen, and he was too ill to be sent out for an x-ray, and there was no portable x-ray in the hospital. I wanted to take some blood but I could not get into a vein anywhere. I called for my boss to deal with the situation but he was indecisive. He did not take any drastic measures to help the man, who died the same night. In retrospect, I think the patient was in shock, probably from a pulmonary embolism, and could have been saved with appropriate treatment.

But on the plus side, during my six-month stay lots of patients came from my village and surrounding areas and they were well looked after, received successful treatment and returned home full of praise.

My father had always suffered from peptic ulcer-related problems and fell seriously ill, so I went to my village home and brought him to the Kumudini Hospital. He was with me for two weeks, got better, and I managed to discharge him in excellent health. I remember the day I took him home. He looked so happy, so full of life and was so proud of me. I too felt immensely happy that after all those years of suffering and deprivation, I was able to repay something to my father. To this day I still remember his happy and smiling face.

Life was good in Mirzapore. I had enough money to support myself. I was young and a bachelor, and had friends including Salim. For the doctors' relaxation, there were both indoor and outdoor games like billiards, table-tennis, lawn tennis and badminton.

The nurses of the Kumudini Hospital were overwhelmingly Hindus and they were very friendly and cultured. I became friendly with one of them during my stay there. Friendship in those days just meant that. There was no scope for meeting by ourselves and certainly not for intimacy. She was a good girl, but whenever we met she would keep on about the future and marriage. She was insecure and I could see that she was trying to get some security by marrying a doctor, even if it meant a Muslim. When I left Mirzapore, she still visited me at Dhaka once or twice.

I realised that my stay in Mirzapore was a bit of a dead end, with no prospect of higher studies or furthering my career. It was fine as a stop-gap, but not for more than six months, although there were doctors who fell in love with Mirzapore and stayed there for many years. I was determined not to fall in the trap of an easy life in Mirzapore and looked for a job with a Government hospital.

I applied for such a job through the usual channels and was asked to attend an interview in Dhaka, but I kept the whole thing secret from my colleagues.

There was a national shortage of doctors so Government jobs were available in plenty. But I would have to take a chance on what vacancy turned up. It might be in a rural dispensary with a whole range of tasks, or at a teaching hospital in a subject of my choice. But a teaching hospital job was impossible, unless you were a talented student with a gold medal, or connected with ministers or people holding positions at the top. I was none of these and so prepared myself mentally to accept any job, in any subject and in any part of the country. But my dream job was in medicine in the teaching hospital in Dhaka though I knew this was impossible.

On the day of the interview I slipped away to Dhaka, some three hours by bus. As luck would have it, I found myself appearing in the interview in front of my teacher from Chittagong Medical College. He knew me well as a student and was pleased to see me. This was a new post and promotion for him as Under-Secretary of the Department of Health. At Chittagong he was our professor of hygiene and public health.

At the interview he asked me what I was looking for. I told him that I really wanted a career in medicine in a teaching hospital. He said that in medicine it would be difficult, but would try his best to place me in a good hospital. Thanking him, I left.

A week later, I got a letter telling me that I had been appointed a Gazetted Officer at the famous Dhaka Medical College Hospital in the department of Clinical Pathology. Like other appointments it was also published in national newspapers.

I was thrilled. The appointment was beyond my wildest dreams. When I broke the news to other medical colleagues, they couldn't believe it and some of them were under the impression that I had some influence at the top. Whatever they may have thought, I am so grateful to the professor who let me into the doors of Dhaka Medical College, an event which shaped my future.

I handed in my notice to the hospital authorities. My friends, particularly Salim, were sad, but he left a few months after me and got a job as an anaesthetist in the West Pakistan Health Service. We would meet up again in England.

It was while I was at Mirzapore and the Kumudini Hospital, that we heard of the terrible Hindu/Muslim riots in 1964.

The problems had started in Kashmir in early 1964 when the well-preserved hair of the Prophet Mohammed in a mosque in Kashmir was stolen and the blame fell on the Hindus. The situation in India between Hindus and Muslims were like a powder keg and it didn't take more than a spark to ignite it. There were riots in parts of India, and Muslims were massacred, and it was a only matter of time before reprisals started in the main towns and cities of East Pakistan. The worst affected areas were the suburbs of Dhaka, largely an industrial area. The inhabitants were mainly Punjabi/Urdu speaking from West Pakistan along with Urdu-speaking refugees from the Bihar state of India. These people had their own community, and the only thing they had in common with the natives of East Pakistan was that they were all Muslim. Other than that, their food, language and culture were quite different. And these Biharis were fiercely anti-Indian or anti-Hindu, probably because they were had suffered from racial and religious hatred and were uprooted from their homes during the Partition of India in 1947.

We heard about these riots and the killing of Hindus through radio broadcasts and newspapers. We knew that there had been terrible atrocities and saw crowds of people flooding in to our hospital with knife-wounds and gun-shot wounds. Every victim told us of killings and rape that had gone on for several days.

The doctors in the hospital, mainly Hindus, were terrified. They wouldn't venture outside the walls of the hospital. They were naturally anxious about what might happen. There was no protection from the authorities and at any time anyone could have been attacked, so the Hindus organised a vigilante group who patrolled the area at night. A few days later an army platoon was dispatched and stationed within the hospital compound, giving some reassurance to the hospital staff.

As a Muslim I did not feel at all apprehensive. One day, one of my Hindu doctor colleagues wanted to go to the bazaar and the post office, which was only half a mile away from the hospital. He wanted me to accompany him for protection so we hired a rickshaw and drove to the town centre. There was an eerie atmosphere. No one was laughing or talking much, though some of the shops were open. In the market we saw a man's body, obviously dead and covered with a white sheet, and people were waiting for the police to arrive. I felt uncomfortable but my colleague even more disturbed. We went to the post office, where we met the postmaster, whom I knew. He told me that the situation was grave and I should return to the hospital compound without delay. I also saw the Officer-in-Charge at the local police station. He was sending a telegram to his superior saying: "Situation grave – send reinforcements". We returned to the hospital compound, thoroughly shaken.

One day, the consultants decided that we should go out to the villages to give medical aid to the victims of the religious riots. We fixed up a date, the hospital authority gave us a mini-bus, and we collected medical supplies, bandages, injections, and antibiotics.

All of us being Muslims, we had no apprehension. As a young doctor, in the company of other young doctors, and led by a foreign qualified consultant surgeon I had no worries and just took it as a sort of adventure.

When we reached the stricken area, I was not prepared mentally for the sights we saw. In one village, there were few houses standing, most burnt to the ground with the inhabitants either fled or killed and burnt along with the houses. The stench was overwhelming. However, we did see a few intact houses, completely untouched and with Pakistani flags flying. When we reached them, it transpired that they all belonged to the Muslims. Some of the Hindus, who had been neighbours for centuries, took shelter in those houses, and many of them had knife wounds which we attended.

We heard the full horrors from the Muslim elder of the house who told us that both the Hindus and Muslims had lived together in harmony in the village and there had been no animosity between them. But marauding factory workers from the industrial suburbs of Dhaka had descended on the village at night and carried out inhuman massacres and destruction of property and decimated the Hindu population. We asked how the Muslims could identify the houses that belonged to the Hindus and the answer was that there were a few collaborators among the Muslims who carried out personal vendettas by identifying the Hindu houses for the mob

We left that village and went to another one nearby, which was a bit more well-to-do. There were many brick-built and corrugated tin-roofed houses, a sign of wealth in rural Bengal. The houses were surrounded by coconut trees with ponds nearby. The village had a secondary school and the headmaster was a Hindu. His house was untouched, because some of his Muslim students had defended him, his family and property. However, his neighbouring Hindus were not so lucky. When we reached his house and told him that we were a group of doctors from Kumudini Hospital, Mirzapore, he ventured outside. He was an educated man in his fifties, unshaven and still in shock and he told us that there were some injured people who had taken shelter in his house. One of us went inside the house and in one room there were a few people huddled together, too frightened to come out. I remember distinctly that there was a girl of not more than ten or twelve hiding under a bed, who would not come out fearing for her life, for she had seen the death of her parents at the hands of the rioters. However, when she was persuaded to come out and told that we were all doctors who had come to help her she emerged totally shocked, holding her left hand with the right, and we saw that there was a deep knife wound in her left hand which was infected. That had happened three days earlier and she had been in hiding since then without any food or water. We attended to her wound, cleaned and bandaged it, gave her an antitetanus jab and left some antibiotics.

The headmaster was grateful, but I never saw any bitterness in him against the Muslims.

It was getting dark, and there was an eerie atmosphere of burnt-down houses, death, damage and destruction. Somebody said that we might even be a target because we had given aid to non-Muslims. It did not frighten us, for we had enough self-confidence.

As we were driving back to our hospital I thought to myself that in a way it would be better for the Hindus to leave *en masse* to India, rather than stay here and risk suffering death, damage and psychological trauma.

In fact, when the riots declined, my Hindu friends and colleagues from Chittagong and Mirzapore left. I never knew what happened to most of them, but I later heard the stories of two of them who left for India.

One of them was Samar Chowdhry, a friend from my class in Chittagong. After the riots he went to India and did his finals in Calcutta. After qualifying, he joined the Indian Army Medical Service and was with the Indian Army when they entered East Pakistan in 1971, which culminated in the creation of Bangladesh. It appears that during that conflict he was involved in a road traffic accident and lost his life. I remember him very well. He was from a well-to-do family and in our third year he had an air rifle with which he used to shoot birds in the nearby hills. One day, he was showing off with his air rifle to a group of teenage boys and it accidentally went off, hitting the son of the college principal The principal was a very powerful authority within the hospital and both the students and teaching staff were afraid of his ill-temper. Some people also accused him of being anti-Hindu. So when his son was hit there was a great commotion and as the prefect of the hostel I was in the front line.

I took the boy to the A&E Department of the hospital, where the casualty officer was himself shaken to see the principal's son, bleeding through the back of the ear. I had to tell the principal that his son has been taken to the A&E Department with a gunshot wound, and the whole hospital was waiting to see how he would react. Meanwhile, some of us suggested that Samar keep a low profile. At the hospital, an x-ray showed a pellet lodged behind the ear, just under the skin, so it would not be a problem to extract it.

The principal arrived with his eldest son who had just entered the medical school. He was subdued and he didn't raise his voice, but just asked whether his son's vital organs were spared. The pellet was removed under local anaesthesia and all was well. Eventually, Samar's father approached the principal and personally apologised and so did Samar who wrote a letter of apology. After this event, everything settled down until the Hindu-Muslim riots of '64 when Samar, along with others, emigrated to India.

Some other medical students who migrated to India also joined the Indian Army Medical Services and were posted in the western front, between East and West Punjab. It was in 1972 when Bangladesh had already been created and many of the Bengali military personnel were trapped in West Pakistan. They were prisoners of war and were being detained in various POW camps. One of my friends, a doctor, decided to escape. He, along with some others, left the camp and walked miles and miles to reach the Indian border. When they reached it they were totally exhausted and were unable to go further. They surrendered to the Indian Army, who of course had received many P.O.W's during the conflict and actively helped them transfer to the Bangladesh border. My doctor friend was so weak that he had to be admitted to a nearby field hospital and the medical officer who attended him was Jadu, a class-friend from Chittagong. They were excited at meeting in such a way, so many miles from home and from the same medical school. My friend returned to Bangladesh and is still in the Army Medical Corps occupying a top position.

So my time in Mirzapore at the Kumudini Hospital came to an end, which was a good and exciting time. I was young, a bachelor and for the first time did not have to worry about money. I developed a friendship with many of the doctors and nurses, and the topic of marriage came up with some of the young women I knew. But I was not prepared to commit yet, so the relationships fizzled out. When I left for Dhaka to take up my job and start yet another life in different surroundings, one or two girls followed me but I made it plain that there was no prospect of marriage and they returned home.

It was some time in the autumn of 1964, that I took up my job as a Government Gazetted Medical Officer at the prestigious teaching hospital in the capital. I was a clinical pathologist, which meant that I had to examine clinical specimens from patients, such as blood, stools, urine, sputum and other materials. There were four of us in the department and I was the most junior. I had no real contact with the patients, apart from taking occasional blood samples from private patients. The only perk of the job was that there was a little private income which was divided among the doctors and technicians. As a newly qualified doctor this was very useful additional income. Although pathology was not my chosen speciality, I was fortunate to have got the job.

This was the first time in my life that I had more money than my immediate needs, so I opened my first bank account and had a cheque book with my name on it. I felt very proud.

I had accommodation within the hospital compound, along with other bachelor doctors. I shared a room with another doctor and there was a communal bathroom. The cooking was done by a servant, who was shared by a few of us.

The winter approached and with my increased income I bought a new suit. I had had no winter clothes in the past apart from a sweater, so this was the first time I was appropriately equipped for the winter. It also made me feel good to wear a suit and tie.

Life was reasonably comfortable. I had a group of friends who were of a similar age. There were no sporting activities – all we would do was go to the new shopping precinct called New Market and just wander around looking for beautiful girls. But, of course, there was no opportunity for social contact and certainly no eye contact or conversation. The girls would go home in cycle rickshaws and we would come to our rooms and discuss which girl was beautiful and whose daughter she might be.

At this stage of my life, two vital decisions needed to be taken: one was about my future career and the other was the question of marriage. My other friends and colleagues were in the same boat. This was a stop-gap situation and my next move was vital for my future. At that time, a number of doctors went to Saudi Arabia with very high salaries, but it didn't appeal to me because I wanted to go on to higher studies.

Within the country, the army paid better salaries than the civilian health service. But the army was dominated in all ranks by West Pakistanis. There was discrimination against the selection of Bengalis as well. Nevertheless, the salary was good, so when the opportunity arose, I decided to apply.

In 1965, when nearly a year had passed in my Government job, I had some savings in the bank and generally felt contented with my life. The army recruiting team came to carry out short service medical commission recruitment. Fourteen of us went for the interview, including rigorous physical, mental and aptitude tests. I was among six who were selected. I was delighted to join the Army and be posted in West Pakistan, where I would see the other parts of the country and other friends from West Pakistan who had been at medical school with me.

But when I told my father, he rejected the idea outright. Though he was not highly educated and his advice for my future career was uninformed, in Eastern culture children don't go against the will of their parents. And I am glad that I did take his advice, because those who joined the army didn't fare well and none had the opportunity to go abroad for higher studies. After the creation of Bangladesh, some of my contemporaries did rise up the promotion ladder in the army and had status within the country but this largely depended on who you knew rather than how good you were at the job, as in many underdeveloped and impoverished countries.

One of my close friends, who was from the same rural background as me, could not rise above the rank of major even when he returned to Bangladesh after being a POW in Western Pakistan. He became disillusioned and left the army and led a very ordinary life in Dhaka.

I worked in the Dhaka Medical College for another year, and had to face up to my responsibilities as the only member of my extended family who was financially self-sufficient. I had the overwhelming duty of looking after the welfare of my elderly parents, and the families of my two brothers. My eldest brother had five sons and one daughter, and my second brother, who had supported and funded my quest to become a doctor, had eight sons and one daughter. I was expected to be responsible for their upbringing, welfare, education and – in the case of the girls – marriages. Also as a doctor I was duty bound to look after any villagers, relations, relations' relations, and acquaintances who might require treatment and medical consultations in the capital, Dhaka.

The first of these obligations arose when my elder brother's family planned for his daughter to get married, so I had to contribute massively to that occasion. The groom was from another village and he demanded a number of things, including a radio and a bicycle. I was expected to provide these without question. Everybody in the village was certain that I earned lots of money and that the cost of these presents would be insignificant to me, but the truth was very different. I did manage to afford to buy a radio and a bicycle and I took them myself to the village to deliver them in person, whereupon I was told that the brands of the radio and the bicycle were inferior to the best.

Life as a bachelor in Dhaka was ticking over but going in no particular direction. I was not keen to make a career in pathology, though that is what my boss wished. I wanted to treat patients and be in direct contact with them as a proper doctor. I also wanted to go abroad for post-graduate studies, but how could I do that? I saw no way to change the situation.

Meanwhile I was getting older and had to look for a suitable wife. My father kept on writing to me and urging me to find a bride. He also suggested many girls within his own community. But none of them would fulfil my criteria – beauty, education and intelligence, in that order – and I therefore rejected them.

I started looking for a bride myself, but it was not easy. My poor background meant that I was handicapped at the start in the eyes of some girls and their families.

Ever since the partition of the Indian sub-continent in August 1947 into India and Pakistan, relations between the two countries were bitter. Muslim communities were imbued with hatred against India and the state machinery was rooted in anti-Indian sentiments. Because I was born and brought up in a mixed Hindu/Muslim society I did not necessarily believe the anti-Indian propaganda. Nevertheless, we were told to believe that Kashmir, which was more than 3,000 miles away from my home, was "ours" and that we had to be prepared to sacrifice our lives for it and that even the nearby village, where my school was, was now part of India and therefore my "enemy".

A few months after the Partition of India, there was a war between India and Pakistan over Kashmir which culminated in the division of Kashmir, still in operation after 70 years, and internationally known as the Line of Control (LOC).

In 1965, a military government in Pakistan led by Field Marshal Mohammed Ayub Khan, in power since the coup in 1958, believed that it was the time to recover Kashmir by force and felt sufficiently strong militarily with American weapons and aeroplanes.

The Line of Control had never been quiet at any time, but in the summer of 1965, there was a full-scale war. Pakistan attacked the Kashmir border and continued to progress deep into Indian-held Kashmir, which India considered an integral part. The radio and the fledgling TV service brought news of the continued success of the Pakistan army and air force. The whole population of East Pakistan was excited at the prospect of capturing the rest of Kashmir. But India had other plans. When she saw that her forces in Kashmir were beleaguered she decided to attack West Pakistan near the provincial capital of Lahore. Pakistan was neither prepared nor expecting it. There many heroic stories at that time about how the Indian advance was stopped by suicide bombers and others, and India was condemned by the British Prime Minister, Harold Wilson, for attacking Pakistan.

The conflict remained confined in to West Pakistan, but the Pakistan government tried their best to spread the conflict to the eastern half of the country. It is now known that East Pakistan was totally unprotected and India could have marched to Dhaka if she had wanted. Indeed, the then Prime Minister of Pakistan was reported to have said that if India had attacked East Pakistan "China would have protected it". This particular comment added fuel to the fire which led to the dismemberment of Pakistan six years later and the creation of Bangladesh.

Pakistan tried to stir up border conflict with India in East Pakistan, through the border security force, known as East Pakistan Rifles. Our village home was just on the border and we were aware of some border skirmishes between the border security forces of the two countries. In our village there were some exchanges of fire but no casualties. Nevertheless, there was some panic among the population, and the women, children and older people were evacuated to relatives' houses away from the border. But many people stayed in the village, to cultivate their land and life was fairly normal. There were reports of the conflict in all the national newspapers and my own village was mentioned.

But from Dhaka, I was not in a position to find out what exactly was happening in my village. in those days, the only way you could communicate was by letter or by actually going there. I was concerned about my elderly parents and wondered whether there would be a way to bring them to the capital to stay with me. But I was living in bachelors' quarters, sharing a room with another doctor. Then I suddenly realised that I could try applying for staff quarters, even though they were mainly for married doctors and there was a waiting list. But I thought I would take a chance.

I went to the Principal-cum-Superintendent of the hospital, an army colonel who knew our area well. As a young doctor, before joining the Army, he had been posted in a nearby hospital. I took the newspaper cutting with me and told him that my family, including my elderly parents, were displaced as a result of the border conflict and I wanted to shelter them here in Dhaka. He listened carefully, saw the cutting and said that I would get a flat as soon as one came vacant.

As luck would have it, I knew of a doctor who was occupying a top-floor flat and was being transferred elsewhere outside the capital. I mentioned to the Principal that this flat was becoming vacant and he called his personal secretary and authorised that the flat would be mine. I kept an eye on the flat and the morning the tenant left, I occupied it immediately.

The flat was an excellent one. It was on the fourth floor, overlooking the lake and the posh Dhanmondi residential area. I was delighted. My colleagues, friends and others were surprised that I, a bachelor, could get such accommodation but no one knew the inside story. I gradually furnished the flat and went home to bring my parents and my nephew, who would study in Dhaka.

Now life was good. My parents were with me, and my income was not only adequate but I could even save a bit each month.

By now the war with India had stopped after eighteen days, after American intervention and there were bilateral talks with India mediated by the Soviet Union in the Asian city of Tashkent. Nothing was achieved. Each side had to give up the position they occupied. The Indian Prime Minister Lal Bahadur Shastri died of a heart attack at that meeting. His funeral was attended by the Pakistani Foreign Minister as a gesture of reconciliation. That is how the war ended and I was the winner by a long chalk by getting a flat in Dhaka.

Looking for a bride

Now that I was earning enough money to support myself and live in a beautiful two-bedroomed newly furnished flat in the centre of the capital, there was no reason why I should not get married.

Because my parents were basically village people they did not want to stay in my flat for more than a couple of months. Both of them felt it was like being imprisoned in a concrete jungle. I looked after them well, attended to their physical complaints, had my father's cataract operation done, dealt with my mother's backache, a chronic problem, and dealt with her dental problems. All these were carefully and dutifully attended to at the best hospital in the country. There was a servant who not only cooked food and did all the washing, but would take my father down to a nearby mosque for prayer. Despite all these facilities, they were unhappy and wanted to return home. One day, I came home from the hospital and found them all packed up and ready to return to the village. I could not allow them to travel on their own, but arranged for them to return by air. There was a helicopter service from Dhaka to our district, and from there they were collected by my brother.

Now that my flat was empty, there was pressure from my parents, friends and colleagues to get married and start the search for a bride.

Marriages in Muslim cultures are all arranged, since there is no scope for boys and girls to intermingle. What usually happens is that if there is a marriageable boy or girl in a family a proposal will come to her parents, from known or unknown people. Preliminary enquiries are made by the parents or an elderly relative and if there is compatibility of families at the social level then arrangements would be made for the boy to see the girl, either formally or informally, in the presence of parents or relatives. There would be no possibility for the boy and girl to meet on their own. If the boy likes the girl, further negotiations could proceed; if not, the proposal would end there. Usually the girls have no say in the matter. If a girl refuses to go ahead with the marriage it would bring disgrace on her family. Sometimes this happens, as when the girl is secretly in love with another boy, and if she refuses to consent to the arranged marriage, there would be tremendous unhappiness in the family.

Such arranged marriages are often very destructive of family life. The brother of one of my cousins had three daughters. All of them were good-looking and – by Bangladeshi standards – educated, which meant they had been to primary school and could read and write, as opposed to 90% of women who were illiterate.

The eldest daughter was married to a member of the air force, based in Dhaka. This was an arranged marriage: the family was good, the bridegroom was handsome, they had a flat in Dhaka – all seemed well. One day we heard that the girl had disappeared and it later transpired that she was in love with a neighbour, an unmarried man with no means to support her. Both of them absconded and were later traced in India. Because of the lack of financial support, they had to return to her home in Bangladesh where all hell was let loose. Her marriage was already broken; she brought the family into disgrace. She was beaten, tortured and kept in solitary confinement. In this way, two years passed and then an elderly man who was widowed married her and they started a family which was apparently happy. There are many other examples of such incidents.

In my case, I decided to choose my own wife, someone attractive and educated. I wasn't looking for an exceptional beauty but even so, I didn't realise it would present so much of a problem. Here I was, a young man, intelligent, with a bright future, earning enough money to support a wife, and pay for a lovely flat in the heart of the capital, but still a suitable bride eluded me.

Usually news would come from a friend of a friend about an educated and beautiful girl, someone's daughter or other relative. Arrangements would be made for me to see the girl, perhaps in a restaurant or at a friend's house, or at someone else's wedding reception, or simply in the New Market in a designated shop, pretending to do the shopping. In this way, I saw about thirty girls, but none made my heart beat faster. Some might be attractive to look at but uneducated. I was also myself rejected by a number.

It was difficult to find a bride among the women doctors at the hospital, because there were so few of them. There were, of course nurses, some of whom were attractive and dedicated, but in Bangladesh the nursing profession was looked down upon, and so the family would not have agreed, and I myself was not keen.

One day I was told about a girl whose father was a retired doctor, and her brother was also a doctor and was a good student at the Dhaka Medical College. The girl was a science graduate and I thought it could be a good match. My colleague who suggested her spoke to the father of the girl. He came to the pathology department and started questioning me. He was particularly interested in knowing what my father did, what my brothers did, where my sisters married and the status of my maternal uncles. Of course, the answers to all these questions were not pleasing to his ears, for none of my relations had been to university or held any high post in government service. They were all from a farming community and lived on the land and what it produced. I was rejected. I hadn't even had an opportunity to see the girl, and of course, who knows whether we would have got on? It later turned out that, after I got married and settled in my flat with my beautiful wife, a colleague informed me that the father of the prospective bride, a doctor, who had rejected me, had been seen dancing naked in the college compound. He had had a mental breakdown, and I thought that Providence had saved me from being connected with that family.

One day, a colleague of mine told me about a girl, good looking, educated, religious and from a good family. I was lukewarm. He suggested that the girl come to my department and we would have an informal talk in front of other colleagues, including a married lady doctor. The girl indeed came but was clad in a *burqa* which meant that no one could see what she looked like, and she did not take part in the conversation. She sat in the doctor's rest room and was observing my every movement, but I could not see how she looked. I also asked a close friend of mine, a non-medical person, to come along. When he arrived, I pointed out the girl in the waiting room. As soon as he looked at her, she retracted her hands and feet inside the veil, so there was no way of telling what she looked like. So that was the end of the matter.

In this way, days and months, even a year or more passed. There seemed no hope of finding a girl fitting my criteria. My father was constantly telling me in his letters to find a girl, but it was a nightmare.

One day, somebody told me that there were two sisters from our neighbouring district studying at the university in Dhaka; one doing her M.A. in Bengali and the other studying biochemistry. The backgrounds of these two girls were very similar to ours. The older sister was slightly short and the one studying biochemistry was a little more attractive and a bit taller. I thought it would be a good idea if this marriage could be arranged through an intermediary. I went to the biochemistry department a number of times with the hope of seeing the girl, but this didn't happen. However, whoever I asked about this girl spoke highly of her. As is the custom in Muslim culture, the younger sister would normally not get married until after the older one. So I convinced a bachelor friend of mine from a similar background to me and a law graduate to take interest in the older girl while I would approach the younger one, the biochemistry graduate. It could have been a wonderful match. My friend was very handsome, taller than average, with high hopes of becoming established in society and in need of a partner who would contribute to that aim. Both of us were intelligent, self-made men, keen to succeed in life. Our backgrounds might not be rich but we were determined to make it in society through our own efforts. So we sent our proposals to the father of the girls, believing these two gems of boys would be a perfect match for the gentleman's daughters. My prospects were a bit stronger than my friend's, because I had a faint hope of getting a scholarship to go abroad to England for higher study.

The marriage proposals went through an intermediary. If the parents of these two girls had met us and talked to us, I have no doubt they would have liked us, but as so often happens, the girls' parents were looking for eligible bachelors from well-to-do backgrounds, and weren't worried about education or moral character. When they found that we didn't come from rich families, we were immediately rejected.

I don't know who the eldest one got married to, but my friend became a successful lawyer in my home town, happily married with two sons, both of whom graduated in engineering from a prestigious engineering university in Bangladesh.

The other one that I was interested in also got married. I found out a long time afterwards when I came to England, that she married a man I had known very well, from a family in the same region as me. His father was from a middle-class family, a local politician with two sons. The elder was an engineer and the younger was admitted to a medical school where I got to know him because he was my roommate in the students' dormitory. It is no exaggeration to say that I have never seen a man with such a low moral character. While we were all busy studying the difficult subject of medicine, he would copy the material out in tiny handwriting and take it to the examination hall where he would copy it to supply the answers. During his medical studies, he would regularly go to prostitutes and later brag about his sexual prowess. One night, he took a motor-rickshaw home from seeing a prostitute and stopped in front of our room. While settling the fare there was haggling and the driver, knowing where he had come from, demanded more money. He, of course, refused and during the altercation the driver insulted him in front of fellow students, saying "You can spend money on a prostitute but not pay enough to the rickshaw driver". The onlookers were stunned, but I was not surprised because he had told me where he was going.

So this was the nature of the man. Eventually he passed his exams somehow and married the younger sister. He managed to get to the UK with his new wife and in those days no exam was necessary to become a GP so he got a job in the Midlands. His nature did not change. When I saw him later at meetings or reunions, he bragged about having affairs with many women, including some of his patients. Eventually, his wife found out and there was a separation.

This is the woman whose family rejected me.

My parents were getting frustrated that I had not been able to find a bride and they knew that, with my status as a doctor, they couldn't get one from the social circles in our village. I was a bit disappointed but not really bothered because I hoped to get a scholarship to go abroad to the UK and perhaps it might be better to remain unattached.

My brother in Kushtia who had been my main mentor was too busy coping with his own family and there was nothing much he could do.

Then, a new opportunity arose. There was a highly respected and qualified doctor practicing in Kushtia. He had been our family physician and I knew him from the days of my adolescence. Everyone in the Kushtia District knew his name. He was a towering personality, a model citizen, and even in those days he had a car, which was a rare sight in Kushtia.

My brother wrote to me that this doctor had a daughter and he was interested in me. For my brother and my parents, this was the best proposal so far and must be grabbed with both hands. I was told in no uncertain terms that I must not reject this proposal.

But the problem was that I hadn't even seen the girl. I heard that she was beautiful, which I believed, because the doctor and his son were handsome and tall, and fair-skinned in comparison to fellow Bengalis. I didn't know how educated she was, but she had not been to university, although she may have taken her GSCE. When I tried to see her, for a combination of reasons it turned out not to be possible. Meanwhile, astonishingly to Western eyes, the date of the marriage had been fixed.

I was really at a loss as to what to do. I hadn't seen the girl, and knew little about her, but now had a date for my marriage to her. If I didn't turn up for my own wedding, my family's honour and the honour of the girl's family would be ruined. Rebellion was out of the question – if I said 'no', I would have been considered disobedient. So I agreed.

Meanwhile a friend of mine said that the girl was actually visiting Dhaka, and if I wanted I could go and see her at least, from a distance. He gave me the address of the house and I went there and hung around for an hour or so in case she came out. But if a girl did come out how would I know if it was the bride? In fact, nobody came out of the house, but I saw a girl standing on the first floor with her back to the road to where I was standing. I could not see her face, but saw curly hair from a distance. I am still not sure whether this was the girl. Whoever my bride was to be, I would meet her for the first time in the bedroom. This is not unusual, particularly in village communities.

So the time came for me to leave Dhaka for Kushtia to get married to a girl I had never seen. At the time, my mother was living with me.

She was a frail, old village woman, who could not stand upright because of collapsed vertebrae. She was happy that I was going to get married to the daughter of a renowned doctor but I was entirely unhappy about the whole business. I didn't bother to go shopping for new clothes but instead borrowed a wedding suit from a friend of mine who had got married recently. My friends and colleagues were happy that I was going to get married, but no one knew that my mind was in turmoil.

In Bangladesh, the wedding preparations start a week before the wedding but I told my brother that I would arrive the evening before the wedding day, just to let them know of my disapproval.

I doubt if anyone has ever taken such a complicated and disrupted journey to his wedding as I did with my mother.

On the day of my travel to Kushtia from Dhaka, I asked for hospital transport to take me and my mother to the coach station. We were offered an ambulance, the only transport the hospital could provide. We set off early in the morning to the coach station which was about five miles from my flat. The coach was a minibus, with accommodation for about twenty people, and the luggage was secured on the roof.

My mother always suffered from travel sickness. Even before the bus set off, she felt nauseated and in fact was sick outside on the pavement. She asked for water and washed her face and put some on her head. She said she felt better. The coach started. While the coach was still within the city, she was sick once or twice more with obvious inconvenience to the other passengers. She was given a seat near the window and wanted to put her head through the window to get some fresh air, but there would be danger from oncoming vehicles. By the time the bus had travelled about five miles, she was very sick and barely aware of her surroundings. And there was only another 130 miles to go...

After sixty miles or so we had to cross the mighty Meghna River on a ferry. During this crossing we all disembarked from the coach. My mother felt much better with the fresh cool breeze of the river and the slow and steady speed of the ferry. It was winter, so the sun was enjoyable. It was midday. She had some green coconut water and I had some lunch. The ferry took nearly two hours to reach the other side of the river, and we then got back into the coach, for a two-hour journey to the railway junction.

As soon as the coach started speeding up, my mother felt sick again, although she had nothing to vomit. When the coach reached the railway station at Ishwardi Junction, it was already dark and we had to cross a bridge to go to the other side, to catch the train to Kushtia. My mother was so ill by this stage that it was impossible for her to walk over the bridge, and yet the train was about to arrive. If we missed that train we would have to wait till the following morning.

My mother's main worry was not herself but the trouble she was causing me. And my immediate concern was how to catch the train.

I hired two coolies: one to take our luggage and the other to hold my mother's hand. I was on one side of her and on the other side the coolie held her, and we virtually lifted her off her feet and carried her over the bridge to the other side of the station.

We managed to catch the train, and once inside, my mother put her head on the window, and the cool, mild winter air soothed her down. The trains in Bangladesh do not run at great speed, so it was not much of a worry.

We arrived in Kushtia, at about 10 p.m. and took a rickshaw to my brother's house. As soon as I arrived I was puzzled not to see any signs of marriage preparations. My brother greeted me and said: "Haven't you heard the news?" My first thought was for my father's health, and I said "No". His next words were music to my ears. "The marriage is off!" he said.

I felt a tremendous relief as if a ton weight had been lifted off me. I had started my journey from Dhaka at around 7 am and it took over fifteen hours to reach home with my elderly and sick mother, but I did not feel tired. Instead I felt elated that I was once again free!

The following morning, I woke up fresh and happy, but not so the rest of the family. My brother and his wife were very disappointed that such a good relationship has slipped away. My mother was also unhappy, worrying about when I would find another girl to marry.

I wasn't told the reason for this rejection. No one knew and I was not particularly interested in finding out either. But years later, I was told that the cancellation was due to my "social inequality". In the bride's family's view, they were only getting a doctor as bridegroom and nothing else. My brother was merely a lower division clerk in a Government office, who lived in a rented house with lots of children, and we came from a rural village and none of my brothers and sisters was married to a prestigious member of the local community.

My near-father-in-law suffered a set-back during the Bangladesh War in 1971. His pharmacy was burned down and he lost his medical practice to young and upcoming doctors. I met him in 1973 when my homeland had become Bangladesh. By that time, I was not only married, but blessed with a son and had already done my MRCP. So I went to see him in Kushtia out of respect for being our family physician. He was then old, and looked haggard and was suffering from severe Parkinson's disease. I suggested some new medication which he appreciated, but it was not available there. That was the last time I saw him, and he died soon after, and with his death all the glory of that family went down. His sons had never been to university and certainly his sons-in-law were not known to be particularly well off.

It was December 1966, and after that rejection, I thought there was no chance of getting married before I left for the United Kingdom.

I had taken a week's leave to get married, so now I stayed in Kushtia and had some time on my hands.

Two further proposals arrived. One was from a distant relative of mine who said there was a beautiful girl in town, a daughter of one of his colleagues. Another was from a cousin who lived in Rajshahi, a divisional headquarters where he was a police Inspector. He had a colleague with three daughters.

First, my brother decided that I should see the local girl who had just passed her GCSE, and was from a middle-class agrarian society like ours. She was the eldest of nine children, beautiful, and about ten years younger than me. So one day, my brother and I went to see this girl who lived quite near to my brother's house.

We waited in the ground floor drawing room and the girl came in wearing a sari. I looked at her and found her extremely pleasant and very beautiful. She was young, full of life and nervous. Courtesy demanded that I didn't look at her too often. My brother asked her some questions and she answered. It was all over within ten minutes and we went home and discussed it among ourselves. There was no question that the girl was attractive and the family was respected. But against marrying her was the fact that she was too young and virtually a school-leaver. I was asked to mull it over.

Then I went to Rajshahi to meet my cousin's colleague and explore the other proposal. This gentleman, an educated man, had three daughters. The eldest was studying for an M.A., the middle one a BSc, and the youngest one was a schoolgirl. They were all invited to my cousin's house to meet me so that I could see his daughters. I wasn't attracted to the eldest girl, but the middle one, called Hashi, was beautiful, fair-skinned and very lively and she caught my eye. Probably she was more relaxed and natural because the proposal being discussed was for her sister and not for her.

I returned to Kushtia from Rajshahi and before I left for Dhaka the parents of the local girl invited me to have a cup of tea with them. Obviously, they were interested in me as a potential son-in-law.

I returned to Dhaka and all my colleagues were surprised to find that I was still a bachelor. Now I had to make a quick decision about marriage. My parents insisted that I must get married before leaving for abroad. The Kushtia girl was very beautiful but not educated enough. The Rajshahi girl, the eldest one, did not attract me. In the meantime, a message came from Rajshahi that if I liked the second daughter, they would be willing to consider it. So there were two beautiful girls and I could marry either of them. I felt that the Rajshahi girl would have been a good match because she was beautiful and educated. But her family were far from my home.

My father wrote to me urging the advantages of the Kushtia girl. My brother was non-committal. So once again I listened to my father and that girl became my wife.

I had met Hashi for less than ten minutes in one afternoon in the presence of the elders. I had never had the opportunity to talk to her alone, which simply would have not been allowed. But at least it was better than marrying the girl I had never seen at all.

It was decided that the wedding would take place within the next couple of months, as soon as the formalities could be agreed.

Although in Muslim marriage there is no dowry, usually the bridegroom asks for money or a gift depending on the financial status of his bride's family. The usual sort of demand in those days was a motor-bike from a relatively middle-class family. I never made any such demand and actually abhor any such requests made under duress. My would-be father-in–law came to see me in Dhaka and told me that the date of the wedding had been fixed for 18th February 1967. He wanted me to go to a tailor to buy a suit. I already had one but he insisted that I must have another. I felt it would actually be convenient to have another suit particularly if I should get a scholarship to go to England, so I ordered a three-piece suit which to be tailored. Also, he wanted to buy me a watch, although I had one already, and I acquired a Tissot, which I wore until I went to England and it gave accurate time for many years.

My brother told me that there should be a post-wedding reception which required money. I handed over all of my savings for him to arrange whatever was required. Off he went the following day.

The date of the wedding came near. I bought a beautiful sari for the bride to wear on the wedding night. That sari was liked by everyone, and is still a proud possession of my wife fifty years later.

I did not have any more money to buy my wedding costume and so I borrowed the same one from my friend as I had on previous occasions. Two days before the wedding, I arrived there with my parents. My brother's accommodation was crammed with his huge family but somehow we squeezed in.

On such occasions there are meant to be lots of formalities on both sides – exchanges of gifts and preparation of the bride and bridegroom. Who was going to arrange and pay for these? Where was the money to come from? My brother was busy making arrangements for the post-wedding dinner, organising a marquee, chairs, tables, cooks, etc., etc. My brother's wife was busy looking after her own family with so many small children. So we had to do without all of fanfare of the usual pre-wedding ceremonies.

The wedding was to be at night and I had to wear a turban with my borrowed wedding costume. Now who was going to get a turban for me and where from? One of my nephews said there were some Pakistani policemen who might be able to help. So I went to the police station and asked whether anyone could help me with a turban. Someone was happy to help me, and so I had a turban.

In the evening, after wearing my borrowed wedding dress and an impromptu turban, off I went to the bride's house to get married. I was accompanied by a procession of people, some of them from my village, and a few of my college friends.

I was given pride of place to sit and I looked around at the gathering. There were some eminent people among the guests. Then, I started to get an intolerable headache, perhaps a migraine attack caused by stress. I asked a friend to buy a painkiller for me, which helped a lot.

Just before the actual wedding, my brother made a fuss and demanded 2,000 rupees from the bride's family, the price of a motorbike. I was not prepared for this. I had no need for a motorbike and was not aware that he would ask for this. But there was a row and my brother said that the wedding would not be formalised until that money was paid. It was handed over that night and the wedding went ahead.

The Islamic ceremony was simple and took only a few minutes. Hashi was in another room and her consent was brought by three people and I was asked to agree three times. This was followed by signing some documents. That was the end of the wedding and I was now a married man.

Following the marriage there was a dinner and, as custom demanded, the bridegroom was served the best food in the best place.

When the ceremonies were over, it was well past midnight. My father-in-law placed his daughter into my hands, "giving her away", and with tears in his eyes he asked me to look after her.

The following morning there were the preparations for the wedding reception. People were erecting a marquee, and preparing food. The house was full of guests, some known and others unknown, many of them from the village to see my newly-married wife. Everybody had high hopes that I would marry a beautiful girl from a good family and they were not disappointed. I was busy with helping with preparations for the reception that night, and it was not customary for me to talk to my wife. Coming too close to her under public gaze was not acceptable.

In the evening, the guests started coming and I was wearing the three-piece suit my father-in-law had bought for me. I was also wearing many rings on my fingers, which had been given by relatives, and the new watch. It is the custom that guests who can afford it bring presents. There is no organised wedding list as there is in western society, because it would look rude and unacceptable for a list to circulate among the invited guests. So the presents are mostly wasted, because of duplications or triplications of presents. I remember there were three or four cold drink sets and more than a dozen table lamps. They all stayed in my in-laws' house and never got used.

The reception was traditional. The usual food and sweetmeats, then those who wished saw the newly-wed bride inside the house. Hashi was wearing the sari and other jewels presented to her and sitting in a room surrounded by female friends, relations, and elder women also in their best clothes. The bride usually sits with head bent forward and eyes closed. If any man wanted to see her, her head would be propped up by a friend manually then he would see her from a distance. It would be rude for her to open her eyes and look at the men.

All the guests left by midnight. I remember a few people came and blessed me and remarked loudly what a mistake the doctor had made in suddenly cancelling the wedding to his daughter.

The custom is that after the reception was over I and my wife returned to my in-laws' house, where the accommodation was good and the young brothers- and sisters-in-law welcomed me wholeheartedly with garlands and confetti. For the first time I felt relaxed.

But what about the honeymoon?

In fact, the word was unknown. Nobody could imagine that we would go away on holiday. It was not the custom among the Muslim families, and in my case it wouldn't have been possible, because all our savings had gone towards the wedding itself. So everybody expected that we should leave straight away for Dhaka and start family life like any other newly-weds.

My one week's holiday was coming to an end and we were preparing to return to the flat in Dhaka. It was expected that an elderly and experienced woman from my side of the family would accompany us, to show the newly-wed wife how the system worked, get her acquainted with family life, cooking and housework, and generally tending to the needs of the husband.

The natural choice would have been my mother. She knew the way round my flat, and her presence would have reassured me, and also she would have treated my wife as her daughter. But there ensued an argument. My brother wanted his wife to accompany us, the sister-in-law who had been so hostile to me when I stayed in their house. Although my father agreed with me and wanted my mother to accompany us to Dhaka, the wishes of my brother prevailed and his wife accompanied us instead.

We had a servant, whose job it was to do the shopping, cleaning and preparing the vegetables, cut the fish or meat and help Hashi with the cooking. In the flat my sister-in-law watched my wife's every move. Instead of helping her, a young college girl, in her work in the household, she took a critical view and started criticising her work and performance. She stayed for a couple of weeks, and when she returned to her house in Kushtia, she fabricated various malicious stories about my young wife. My brother was very influenced by her stories and even after nearly forty years of marriage I have never heard a kind word spoken to my wife by my brother.

I hardly visited Kushtia after my marriage, but whenever I did I always went first to my brother's house and would then go on to the in-laws' house. I distinctly remember on one occasion my brother told me not to be too subservient to my in-laws because he didn't want to be under any obligation to them. I found this very upsetting, for I had always been polite and decent to everybody. But what he was trying to do was to ask me to be "nasty" to them, which I couldn't accept.

I remember one evening I arrived in Kushtia on a short visit to see my wife, who was taking a break from Dhaka life. As usual I went first to my brother's house, although news had reached my in-laws that I was in town. I was keen to go and see my wife and have a pleasant evening with her, and her relatives kept on coming to remind me that their sister was waiting anxiously to see me, but my brother took no notice, almost as if I come all this way to spend the evening with him and his family rather than with my wife. In the end, I had to make my excuses and leave, in spite of their obvious desire that I would stay with them.

I stayed in the flat with my wife for over a year and, looking back, it was a wonderful time. I was still young, just past thirty and my wife was ten years younger than me. Sometimes my mother stayed with us, as well as my elder brother's son, who left his school in the village and came to stay with us. He was the same age as my wife and I got him admitted to a nearby school and supervised his study from my flat. I was the master of the house and my word was law as it is the case in all Muslim households.

My daily routine was as follows: I would have a hearty breakfast in the morning, then I went to the hospital in a cycle rickshaw and would return at two p.m. Everybody would wait for me. I would have my lunch and then others would follow. I used to smoke in those days, and I would light a cigarette after my heavy lunch and look through the window to the horizon. It was a wonderful feeling.

Invariably there would be a siesta and after that, we would have some further refreshment and tea, then I would go out with Hashi. We would either go shopping or visit friends or relatives. Dhaka was a very safe place in those days and Hashi would wear her decorative saris and jewels to go out in the afternoon. I felt very proud walking by her side. People would comment how beautiful she was. Sometimes I thought to myself 'I am not that handsome how do I deserve Hashi as my wife?' On the other hand, my in-laws were also thankful and appreciated having a well-qualified and established son-in-law.

Life was good and, what's more, Hashi got pregnant in the very first month of our marriage. There was no family planning and nature took its course. I was happy and proud, but some of my friends commented that I was a fool to "destroy" that beauty at such an early stage. But another of my friends, who himself was married and a father, encouraged me to believe that there would be different pleasures in being a father. I felt better in myself and for the first time I put on weight. I gained nearly a stone so that my old suits didn't fit me!

Hashi stayed in Dhaka throughout her pregnancy, apart from the odd trip back to Kushtia to see her family.

Next steps

Although I was doing a job in clinical pathology, I never intended making a career out of it. I was always looking for an opportunity to change course and do proper medicine where I could come into contact with patients and diagnose and treat them. But changing course was impossible in that setting.

Nevertheless, my job at the Dhaka Medical College was a blessing because it kept me in contact with the Government Secretariat. I went out of my way to make friends with one or two of the clerks in the office and I would invite them to the canteen for refreshment and tea and ask them whether there were any scholarships, in any subject or to any country. Pakistan, being a developing country, received plenty of offers of scholarships and financial aid for the postgraduate education and training in various subjects. But usually these scholarships would be distributed clandestinely to the relatives of people in power rather than being awarded on merit.

At about the time I got married, I was told that there were scholarships under what used to be known as the Colombo Plan to study Physical Medicine in the United Kingdom. Not many people knew about this subject and many of the medical practitioners thought it was similar to physiotherapy. But I showed an interest, because after all it was a form of medicine and I would have the opportunity to go to the UK. I was told that few people were interested in it, because everybody wanted to go to the UK for degrees and diplomas like the MRCP or FRCS or MRCOG.

Anyway, I decided to apply, not pinning my hopes on getting it. I remember there was a form from the British Council in Dhaka and I had to fill in five copies. I was so tired from writing them that I asked my brother-in-law to help me, because he had good handwriting. I submitted the application by the due date and virtually forgot about it. I still went regularly to the Secretariat and ask the clerks whether there was any news about scholarships from U.K.

During the last stages of Hashi's pregnancy I got a letter from the British High Commission in Pakistan telling me that I had been offered a place to study physical medicine in the UK and I would have to start the course in January 1968, barely a month away. It seemed daunting. I was delighted but I had so many responsibilities. My wife was heavily pregnant and there were so many formalities to be completed before I could proceed to the UK. Of course, everybody else was very pleased with the news and my father-in-law was particularly helpful and gave every encouragement to concentrate on my scholarship rather than anything else. To make matters worse, I was suddenly transferred to another post. Because I was a government employee I was transferable from one area to the other. People who have high level connections can usually avoid these transfers but someone like me had to find another way.

I went to the appropriate department and showed them the papers received from the British High Commission about my impending departure abroad. They were not helpful. I had been offered a place abroad, it was true, but it was in an entirely different subject from the area I had been working in for the past four years, so the Directorate of Health would be unlikely to approve it. Also, getting an offer of a place abroad was not enough. I had to be released from my post on secondment; otherwise they would not be able to require me to return to Government Service. My wife's expected date of delivery was approaching fast and I was bogged down with official bureaucracy about my transfer and release from the job. The only solution is to bribe someone, in cash or in kind. That was how I managed to apply and ultimately get offered a scholarship to go abroad. But now I was dealing with an entirely different department and I knew no one there who was willing to listen to me.

I sought the advice of a friend who suggested I bribe the Head Clerk on whom transfers and appointments largely depended. The clerks do the work and the signatures of the Directors are obtained later. In many instances, the Directors do not even read what they are signing. My friend knew the home address of this clerk and obviously was familiar with the business and had done this sort of thing before, so though it was against my conscience, I had to resort to bribing in order to get anywhere.

I took some cash, not more than fifty or sixty rupees, in a brown envelope and went to the clerk's house in the evening. He was courteous, and offered me tea and biscuits. I then showed him the letter from the British High Commission about my scholarship. I asked him to stop or cancel my transfer order and release me from my post for higher study abroad. For services rendered, I presented him with the envelope with the money. He "objected" vehemently but I left the envelope on his coffee table and said 'Good night' to him.

The following morning when I met him in his office he was a different person. Polite, all smiles and helpful. He ordered his junior clerks to cancel my transfer order and advertise the post. So I was saved from one worry.

Because the time was short I spent most of the day in the Secretariat with various departments, pleading, begging and bribing with cigarettes and refreshments to expedite my release and issue the all-important "no objection certificate" or "NOC". Without the NOC I would not be able to do any of the things I needed in order to travel, such as apply for a passport, an airline ticket, and foreign currency and so on. After taxing their patience and begging and cajoling I was issued with 'NOC'.

While I was extremely busy getting things sorted out for my trip abroad, my wife was being looked after in my flat by my mother-in-law. Also at home were my two sisters-in-law, who were small girls. I was reassured that someone was looking after her while I was away from home. My mother-in-law was young, may be in her early forties and as my wife was her eldest child, she was excited for her first grandchild.

Hashi was taken in one day with false labour pains, but was returned home. It turned out that her expected date of delivery was uncertain and because her blood pressure was raised, the obstetrician decided to admit her to be induced.

She was admitted to what was called a 'cabin', reserved for higher officials. Labour started at midday on the 13th December 1967 and reached its climax at night. There was an inexperienced junior doctor who did what is called an episiotomy, a cut to increase the birth canal, unnecessary in my view. The baby was born, a cute and lovely boy. Immediately after the birth, he was taken to a side room for washing and given an identification tag while the doctors were tending my wife and suturing the episiotomy incision. I stayed with the baby all the time in case there was a mix-up. The identification tag said "Baby Wajed", because we hadn't decided on a name. In our culture the name was decided later as there was no system of birth certification. The only proof of birth is a hospital counterfoil receipt which simply says the date and time and the name of the father.

My wife was taken to the cabin where my mother-in-law was waiting for her. One of the nurses took the baby in a carry cot to show my wife and my mother-in-law. I followed the nurse all the way. In the cabin my wife saw the baby for the first time and her pain lessened by seeing such a beautiful baby boy. My mother-in-law took him in her arms and said in Bengali "Look at your dad" pointing towards me! The word 'dad' gave me an unfamiliar feeling. Me, a dad! How strange. According to Islamic custom the boy was given Islamic rites.

Unfortunately, the following days were very traumatic for Hashi. The suturing of the incision was done in the wrong way and it got infected. She had to stay in hospital for at least a week after the delivery and needed secondary stitches under general anaesthesia. By the time she was discharged, she had lost a lot of weight, and felt and looked really ill.

However, with my mother-in-law's tender, loving care, the baby and his mother were recovering well and, meanwhile, many relatives came to see the newborn. We decided to call the baby "Sajal" a pure Bengali name, meaning "fresh and bright", like the morning star.

Meanwhile, the baby was two weeks old and I had only another two weeks before leaving for the UK. My father-in-law, a very capable man, came and asked me to concentrate on the formalities to do with the scholarship and he would take Hashi and Sajal to Kushtia, leaving me a free hand, which was a great help.

So my wife and son left for Kushtia, and I stayed in my flat with the servant and my nephew who was admitted to a college nearby.

It was January 1968. Winter in Bangladesh is pleasant if you go there from European countries. The temperature could go down to 8°C but no more. There is never any frost, and certainly no snowfalls. But for the ordinary people who have no winter clothes and sometimes no proper homes, the winter can be very hard. It is not unusual for people to die from hypothermia, particularly in the northern districts, which are hilly and closer to the Himalayas. But for those who are well off, the winter months are enjoyable, with plenty of winter vegetables, fewer creepy crawlies, and a chance to wear light-weight suits and ties. After coming to the UK, like everybody else, we visited Bangladesh in December and January since it is the most enjoyable time.

My family now left for the in-laws' house in Kushtia while I concentrated on getting things sorted for going to the UK. My first task was to go to the Passport Office for an International Passport. There was barely two weeks before my departure. At the Passport Office I was handed a form, which needed a photograph and police verification about my past, including whether I had taken part in any anti-state activities.

I took the form and the following day went to the Passport Office again, to submit it with a photograph. I was horrified to learn that no passport could be issued until the police verification was at hand. This is the job of the passport office who would write to the relevant police stations, including my village police station as well. This all could take months, whereas I needed the passport now. I could not see any way out of it, since I didn't know anybody in the Passport Office or the relevant Ministry who could help me, and without a passport I could not buy an airline ticket or get currency from the State Bank.

On scanning the various clerks working in that office, I found a familiar face. He was a junior clerk, the younger brother of a classmate of mine at Kushtia school. He didn't recognise me, because I left Kushtia in 1957 for medical school in Chittagong. However, I introduced myself and asked about his brother. Then, I came to the real point and explained to him that my passport was required that week and I couldn't wait for the lengthy process of police verification.

He was a very nice young man and very helpful. Because I was his brother's friend, he addressed me as a brother. He said that it was true that police verification was needed for an International passport, but because I was a Government Officer and I was going abroad on a scholarship for higher studies, the passport would be given a stamp showing that I was on government business, and the police enquiry was not essential. But he said that I must see the Officer-in-Charge directly rather than dealing with the clerks, as I had been doing over the past couple of days. I was very encouraged with that information. He also told me that the Officer-in-Charge was a very nice man and would be helpful.

The following day, the third day of visiting the Passport Office, I took with me the papers from the British High Commission, and the relevant documents from the Ministry of Health, . agreeing to relieve me of duties for five years to study abroad.

I went in the morning since there was no appointment system. The Officer-in-Charge was a short-statured man with a goatee. I showed him the usual courtesy and greetings, and he indicated to me a chair in front of the desk. I told him that I had already submitted my application form and been told that it would take two to three months before a passport could be issued. He listened very carefully and then pressed a bell.

A person who was outside his office rushed in. The Officer ordered him to call a named clerk, who arrived within minutes. He ordered the clerk to issue the passport within 24 hours.

This was unthinkable. I could not believe that such an honest officer existed in government service. I thanked him profusely and left his office. To this day, I remember his name and face and will always remain grateful to him for his act of kindness. As I left the office, I also thanked the junior clerk, the brother of my schoolfriend. Two days later, I went again to the Passport Office, where the passport was waiting for me, a Pakistani passport and beautiful to look at. I was now a Citizen of Pakistan!

My next task was to get permission from the State Bank of Pakistan for the foreign currency that I would take with me, as I was still technically on full pay, and needed to transfer some of my salary for my maintenance.

Most of the offices I had been dealing with so far were part of the Provincial Government but the State Bank was under the control of Central Government. That meant the senior officers and heads of department were from West Pakistan and non-Bengali speaking. The State Bank of Pakistan was an impressive building in the heart of the commercial area of Dhaka which I had passed many times, but never been inside.

My departure date for the United Kingdom was drawing near, and there was hardly a week left. By now I had stopped going to the hospital and everybody realised that I was too busy to concentrate on my work. So I was on unofficial leave and going from one office to another. I was very stressed and felt a few extra heartbeats which unnerved me. One evening I went to one of my teachers who had a huge private practice, a man I used to hang around in the hope of getting some private patients for investigation. I went to see him for two reasons: to tell him of my imminent departure to the UK and to seek his help with my ectopic beats.

He was busy and in between talking to patients, he took a moment to wish me luck and warned me it would be very cold in the UK at this time of year, as he himself had been to the UK for higher studies. And for my extra heart beats he suggested some Valium for a week or so.

The following day I went to the State Bank of Pakistan. Inside there were hundreds of people working. I approached a clerk and asked him who dealt with the "clearance section". He indicated another clerk. He was obviously a fellow Bengali, and he was reading a newspaper. He was middle-aged, and a few of his teeth were missing, with the remainder unhealthy and stained dirty red due to the chewing of 'Pan', a leaf which is chewed by everybody. I greeted him and he glanced at me and then turned back to the newspaper. Once again, I let him know I was there, and explained to him the purpose of my visit. He listened and in a very irritated voice pointed out another officer I had to see.

That man was sitting in a cubicle which was isolated from the rest of the people working there, and outside it there was another man, his orderly. I saw the name on the door and it was obvious that the officer was a retired army officer from West Pakistan, but the orderly outside was a Bengali. I told the orderly that I needed to see the officer and I was allowed in. He was healthy-looking man with a moustache and wearing a nice shirt. I greeted him and explained in English what I needed. He showed no interest and asked me to come again.

I had hardly three or four days left, and I still had to go to Kushtia to see my wife and son, as well as visit my village home to see my elderly parents. I might not be able to carry out those visits if I had to spend all this time getting permission from the State Bank of Pakistan. I really didn't know what to do.

The following day I again went to the bank. If I could not get permission that day there would be no possibility of me making the trip to my home region. In the office, I saw no familiar faces, and didn't know who to approach. So far I had met two people, both of whom had cold-shouldered me. Then, in desperation, I asked a young Bengali clerk who the Governor was and what he was like and where was he from? He said the Governor was not usually approachable but he had his private office on the fourth floor. He also said that he was a Bengali and, by and large, a good man.

I thought, come what may, I must see the Governor. I gathered my courage, took a lift to the fourth floor and found his office. There were several orderlies waiting outside his office and I told one of them that I was a doctor and wanted to see the Governor for five minutes on a personal matter and would he kindly grant an interview. I wrote my name on a small card and simply said "Seeking interview". It was in the morning and perhaps the orderly was in a good mood. He asked me to go in to the Governor's office. I never saw such an impressive office in my life. There were several telephones, one of them red. He was short, softly spoken, middle-aged and, I thought, he might have a son of my age. I explained to him the purpose of my visit, which was to get the State Bank's permission, and it had to be done today, otherwise I would not be able to see my elderly parents and my three-week old son. I showed him the papers from the British High Commission, my "No Objection Certificate" and my International Passport. He was convinced. He pressed a bell, and in came an orderly who stood to attention. The Governor spoke to him in Bengali, and asked him to take me to the relevant officer for the permission. The orderly took me to the same officer who had ignored me yesterday, the retired army officer from West Pakistan. Now that I had come directly from the Governor, he did not say anything, but simply ordered another of his subordinates to issue the necessary permission. It wasn't possible to get the paper on the same day but I did so on the following day.

When I had all the documents ready, I had to go to Pakistan International Airlines to buy the plane ticket. I had all the documents with me and there was a clerk there who was my school friend in Kushtia, so my ticket was ready for travelling to the UK. The date for departure was the 26th January 1968. I had three days left.

I was now totally exhausted, but I had to make the trip to my village to see my parents. Who knows whether there would be any further chance to see them, as they were getting on? Also, I had say goodbye for now to my son who was a little over a month old.

The journey from Dhaka to Kushtia alone would take the best part of a day, and from there to my village home another half day.

Early in the morning I started for Kushtia using the shortest possible route, by coach, ferry, and train and I arrived in the evening at my in-law's house. I saw my son Sajal, who, by now, had grown and was crying less than when he lived in Dhaka. He was being well looked after by his maternal grandparents who were young and had had experience in raising their own children. I held my son and felt that one day he would be a handsome young man. I stayed at my in-law's house overnight and in the morning I left for my village home.

Once again I took the shortest possible route, which meant going by bus for about thirty miles and then cycling the remaining six miles to my home. But where would I get a bike? I knew the village where the bus would drop me was pretty impoverished but I had a very good friend who came from the village but lived and worked in Dhaka. His family must possess a bicycle which they could lend me for a day. The bus dropped me off in a village I had never been to before, but I knew the name well. From there to my village was six miles and a bicycle was the only way to get me back on the same day.

It was winter, and the sunshine was pleasant, but the road was full of dust. After any motor vehicle passed there was a cloud of dust which lasted quite a long time. It settles on the road-side trees, so that the leaves look white and dirty. After getting off the bus, I asked people where the house of my friend was. It was within walking distance. There I asked to see the brother of my friend and he insisted that I must rest and have some food. I asked if he could lend me a bicycle to go to my village and return that afternoon. He was astonished to hear that I was intending to return all the way to Dhaka that day. He lent me his bicycle and I hopped on it and started pedalling like mad towards my village. I had to cross a river by ferry and the ferryman knew me and had heard about my imminent departure to the UK. He wished me luck and he too was surprised when I told him that I was going to return today.

I arrived home, where everybody was expecting me. I sat with my father, and my mother now unable to stand upright came up and kissed me with tears rolling down her cheeks. She asked me how my Sajal was and I told them that he was fine and well looked after. My brother and his wife, nephews and cousins all came to see me and we had lunch.

It was now time to leave. Nobody said much. What could they say? On the one hand they were happy that I was going to the UK for higher study, on the other hand it was far away, so far that it was known locally as "seven seas and thirteen rivers away". As is the custom, I touched the feet of my parents and brother and took leave of them. I myself did not know whether I would ever be able to see my parents again because my stay in the UK would be five years at minimum. The village folk crowded around me, some in tears including my mother.

I set off on my borrowed bike and this time I was escorted by two other cyclists, a friend and my nephew. They escorted me to the village six miles away, where I got the bus to Kushtia.

My wife, in-laws and my brother all assembled and insisted that I stay overnight and travel to Dhaka the following morning. They meant well, but I knew I needed a whole day for tying up loose ends, getting some travellers' cheques and packing. I ignored everybody's advice and decided to return to Dhaka that night.

The last train to Dhaka was at 5.30 p.m. Once again, my plan was to take the shortest possible route, no matter how tedious the journey might be. At the station there were well over a hundred people assembled to say farewell. I got on the train and stood by the door as it moved out of the station, until Kushtia receded and I could no longer see their waving hands. When I sat down, one of the other passengers asked me if I was going far? I said "To Dhaka and then to England". He replied "I guessed it must have been something like that, otherwise there would not have been such a crowd". Then someone asked what I was going to study, and other people joined in. All of them had a tale to tell, and some of them already had relations in England.

After a two-hour journey the train would arrive at the ferry. I would have to catch the last ferry of the day and if I missed it, there would be no way I could cross the river and no place to stay overnight. I was young and confident and full of hope. As soon as the train stopped I ran towards the ferry terminal and heaved a sigh of relief when I saw that it was still moored and passengers were boarding.

It would take about an hour to cross the river, much narrower because it was winter. The ferry was comfortable and I had my evening meal there on board. I could not see the coast, only a few flickers of light from distant villages. I used to smoke in those days and liked a cigarette after dinner. I was really enjoying the moment. It was rather peaceful – not very many hawkers pestering, because it was late and cold. I reflected on the events of the past fortnight and how in the end it all worked out. I knew my wife and son would be well looked after by my in-laws and I would be venturing across a new frontier to fly to England, the dream of every parent for his children if they do well in their education. I lost myself in wondering what England would be like, knowing that I would find out in two or three days.

After an hour or so we reached the ferry terminal on the opposite coast of the mighty Meghna. In those days it was only a village and I now faced the problem of how to get to Dakha, sixty miles away. There were buses but they usually plied only in daytime and then only when it they found enough passengers to fill them. There were a few people who got off the ferry with me but they vanished into the darkness. It was around 9 p.m. – cold, wintry and dark. I found myself standing in the middle of nowhere. On one side, the river and on the other empty ground interspersed with small huts, which were all shut. I was marooned in a god-forsaken place far away from my destination. There were no houses nearby and even if there had been, who would give me shelter? I felt helpless. I asked one or two people about how to get to Dhaka and the answer was always the same – "There is no way you can get there tonight".

I was desperate. I was thinking perhaps I should have listened to the elders and stayed the night in Kushtia. But I believe in Allah the Almighty and that night He saved me, as He has done on many occasions.

In the distance, above the howling of wild dogs in the dark winter night, I heard the sound of a heavy lorry starting up. I ran towards it in the dark. It was a three-ton truck and must have just unloaded some cargo. As the truck was about to leave, I ran in front of it and raised my hands. The driver was surprised to see a smartly dressed man in jacket and trousers in that deserted terminal looming out of the dark. I asked him where he was going and he replied "To Dhaka!". I explained to him my situation, that I was a doctor and had to return to Dhaka that night, and he was kind and helpful and invited me to get in the front next to his assistant.

It was a long journey by Bangladeshi standards. Though sixty miles is not that far, the road was rough, and the truck was old, and not fit to drive very fast. I asked the driver what would have happened to me if he had not turned up and I still remember his words: "If you hadn't found us you would have faced certain death!" It might have been an exaggeration, but I certainly would have had a difficult time and might have been in danger.

The truck arrived in the suburbs of Dhaka and it was nearly midnight when the driver dropped me near my flat.

In the flat was my nephew, a student, and when he opened the door he was astonished to see me. He could not believe that I made it in one day to Dhaka from my village home.

The following morning, I could at last relax, secure the knowledge that everything was now under control, all preparations made, all the loose ends tied, and I was ready to fly to England, to a new and unknown land, and to an uncertain future.

I went to the Secretariat Building for the last time to say a personal thanks to the clerical staff, who by now knew me so well, after my weeks of pestering them. I invited a few of the closest ones to the canteen and we enjoyed snacks, tea and cigarettes. As I told them about my hectic trip to and from my village home, one of the junior clerks happened to mention something called a "Police Verification Certificate" which he said might be necessary at the airport, in order for me to leave the country. This apparently had to be obtained from the Dhaka Police station. I was flabbergasted. How could I get this now within a day? Knowing about the Police Department and its reputation for bribery and corruption, I knew that no one would even listen to me, let alone issue a certificate of good behaviour. This certificate was apparently needed to confirm that someone has no anti-state activities against his name and no criminal record, and that he was not slipping out of the country with ill-gotten gains.

Faced with this final hurdle, I had to find a way to get the certificate.

I had a close friend, the son of a well-to-do family who had been to England to do a diploma course. He was the only friend who had a car, a 'Ford Anglia'. I knew that his elder brother was a very high ranking police officer, perhaps a Deputy Commissioner of Police. I had no idea how close he was to his brother and whether he would appeal to him on my behalf, but this was the only avenue left. That afternoon, I went to his flat and explained everything to my friend, who incidentally is now a very successful businessman and one of the richest men in Bangladesh, and he agreed to take me to his brother's house.

His brother's house was in an exclusive area of Dhaka and had a policeman at the gate, who obviously knew my friend and let us in to meet my possible saviour. The man was highly educated, extremely handsome and was relaxing at home in ordinary dress. He looked on me as a brother, as I was a good friend of his younger brother.

He listened to me very carefully but explained that such a certificate usually takes three to four weeks, and I had less than a day. I told him my background – selected for the army, a bona fide government health official, and holder of a government scholarship – and said that all of these organisations must have looked at my past record. I felt he was convinced. Servants offered us tea and refreshment. As we were leaving, he asked what time my flight was tomorrow and I said it was in the evening. He replied "I can't promise anything, but I will see what I can do". I paid my respects and left his house.

The following day was the 25th January 1968 and my last day in Dhaka. All my bags were packed, and my travellers' cheques, passport and entry documents were ready.

I decided to go to Dhaka Medical College to pay my respects to some of the teachers and say goodbye to my colleagues. It was nearly midday. To my surprise, on the medical college lawn I found a collection of all the professors, teachers and administrators in the winter sunshine, assembled in the hope of greeting the governor of East Pakistan, Abdul Monem Khan, a hated figure during the Bangladesh struggle, who would pass along this road and might or might not stop over at the medical college. I found my pharmacology teacher nearby and he advised me that whatever I do in the UK I must sit the MRCP Examination because it is looked on very highly when applying for jobs.

I returned to my flat, where friends, well-wishers and flatmates were waiting to say goodbye, along with my father-in-law and one or two of my brothers-in-law. I asked them to take the contents of the flat back to Kushtia for safe-keeping, including some suitcases which had my papers, including an account of "days of torture" during my school days in Kushtia. I was, of course, unaware that within three years of my departure the country would undergo a civil war, my family would be uprooted, and all the contents of the house, including my personal papers would be looted.

My flight was at 9.30 p.m. and as our rickshaw stopped near the steps of the departure lounge, I saw a policeman on a bicycle coming towards me. He asked me "Are you Dr Wajed?" I said "Yes", with some trepidation, fearing a final obstacle at the eleventh hour. He produced a letter from the office of the Dhaka Police with the certificate I needed. The visit to the Police Commissioner's house had paid off.

At the airport, one or two people commented how cold it would be in England at this time of year and what warm clothes had I got? I pointed out that I had a three-piece woollen suit, but I was told it was not enough. I was too late to do anything about it and I resigned myself to facing the situation at the other end.

I boarded the aircraft which would take me to Karachi in West Pakistan, the main Pakistan International Airport, where I would change planes to a bigger aircraft for the flight to London. The plane would cross India, which was an enemy territory. Half an hour into the fight the plane was over Calcutta and I could see the lights of the city below. Calcutta is barely a hundred miles from my house in Kushtia and in pre-Independence days people from my area would visit the 'Great City', second in the British Empire. Villagers who had been to Calcutta would come back to tell the others that "He who has not visited Calcutta is still in his mother's womb!" I had never visited it, because of the enmity between India and Pakistan and the further deterioration following the war in 1965. But as young men we were avid listeners to the radio from Calcutta, which was far superior to the infant Dhaka Radio. We used to listen to Bengali music, drama and of course some political propaganda as well.

While the plane flew westwards towards Karachi, I looked around at my fellow passengers. The vast majority were not like me, young and educated, but rather middle-aged, not well dressed and of rural background. Some of them were carrying bags of onions. It was a revelation, because I always imagined that people went to the UK for higher studies but in fact there was a large Bengali community in the UK, most of whom came from Sylhet, an important industrial region and city, and on the plane the overwhelming majority of the passengers were from Sylhet.

I talked to a fellow passenger in his mid-forties with a black and white goatee beard and teeth stained red from chewing betel nuts. I could not understand his dialect fully, but what I did understand was that he was living in the UK and worked as a kitchen hand in a restaurant, mainly washing plates and utensils and preparing the vegetables. He lived in London, but had been on holiday to Sylhet and was returning to the UK after a year. He was one of those carrying a bag of onions, which he believed to be much tastier than the ones available in the UK. During the conversation, I asked about the weather and how cold it would be. I also told him that I did not have an overcoat. His jaw dropped and he said "Doctor Shahib, it will be terribly cold, and I don't know how you will cope". I told him that since the plane would be landing in the daytime at Heathrow, surely the cold wouldn't be a problem. He replied "Doctor Shahib, there is no difference between day and night!"

After three hours of flying, the plane landed at Karachi. It was still night and we were taken to a transit lounge where there were many West Pakistanis waiting, tall, well-built, and well dressed. There was a bar at the corner where I saw a few of them sipping whisky. There were also a few Europeans waiting to board the London bound plane.

After waiting a couple of hours, we were ready to board the London flight. At the check-in counter, a hefty official looked at me and said "You are a doctor and leaving the country – where is your 'No Objection Certificate'?" I think he was trying to create some trouble and perhaps receive a bribe. But I showed him all my papers and told him I would be returning to Pakistan after completing my studies and he allowed me through.

On the plane, my fellow passenger was an Englishman this time. I had read the various instructions provided by the British Council about the weather and life in general in England. I still remember one comment, that "the girls in England are friendly and mix freely, which does not necessarily mean they are easily available". I think this was a wise precaution, because in Islamic countries there is hardly any social mixing with the opposite sex, but in Western society a Muslim man can find himself freely talking, joking and laughing with women and this could easily be misconstrued.

I started to talk to the Englishman and it turned out that he was an engineer working in West Pakistan and was returning home for a visit. I was still worried about the weather in London and I asked if, since I didn't have an overcoat, would I freeze at the airport. He said it is of course cold, but not any colder than Murree, a hillside town in Pakistan. I knew that Murree was a ski resort but had never seen snow in the eastern part of the country. The engineer thought that I would probably survive, but another passenger who overheard our conversation said that I could wrap newspapers under my jacket which would protect me from the cold.

PART II
MAKING MY WAY

A new world

I took off from Dhaka in the evening, then at Karachi it was midnight but to me it seemed the night would never end. On my watch it was 10 a.m. Dhaka time, but I was still in the plane, and it was pitch dark outside.

The plane landed in Rome for refuelling and from the window I noticed the dawn was breaking. I could not sleep and never can on an aeroplane. Breakfast was being served. The air hostess of Pakistan International Airline asked me whether I would like ham. I did not know what ham was. She explained it was from a pig and an English person's favourite. Of course, I could not eat ham but was surprised to find that it was being served on the national airline of Pakistan.

In retrospect, it seems that in those days there was not such strict adherence to the Islamic code of practice. It was much more liberal. I remembered an incident when, as a young medical student, I happened to visit Chittagong cantonment at the invitation of a friend who was an officer in the Pakistan Army, which was dominated by Punjabis from West Pakistan. This friend of mine was a captain in the prestigious Baloch Regiment, and later became a war hero in the liberation struggle for Bangladesh in 1971, going on to become Army Chief of Staff, and then President of Bangladesh for a few days before he was killed in a counter-coup. I remember that in the cantonment he took me to their bar which was well stocked with alcoholic drinks of various sorts. He ordered some beer for both of us. That was my first taste of an alcoholic beverage – in the Islamic State of Pakistan's Army cantonment, of all places.

The tradition was maintained from the days of the British Raj, though this practice has been discontinued now, both in Pakistan and in Bangladesh.

The plane landed in Rome in the early morning. We disembarked: my first step on European soil. I remember the transit lounge was very long and spacious with few people there. I walked, full of confidence and hope. I was a young man, looking forward to the challenge of a new life in a new environment and above all had a burning desire to get a post-graduate degree from the British Royal Colleges, the dream of every medical graduate. That I left my young wife and one-month-old son back at home was the least of my worries, for I knew they would be well looked after by my parents-in-law, who themselves were young, and our son was their first grandson. I bought some picture postcards and sent them to my wife, brother and other friends from Rome Airport. The plane took off and headed towards London.

It landed at Heathrow at 10 in the morning. It was 26th January 1968. Little did I know, that day, that England would be my home for the rest of my life and that I would perhaps die and be buried here.

It was a dry, crisp morning and very cold. I had a three-piece woollen suit and could withstand the cold without an overcoat. Certainly, it was not as bad as I had been told it would be by various people, both on the plane and before boarding it.

Before Immigration there was a health check, to show proof of vaccination and inoculation against TB and smallpox. Only a few years before, a Pakistani man had been found to have smallpox. There was much adverse publicity in the press in England and we felt very bad about it in Pakistan. Of course, my paperwork was up to date, so I proceeded to Immigration. I had a passport with a student visa and was confident in speaking and understanding English, so I did not anticipate or experience any problems. In front of me, there was a man from Bangladesh, from the Sylhet District, and he was having some difficulties. The Immigration Officer asked me to ask him why he could not speak English though he had been in England for many years and was returning from home after a sabbatical. His answer was that he "washed plates and utensils" in a restaurant, and had no contact with any English-speaking people. I told this to the Immigration Officer, who then produced a coin from his pocket, showed it to the man and asked him to tell him what it was.

I had just landed at the airport and had not had any chance to see English money. The man, to my surprise, immediately said the coin was "half-a-crown", worth 2½ shillings as I later learned. He was allowed through Immigration.

I had been told to take a bus to the Victoria Bus Station, where a British Council representative would be waiting for me.

I sat in the bus and looked outside. It was cold and dry, the trees bare of any leaves. No sunshine. It was so gloomy. I felt uncomfortable. At the back of the bus there was a young couple passionately kissing and cuddling. To me this was a strange experience. I had never seen people kissing in public, which was totally unacceptable where I had just come from. Even to hold hands with a female companion would be frowned upon. I was to learn within days that this was normal social behaviour.

At Victoria, I found a middle-aged man wearing a yellow armband with "British Council" written on it. I introduced myself and he was expecting me. His name was Robert and he took me to the British Council offices, where I met my supervisor, Miss Pritchard. She asked me to join her for lunch. I ate fish and chips for the first time, and she paid for me. I was told that Robert was a guide, who would take me to a shop to buy some winter clothes, and then take me to a hotel for an overnight stay.

I needed an overcoat and Robert found a good one for me. I remember the sales assistant said, "You could go to Buckingham Palace in it". Robert took me to a hotel. Though it was terribly cold outside, inside the hotel and the room it was warm and comfortable. Robert explained to me that this was because of "central heating" and showed me those wavy metal things near the wall called "radiators". I fell asleep, not knowing what time it was.

In the morning, Robert came to take me to an International Students' Hostel and also to show me the route to go to my hospital.

The hostel was mainly for undergraduates from overseas. Only I and another fellow medic from Ghana were postgraduates. My room was small with only a sink. No heating, except for a coin-operated electric heater. As I was short of cash and the heating was ineffective, I chose not to use it. The difficulty was at night, when the bed was as cold as if the sheets had been in the freezer. It continued for days like this until somebody suggested that I buy myself a hot water bottle.

Apart from breakfast, no food was supplied at the hostel. We were told that there was a restaurant nearby, where we could have our evening meals.

Paul's Restaurant was a family business, run by a husband and wife with a teenage daughter. The food was very basic and had to be finished by 6.30 – 7.00 pm, whereas we had been used to eating supper late at night, so by the time I went to bed, I was hungry.

The bitter cold weather, inadequate and alien food, and homesickness for my wife, children, parents and relations made me very uncomfortable indeed. I wrote in my diary "Every moment, I feel like returning home." I cried and cried, wondering why I had come to this God-forsaken country. At Paul's Restaurant I felt that the wife was deliberately sending her teenage daughter in "hot pants" (these were fashionable in the sixties) to serve me, to attract my attention. I was a good-looking, aspiring and ambitious foreign student and they did not know I was already married, with a child.

This is how I started my life, and I would visit the International Students' Hostel again twenty-seven years later, when my son Faisal got a place at the nearby Greenwich University.

It was half-an-hour's bus journey to Lewisham Hospital, where I was supposed to do a course in medicine for two months to orientate and refresh myself, and get acquainted with British medicine. My travelling companion was Dr J.A. from Ghana. He was the same age as me, over six feet tall, with an athletic build and scars on both sides of his face which I was told later were the marks of an initiation ceremony in his native Ghana. Dr J.A. had qualified in Nigeria and had come to the UK for higher studies. Because we were staying in the same hostel, travelling in the same bus and attending the same course, I became friendly with him and learned more about him.

In all there were nine postgraduates at the hospital and this course was meant for those intending to do the Membership (MRCP) Exam. This exam at that time had two parts. The first part was a written exam, in multiple-choice form, and those who qualified in that proceeded to the Final, which was clinical, meaning that candidates would be examined thoroughly about their skill as aspiring consultant physicians. It was, and still is, a very tough examination and only 10% of the candidates succeed. What's more, in those days if someone failed the First Part six times, he or she would not be allowed to sit for any further attempts, as they were considered not up to it.

However, every doctor who wants to do higher studies in medicine aspires to attain Membership, for success in this examination is the gateway to a better future, whether that person stays here in the UK or returns to his own country. Because of the legacy of the British Empire, postgraduate degrees are highly valued in Commonwealth countries and with MRCP after one's name, one is bound to get a good position in the government hospitals and be assured of lucrative private practice.

Amongst the other eight postgraduates, one was from India, one from Sudan, one from West Pakistan and myself from East Pakistan. My friend, Dr J.A. was from Ghana, another one was from Nepal and I forget where the other two came from. All of them except me had been in the UK for some time working in the hospitals, and some of them had taken the Part I exam a few times. All of them had had some preparation and knowledge of current developments in medicine. I was the only one freshly arrived from abroad and ill-prepared for any sort of examination, for I had been out of touch with academic medicine since qualifying five years previously. I had never touched a medical textbook since medical school. I had been doing my job as a clinical pathologist in Dhaka Medical College Hospital, which did not need any book work as such.

Anyhow, on the first day at the hospital the supervisor of the course, Dr S., a dignified consultant and examiner of MRCP, gave a talk on what the course was about. After the introductory talk, he handed over a multiple-choice questionnaire. He told us that he would like to "gauge the depth of our knowledge of medicine" before the course started – a very valid point - and he intended to do it again at the end of the course.

The questionnaire was handed out. It was for half an hour and one had to answer by ticking the box: yes/no/don't know. There were fifty questions, carrying fifty marks.

I do not remember who got the top marks or what they were, but I do know that I got only eight out of fifty, a dismal failure, and in the eyes of the supervisor and the participants I was the worst candidate, with little knowledge.

On my way back to the hostel with Dr J.A., I could not talk much. I felt inferior, humiliated and good for nothing.

On subsequent days, whether in class or interpreting an X-ray or discussing a patient at the bedside, I would be the first to be asked and invariably I either could not answer or gave the wrong answer. My morale broke down completely and I thought that this course was not for me. I was afraid that the supervisor might report my dismal performance to the British Council, and that they might in turn stop my scholarship. After all, why would the British Council spend so much money on a "good-for-nothing" candidate... But I was much more concerned about the daily humiliation in front of everybody of not being able to answer at all. I knew I had been able to when I was a medical student, but five years of being out of touch with study had made me forget everything I had learned.

At the beginning of the second week of the eight-week course, I made an appointment to see the supervisor. I told him frankly that I felt humiliated that I could not answer the questions, and this was because I had been out of touch with medicine for so long and that I did not intend to do the Membership Exam. I had been sent for a Diploma in Physical Medicine and I told him I would prefer not to be asked any questions either by himself or by any other consultant. Dr S. was understanding and advised me to stick it out to the end of the course and try to learn as much medicine as possible, which would help me in the future, whatever I did. He promised that I would be spared being asked any questions, but if I wished I could volunteer an answer if I knew it.

Life at Lewisham Hospital became a bit easier for me. I attended all the lectures, ward-rounds, and did try to catch up, by reading in the library. I tried to avoid other participants of the course, particularly when it came to discussions about any patients or any clinical problems. Among all the participants, Dr J.A., was regarded as the best. He would answer all the questions correctly and would diagnose a patient with accuracy. Somehow, I felt I couldn't keep up with him in any conversations about medical problems and tried to avoid him as much as possible. Certainly, it was everybody's expectation that if anyone succeeded in the membership exam, he would. As for myself, I did not consider that it would be remotely possible for me to sit the exam.

As it turned out many years later, I was the only one from that group that did pass that wretched exam and succeeded beyond all expectations in getting a consultant's job in the United Kingdom. I know this for a fact, because all the candidates who pass are entered into a Register and I never saw in it any of those names with whom I did this course at the Lewisham Hospital in the winter of 1968.

I met Dr J.A. from Ghana later, at a medical meeting. I enquired about his situation. He said he did take Part I of the Membership once or twice, failed, married an English girl and settled in this country as a GP The doctor from Sudan did not take the Exam, returned home to his own country and much later I learned he had died.

We had our lighter moments at Lewisham Hospital. At lunchtime, we would talk about various things, including sexual relationships. This being the "swinging sixties" and we being young, the inevitable discussions about success with girls would come up. I was the only one in that group who was married and very new in England, and I only knew decades later that the sixties had been swinging at all. The Indian doctor was very conservative and would not open up. The Pakistani doctor had a relationship with a nurse and would spend time with her at the weekend. Dr J.A., who was good looking and intelligent, would talk about his sexual experiences in Ghana and Nigeria, but not in England. The doctor from Sudan was the oldest amongst the group, short and obese. He was a chain-smoker and talked about marrying a virgin on returning to Sudan.

A doctor from Nepal was handsome, short, like a Ghurkha soldier, and very articulate and well dressed. During these discussions, it turned out that he was a vegetarian, which many Indian/Nepalese are, because the Hindu religion forbids the eating of beef. He also drank no alcohol and had no girlfriend. After this disclosure, Dr J.A. commented, "You do not drink, do not eat meat, do not have a girlfriend - so what is this life for?" We all burst out laughing.

The bitterly cold weather continued; it was mid-February. One day while at the hospital, I looked through the window and found that something like cotton wool was falling from the sky. It was relentless and settling on the ground, which looked as though it was covered with white flour. One of the other postgraduates explained to me what it was and how it could be dangerous to walk on it. In Bangladesh I had never seen snow. We only had hail, and I had imagined snow to be something like that. I went out and played on the newly fallen snow, and it was one of the most exciting things that I experienced. A few days later, the snow melted. It was the weekend, and from my window I saw lovely sunshine. I thought it must be warm outside, as it would have been back at home. I went out in my shirt and trousers, only to find that it was still bitterly cold.

My days at the Lewisham and Brook General Hospital were coming to an end. It was the end of March; the buds were coming out on the trees that had looked dead when I arrived. The leaves on various trees were fresh and tender and some trees had flowers. I later discovered that many trees, particularly cherries, give flowers first and then burst into leaves of various colours. Back at home the trees are evergreen, but in spring and rainy seasons fresh growth of leaves takes place, and then flowers blossom. I was amazed that, here, the flowers came first.

One day I was walking through the nearby park with another student, an undergraduate from West Pakistan. I saw lots of yellow flowers on the ground, raising their heads. Some were in full bloom, others still in the bud stage. I asked my fellow student what these flowers were. He said they were daffodils. I was very excited, because I had heard and read about daffodils in Wordsworth's famous poem. English was compulsory in my school days, so I knew about Wordsworth's daffodils long before I actually saw them in England. Later on, I had the opportunity to see the site of Wordsworth's original daffodils, and his house, in the Lake District.

We were familiar with other English poets, too. I can still recite many of them after all these years. One line from Shelley's poem "To a Skylark" that made a mark on me was, "Our sweetest songs are those that tell of saddest thought."

The British Council was trying to relocate me after my terms at the Lewisham Hospital. I was asked to see a physician called Wing Commander W.P. This particular doctor was in the Royal Air Force, and was in charge of placing the overseas students at various hospitals for training in Physical Medicine. I went to see him in one hospital in London. He was a very smart, thin, tall man, very friendly and pleasant. After a brief talk he said he would let me know my placement.

I should explain Physical Medicine, a speciality that no longer exists. It was abolished in 1973 and is now called Rehabilitation Medicine. Physical Medicine was born out of the need to rehabilitate servicemen injured in the Second World War. There were servicemen who had various injuries to limbs, damage to their vital organs and were unable to return to their original job. The Physical Medicine specialist's task was to assess the damage, and in the cases of loss of limbs, fit artificial limbs. For upper limb and hand injuries, there were various gadgets and appliances that could be provided to maintain the patient's independence. For the very severely disabled, an appropriate wheelchair had to be provided. So this was not acute medicine, but the practitioner would have to have a wide medical knowledge. My scholarship was given to help me work for a Diploma in Physical Medicine, get as much training as possible and then return home. Five of us were sent for this training. At that time there was no specialist in Physical Medicine in East Pakistan, so we were sent here, with various scholarships. Mine was the "Colombo Plan" scholarship, provided by the British Council. Because there was no provision for training in East Pakistan, all of us were required to have at least three years' training in a recognised centre before being eligible to take the Diploma Examination organised by the conjoint Board of London. This was the reason for my interview with Wing Commander Dr W.P.

It was now early April 1968. The days were longer and brighter. The cold was getting less intense. My course at the Lewisham General Hospital was nearly at an end. Luckily there was no exit examination and I was relieved about that. The other candidates melted away to their various destinations but I still had to stay at the International Students' Hostel, for I had not yet heard from the Wing Commander about my next clinical attachment.

While I was still in the Hostel, I met a postgraduate student from Pakistan. He was staying only for the weekend. He was senior to me and had obviously been in the UK for a while, for he owned a car and knew his way around London. It was Saturday night and he asked me to go out with him in his car. He took me to central London to a nightclub called "Mecca". Mecca is a holy name for me as a Muslim and I was convinced that some sort of religious service would be taking place inside.

Once there, I found there were lots and lots of girls in mini-skirts, just hanging around the corridor and alleyways. My friend asked me to get hold of a girl and dance while he disappeared. I felt like a fish out of water. I didn't know how to dance or who to ask. Instead I just watched what was happening.

There was a dance floor where many people were dancing, with quite a few of them Africans dancing with white girls. When the music stopped they sat and drank. The whole area was filled with cigarette smoke. Most of the girls were white, some African and only a few Asian. Almost invariably they were smoking. I also smoked.

The night wore on. I looked at the dance floor for my friend, who was nowhere to be seen. I didn't have the nerve to ask a girl to dance with me, and even if anyone had said 'yes', I wouldn't have known how, or what to do. So I continued to keep a watch around the dance hall and the vicinity.

I was getting worried in case my friend did not show up. How would I get back to my hostel at that time of the night? Although London was quite safe at that time and I was a young man full of confidence, I was still getting apprehensive. It was nearly midnight when my friend appeared from nowhere and said, "Did you enjoy it?" I could not answer yes or no, for it was a totally different experience for me. We decided to leave the Mecca Club. It was pouring with rain outside. We got in his car and started towards our hostel. I was very new and could not help him with navigation. He got lost. We drove and drove - God knows where we went. Ultimately, however, we did reach our hostel in the early hours of the morning. It was a Sunday and I got up late for breakfast. I intended to meet my friend of last night at the breakfast table, but he had gone. There was no car in the forecourt. I did not even know his name or where he lived. I never met him again, though I wish I had.

On another Saturday night, we were invited to a party organised by the British Council in Central London. It was a lovely gathering with postgraduate and undergraduate students from all over the Commonwealth. There were lots of Asians and Afro-Caribbeans, and some Malaysians. There were also lots of girls, some in their national dress.

I met a young man of my age, from South India, tall and handsome, doing postgraduate work in dentistry. I started talking to him about his origin and how long he would be staying in the UK. A middle-aged lady came and joined us; she was an official from the British Council. She asked us where we came from. I said, "I am from Pakistan" and he said, "From India". The lady jokingly said, "I am glad you are not fighting now". Her comment was appropriate, for India and Pakistan had fought their second war only three years earlier over the disputed area of Kashmir. At the party, I met a few Nigerians; one was an Army Officer at Sandhurst. He must have returned home and occupied a high post in his country.

I finally got a letter from the Wing Commander, saying that my clinical attachment had been sorted and I would be with the Physical Medicine Department at the London Hospital, Whitechapel (now the Royal London Hospital). I told this news to my fellow students at the hostel, who would be staying longer for their studies. A few of them commented that it was an area where "you will meet lots of your fellow countrymen" (Bengalis). Some commented that it was a violent area, frequented by gangsters and where Jack the Ripper was active in Victorian times. I did not have any choice but to accept my offer to go to the London Hospital.

In my opinion, opportunity in life comes only once. One has to capture it with both hands, for it will perhaps never return. This opportunity comes either by design or by pure accident. In my career it has always been by accident rather than design,whether it was the decision to go to medical school, to get a job at the teaching hospital in Dhaka, the capital, to get married, to have my first child, or to come to the United Kingdom for higher studies. Now it was an attachment with the London Hospital for my training.

I had heard many horror stories about the East End, and the activities of the Kray twins were still very fresh in people's minds in the late sixties. I asked myself what I had done to deserve this posting, which could be for as long as three years, the whole duration of my training. The Wing Commander in his letter reassured me that it was the best department in the country at the time.

How right he was, and how fortunate I was to be placed at that great centre of learning. In fact, I was one of the luckiest overseas doctors to be allocated a place in that famous department, headed by a giant of a man called Dr Michael Mason. He was well-known all over the country and abroad for his contribution to this particular branch of medicine.

It was the 7th May 1968 when I went to the London Hospital for the first time. It was a Tuesday, the day the Rheumatology Department, which also used to be called Physical Medicine, had their weekly ward round and clinical conference. Between 12.30 and 2 p.m. I went to the Department to see Dr Mason. He was busy and he asked one of his registrars to look after me, to take me to lunch and then meet at the entrance hall at 2 p.m. for the ward round.

At 2 p.m. Dr Mason arrived, followed by a group of about twelve doctors, from junior consultants to the House Officer. A dignified man, full of confidence, he advised me to stay for the ward round, followed by the clinical meetings, which I did. It became my routine for the next two and a half years.

At the London Hospital, I found even the most junior doctor, that is to say, Senior House Officer (SHO), had got his MRCP. Most of them later became famous in various specialties. In that group of doctors, I was the only Asian, the others being all locals and Caucasians. Dr Mason asked me to come the following day and see his Registrar, who would formulate my work schedule.

On the first day at the London Hospital, I felt a bit lost. It was a huge place, and everybody was so knowledgeable and knew so much about medicine. I felt I was just a small fish in a big pond. But I felt that if I managed to stay there for the whole three years of my scholarship I would learn quite a lot, and I was confident I would at least pass my Diploma, the reason I was sent there in the first place.

I was under pressure from the warden of the International Students' Hostel in Woolwich to leave. It was a long and expensive journey for me as well, so I was looking for accommodation near the hospital. Even at that time there were quite a lot of Bengali people in the area, but I did not feel that I would be able to stay with them, because the way they lived might make it difficult for me to study. I could not find any other International Students' Hostels either. I looked at the notice boards, and local newspapers, but either I could not afford the places advertised, or they were too far from the hospital.

One day I met an Asian doctor in the dining room, a Registrar in the Radiotherapy Department. He was one of the few Asian doctors working there and it turned out he was a Bengali from Calcutta. His name was

Dr Das, and he became a great friend. He later enjoyed his retirement in India, sharing his time between Calcutta and Goa. Dr Das had a three-bedroom terraced house in Woodford, and he suggested we explore the possibility of me taking a room in his house, but it did not happen, so with his help I kept on looking.

At that time, there was a lot of racial prejudice in Britain. I was told that it was unlikely that I would get a tenancy with a white landlord or landlady, particularly as I wanted to bring my wife and small child over as soon as possible. So Dr Das and I concentrated on looking for houses with Asian landlords, of which there were not very many.

One day we knocked on door in Queens Road in Leytonstone. A pleasant man, a Sikh with a beard and turban, opened the door and said that he had a room that he could let. It was a three-bedroom terraced house, in which he lived with his wife, three children, mother and two younger brothers. There was only one bathroom and two toilets, one upstairs and an outside lavatory downstairs. The man was prepared to let the room at the back, where there was only a single bed. How they were going to manage the rest of the house with so many people, God only knew. We settled the rent: it was £3.50 per week.

I moved into this gentleman's house on 26th May 1968. They welcomed me with open arms. My room faced the back yard, near the family bathroom. The landlord was middle-aged, and his mother elderly and I called her "Mataji" – "mother". The kitchen was downstairs, and was in constant use. I had never learned how to cook, so most days I ate in a Bengali restaurant called "Star of India". During my first months in Britain, I had eaten in many "Indian" restaurants, which were all owned by Bengalis, East Pakistanis. Being a nationalist and because the Indo-Pakistani war was still fresh in the memory, I asked the owner why it was that all of them were called "Indian" though they were all in fact Pakistani. He smiled, and said the image of Pakistan was not good, and so for the sake of business they call it an Indian restaurant.

Mataji at the Sikh house was very kind and affectionate to me and treated me like her own son. There were many days when she would provide me with their food, which was mainly vegetarian. I am mainly a rice eater, but Sikhs, like other Punjabis, are mainly chapatti eaters.

Before I came to England I had never seen a Sikh man, only heard that they wore turbans, grew beards and wore a bangle called a Kanga. For the first time, I realised that the main reason for wearing a turban was long hair, which is neatly tufted and then covered with a smart turban. At night the men would come home, take off the turban, wash their hair and dry it as the women do. I saw this for the first time when my landlord let his hair down completely, relaxing with a glass of whisky while his wife was ironing the turban for him to wear the next morning.

My routine to go on the Tube to the London Hospital and hang around the departments, observing how the consultants saw the patients. I noticed how nicely they talked to them, with no sense of urgency or impatience in their manner, even though the patient might be illiterate, unshaven, and wearing ragged clothes, as was often the case in the East End. It was all quite different and a somewhat new approach to me. Where I had come from, the doctor/patient relationship was one of intolerance and 'getting on with the job as quickly as possible'. No one cared about patient satisfaction and the doctors were not answerable to anyone except their supervisors. There was no governing body, like the GMC in England, to safeguard the patient. Back home, the doctors' behaviour to private patients might be somewhat more deferential, but even then, not always.

I remember an incident when I was a final year student in East Pakistan. I came across a young man who took his elderly father to a specialist to consult privately. The father, being an old man, was speaking rather slowly at his own pace. In the consulting room, apart from the patient, there were some young doctors as helpers and of course the son of the patient. The professor suddenly lost his temper and shouted at the old man, saying "Hurry up! I am a busy specialist with higher degrees from the UK, and lots of people are waiting outside to consult me." The patient didn't say anything. His son maintained a dignified silence. The prescription was written. The son collected it, gave the professor his fee in cash (as is the custom there) tore up the prescription, put it on his desk and left the consulting room.

So after coming to the UK, the first thing I noticed was the general behaviour of the physicians. However qualified and internationally famous they were, they gave their patients top priority, and I quickly learned it and practised it.

I was settling down in the East End of London. It was my first summer in the UK. I noticed such a contrast in the whole atmosphere. It was unbelievable that the trees that had seemed dead to me were now alive with green leaves. The parks and the front garden of every household which had looked lifeless were now full of flowers and green grass. It gave me a tremendous lift and I took as many photographs as I could and sent them to my wife, parents and relations. It was not easy to come to the UK in those days and a photograph of me in midsummer would have given them, particularly my elderly parents, immense satisfaction.

It was June 5th 1968: Robert Kennedy was assassinated in the United States. It made me sad for the family for I distinctly remembered the day his brother President Kennedy had been assassinated in Texas. The picture of Jackie Kennedy with her two orphaned children was etched in my memory, and now another Kennedy was dead.

The political situation in East Pakistan was not good. Anti-Pakistani feeling was crystallising. There was unrest, strikes and demonstrations almost every day. I was trying to get my wife and son here to join me, now that I was in a stable situation for at least the next two to three years. I wrote to my father-in-law to start the ball rolling with arrangements for my wife to join me. Life would be a bit easier with my family around. All the friends and colleagues in my situation were with their families. I felt very lonely in a foreign country. While the preparations were afoot for my wife and child to join me here, an obstacle was put in our way by my brother. I respected him so much and owed so much to him because he gave me moral support to study medicine but his attitude towards me changed overnight after I got married. He felt that his full control over me had been slipping away since my marriage and also that I was under too much of obligation to my father-in-law, which was totally untrue.

My brother did not like the idea of me bringing my wife and son over here to the UK. I think he thought life here in England was all roses and that once you step out of Heathrow Airport it's all cosy and problem-free. He thought that I should stay here on my own with the meagre scholarship money, and that my salary from the East Pakistan Government should go to him, for his family expenses. Once I brought my family here, I would need all the money, and he would be deprived. It was an entirely selfish idea of which nobody could approve.

11

Finding my feet

I n mid-July 1968, clouds were gathering over East Pakistan. There were demonstrations, processions and strikes for the release of Sheikh Mujibur Rahman, the furious, charismatic national leader of Bangladesh. On 14th July 1968, there was a meeting at Hyde Park Corner, which I attended. There was trouble at that meeting: the agents of the Pakistan Government interfered and the meeting was broken up. Still the procession went on and I was part of it.

I also took part in the clinical activities at the hospital. Dr Mason asked me to see patients independently but under supervision. I remember my first case, and the first time I donned a white coat in this country. It was Monday July 15th 1968. The usual practice after seeing a patient was to write a letter to the General Practitioner about the consultation. All the doctors used to dictate the letters to the secretary, who would take it down in shorthand and then type it up the following day for signature.

I was a newcomer, my English was poor, and not easily understood by everybody, including the secretaries. So I wrote the letter in longhand, showed it to one of the consultants, then gave it to the secretaries for typing. Dr H.L.F. Currey, who later became a Professor of Rheumatology, was my mentor in this and I owe a great deal to him in my career. He was a tall, handsome, upright man, with a no-nonsense attitude. He was of British extraction, born, brought up and qualified in South Africa. His father was a famous headmaster in South Africa and a strong opponent of the apartheid regime. I read his obituary in the *Times* in the mid '80's. Harry Currey had left South Africa because he was opposed to the apartheid regime and made England his home.

At my landlady's house I was comfortable; they all respected me because I was a doctor. One day Mataji asked me to look at her wrist, which had been very painful and she was unable to do much housework. I was a novice and could not help her. Her own GP was also not very helpful and x-rays did not show anything. So I asked Harry Currey to see her on my behalf. At a glance, he diagnosed the condition and gave an injection which cured the problem once and for all. Mataji was so happy that she would point to the portrait of Guru Nanak hanging on her wall, saying it was the God's wish that I took up residence in her house. This situation however, was to change when my wife and my son joined me.

There were further complications back at home, which I need to explain in a bit of detail. My nephew, the eldest son of my eldest brother, lived in my paternal home in the village. In the Indian sub-continent, the family means the extended family. In my case I had two brothers and two sisters. My sisters moved away after marriage and started their own families in other villages or towns. But my brothers stayed in the paternal home and their children were part of the family. My eldest brother, the backbone of the family, was a very pious man, only happy in his village surroundings and looking after the land and crops. When I went to medical school, 70% of my expenses were paid by my father and was the proceeds from the sale of crops grown by my eldest brother. Neither he nor his wife nor any of the family raised any question about the severe hardship they had to endure for my expenses. This is the norm. No question would be asked and if anyone dared to ask he would be the black sheep of the family. In turn, it was my duty to bear the expenses of his children and help him financially whenever needed. For example, when I became a doctor and started earning money, my first expense was to provide money to buy presents for the bridegroom of my niece. My eldest brother has five sons and one daughter, so when his only daughter was getting married it was my responsibility to bear the lion's share of the expenses, though I myself was not yet financially solvent, being only recently qualified.

Out of the five sons of my eldest brother, the eldest became a problem and to this day remains a problem, though he is now a grandfather himself. He is probably ten years younger than me. While I was a medical student, he was studying in the village school, where everyone, including myself, studied. At the school he was a bully. He would pick a quarrel with anybody and would not concentrate on his studies. He was intelligent, but used his intelligence not in learning but in creating mischief for others. I was far away in Chittagong, and my middle brother in the district town struggled with his unplanned family. At home, my father was an old man, mainly preoccupied by the question of how to find the money for my next month's expenses. My brother, the boy's father, was busy tilling the land and trying to keep the family moving forward. In this situation, my nephew Idris grew up unsupervised and unguided. Though everybody expected that he would follow my path, in reality he was a spoilt child. He failed his GCSE a number of times and moved from one school to another, still not doing well. To all intents and purposes his education came to an end. It was at this time that I qualified as a doctor. It was a great relief for my father and the extended family that at least they would not have to support me financially.

I, as a newly qualified doctor, was on my own. I had some debts as a student, I had to support myself, buy some good clothing, find somewhere to stay and pay rent. It was an uphill task to meet these needs, but on the immediate horizon I also had to repay financial assistance to my elderly parents, and see to my eldest brother's family needs, such as the wedding gifts for his daughter. There were also enormous demands from my elder brother's family, with eight or nine children living in rented accommodation not fit for human habitation. Then of course, I had had to look to my career, find a wife and set up my own family. I felt myself that, as a medical student, poverty was my constant companion, and I was busy with only one goal: to qualify as a doctor.

So when I had got a government job in the capital and a flat "through the back door", it was quite natural that my nephew who was growing up as a wild child in the village, should join me in Dhaka.

I was a bachelor at the time, so Idris came and was admitted to a school. My parents did come from time to time but would only stay for a few weeks, so in the flat there was me, a servant who would do the shopping and cooking, and of course Idris as a student. He was under my supervision and had to study, away from the distractions of the village.

I knew his needs and provided him with the best care that I never had when I was in my brother's house in Kushtia. He passed his GCSE with good grades. We were all delighted. He grew up as a handsome teenager. He was then admitted to a prestigious Government College not far from my flat. I was convinced that after graduating from this college he would find a niche in society.

In my own life and career there had been some changes, in which my newly married wife became pregnant and my scholarship to the UK had nearly matured. My nephew continued to share the flat with myself and became friendly with my wife. It was as good as one could imagine.

So when I went to England, the apartment had to be vacated for another employee of the hospital. My wife and child would go to live with my parents-in-law, Idris would move into a hostel for students and I would continue to bear his expenses until he graduated.

For the first six months, this arrangement was working perfectly well. He continued to receive the money from my bank and I was satisfied that he was continuing his study. But it was not so. He had ready money and was unsupervised, in the capital city, with lots of newly acquired friends. He neglected his studies and demanded more and more money from me. I provided the money, not only from my salary from East Pakistan but I also had to remit money by telegraphic money order, because he would fabricate a story that he had been pick-pocketed and needed money immediately. There were times I would have to ask a friend in Dhaka to bail him out. I still did not suspect that he was totally out of control and had no inclination to pursue his studies.

However, there was another twist to this story. Because of some administrative bungling as was so common in the government offices, my salary from the East Pakistan Government was suspended, so there was no money in the bank. Idris assumed this was done by me deliberately. He did not wait to find out, neither did he ask any of my friends and relations to help him out. He left Dhaka and reported it to his uncle, one of my brothers in Kushtia. My brother was already unhappy and upset with me, because I was not helping him financially, and when he learned that Idris had had no money for that month he was simply furious. In normal times, my brother would not give a damn for my eldest brother or his family, but on this occasion he became so sympathetic towards him and so infuriated with me, that he wrote a letter to me in the U.K. I will never forget the language he used and from that day I lost all the respect I had for him. I showed that letter to my friend Dr Das, who had been so very helpful in finding my accommodation in London. He simply could not believe the language uttered to a younger brother, on his own in a far country. The gist of the letter was that I had become "obsessed" with bringing my wife and child over, and had forgotten all my duties and obligations back at home.

After this letter, I did not care what others thought. I made arrangements for regular money to be sent to Idris and asked my father-in-law to expedite the application for my wife and son's passport and travel arrangements.

The summer of 1968 was good, and I took lots of photographs with my new camera, intending to return home, so capturing as many images as possible. I continued to get letters from my wife telling me the passports were ready and giving the possible date for their arrival sometime in December.

I continued my studies and clinical duties at the London Hospital. I was getting better and better and was able to answer questions and comment on some of the problems. My English was improving too and I could understand what people were talking about. In the department I would see patients, attend ward rounds, watch post-mortems and spend as much time as possible in the library, because trying to study in the Sikh house was impossible.

The political situation in East Pakistan was bad. General Ayub Khan's regime of martial law was coming to an end. The Awami League, under the leadership of Sheikh Mujibur Rahman, was agitating for the equality of the people of East Pakistan. Because of this upheaval, my wife's arrival in the UK was delayed.

Christmas of 1968 came and went. There was so much hype about it beforehand, but on the day it was so quiet it was unbelievable. There was nothing much I could do, apart from visit one or two friends who felt the same way as I did. I never received any Christmas cards from anybody nor did I send any. Boxing Day was also very quiet.

The year ended and I wrote in my diary on 31ˢᵗ December that it had been "a remarkable year – for it was in this year I got the opportunity to come to England. What lies ahead, only Allah the Almighty knows". I also wrote, "This day my son is one year and eighteen days old. I left him when he was eighteen days old; he only cried and cried and I hardly remember his face".

In the first week of January 1969, I had to travel to Clacton-on-Sea to stay for a week and observe the facilities at the Rehabilitation Centre. I immediately liked the place with its wide-open spaces and on the coast. The Director there was very friendly and helpful. He treated me with respect and offered me the appropriate facilities for a foreign postgraduate student. I was most impressed by his attitude towards me. He was obviously a well-known person in the town and chairman of the local Lions Club. He invited me to their lunch and toasted me. I didn't know the etiquette, so he told me to remain seated while others stood and said my name. One evening, he invited me to his house, where his in-laws were also present. This was my first opportunity to visit an English person's home. It was a wonderful feeling. The house was well decorated, nice and clean with expensive furniture. Mrs Millard, the housewife and host was most elegant. During the conversation, I asked the father-in-law about the impression Englishmen have of Asians. He was obviously an educated and experienced man. He took his time to answer, then said, "We regard Indians" (i.e. including Pakistanis like me) "to be slightly inferior to us in every respect, but much superior to Africans". I was not surprised by this honest and straightforward answer.

During my stay in Clacton, I became friendly with two female occupational therapists and one physiotherapist. We played billiards, went for an "Indian meal" and fish and chips. We had photographs taken while sitting on the beach in very cold weather. I was proud of this photograph, sitting in between two beautiful young English girls. I myself was young and lonely. I sent this picture to my wife and sister-in-law in East Pakistan, but later I learned that they did not like the photograph because I was sitting too close to the girls.

On my return to London, I got a letter from my wife, saying that everything was now ready for her to join me in England, and the date was fixed for 31st January.

By this time, political agitation in East Pakistan had worsened and I thought it would not be possible for them to travel from Kushtia to Dhaka, then from Dhaka to the airport, because there was almost a complete shutdown of the transport system. In those days it was not possible to telephone, so on arrival day I half-heartedly started for the airport, not knowing whether they had been able to come.

At the airport, I asked for the passenger list at the Pakistan International Airlines counter, and to my surprise and excitement I saw listed: "Hashi Wajed and child". I was ecstatic and all the tiredness, despair and uncertainty vanished. I waited outside, and saw Hashi coming out looking tired and exhausted. Then there was Sajal! My son looked clever, started smiling and I saw four teeth, two incisors up and two down. I took him on my lap, covered him in warm cloth and we boarded a coach to Victoria. That was the beginning of my journey in this country with my wife and family.

My wife was only twenty-one and had not been exposed to the outside world, not even to university life in East Pakistan. She came from a sheltered life in her parents' house, straight to the practicalities of a foreign land, with a baby son just one year old. I myself was not at all sure in what direction my career would go and what would happen back in our country, where so much turmoil was going on.

My usual routine was to spend most of the day in the hospital, attending outpatient clinics with the consultant, ward rounds, clinical meetings and post-mortem sessions, then reading and reading in the library. I would have an excellent lunch in the hospital canteen, although unconscious – or conscious – racism was rife. I noticed that when I sat down at a table no one would share the table with me, even if I was alone there. On the other hand, if there were no chairs at all at an occupied table, a chair would be grabbed from mine and somehow they would squeeze a seat in for someone else. I could not understand why. In those days, almost all doctors, both junior and senior, were white, particularly in teaching hospitals such as the London Hospital. Occasionally, I would sit with a group of doctors at their table and join in the conversation, but I didn't like their body language and answers. I realised this was because of the colour of my skin. So in the dining room I would look for foreign faces. There were a few like me doing clinical attachments in various departments, financed by their respective Governments. I met a gynaecology student from Saudi Arabia and there were postgraduates from Iran. Iranians were very rich and many of them were from the army and had scholarships which were handsome compared with mine. There were Nigerians, Sri Lankans and a few Indians; one of them was my friend Dr Das.

So we knew where we stood: all of us were in the same boat and would enjoy our lunch sitting at the same table, under the gaze of our white colleagues

After three months in the Sikh house with the family, there were certain changes in their attitude to my wife. The house was full of people, from grandmother down to the young children, and I would have expected the women folk to accept my young wife like a daughter and give her a helping hand, since she was new in this country, without any relatives and not even anyone she could speak to in her own language. Mataji asked my wife to clean the cooker and the kitchen floor. They took the view that she was using the same cooker as their whole family used, so should share the cleaning. My wife did clean the cooker and the kitchen without telling me but one day I found her upset; one of the women had scolded her because she had spilt some gravy on the cooker. When she told me, I decided that we should move.

I found a house, this time belonging to a Pakistani man of a similar background. Father and son worked in a factory and lived with the son's wife and two young children. This was at Grove Green Road, about one mile from where we had been living. When I gave notice to the Sikh landlord, a good and friendly man, he was very surprised. I did not have to tell him the reason for our going.

At Grove Green Road, we were given the downstairs front room, really a drawing room, but to let it they had put a bed in there. We shared the kitchen and the toilet, both on the ground floor. Two upstairs rooms were occupied by the landlord and his son and the third was let to another single man, also from Pakistan. The kitchen was shared by us all, there was no central heating and the toilet was outside. With the money that I could afford for rent, this was the best I could manage.

From the Sikh house to a Punjabi house was like jumping from the frying pan into the fire. No Englishman would let any room to Asians, particularly when there were small children. Although, as I was a doctor, the British Council did their best to find reasonable accommodation, in the end I had to find my own. The answer was to look among the Asian community.

In both the Sikh house and the Pakistani house the men folk were excellent. In both places they were factory workers, and they respected me enormously as a doctor. In turn, I behaved impeccably and always paid the rent on time. But the problem was with the womenfolk. At Grove Green Road, the landlady was as young as my wife – perhaps she felt jealous. Because of the shared kitchen there would inevitably be an overlap at cooking time but the landlady would have none of it. She would not tolerate any inconvenience at all, forgetting the fact that we were paying money to stay in their house. The menfolk were very well behaved and were kind to my wife and my son.

When I came home in the evenings, I found my wife unhappy. Almost always there would have been some argument or unnecessarily harsh words had been spoken to her. It was affecting her, and also my studies. So we decided that we would have to look for yet another place to live, although we had been at Grove Green Road hardly three or four months.

While we were at Grove Green Road two important events happened which in many ways furthered my career in the UK.

I had been in the UK now for one and a half years. My scholarship with the British Council was for three years initially and could be extended depending on the circumstances. The initial three-year scholarship was purely for training and gathering experience in the UK before I became eligible for sitting the Diploma Examination, which It was not possible to do in East Pakistan. This was the regulation set by the Examining Board for overseas graduates. By now I had already been at the London Hospital for more than a year and had the opportunity to talk to other postgraduates who either had passed this exam or were preparing for it. I also had the past question papers and was capable of answering them. I felt confident in my own mind that if I was given the chance to sit for the Examination, I would succeed, but I was still short of another one and a half years' training. One day I was talking to a candidate from Mauritius, who had already been in this country for a while, having qualified in France, and who was ready to take the exam. I discussed the situation with him of my not having had the required three years' experience, but feeling confident enough to take the exam. He suggested I should talk to my boss, Dr Mason, who was not only a very influential man in medical politics, but also the examiner for this Diploma Examination. During my stay at the London Hospital, I had created a good impression on him and other colleagues at the department.

So I made an appointment to see him and explain the situation and asked if he could write to the Examining Board recommending me to sit the next exam, even though I had not completed the required three years of training. He was very kind and sympathetic, for he knew I would do well, and the time saved, another one and a half years, I could devote to a higher Diploma such as Membership of the Royal College of Physicians. He wrote to the Examining Board and to my surprise and delight the Board agreed and gave permission for me to sit the next exam. I was excited and submitted the fees for it.

The time came for the examination, with the written part held at the Examination Hall in Queen Square. The nearest tube station to the Examination Hall was Russell Square where there is a lift rather than escalators. Because I was late, I decided to take the stairs rather than wait for the lift. What a mistake! I did not realise that the platforms were so far underground. I was totally breathless when I reached the top and at the Examination Hall the papers had already been delivered and candidates had started their answers when I arrived, out of breath and tense. I could hear my own heartbeat going faster and faster from exhaustion and worry. I settled down in my place and said to myself that it was not a good omen.

It is often said that you never forget your first experience, whether it is your first day at school or university, the first time you met your girlfriend, your first kiss, and so on. It was the same with this, my very first exam in England, and being late. The exam consisted of two papers: the first paper before lunch and the second paper after lunch. I found that the questions in both papers were not straightforward. In fact they were nothing like I had expected and not much like the past question papers I had used for practise and had found I could do. Still, I thought I had done reasonably well.

However, after both the papers were over and when I was discussing with my fellow examinees, most of whom were from overseas – India, Pakistan, the Middle East and Africa – I found that some of my answers had not been right. Many of the examinees were sitting the exams for a second, third or even fourth time. There was even a fellow Bengali, from West Bengal, for whom this was his *eighth* attempt. I felt disheartened and there was nothing I could do about it. In all there were twelve candidates taking the exams. If I remember correctly there were two British, from the Services.

However, the exam also had a practical part in which you had to demonstrate your ability to diagnose and treat patients suffering from a disorder of the locomotor system. This was purely a clinical exam, though there would be some questions about various appliances used by physically disabled people, such as splints, callipers, wheelchairs and suchlike. I was told beforehand that this was the part where most of the students fail.

The date and the place of the practical exam arrived by post and, as luck would have it, it was the turn of the London Hospital to hold the exam and my boss Dr Mason was the head examiner. I felt happy about this, for the surroundings were familiar. Once again the clinical and practical exams were not as I had anticipated. I realized I could not answer all the questions and that they should have been answered more confidently. Apart from Dr Mason, there were three other examiners, and from their facial expressions I did not get the impression that I would pass. The exam finished and I went to the doctors' mess to reflect on the examination. I told myself, "If I pass, it will be an excellent achievement for me and I will have one and a half years' scholarship left. On the other hand, if I do not succeed, I have another one and a half years in which to try."

At about 3 p.m. another doctor who worked in the Department, and a close friend of mine, from Iran, ran towards me to congratulate me on my success! Apparently he was present when the examiners were having tea after the exam, and he overheard that six candidates out of twelve had passed, including me. I was obviously overjoyed with the news and phoned my wife to let her know the result. Still I could not believe it and thought I must wait until I got the official result from the Examination Board.

This arrived just over a week later. I was over the moon with this news of personal achievement – and coincidentally, on that very day,

Apollo 11 landed on the moon. Though Neil Armstrong and Buzz Aldrin were still inside the capsule, they stepped on to the surface a few hours later, and stayed on the surface for twenty-two hours. The following day, all the newspapers carried pictures of those two astronauts walking on the moon.

12

Over the moon

A t the end of July 1969, I wrote in my diary that it was a memorable month in many, many ways. It was the month that I passed my first examination in England. It was the month that the first man landed on the moon, a great achievement for mankind. I wrote that it was the beginning of space exploration, and who knew where it would end? It was the month Prince Charles had his Investiture as Prince of Wales. I was 32 years old.

There was all round happiness about my success in the exam and I was full of confidence for the future. The news of my exam success reached my scholarship provider, the British Council, and they wrote to me congratulating me on my success, but with a sting in the tail. The letter concluded by saying that since I had already completed the Diploma Exam, for which I was sent to the UK, and as the scholarship was using taxpayers' money, there was no need for me to stay in the UK and so I should return to my home in East Pakistan. I was totally disheartened by this letter, yet I always trusted, and still trust, in British fairness and justice. I showed this letter to my mentor, Dr Mason, who was also aggrieved. I explained to him that the reason I took the exam early and succeeded was so that I could spend time on further training in the UK to try for a higher exam, such as Membership of the Royal College of Physicians. Once again, he was kind and sympathetic to me and dictated, in front of me, a letter to the Director in Charge of Education for Foreign Graduates at the British Council.

A few days later, I got a call from the British Council saying Dr Russell wanted to see me. I met him at his office and he gave me the excellent news that the Council had agreed to continue my scholarship for another year and a half and I could devote myself to further higher studies. I was delighted and felt financially secure for the time being.

It was while we were still in Grove Green Road that we invited an English person to supper in our house for the first time.

I decided to invite my British Council supervisor Miss P. She was the person to whom I submitted my monthly mileage claim and it was she who was responsible for sending the monthly scholarship to my bank. She was a pleasant person, maybe a bit older than me, and she walked with a slight limp.

We had only one room, which was our bedroom, and it had a second-hand two-seater settee for the guest. We used to share a table in the kitchen with the landlord and the other tenant for evening meals. I informed the others that a guest as coming to have supper with us, so they left the table to us. Miss P. came on time and the only seat we could give her was in our bedroom, on the two-seater settee. During the conversation, it turned out that Miss P. was from Wales. I was not at all aware of what the implication would be, but in my innocence I asked her whether she was a Welsh Nationalist. The Welsh Nationalists were very much in the news in those days, as there had been some attempt by them to disrupt the Investiture of Prince Charles. Miss P. was taken aback by this question and vehemently replied that she was *not* a Welsh Nationalist. I felt uneasy at having put such a question to her. I don't think she enjoyed the meal, curry and rice as usual, and as it was a Muslim house, no alcoholic drink was offered. Also, my wife was not yet able to converse in English so couldn't communicate with our guest. We have given better dinner parties since...

In the summer of 1969 I was young, with my young wife and eighteen-month-old son, who even then was quite bright and very talkative. One afternoon when I returned from the hospital, he looked very concerned and as I picked him up, he was in tears and tried to say in broken Bengali, that the landlord had cut the trees in the back garden. I went out to inspect the garden and found the trees at the back had been pruned. I assured him that this was necessary and it would be all lovely, because young shoots would come out next year. He was very happy with the explanation and relayed this message to his mother.

Our plan had never been to settle in England, and indeed those who came to England for higher studies before me all returned home. It was unthinkable that after obtaining higher degrees and diplomas anyone would stay here, because the job we had left was waiting for us. With a UK degree in Bangladesh there would be promotions and prospects of staying in the capital or other big cities, with lucrative private practices. Needless to say, there would be servants, and a chauffeur. Therefore, the question of staying in England did not arise, for the standard of living would be much better than we could expect in the UK. With this at the back of our minds and after my early success in the exam we made full use of the summer, visiting various parks such as Regent's Park, Hyde Park and Kew Gardens, enjoying many other outdoor activities and taking photographs. The idea was to capture as many memories of England as possible before our return home.

Our sojourn at Grove Green Road came to an end in September. The landlord gave notice and once more we were on the lookout for yet another place to live.

This time we found another house belonging to a fellow Bengali. Once again, it was a two-bedroom terraced house with a shared kitchen and toilet. We were given the upstairs room overlooking the garden. It was a small room with a double bed, which we had to share with our son. There was a small two-seater settee in the corner, and no central heating. We were concerned about the cold, with the winter coming on. Downstairs, the front room had been converted into a bedroom for a bachelor tenant. The toilet was outside and was shared between all of us and the kitchen was shared between the three families living there. There was no dining room, but adjacent to the kitchen there was a temporary shelter with a corrugated iron roof. It meant that there was condensation from the metal roof falling on the plates while we were eating.

Winter approached. The only heating was an old-fashioned second- (or perhaps third-) hand paraffin heater. It gave out a horrible smell and soot, and needed to be cleaned every day. The room was damp: there was condensation all over the windows and wallpaper. There was nothing I could do with the meagre money I had at my disposal. My son, Sajal, who was a very receptive and intelligent two-year-old, fell ill one day. I took him to the GP, who, when he learned that we had only an old paraffin heater for warmth, was very displeased.

All these inconveniences were as nothing compared with the ill manners of the landlady. She thought that she had all power over the newly arrived housewife with a small child. She would pick an argument over the slightest inconvenience, forgetting the fact that we were paying rent.

One day we were saved by the common sense of my two-year-old son. Only God knows what would have been the consequences otherwise. A friend of mine came with his son of the same age. My friend was a doctor and was in the same situation as I was, preparing for the exam. My wife and my friend's wife were busy talking and preparing lunch. I too was talking with my doctor friend. None of us had any idea where the boys were. The wives thought they were with us, and vice versa. But the fact was that both of them were in our bedroom. It was winter and the paraffin heater was on. The other boy had a plastic toy camera, which he threw into the fire of the paraffin heater. It melted on the heater, emitting acrid black smoke. My son shouted at the top of his voice, "Fire! Fire!" and started crying. I rushed upstairs and found the room full of smoke and the boys huddled in one corner. I had a towel nearby which I put on to the heater, which stopped the smoke. The windows were opened, the boys were taken downstairs, their lives and the house saved from perhaps a catastrophic fire.

Life was becoming intolerable at that house. There was no peace in which to study, the accommodation was barely habitable and the 'landlady' was grumpy all the time, for no apparent reason. Still the winter passed, spring arrived, followed by summer. There was a small garden but nobody bothered to keep it tidy, let alone plant any flowers. The adjacent house, however, had a beautifully kept garden with a variety of roses. An elderly Englishman lived there and I used to have conversations with him about gardening. At that time only a few Asians owned houses, and even if they did, the concept of gardening was alien to them. They were happy to have a house and that was it. I never thought – and for that matter nobody in my generation would have thought – that we would settle in this country and that gardening would be one of our passions.

We decided to leave this house and in the late summer of 1970 we moved to another house nearby, in North Birkbeck Road. This belonged to a Pakistani-Kashmiri immigrant. The man was a factory worker. He had a wife, three daughters and one son. All of them were crammed downstairs. Upstairs, there was a master bedroom, which was rented by another doctor with his wife and son of about five years old. The second room, much smaller, with a double bed, was given to us. The room was so small that there was no space for even a single chair. We shared the bed with our son. There was a kitchen and bathroom also upstairs, shared with my Bengali doctor friend. Another room at the rear, overlooking a cemetery, became our sitting room/study So we were in a self-contained apartment, not shared with the landlord, but with another fellow Bengali. Although our bedroom was rather small, for the first time we were happy. We were happy because the landlord and landlady and their behaviour towards us was friendly.

They were the Darr family from the Pakistani part of Kashmir. The husband was a simple, sincere and humble man, softly spoken and always with a smile on his face. He worked in a factory which produced plastic toys, mainly small farm animals, and he treated our son like a grandson, so he was showered with many toy farm animals. The landlady was a superb person. My wife, for the first time since arriving in the UK, got some motherly affection from her. She would always ask about the welfare of the family and would provide us with food almost every day and certainly over the weekend when special meals would be cooked. This was early 1971 and the political situation in East Pakistan was going from bad to worse. It reached a point of no return, in fact. All the meetings between Sheikh Mujibur Rahman, Mr Z.A. Bhutto and General Yahia Khan came to nothing. All the West Pakistanis blamed Sheikh Mujibur Rahman for the failure and all the East Pakistanis knew in their heart that the responsibility for this failure was squarely on the shoulders of Mr Z.A. Bhutto. Gen. Yahia was a drunken dictator who did not understand the nuances of politics.

In those days, we had neither TV nor a radio. The black and white TV was in the sitting room belonging to the landlord. Almost always there would be news from East Pakistan, which it became intolerable for us to watch. The Darr family were tactful enough never to watch the TV news when we were watching. They would simply leave the room so that we could watch. They never ever discussed politics. We also kept a brave face, and despite the fact that our family house and my wife's parents' house were burnt down, we never told them. Some friends would come and we would discuss politics upstairs in our bedroom or in the study room. Those were very traumatic and uncertain days, but our landlord behaved impeccably. We never told him about the suffering our own families were undergoing, for most of the West Pakistanis would not believe it. They thought this was 'Indian propaganda', whereas we knew that my own family and my wife's family were refugees in India.

However, one day it could not be kept secret; I got a letter from my father-in-law in India with the news that my wife's maternal grandfather had been killed and her grandmother seriously wounded. My wife, being the first grandchild of her grandparents, was particularly close to them. Her grandfather was a well-to-do man in his area and refused to leave his house when everybody else, young and old, left their houses and headed for India. Initially we thought he had been killed by the Pakistani Army, but then I reflected that he was an old man with a white beard and a *haji*, one who had done pilgrimage to Mecca, so this was simply incredible. He could not have been a threat to the Pakistani Army. It later turned out that he had been murdered for his money by criminals, and that they were known to my grandparents-in-law. They killed the old man by rifle fire, and also shot my grandmother-in-law, who tried to protect him. Both of them were left for dead. The old man died instantly but my grandmother-in-law survived her injury and lived to tell the tale.

When I got this letter, I did not have the nerve to break the news to my wife. I waited for a day and then in an opportune moment I had to tell her. She was young and in a foreign land and I was the only one she could rely on. She burst into a loud cry, which was heard by the landlady who rushed upstairs. I had to explain to her what had happened. She consoled her and me to the best of her ability. There had been other bad news from friends and relations both from inside East Pakistan, from India and from West Pakistan.

Since passing my Diploma Exam in the summer of '69, I had been busy preparing myself for the MRCP Examination. It had two parts: Part I was entirely based on book knowledge with no clinical involvement. I would spend hours reading the heavy medical textbooks at the London Hospital library. At this time, there were a few doctor friends from East Pakistan, renowned for their talents back at home, who were also in the middle of doing this exam. Some had already got their Part I and had become frustrated by not being able to pass the Final and there were a few who had perhaps been trying and failing Part I. It was at this point I started a partnership with Dr K. a brilliant student from Dhaka Medical College, who had been sent to do an MRCP specialising in cardiology. He was a married man with two children. My wife and Mrs K. became friends and we would spend countless hours studying together. I was overwhelmed by the amount of theoretical knowledge he had and asked myself what chance I had got, when Dr K., who had so much encyclopaedic knowledge, had failed as many as four times. In those days, those who had failed Part I six times would not be allowed to sit the Exam anymore. So Dr K. had two more chances left and I was just beginning.

At the London Hospital, even the most junior doctors had to pass their MRCP examinations, so I was in good company. I decided to try for Part I in early 1971. A colleague of mine at the London Hospital advised me not to guess, when dealing with multiple-choice questions, but only to put a cross in the box when I was absolutely sure. That advice was invaluable. I paid the hefty fees for this exam, and was reimbursed by the British Council.

The exam was held at the Royal College of Physicians in Regents Park, and I answered the questions only when I definitely knew the answers were correct. There were approximately 300 questions, covering the basic sciences, therapeutics and clinical. I didn't count how many of those questions I answered.

Dr K, who had had previous experience of this exam, told me that if you had failed then the envelope with the news would be thin, so that you knew the result even before opening it. If one had succeeded, then the envelope would be thick, for there would be instructions for Part II of the Exam. It would take about a month before the result was declared. We already knew the date on which we expected the result by post. I was certain that I would fail, because if Dr K. with so much knowledge failed four times, what chance had I got? Dr K. was also under the impression that I would not make it.

On the appointed date, my wife and I were waiting anxiously for the postman to come. Lots of things were going through my mind, for success would stand me in good stead, whereas failure would make my status uncertain, the scholarship would stop, and the political situation back home was deteriorating by the day

I told my wife to keep an eye on the door and the letterbox. I was waiting upstairs and she was at the end of the stairs. The postman dropped the letters. Hashi went down and picked up the one addressed to me. She shouted from the bottom of the stairs that it felt thick. When she brought it upstairs I also felt it was rather bulky. I opened it and was extremely happy and delighted to know that I had passed. The letter started with a word of congratulations and enclosed various forms for Part II and the Final.

We could not believe that I had passed Part I of the MRCP Exam. When so many others who had been such good students had entered and failed, here I was, qualified from Chittagong Medical College and sent to the UK for a Diploma in Physical Medicine, having now passed Part I of the MRCP on my very first attempt. Both of us were absolutely thrilled.

We decided to go to Dr K's house, which was a ten to fifteen-minute walk, to tell him the result. It was nearly lunchtime. Dr K. also knew that the results would be available today. I pressed the doorbell and his wife opened the door. Dr K. was in the kitchen. He had never ever imagined in his wildest dreams that I would pass. He almost nonchalantly asked me, "Have you passed?" I answered, "Yes". He thought I was joking. When I showed him the letter he was simply astounded. He congratulated me and we had lunch with them as I had had so many times before while we were studying together.

From that day onward, Dr K. and I saw less of each other. Perhaps he took badly my success at the very first attempt or perhaps he gave up hope of success after so many failures and focused his attention on going into general practice, where no further training was required. The worsening situation in East Pakistan also played its part, when most families were uprooted and displaced. He had told me, "I would not be surprised if my widowed mother goes to bed at night without food", and it was vital that he take a paid job, for so far he was on a Pakistan

Government scholarship. Dr K. did join general practice and also did his MRCP from Ireland to satisfy himself.

At the London Hospital, everybody in the Department was happy at my success and congratulated me. I felt on top of the world. One doctor, a senior registrar named Derek, originally from Kashmir but qualified in the UK, took special pride because he had given me lots of advice before the exam. He invited me to supper in a Jewish restaurant. I remain ever grateful to him.

In the spring of 1971, the political situation was changing rapidly for the worse in East Pakistan. The National Assembly session was due to be held on 3rd March but Mr Z.A. Bhutto boycotted it. This had been the main news on the TV and radio. The whole world was disappointed by his selfish decision, and the country was about to be thrown into turmoil.

On Friday March 5th I wrote in my diary "The President is going to broadcast to the nation tonight. Don't know what he has got to say. Never before has the existence of Pakistan been threatened so much". In that broadcast he declared that he would "stop the split" and the new Assembly session was called for the 25th March. It is now history that this was his ploy to gain time for the deployment of the armed forces to crack down on 26th March 1971. Sheikh Mujibur had given a historic speech on the 7th March when he said, "This struggle is the struggle for Independence" – but wisely he did not declare independence unilaterally.

26th March 1971 was a traumatic and unforgettable day for Bangladeshis all over the world. It was on this day the Pakistan army, which was our own army and of whom we were so proud for their performance in the Indo-Pakistani war only six years earlier, turned their guns on us.

It was a Friday. I took our son Sajal to start his first day at a nursery nearby, and on the way I bought a copy of the *Times*. The main headline was: "Shots in Dakha as troops land by air and sea". Sajal would not leave me, so I sat in the corner of the nursery and finished reading the whole report and the editorial.

On that day, I started writing my daily diary in red ink because of the blood being spilt in my homeland, and I reverted to black ink on 16th December 1971 when the country was liberated. Because the Pakistan Government expelled all the foreign journalists, there was no accurate reporting and when I look back, lots of the news was exaggerated. It was reported that Sheikh Mujibur was leading the uprising, whereas he was in custody. There was one journalist, Simon Dring, from the *Daily Telegraph*, who was hiding in the roof of the Intercontinental Hotel and who, three days later, managed to reach Calcutta, from where he sent the news and photographs of the Pakistan army's massacre of the civilian population.

From that day on it was not possible to concentrate on my studies, I stopped going to the hospital, bought all the newspapers and not only read the news, editorials and comments, but also cut them out and put them in albums, which were later digitised and deposited in the Liberation War Museum in Dhaka. It was a time when I was confused, not knowing how to help the liberation struggle. Had I not had a wife and child to support, I would have left England to join the struggle, and many of my bachelor fellow doctors did just that. They returned as heroes after the liberation of Bangladesh.

In England, the news media were all in favour of the Bangladesh movement and I joined a group of doctors and others to lobby MPs, demonstrate, and attend a rally in Trafalgar square. We were demanding that Bangladesh should be recognised, but it was not possible for any government to do so, with the leader under arrest. Though there was resistance in almost all the towns and cities, the Pakistan Army was in overall control. Wide media coverage continued and on the 28th March we heard from All India Radio that a Major Zia, had declared independence on Chittagong radio, with the help of local radio technicians and a resistance fighter. Later, following a coup and counter-coup, he became President of Bangladesh. We were encouraged by the fact that some resistance was going on. At that moment, the most hated figure was General Tikka Khan, dubbed 'the Butcher of Bangladesh'. It was on his instructions that systematic killing of the civilian population continued unabated. On the 30th March '71 I wrote, "India has raised the issue of Bangladesh at the United Nations, but it seems nothing will come of it. If the Punjabi domination stays – what then?" By the 31st March, virtually all the resistance was crushed; the *Daily Telegraph* said "It will take a generation for the Bengalis to stand on their own feet".

On the 18th April 1971, the *Times* correspondent, Peter Hazlehurst, reported from the Indian side, opposite my village, Shikarpore, that heavy fighting was going on inside East Pakistan and countless refugees were pouring in to India. At the height of the crisis some ten million people crossed to India for shelter, including my family.

At about the same time, Pakistani TV showed a picture of two captured Indian soldiers from inside East Pakistan and my village of Dharmadaha was named. I was horrified and totally bewildered. If this had been happening in my village, which had become a battleground, what had been the fate of my elderly parents, brothers, nephews and other relations? I could not think straight.

However, I realised that whatever might have been their fate they were definitely displaced and would need money to support them. Here in the UK, I was just about surviving on the meagre scholarship from the British Council.

I decided to take a job. With the help of my superiors at the London Hospital, I managed to get a locum job of senior house officer (SHO) at the busy Whipps Cross Hospital, also in the East End of London. I asked my wife to take a job, which she did, in an assembly factory for transistors. Sajal, now two years old, was looked after by the landlady. This arrangement worked well and we were able to earn some money and were in a position to help financially.

Before I took up the job at Whipps Cross, I had to go to Edinburgh to attend a course, which had been arranged three months previously. The registration fees, hotel accommodation and travel expenses were all paid in advance by the British Council. I arrived at Ben Doran Hotel in Edinburgh on 4th April, but my mind was all the time preoccupied with the affairs back at home 5,000 miles away. During my stay in Edinburgh, I was always glued to the TV set in the hotel and there was saturation coverage of the fighting in East Pakistan. One European evacuee from Chittagong gave a graphic account of the fighting by the Bengali soldiers who defected to the resistance. He said there was no doubt in his mind that the determination he had seen in the eyes of the population of East Pakistan was bound to win the struggle they were fighting for. There was also a comment that the resistance movement was leaderless, which was true, for Sheikh Mujibur Rahman was in custody and his close associates were hiding and trying to make their way to India.

When I returned to London there was no letter, no news from back home. I was worried stiff for everybody but above all for Idris, my nephew at Dhaka College whom I was supporting. There had been large scale student massacres and I was not sure whether he had survived.

The following day, it was with great relief that I received letters from Idris and my brother. Both letters had been written from Shikarpore, on the Indian side of the border. I was relieved that they were physically safe and well in India, but hey needed financial help.

In mid-April I took up the job of SHO at Whipps Cross Hospital as a locum for two months. Although I had done one month's locum at another nearby hospital, I found that Whipps Cross Hospital was in an entirely different league. I had had no idea what I was walking into. Whipps Cross Hospital A&E Department was like a battlefield, particularly at night. On my first night, being first on call, I had to attend every acutely ill patient, give emergency treatment, do the necessary investigations and then inform the Registrar. The Registrar post is a highly responsible post and he has to supervise many other SHOs like me. Being very new and having little knowledge about dealing with acutely ill patients, I was often at a loss, and had to depend on fellow SHOs. The Registrar did not like to be called very often, but I explained my situation, after which he did not mind. I started work on Friday morning and finished on Monday evening, with little sleep. I survived my first weekend on call, but when I returned home I was totally exhausted. Fortunately, this type of duty was to be only once a month. In those days the SHOs would work non-stop for 92 hours without any extra pay. The situation gradually changed. Firstly, the doctors were paid for the extra time, and then the European Work Directive (EWD) forbade doctors to work for more than 56 hours.

When I was not on call, I had to look after the ward patients who had been admitted either from the A&E or from Outpatients. My job was to take their history, take blood, arrange other investigations, and prescribe medication. It was a busy undertaking but manageable and I was not able to finish my work until the consultant's ward round, which could take a long time. Because of my theoretical knowledge from Part I MRCP, I was able to answer the questions in the consultant's ward round. So within two weeks I created a good impression with the consultant, other doctors and nurses.

While at Whipps Cross I came face to face with racial abuse. In those days, the National Front was very active. Very often they would march through the East End with the Union flag, shouting anti-immigrant slogans. First generation immigrants were, in the main, peace-loving, hardworking people and they would never retaliate, even when there had been physical assault. I remember that an East Pakistan restaurant worker was killed in the East End, and his body was sent to Sylhet, in a ceremony attended by the High Commissioner of Pakistan. The oft-repeated term was "Paki-bashing", used in various newspapers. I don't know how or where the word originated, but it not only meant Pakistanis but applied to all the immigrants from the Indian sub-continent.

One day, I went as usual to check on a patient who had been admitted from Outpatients. He was a middle-aged Caucasian man, who needed some investigation for a weakness in one side of his body. I was assisted by a student nurse, who was also Caucasian. The nurse pulled the curtain around and when the patient saw me, an Asian doctor, he said to me bluntly, "I don't want to be examined by a coloured doctor". I was stunned. I did not know how to react or answer him. Also, I was not sure that I was "coloured". I thought this term was for Afro-Caribbeans. Nevertheless, I moved on to another patient and continued my work. However, the student nurse did not take this insult to me kindly and she reported it to the sister in charge of the ward. Sisters-in-charge were very powerful individuals and not only did the patients and nurses obey her but the doctors, including consultants, had to pay her due respect. The sister was a very efficient, middle-aged Irish woman, who saw me personally and apologised profusely for the offence caused by this patient. The following day the consultant came for his ward round. The patient had been examined, as demanded, by a white doctor. Before the ward round the sister obviously briefed the consultant about the patient's refusal to be examined by me. The consultant was a very gentle Englishman with superb manners and a mild nature. He was highly respected by all the junior doctors, particularly the overseas doctors. I remember when he had interviewed me for the job, he asked me what it was I wanted. I answered, "I have come to England in order to get the higher Diploma of MRCP and then return to my country". He was not happy with the answer and corrected me to saying, "No, you have come to this country to learn medicine, and in the process you will acquire the MRCP". I thought what a wonderful person and what a wonderful answer. The consultant called me in to his office and apologised again and again for what had happened the day before. The ward round started and I avoided going to the racist patient. The consultant did his usual work with the help of other junior doctors and nurses, but never, ever mentioned to the patient that he had offended me the day before. So, though both of them profusely apologised to me, neither of them mentioned the incident to the patient. This was in the days before the Race Relations Acts were passed. I took the whole episode in my stride and moved on.

Other minor racist incidents happened in 1975. For instance, my first car was a new Ford Escort, a nice car. One day I stopped at a pedestrian crossing in Leytonstone High Street to let a woman pass. She looked at my car and could not control her envy that an Asian was driving a brand-new car. She spat on the bonnet. A few months later, a man threw a cigarette butt on the bonnet of my car. On this occasion, my brother-in-law was sitting in the passenger seat and I felt offended, particularly in front of him. On other occasions a total stranger would say, "Go back where you came from". However, as time passed, things improved and as I write this in the early 21st century, open hatred and open racial abuse has largely disappeared.

My two months' locum appointment was coming to an end. The post would be advertised for a long-term appointment. I thought I had a good chance of getting it. A fellow SHO overheard a conversation between two consultants about me and the chances of appointing me for the regular job, and one of them said, "Very good". I was gaining immense clinical knowledge at Whipps Cross and in my view it was the place for learning acute medicine. But the workload and long working hours were hampering my studies, which was my main aim. The post was advertised in the *British Medical Journal* but I did not apply. My fellow SHOs and the consultants were surprised.

I got to know a highly respected and extremely knowledgeable consultant, named Miss Hanson. She was in charge of acutely ill patients in the Critical Care Ward. I happened to visit that ward from time to time, to see and follow the progress of the patients we had referred. I still remember with awe her efficiency, depth of knowledge and bedside manner towards the patients and their relative. I sometimes wished I could be like her. I left Whipps Cross and never met her again. Maybe twenty years later, I read her obituary in the *British Medical Journal*, describing how was on holiday in Nepal and after a minor cut she developed septicaemia and died. I said to myself, "She had treated so many patients for septicaemia but had to succumb to the disease she was so good at treating."

There were times when the work could be very harrowing. In those days whenever a patient needed an Intravenous pylography (IVP), a type of x-ray to be taken of the kidneys and bladder, the contrast medium had to be injected by the SHO in charge of the patient.

A patient of ours, a teenage girl, needed kidney x-rays. I went to the x-ray department where the patient was already lying on the examination couch with all the x-ray equipment hanging overhead. The contrast medium solution was already in the syringe and I had to inject her intravenously in the arm, which is one of the easiest of the practical procedures. As I introduced the needle into her cubital vein, at the elbow, and pushed the drug in, she kept quiet. Her mother and the radiographer were watching me introduce the drug. Within a few seconds, I saw the girl roll her eyes upwards, twist her neck to one side and go as pale as blotting paper. I immediately knew she was having an allergic anaphylactic shock and withdrew the needle. It was a medical emergency: I was faced with a matter of life and death for a young girl. Fortunately, the radiographer was experienced and had another injection ready. It was adrenaline, but the ampoule needed cutting, which was an effort in the panic situation. Nevertheless, as soon as I gave the injection of adrenaline, her colour changed, and she became flushed and opened her eyes. Somebody informed the consultant radiologist next door, who came running, by which time the patient had recovered and I was totally relieved. I wrote in red ink at the top of the notes, "Allergic to contrast media".

After working for two months and learning a lot of acute medicine, I left Whipps Cross Hospital, not knowing what I would do next.

I went back to the British Council, met the Director and told him that in order to concentrate on my studies I had given up the job at Whipps Cross Hospital and would like him to reinstate my scholarship, which had been suspended during my locum job. He was very kind and sympathetic and taking into account that my family were now refugees in India, he agreed to reinstate it until the end of the year.

The situation in East Bengal got worse. The resistance crumbled and the Pakistani Army was in total control of the country. There was a Government in exile formed with Mr Taj Uddin as Prime Minister who passionately wanted India and other countries of the world to recognise Bangladesh, but this didn't happen. This was mid-May when the resistance force was not yet strong enough to face the mighty Pakistani Army, though there were sporadic guerrilla attacks on various parts of the country.

I started getting letters from my friends, relations and brother all written and posted from India. I also started getting letters from West Pakistan, from friends who were imprisoned there. They had no idea what was happening to their families, as there was no communication between East and West Pakistan. So during the whole nine months of the liberation struggle, I was working as a *de facto* post office, forwarding letters from West Pakistan to India to let relatives there know that the writers were alive. Similarly, I would forward the letters from India, in an envelope addressed to the military personnel in the POW Camp in West Pakistan. Because these letters were from England, they would not be subject to much censorship. In this way I was able to help with communication between the people of the two wings of Pakistan.

I continued to get sad news from East Bengal, which included the burning down of our house and those of other neighbours. The house of my parents-in-law was completely gutted and looted. I had some valuable documents there, which were burned. But the saddest news was the death of my cousin. He was a police officer, posted in Rajshahi, and a very close friend of my elder brother. He was one of my role models and had been of tremendous help when we were stricken with cholera in 1942. Though I was only five years old at the time, I still remember him coming to our house to comfort us. Now he was in a position to leave his post and slip off to India to join the resistance movement, but many of his generation believed in Pakistan and thought somehow Pakistan would still remain united. So, when many other officers deserted, he was still holding on to his post, to show the Pakistani Army that he was loyal to Pakistan. However, in May 1971 the Pakistanis did not trust any Bengalis and killed anybody and everybody at random, particularly those who were in uniform, such as East Pakistan Rifles personnel, police and, of course, the army. So when the Pakistani Army came to Rajshahi and surrounded the police station where my cousin was working, without asking any questions they shot him on the spot and his dead body was left on the street for three days before his family were allowed to bury it. I continued to get news of many other casualties.

The summer of 1971 was a time where all the Bengalis from East Bengal, wherever they were in the world, were on tenterhooks, not knowing what the future would be. The liberation forces were active and were carrying on guerrilla attacks on the Pakistan Army, but there was no sign that they would be able to capture and hold any part of East Bengal, without which there was not going to be any recognition by the international community. We were looking to India to help, not only by giving shelter to the refugees but also by providing political and military support. We were all grateful to the then Prime Minister of India, Mrs Indira Gandhi, for her active support culminating in the invasion of East Pakistan. After a brief fight the Pakistan Army surrendered on the 16th December 1971. Bangladesh was born and we were all absolutely delighted.

On December 31st 1971, I wrote in my diary thanking Allah the Almighty that my parents and all the family members were safe, that Bangladesh had achieved independence, and that I was still hoping to gain membership of the Royal College of Physicians.

So the year ended on an optimistic note for my family and for my country. I was also fortunate enough to get a job as a Registrar at King's College Hospital; again thanks to my boss, Dr Michael Mason.

My next task was somehow to get through the exam. Attempts once or twice in London were not successful.

We stayed in the house of the Darr family throughout the struggle for the liberation of Bangladesh. They never brought up the subject. Being Pakistani, they maintained a dignified silence. We, too, though we felt happy and relieved, never showed this to them.

My wife made some local friends and our son was at the local nursery. They were happy in that place, though it was the heart of East London. So when I got the job at King's College Hospital in Denmark Hill, I still decided to stay in that house and travel the long distance by underground and then by bus. I got used to it and started earning a reasonably good salary, which was just as well because the whole family back in independent Bangladesh needed my financial support.

As I was settling down at my work and trying to prepare for the exam, I had a health scare. While shaving I noticed a lump in my neck. I had noticed it a year earlier, when it was small. At that time I consulted an eminent physician at the London Hospital. He reassured me it was nothing and did not need any investigation. However, when a year later the lump was bigger, I got scared. What if it was a sinister lesion? My wife was young, the child was only four years old and the situation back at home was precarious, so what was going to happen if anything happened to me? Who was going to look after them?

With much apprehension, I made an appointment with the professor of surgery at King's College Hospital. He saw me and immediately told me the lump was coming from the thyroid gland and needed investigation. Doctors are the worst patients. We know too much, and always think the worst. I remained in a state of the highest anxiety while the investigations were being conducted. At each stage of the investigation, I kept asking the technician for the result, before it was even reported. By the grace of the Almighty, the lump proved to be non-cancerous. I felt immense relief, but the professor advised me to have an operation to remove the lump and other smaller cysts within the thyroid gland.

I knew how delicate the thyroid operation is and what could be the complications, but I did not object to the surgery, and I returned home after five days.

Many doctors of my generation were here for the sole purpose of acquiring postgraduate degrees/diplomas and returning home. There had been hardly any instances of doctors from East Pakistan staying in the UK. This was because on return they would be walking straight into a Government job with a lucrative private practice and a high standard of living. In the process of obtaining these degrees there had been suffering and sacrifices. Many were able to withstand these rigours of hard life and got through; others gave up and entered general practice where no further examinations were required; and for yet others, high ambition and repeated failures led to mental breakdowns.

I was friendly with a doctor from Dhaka, who was a bright student and qualified in the same year as I did. We had stayed in the same bachelors' quarters when we started the Government job. He was awarded a scholarship to do the MRCP Exam in the UK. While I was still back at home, the news filtered through that Dr H. was doing well and had passed Part I of the MRCP Exam from all the three Royal Colleges of Physicians, London, Edinburgh and Glasgow. So it was only a matter of time until he would take his Final from at least one of the colleges.

I met Dr H. in a friend's house and I congratulated him on passing Part I from all the Colleges, but he was subdued, passive and showed no enthusiasm for the fact that we were meeting after three years or so. He seemed to me to be frustrated. I asked him why. His reply was, "I am ready for the MRCP, but they are simply not giving it to me". He was not married and was still living on a minimal allowance given by the British Council.

I was busy with my career, family here and extended family back at home, so I lost contact with him.

One Saturday in 1972, while we were still in bed in the morning, the doorbell rang. The landlady opened the door and was surprised to see a man in shabby and filthy clothes, unshaven for many weeks, unkempt, wanting to see me. She would not let him enter the house, but instead asked me to come down and meet a man who claimed to be my friend.

I went down and found Dr H., a brilliant student, standing in front of me like a vagrant, with dark, long beard, hair not cut or washed for many months, and wearing an overcoat in the middle of summer. I could not believe that this was him. He did not want to come in. Instead he asked for £10, which was a lot of money in those days. Obviously, I understood that the £10 was not the problem, but he himself was the problem and needed help.

I invited him to come in. He shaved, washed and had a hearty breakfast, maybe the first he had had in a long time. He took a nap on the settee. Then, about mid-morning, I asked him how he came to be in this state. He would not talk much, but said it was because he had no money and no job that he had become penniless and slept rough in a railway station in empty wagons. When there was no money at all for buying food he decided to seek help from me. He had no money to pay for the underground fare, so he travelled without a ticket and at the end of the journey he begged the ticket collector to let him go. When I asked him what he intended to do, he only looked helplessly at me and begged for £10.

I felt he needed not only financial help but desperately needed psychological support. My house had only one bedroom and there was no way I could accommodate him. I frantically phoned two friends who I knew had bought houses and had spare rooms. Both of them declined. After lunch I was worried about where he was going to spend the night. I phoned another friend, also a doctor, a bachelor, who lived in a Doctors' Mess within the hospital compound. He had a car. I was most grateful to him. Dr Ali came that evening, collected him and gave him shelter for that night.

The following day, we informed a few more friends and because there was no way we could approach the Pakistani Students' Hostel, we decided to take him to the Indian YMCA. We explained to them that I would pay his rent and other expenses. He stayed there one night and then absconded. In the end, to cut a long story short, we had to admit him to a psychiatric hospital and while he was there I contacted the British Council and asked them to repatriate him to the newly independent Bangladesh. The British Council was very co-operative and within a few days of his discharge, he was sent back to Bangladesh.

I have never met him since, but I know he was alive, never married and remained mentally ill in Bangladesh.

I got used to my life as a Registrar at King's College Hospital and my next task was to go for the Final MRCP exam. I had already sat the London Exams twice and failed so I thought I should try the Scottish one in either Edinburgh or Glasgow.

The year came to an end. I was still in the house in North Birkbeck Road and had become used to the long journey to King's College Hospital, Denmark Hill.

I wrote in my diary on 1st Jan. 1973: "Praying to Allah the Almighty that I succeed in my Exam in this year and intend to visit home to see my parents in their old age".

My exam was scheduled for 9th January in Glasgow. I went there the day before and stayed with a doctor friend from my year at medical school, who was practising oncology in Canada and came for further training in the UK. He was a friendly young man and came to us at the students' hostel at the medical school and we would pass the time playing cricket or badminton. He was not known to be good in his studies, and when we took the 2nd year Final Exam he failed for the third time. The regulation at that time was that if anyone failed in three successive attempts then he would fall into what was called "automation". This meant he would be judged as not suitable for a medical career and would have to leave. This was in 1959, when I was the President of the Students Union, which carried lots of prestige, and it was one of my duties as student representative to support students with grievances.

So it fell on me to approach the authority on his behalf. There was martial law and the martial law administrator was a military man from West Pakistan. I made an appointment to see him with the student and in his office, the administrator, a lieutenant colonel, was in full military uniform. I entered the room with this hapless boy who was shaking like a leaf and I put forward his case strongly: that he could not study well because of his sister's illness and other factors and asked whether he could be given a further chance to sit the exam. To my surprise, the administrator relented, and the student passed the exam on his next attempt.

He qualified as a doctor and remained grateful to me for that day and for my forceful argument with the authority. After qualifying he went to North America to make a career in oncology and became one of the highest earning oncologists in North America.

I finished my exam on the 9th January and phoned my wife from Glasgow. She told me my son Sajal had started school on that day. I prayed to Allah: "Let this day be the beginning of my son's education and let it be my last examination". Allah heard my prayer.

I was expecting the result by post on Saturday the 13th January. Waiting anxiously for the postman, I wrote: "Postman came and we heard he had left some letters. Heart rate went on increasing and I could feel my carotids beating. My wife went to collect the letters, but to our surprise there wasn't anything from the Royal College. It was a relief! At least we could wait until Tuesday. A few friends phoned and I told them frankly, 'I have failed!'"

On Sunday I felt a tremendous urge to see my parents. I had not seen them for five years and they had been through so much suffering. What could I do? Everything was on hold for the wretched exam. But that Sunday, 14th January 1973, was one of the most memorable days of my life. At about 11 p.m. I received a telephone call from a friend of mine from Edinburgh. This doctor friend was two years junior to me at the medical school and was also preparing for the same exam. He said 'Wajed Bhai', ("Bhai" means "brother" and is the customary address to one's seniors) and asked, "Did you take the exam this time?" I replied, "Yes". He said, 'You have passed; I saw your name on the list at the Senate House!"

It was such a relief that even today I cannot describe the feeling. At that time of the night I could not share this excellent news with anyone else but had a totally sleepless night with joy and excitement. All my effort had borne fruit and the door to the next stage of my career was open. Hashi and I pondered our future while little Sajal was fast asleep. I thanked Allah the Almighty for His kindness and infinite mercy in listening to my Prayer on the day of the Exam.

The following day, Monday, I went to the hospital thoroughly pleased and excited. In the corridor I met my boss Dr Hamilton. When he heard that I had passed, he grabbed me, embraced me warmly and took me to his office to share the moment of joy. Later that day when I went to the coffee room, some non-medical staff, physiotherapy and occupational therapy staff, were there. One of them asked me, "What have you done? I thought Dr Hamilton was so excited he was going to kiss you!"

That day I sent a telegram to my father, brother and father-in-law about my result, for in those days telephone communications were not easy. I also phoned local friends and on my way home I bought sweetmeats and distributed them to friends and the landlord. By the time I went to bed on Monday I was totally exhausted.

I spent the following day and the rest of the week full of happiness at the result. One of my colleagues said that this "euphoria" would last for six months. He was probably right.

The following Sunday I went to see my friend, the doctor who was with me in Mirzapore and my roommate at the medical school at Chase Farm Hospital. We talked about the past, and remembered how we had passed our MBBS Exam ten years ago and both of us were now married and had children and both of us had done our postgraduate degrees, I in medicine, and he in anaesthesia. Salim was from the Pakistan Army. He went back to Pakistan and became famous in his specialty. He retired as a Brigadier and I am still in touch with him.

Now that the worry of the exam was over we had to think about the future.

13

Back home

1973 was in many respects a turning point in my life: at a grand ceremony at the Royal College of Physicians in Regents Park, London, I was handed my MRCP certificate. Normally this ceremony is watched by parents, relations, wives and girlfriends. I had no relations, my wife was busy looking after my son, and she did not have the inclination to go either, so I went on my own. The ceremony was followed by a sumptuous dinner and I sat beside another doctor, who happened to be also from Bangladesh.

I had to decide on my future: whether to return home to newly independent Bangladesh, stay here in the UK or go elsewhere such as the Middle East, which was awash with petro-dollars, or to North America. But my first duty was to go to Bangladesh to see my elderly parents. So I made preparations for travelling to Bangladesh on my own, because my wife was pregnant again and was not in a position to accompany me. It was the correct decision, though it was not easy for my wife to cope on her own. I am glad I went that year, because I was able to talk with my elderly father and mother in a rational and coherent manner. The next time I saw them they were on their death beds.

As I started preparing to travel to Bangladesh, I got letters from back home with demands from relations, friends and acquaintances. Among the requests were a car, binoculars, and cassette recorders. My nephew demanded sponsorship for bringing him here; my father asked me to return home and at the same time asked me to bear the expenses of my other nephew. I was only working as a registrar, with a non-working wife and a child to support. We were living in rented accommodation with shared kitchen and bathroom. Nobody back home realised how difficult my life was here. Everybody wanted and expected something from me. But it was beyond my capacity to meet all their requests and demands, though I tried my best to give presents to everybody I thought I should. This has been the case throughout my working life. Whenever I expressed the intention to visit home, there would be demands from all quarters, nobody realising that, apart from the cost, there is a weight limit for luggage. On many trips later on, we had to devise various ways to carry extra weight.

My last working day at King's College Hospital was Friday 3rd August and I thanked everybody for being so kind and helpful. I had decided to travel home via Calcutta, West Bengal, India, because transport from Dhaka to my home in the Kushtia District was disrupted. It was nearer to my home and in fact the journey from Calcutta to my home district was the most convenient before the Partition of India in 1947. The train link was still there, in spite of disruption and a discontinued direct rail service since the India/Pakistan war in 1965.

I knew something of what would be waiting for me back home, but never imagined what I actually came face to face with, in that summer of 1973. The BOAC VC10 took off from Heathrow *en route* to Dum Dum Airport near Calcutta. After a two-hour flight the plane landed at the Rome International Airport, the airport I had passed through five years earlier. There was a bomb alert at the airport, and because of that the plane was further delayed in its onward journey. The next stop was Tehran, in Iran, a thriving city and airport during the reign of the Shah. It was early morning, but we were not allowed to disembark.

When the plane was near Dum Dum airport and about to land, I was impressed with the green landscape down below. My memories flooded back: those lovely coconut trees, banana groves and trees of other tropical fruits, standing on the verge of a green, green paddy field. The jet lag from this long journey disappeared at the sight of Bengal in the rainy season. As the door of the plane opened, I suddenly felt with a gasp the damp and humid weather, as if an oven door had been opened. That feeling continued all the time I was in Bangladesh.

At Dum Dum airport I was met by an old school friend from Shikarpore, who was now a police officer in Calcutta. He took me to the house of another school friend who was working as a clerk in a Writers' Building in Calcutta. The accommodation was pretty basic but their hospitality was superb. I was given a bed with a mosquito net, which I shared with my police friend, while another young man, the brother-in-law of my clerical friend, slept on the floor. So a small ground-floor room, damp and dark, was shared between three people, virtually all strangers. After living in England for five years, the experience of sharing a room in a foreign land with two strangers - even sharing a bed with one of them - was unbelievable. But I was young, full of confidence and had been used to this sort of sharing while I was in Kushtia, during my school and college days.

The following morning it was decision time as to how to get to my village. The authorised route was to travel by train to the border, get one's passport stamped and walk three miles over the disused railway track to reach Bangladesh, where the passport would be stamped for entry. From the entry point to Bangladesh, and to my village, I would journey by train, by bus and then on foot, though the distance as the crow flies would not be more than 150 miles. Communication on the Bangladesh side was chaotic and there was hardly any rule of law, yet this was the legal route for me to reach Bangladesh.

The other route was very convenient. I could take a bus along with my police constable friend who would accompany me to his village of Shikarpore and cross the border illegally to my village just opposite. But it would be unauthorised and illegal entry, and my passport would not be stamped because there was no checkpoint. After a long discussion with my friends, I decided to take the authorised route.

The train took me to the border, then I walked in the midday sun, in hot, humid August, towards the Bangladesh checkpoint. Along the route, there were other passengers, many of whom thought I was escaping from Pakistan. I arrived on the soil of independent Bangladesh, on 7th August, 1973.

I waited at the railway station for the train to take me to Kushtia, my home town. People gathered around me and asked me many questions about life in England. I reached Kushtia at 4.30 p.m. on the same day.

My first trip to Bangladesh in that summer of 1973 was a nightmare and changed the course of my life, ending up with me settling in England. I went to Bangladesh with high hopes that after so much bloodshed we had achieved Independence and this was MY country and no one else's. I would settle in this new country and serve my own people and teach my own students for future generations. But I was so wrong in that assumption.

I did expect some devastation, poverty and lack of essential items, but never in my wildest dreams did I imagine what confronted me.

First of all, I went to my brother's house, which was a rented house with two bedrooms, housing him and his wife and eight children. Most of them were undernourished, not properly clothed and without even the proper medical care for one or two of them when they were unwell. Unhappiness was written on everybody's face, both adults and children. They all expected that I would be able to get rid of all their problems, mainly financial.

I went to my in-laws' house. My father-in-law had just returned from my village, and he reported that there was panic because of my non-arrival. Many were expecting me to arrive via the non-authorised and easy route, but when I did not, the natural assumption was that I had

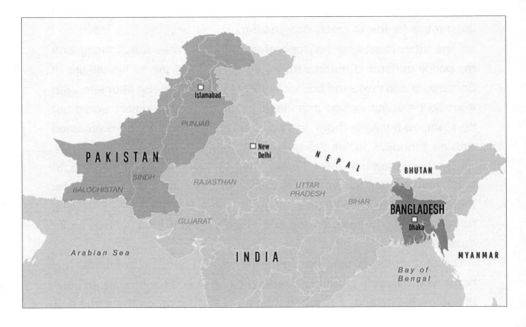

been robbed and killed, considering the lawlessness of the country. My father-in-law immediately sent a messenger to the village to reassure my father and mother that I was alive and well, had reached Kushtia safely, and hoped to travel to the village within the next day or two. In their house there were my sisters-in-law, who had now grown into attractive teenagers. When I had left for England, all of them had been very young. My brothers-in-law were in various stages of their education and I found some peace and comfort there, as opposed to my brother's house, where the whole atmosphere was one of poverty, want and deprivation. In my in-laws' house, there was not that aura of poverty there. I had hoped to find there my photograph albums and diaries of school and college days, but they had been lost to looting during the war.

As I passed my first night in Kushtia in my father-in-law's house, the real situation in independent Bangladesh dawned on me. The main problem was lack of law and order. Everywhere, in every town and village, there was hijacking, robbery and murder. Everybody I met was surprised that I had decided to visit Bangladesh at this time, for there was simply no security at all. The country was awash with illegally possessed arms, and the killing and counter-killings were rampant, some for the sake of robbery, others to settle old scores and yet others for political reasons. I found there were Marxist slogans written on the walls asserting that "Power comes through the barrel of a gun", which simply meant that those who had a gun would kill and take whatever possessions were to be had from one of the slightly better-off families. I went to the town centre and met my old family doctor, the one who had not let me marry his daughter. He was now old. His surgery had been burned down and now he was in a smaller pharmacy trying to eke a living. He looked unwell and suffered from Parkinsonism, and barely survived. He knew I lived abroad and was surprised to see me. He asked me why I had come to Bangladesh at this time. He said it was foolish of me to come and I certainly shouldn't visit the village where my parents lived. I tried to explain that I had come in order to see them, whatever the risk might be. He was not happy and suggested that either my parents should come to Kushtia, or if I did go to the village, I should return on the same day before sunset. I was very grateful to him for this fatherly advice and thanked him for it, but in my heart I knew I had to travel to Dharmadaha the following day, come what might.

I of course consulted my brother, who was non-committal. Road communication from the district town to my village was non-existent. I would have to travel by train, then by bus if available, then on foot. It is only a distance of 36 miles, but it would take the whole day to reach the village.

Anyhow, while I was trying to decide about the journey to the village, a man came and gave me even worse news, which instilled even greater fear and anxiety in me.

He informed me that a prominent man in our area, Wahab Sarkar, had been murdered last night. I could not believe it. Wahab Sarkar was well known to me because my best friend, the son of my first cousin, married his daughter. The man also informed me that many other people had been killed but this was for me the most tragic death. Later on, when I was in the village, I met his son-in-law, my friend Mujibur, and learned all about it.

Mujibur said that there was anarchy in and around the area where his father-in-law lived. His was the only house, well built and well protected. Even so, at night they could not sleep and were always alert for an impending attack by ordinary thugs, either on the pretext of politics or for robbery. That particular night, the family were sleeping upstairs. My friend's wife was in one room and his in-laws in another. In the middle of the night the in-laws were woken up by the noise of intruders in their room. There were two or three intruders with daggers in their hands about to stab Mr Sarkar. In the meantime, the mother on one side and side the daughter (my friend's wife) on the other, rushed from the nearby room and shielded him, so the villains had difficulty in finding a place to stab him. Eventually, they injured both the women, who must have loosened their grip on the man's body, and then stabbed him repeatedly in the abdomen. He died instantly in the lap of my friend's wife. This had a profound psychological effect on her. When I met her two weeks later in Kushtia, she was severely depressed. Usually a happy and cheerful person, she showed no emotion on seeing me. She needed to see a psychiatrist urgently, but there was none available at that terrible time. She never recovered from that psychological trauma and died prematurely.

When I first heard the horrifying news of this event, somehow my system became immune. I decided to leave for the village the following day. One of my brother's sons wanted to accompany me.

It was Sunday 12th August 1973 when I arrived at my ancestral home after a long gap of six years. The village was totally devastated, apart from one corrugated iron roofed house. I could hardly make out the configuration of my beloved old home. There used to be an old coconut tree at the side of the drinking water well. It was gone. At the corner of the house there was a jackfruit tree, which had taken a direct hit from a cannon shell and been totally burnt; only the trunk remained.

I met my parents. They looked very, very old. My mother was in tears at seeing me after such a long time. She could hardly move, because of collapsed vertebrae. She could just take a few steps with the help of a walking stick. My father was at least able to move about independently, but with difficulty. My brother, nephews, cousins and all the other village folk thronged round and wanted to see me. Almost all of them were undernourished; some of them looked like human skeletons. But above all, there was tremendous apprehension and anxiety on everybody's face. All of them wanted to tell me the story of their sufferings and how they had survived during the fighting, but their main worry now was not lack of food, clothing or sanitation, but whether they would survive the following day, because of the lack of law and order. Everybody was eager to tell me who had been killed last night or the night before. An old man, illiterate but intelligent, told me that in the olden days, people would be sympathetic if a dog or a cat was killed, but no such sympathy now existed anywhere, not even for dozens of deaths. All these stories, and the whole atmosphere, made me even more terrified. One or two people in the crowd recommended that I should not stay the night there - but where could I go? I had no option but to stay.

I had my first meal there, and naturally it was rice and curry. There was no electricity. In August it was hot and humid. I settled into my bed for the night; it was pitch dark outside, hot and humid inside. I could not sleep a wink. I was awake all night, waiting for footsteps and the noise of doors opening. It was a nightmare. I passed that night almost sleepless until the early morning, when the muezzin called for morning prayer. I thought nobody would come after me at that time, so I dozed off and slept for a couple of hours until I was woken up by the noise of people waiting outside to see me. Some of them reported how many had been killed last night in the adjoining village.

Then I got a message that somebody wanted to see me at the Indian border. I went to the river - my old river - Mathabhanga. The other side was India. There was my friend Dhiren, the police constable from Calcutta whom I had met a few days ago at Dum Dum Airport. Also there was an elderly man we all called Phoni Da who helped the family when they were displaced.

My parents, friends and well-wishers implored me not to stay another night in the village, as the criminals would by now know my whereabouts and would assume that since I had arrived from England, I must have lots of money for them to steal. So I decided to leave for Kushtia at about 2.30 pm, after staying only twenty-four hours. I promised my parents that I would come back.

In all, I stayed in Bangladesh for a month and, as promised to my parents, I went to the village once every week and stayed for one night only, and almost always had a sleepless night.

Since my days at medical school and later while I was working as a junior doctor, whenever I came home my father would arrange what is called 'Milad'. This is basically a get-together of friends, relatives and village folk in the evening. A learned man or suitably qualified Islamic scholar would be invited and he would give a talk, glorifying Islam and praising the life and time of the Prophet. Afterwards, there would be communal singing of the hymn, "Praising the Prophet". It was an all-male affair, though women would also listen from behind a screen. At the very end, sweetmeats would be distributed and close relations would have a feast that night. It was my experience that between 190-200 people would attend, excluding the women.

Following this tradition, my father arranged a similar 'Milad' one night while I was staying in the village. To my surprise not more than a dozen people attended. Most of them were anxious, worried and keen to leave for the safety of their home.

The last visit to the village was the 28th August 1973. I wrote in my diary "It was a pathetic scene. My parents are very old. I know what they are thinking. It was heartbreaking: everyone was weeping and weeping. I could not check my tears. They know that I will not be back for at least another three or four years, so who will live and who won't? This was the question ringing in my ears. However, I had to leave with tearful eyes and a heavy heart". So that was it. The next time I saw my father was in March 1976, when he was on his death bed.

During those hot, humid and terrifying days, life, death and marriage were going on. My sister-in-law fell in love with a young, handsome medical student and my father-in-law decided to hold the wedding with a simple ceremony while I was there. I stayed a few more days in Kushtia before starting my journey back to England and safety.

At the end of August, I started for Calcutta, using the same land route by which I had arrived in Bangladesh a month earlier. I arrived by train at the Indian border. My luggage was full of presents for my wife and family, mainly food produced from our own land. My brother-in-law came as far as the Bangladesh border, after which I had to walk five miles to the Indian border post, and go by train to Sealdah, on the outskirts of Calcutta. I hired a *cooli* to carry the luggage. After crossing the Indian border, I waited for the train. On the platform, I met a man, probably in his mid-thirties, also from my district town. He was a Muslim travelling to Calcutta, to his in-laws' house, and was well-dressed for the occasion. He was originally from Calcutta but had emigrated to Kushtia after Partition.

We sat down in a compartment of the train, which moved on towards Calcutta, stopping at various stations. At one station, a young boy, maybe ten or twelve years old, got in and sat close to us. My companion had a pair of slip-on shoes, which he took off in the summer heat and folded his legs under him on the seat, in the way that many of us Asians sit, a kind of yoga position. After a while, at the next station, the boy left. My companion wanted to put his shoes on, but they were gone. They had been stolen, almost certainly by the street urchin. Now what would my friend do? He was in his best clothing but without shoes. He had no spare ones with him. It was a very embarrassing situation for him and most distressing. We reached Sealdah Station when it was nearly evening. He disappeared at the station – obviously his priority was to buy a pair of shoes.

The stealing of shoes is a common problem. I had my shoes stolen at least twice in East Pakistan, once on the steamer when I was going to the Medical College in Chittagong, and again when I went for prayer at a mosque and then found my shoes gone. Much later in life I had my shoes stolen again at a famous mosque in Saudi Arabia. So whether it is poverty or greed I don't know, but one has to be very careful with one's shoes. At the village level, hardly any people wear shoes, but those who do have to be careful, not only of theft but also stray dogs: the dogs would take them away and simply eat the leather.

At Calcutta Station I took a rickshaw, which was quite different from the usual ones we used. In Bangladesh all the rickshaws are cycle rickshaws, but in Calcutta I found that they were drawn by the sheer bodily strength of a single man. He pulls the whole load and runs towards the destination. I found it very unusual and I must say quite a pathetic sight, for most of the rickshaw-pullers are poor and in ill-health. They are doing this hard job to make a meagre living.

I reached my friends' house in the evening. They were expecting me. My friend and his wife did their best to make me comfortable. I meant to stay there for two nights, so that I had virtually one full day in Calcutta, a city about which I had heard so much in our childhood and adolescent years. I dreamt so much of seeing this city, the second in the British Empire, after London.

In the morning, my police constable friend, Dhiren, came to help me with some shopping for my wife, friends and family. By the time we finished, dark clouds had built up and in no time the monsoon downpour began. We waited in the shop for the rain to stop. When it did, maybe an hour or so later, the whole road was flooded. We had to return to our friend's house for the remaining night. It was a nightmare journey. We got a rickshaw. A poor, skeletal human being offered to take us to our destination, which was maybe an hour's journey. It was still drizzling, so we had to cover ourselves with a waterproof plastic sheet and off he started on his journey.

The water on the road was ankle deep and in some places knee deep. The poor man trundled along cautiously, getting wet. My friend who was with me directed him which way to go. I thought we were doing well and in no time would reach our destination safely. But it was not to be. The road was flooded and in most Calcutta streets there are open drains. We came to a place where there were rows of houses with open drains and on the other side a ditch. The rainwater flooded the area in such a way that the whole road resembled a rivulet. The rickshaw-puller accidentally put his foot on the edge of the drain and tripped and the whole rickshaw tipped over sideways, so that both of us fell into the ditch. Fortunately, the water was not very deep, just about thigh-deep. Up to the knees it was filthy mud mixed with other effluents from the neighbourhood. I was glad that I was on my feet and standing. My friend Dhiren was worse off; he fell sideways, so got soaked all over. I was covered in filthy water and mud up to my thighs. The noise of the fall alerted the inhabitants of the neighbouring houses, who rescued the poor rickshaw-puller and steadied the rickshaw. Somehow, I got hold of the box that contained jewellery and saris from my shopping expedition. I was very shaken, but unhurt. I paid the fare to the rickshaw-puller and walked to my friend's house. They were surprised to see our condition, two fully-grown men covered in filthy mud and smelling foul. We washed and tried to get as clean as possible. Shoes and trousers would need cleaning overnight, for my plane was the following morning. I decided to leave them there and asked my hosts to clean them, if they wished, after I had left.

The following day I arrived at the airport and for the first time, in the air-conditioned air terminal, I felt a bit of peace and quiet. I felt that I had come back to civilisation.

The plane took off on time, and I could once again see the green pastures of Bengal in the rainy season. I thought about the last month and the dangers and risks I had come through. I felt happy and secure in the window seat of the DC10 aircraft and looked forward to the rest of the journey back to England.

During the flight I came across a fellow Bangladeshi passenger. She was well dressed, looked well-fed and was accompanied by her son of about twelve or thirteen years old. During the conversation it turned out that she had flown from Dhaka to Calcutta and was travelling to New York to meet her husband, who was a Minister in the Bangladesh Government. From New York she would accompany her husband on a world tour and would return to Dhaka in two months' time. I was dumbfounded by what she said. I had just seen how Bangladesh was devastated by a brutal civil war, with no food and shelter for most people. Even the dead were buried covered with banana leaves because people couldn't afford the cost of a shroud, and here was the wife of a Minister, with her family, doing a world trip. Then I remembered a headline in the newspaper a few days earlier, about government extravagance. While attending the

Commonwealth Prime Ministers and Presidents Conference in Canada, the Prime Minister of Bangladesh, Sheikh Mujibur Rahman, chartered a private plane for his entourage. The other Prime Minister who arrived in his own plane was Edward Heath, then Prime Minister of Great Britain. So I realised that although I had seen with my own eyes the extreme poverty, deprivation and lack of security within the newly independent and devastated Bangladesh, those who were in power seemed not give a damn for the ordinary people and were keen to enjoy themselves in any way they could.

Later on, I came to learn that the woman on the plane with her son was the wife of the Rehabilitation Minister, who siphoned off aid money from the western donor countries, took the cash and opened a restaurant in New York.

I arrived back on the morning of 1st September 1973. While the plane was circling for landing, I saw the beautiful green landscapes of the English countryside. I felt happy and secure inside. I forgot the racist antics of the National Front, and Enoch Powell's 'rivers of blood' speech five years ago seemed insignificant. I told myself that the country below was probably going to be the place I would call home. So it turned out to be, not by design but by fate, the fate that caused so much death and destruction and which saw the birth of a new nation in South East Asia, called Bangladesh.

At the airport, the friends who had seen me off a month earlier were there to meet me in Dr Ayub Ali's car. We arrived home and I shared with my family the story of my trip to the newly independent Bangladesh.

$$14$$

Looking for a job

On arriving back in England in the summer of 1973 after a month's traumatic visit to war-torn, impoverished and lawless Bangladesh, I contemplated my future. It was obvious that my original dream of returning home, to become a head of department with foreign qualifications, treat my own people, and teach my own students was not going to materialise. The country was so unstable that I couldn't visit the capital Dhaka and even had sleepless nights at my village home, so close to my heart. I had to take the decision myself and live with the consequences.

I had all the necessary qualifications and training by now to apply for a Senior Registrar job in England. If I got one, I would almost certainly eventually get a consultant's job somewhere in the country. But did I want to stay in the United Kingdom? In the early seventies, Asians were treated very much as second-class citizens. There were racist attacks and abuse in various places, which I myself experienced, so in my heart of hearts I did not wish to settle in England. But where? North America was the place to be. A few of my friends made that move. With this in mind, I sat the United States Visa Qualifying Exam for doctors and succeeded in getting top marks, since my preparation after the Membership examination was adequate for this basic exam. Also at that time, the Middle East attracted many doctors from the Indian sub-continent who went to Kuwait, Saudi Arabia, Iran and the Gulf States. There was plenty of money and I had some connection with the doctors in some of the countries, but the Middle-East did not appeal to me. I got a firm offer from Bander Abbas in Iran, but declined it.

My main concern was my wife Hashi, who was pregnant with my second child and was showing early signs of pre-eclampsia, so in the autumn of 1973 she was admitted to the London Hospital's obstetric department, where I was doing a locum job. Since I returned from Bangladesh, I knew I had to find a house of my own, particularly with a newly arrived child. With the help of Dr Hussain, we found a house in Gant's Hill in Essex for £12,500 – a huge amount for me to find at that time. The deposit was £1,000 but where was I to get this money? I had just returned from Bangladesh, spending whatever savings I had on the trip. I had seen with my own eyes the poverty and deprivation being suffered by everyone, especially my brother in Kushtia, with so many young children and felt obliged to help him with money, but from where? In the East End of London I lived in rented accommodation with my son, so who could look after him?

It was a perfect storm of problems: my wife was in hospital, I was working all day, money was needed for a house deposit, and money was also needed in Bangladesh. What added to my despair was the Arab-Israeli War, where the Arabs, after initial successes, were taking a beating and being humiliated. Though I am not an Arab, being Muslim I felt very bad at that time.

So from every corner I had nothing but despair. In the hospital ward, where my wife was an inpatient, she was on her own – not a single visitor to see her or comfort her. After a day's work I was the only one who would go and hold her hand, and some days I would take my son to see his mother. But in the midst of all this, I had self-confidence and believed these things would pass and eventually better days would come.

I was fortunate enough to be in the good books of the department and was offered a locum post of Senior Registrar, with a good salary. There was every possibility that I would get the regular Senior Registrar job in the department, which had to be first advertised nationally in the *British Medical Journal*.

On October 23rd it was decided that Hashi's pregnancy had to be induced and a drip was set up to cause the contractions. She was young, in pain, without any other relations or friends, not good at speaking

English, and had been in the hospital for over a month, so naturally she was emotionally upset. I tried my very best to console her.

24th October 1973 was a remarkable day in my life. On this day, my second son was born, at around 3.30 pm. I was at Hackney Hospital and a nurse passed on the message to me. I wrote in my diary "This day my second son (name not yet decided) saw the light of day on this earth. This is the month of Ramadan and it is just a coincidence that my first son Sajal was also born in the month of Ramadan ... May Allah pour His infinite mercy on him. May Allah give him long-life, intelligence and good health".

We have such high hopes for our children when they are born, but no one can foresee the joys and sadnesses our children will present us with.

Later on that day, I saw my newly born son, later named Faisal, who looked very cute and was sleeping in his mother's lap.

At my rented accommodation, the Bengali family changed their attitude towards me, when they learned that we were about to buy a house. They never visited my wife or my new son at the hospital and what's more, they would not even put the central heating on to keep the house warm. I had to remind them that heating was essential in the cold, dark November days when my baby son would come home.

The day that Hashi was discharged from the hospital was a terrible day for me; I was supposed to do clinics in the morning and in the afternoon. Thanks to a colleague who did the afternoon one for me, I got some breathing space. Around 3 p.m. I collected my son, and Hashi took the suitcase and we travelled by underground to our rented home. My eldest son Sajal was with my previous landlady, who had been so kind to us while we were there with them.

By the time we collected Sajal and reached home, it was dark, dreary, and cold and there was no one in the house. The landlady knew that my wife would be coming home so she deliberately went out, leaving the house dark, cold and unwelcoming. It was a pathetic scene. It was the one day when, if the Bangladeshi landlady or any friends or neighbours had cooked at least one meal for us, it would have been so much easier and I would have remained grateful for the rest of my life. But it did not happen. The days have passed but I still remember that hardship we encountered.

I made the room warm and comfortable for mother and newborn, then went to the kitchen downstairs. I had to cut up the chicken and cook it along with the rice for a main meal, and it was perhaps 9.30 or so when we went to bed, totally exhausted, only to be woken up at midnight by the baby's cry.

To move ahead with the house we liked in Gants Hill, I asked a bachelor friend I knew from Dhaka for help with the deposit. We got the mortgage and moved to our very own home at Avery Gardens in Gants Hill. Dr Ali helped with some money and Dr Hussain helped with various things like buying furniture and other household items. The house was virtually empty of everything, including the door handles and electric light bulbs, which the vendor had taken because we would not buy a few things he wanted to sell. He also wrote racist remarks on the walls, cupboards and various other places. I just had to grin and bear it

To add to our problems, our son Sajal's first day at the Gearis School was marred by dental pain. I had to take him to the hospital where a dental abscess was diagnosed and he had to have a tooth extracted under general anaesthetic. The poor boy was so unwell and I had to keep him warm and we reached home by underground in the evening. I could not tell my wife about any of this because we didn't yet have a phone. When I think back now, I just don't know how we managed.

The house was empty: no carpet, no furniture, no telephone and no car. The only thing I had was a new fridge where we kept the baby's milk. Money was in short supply, but still demands kept on coming from back home and we had to economise on food. We managed the children's clothes and food with child benefit money, but for our own needs there was little or nothing. I remember in those days we survived by buying chicken necks and liver, the cheapest forms of meat available. The combination of these two would make excellent curry, with lentil dal and rice, quite adequate for us. This is the way we continued for quite a while.

In the meantime, I wrote to my father and brother and told them that I had bought my own house which was comfortable, with a garden and a few rose bushes. This was to cheer him up amongst all the gloomy news. Back home nobody realised that the house was mortgaged to the building society and not exactly mine. My brother, who was in dire financial straits with no income and many small children, got the wrong end of the stick. He immediately assumed that I had a lot of cash with which I had bought a house in the heart of London, while they were so much worse off. I knew their situation, which I had seen with my own eyes three months before, but nobody back home realised, or even cared to understand, the truth about *our* situation.

The days somehow passed with me working at the hospital and Hashi looking after two young children and trying to organise the house. The carpet was laid and we bought a bed-settee which could be used as a bed when visitors arrived. We managed to entertain friends who came to see our new home and the neighbours on both sides were good. They accepted us well and over Christmas I presented each of them with a bottle of wine.

So 1973 came to an end. It was a very successful year for me, where I passed my long-cherished MRCP Exam, and a gateway to further success in my career. I was blessed with my second son, and had the opportunity to visit newly independent Bangladesh and see my old parents, relatives and friends.

1974 started with two positive developments – owning my own house, and getting a Senior Registrar post in Rheumatology at the London Hospital. This meant I now had a secure job for at least four years and at the end of this I would be eligible for a consultant's job somewhere in the country.

The job interview for the Senior Registrar post was interesting. This was a coveted job which was rotating with Norfolk and Norwich Hospital, in East Anglia. The first two years would be at the London Hospital, and the subsequent two years at Norwich. I was glad to get this job with the help of my mentors Dr Michael Mason and Dr H.L.F. Currey. There were some English candidates, but I was still appointed, though I felt dissatisfied with my performance at the interview. I did not care about what would happen after two years when the time would be to move to Norwich. My predecessor hadn't gone to Norwich and had managed to get a consultant's job before his two years were up at the London Hospital. This job suited me very well, for the journey by underground to Whitechapel was convenient. My son Sajal got settled at the local primary school with a good reputation. We had at least one or two friends locally, who were helpful in every respect. So there was some stability in my working life and I was well and truly established on the career ladder.

But the financial difficulties not only persisted but multiplied. It was less than a year after my trip to Bangladesh where I had seen the extreme poverty with my own eyes, and now I was getting letters from my father, brother, and nephews asking for money. My father asked me to send money for the family of my elder brother, who had no roof over his head and an uncontrolled family with ten children. Nephews wanted money for their education and the eldest one who had now graduated with my money wanted me to send a lump sum, so that he could start a business. On top of this, my friend who was kind enough to lend me £400 three months ago towards the house deposit wanted it back. Money was in short supply and it dominated my thoughts just having to support my own family to support, with two young children. I had stomach pains, due to a peptic ulcer, palpitations in the middle of the night and on occasion I felt faint during the clinic and while presenting cases. These were all due to anxiety and extreme tension.

To alleviate the financial burden, I took two weeks of annual leave from my regular job and did a locum consultant job at another hospital, where an acquaintance was going on leave. There was a problem about my General Medical Council Registration. Although I had passed so many exams in this country, the GMC would still not grant me the full registration, because I graduated at Chittagong Medical College, which was not recognised by the GMC. I had to get a temporary registration for each job, which meant a letter from the hospital authority and yet more fees. However, it was managed and I did get this job for two weeks which alleviated the financial situation a bit and I was able to repay £200 to my friend, which was my highest priority.

It was mid-1974, marked by significant events in the outside world: India exploded a nuclear device, and there were protests from Pakistan, but it did not matter to us as Bangladeshis; Turkey invaded Northern Cyprus and there were protests all over the world, but that occupation still continues today. And on a lighter note, it was a World Cup year and our favourite team was Holland, but Argentina won.

One day in August, I was in the clinic and got an unexpected telephone call from my wife. Sajal, my son, had banged his head while cycling. I asked her to bring him along to the A&E Department of my hospital, and an X-Ray showed that he had a depressed skull fracture. I prayed to Allah for my son's well-being and the neurosurgeon, Mr Watkins, gave him a clean bill of health and he was discharged.

Because I was still having difficulty in getting the full registration with the GMC, I decided to sit yet another qualifying exam. I passed at the first attempt and it was all over. So though I qualified as a medical graduate in 1963, on the GMC Certificate I graduated in 1974. My contemporaries at the London Hospital were amazed at the fact that I had to take the basic exam again after eleven years of qualifying. But I told them they did not realise how fortunate they were, having qualified at British medical schools.

Then, help with my financial circumstances came from an unexpected source.

While preparing for the Membership exam I met a Muslim doctor I'll call Dr K. and we shared rented accommodation in Leyton.

I was offended when he brought a girl home who stayed the night with him. I thought it was inconsiderate because it was a family house with a Bangladeshi landlord with his family, and I was with my wife and a young boy, sharing the bathroom. It was demeaning for our religion and culture.

Meanwhile Dr K. passed his MRCP and went to India to settle. I got a letter from him telling me that it was not possible for him to settle there. His medical equipment had been stolen and the political situation was not conducive to practice. He intended to return and wanted to stay with me as a lodger for a short time. He had also got married there, but would bring his wife later.

It was a blessing in disguise. We now had a three-bedroom house, so one room was unoccupied but the problem was that it was not furnished, and I couldn't afford to do so. However, we did manage to buy a folding bed and accommodated him there. He paid a small rent and had his meals with us for which he did some shopping. It helped us enormously and I remain grateful to him for lending me £200 to repay to Dr Ali, and I was tremendously relieved with each debt I could repay.

Meanwhile, my brother from Kushtia stopped writing to me. I understood the reason. Obviously his financial situation was even worse than mine, but he was under the impression that I was very well off. I continued to get letters from my father and nephews from the village but there were demands for money from everywhere and in every letter and I did not have any spare cash to give to anybody.

All of a sudden, I got a letter from a friend of mine, who had been my roommate in medical school. He wrote to me from Libya where he was working as a Medical Officer. He was returning home after a fixed contract of five years and before he returned, he wanted to spend a few weeks in England. He, along with his wife and two small children wanted to stay with us for a few days.

It was in the autumn of 1974 when he arrived and we made arrangements for him to sleep in the sitting room, where we had bought a bed-settee. I was pleased to see him after all these years. As I was in need of money to send home, I asked him for help. He already had a bank account here and gave me a cheque for £100, which I cashed and sent off to Bangladesh for the immediate help of my brother's family.

In those days money used to be sent abroad by money order through the Post Office. At lunchtime I used to get some cash from the bank and I would go to the Post Office nearby and send it off. I did this perhaps every two to three months. This time, I withdrew £100 and the cashier was an Indian girl. It was very uncommon to see any Asian employees in those days, let alone a female one. From her name I knew she was a Christian. After taking the money from the counter, I went straight to the Post Office and handed over the same amount to the counter-clerk, but there was only £90. It was my foolishness that I had not counted out the money and she did not either. I was astonished. I immediately returned to the bank, and she was still at the counter. I told her that there was £10 short. Without any comment, she gave me a £10 note from among the papers in front of her. I am sure this was cheating, and she must have done it before with other Bangladeshis, first generation immigrants of which there were many in that area. I did not take the matter any further, but told myself that we Asians are always trying to make a few quick bucks by cheating or fraud.

Towards the end of 1974, the salary I was getting as a Senior Registrar was adequate for me in supporting my family, and paying the mortgage and utility bills, but my mind was elsewhere. Firstly, though I had transferred my debts from one friend to another, I still had to find the money to repay them, and of course, there were the unrelenting demands from back home. It was not possible for me to take further annual leave to do a locum consultant's job, yet I needed some extra cash, even if it meant extra out-of-hours work.

I decided to do GP sessions in the evenings and at weekends. There were practices near Gants Hill which I could reach by public transport, because I did not have a car. I worked the whole of the autumn and winter and had enough money to repay loans to two friends. I was now happy within myself and could walk with head held high.

I started driving lessons, another expense but I managed it. It was now a year since I had moved to my own house and slowly but surely had furnished it. The value of the house went up in one year. Though I was comfortable with my job and there was every chance of getting a consultant's job, I was still not sure whether to settle in the UK. Two of my friends left for the US and encouraged me to cross the Atlantic. I had the necessary qualifications.

I thought if I did emigrate to the US and sell the house, I would be financially well off and the profit from the sale could be sent to Bangladesh to alleviate the poverty of my brother. This was the only way I could help him with a lump sum, since there was no other way I could procure the cash. I got an offer from Chicago, from an English doctor who had settled there. He was satisfied with my CV and, in particular, that I was working at a prestigious teaching hospital under an internationally famous consultant. He was keen to accept me on his team. So I faced an important decision on which my future and the future of my family depended. My wife was not keen to go to Chicago, because of its reputation as a violent city, but the main reason was that my consultant, who helped me so much in my career, advised me to stay in England. He said that the US was not good for everyone and I would be better off staying in the UK. He gave as an example that "If I drop my hat in England, a passer-by would pick it up and hand it over to me, but if I drop it in New York, somebody will kick it rather than hand it over".

I got well settled in my job at the London Hospital, which was for two years after which I was supposed to go to the Norfolk and Norwich Hospital as part of my contract. Since my predecessor had managed to avoid this by getting a consultant's job I was hoping that I, too, would be in a position to become a consultant, and avoid travelling to Norwich, uprooting the family from our comfortable lifestyle at Gants Hill.

On the 2nd January, 1975, I wrote in my diary: "I got a letter from my beloved father. Aged ninety, he still keeps on pouring his love, affection and tenderness in his beautiful handwriting. I read and read. He is so nice. He is my only light – when it fades, one aspect of my life will close. He is intelligent and the main force behind my upbringing. May Allah keep him alive and give me another chance to see him". (He survived another four years and died in March 1979. I was able to see him on his death bed.)

My work at the hospital went on smoothly. The family felt at home in Gants Hill. We had quite a few friends in and around the East End of London and Ilford. Sajal settled in Gearis School, which was not far from my house. But financial worries continued, because the locum GP job I was doing came to an end. In mid-January I received a letter from the bank saying I was £4.25 overdrawn, and a £9 telephone bill. This was a huge sum of money for me in those days. I wrote in my diary on the 14th January '75 "I honestly don't know how I am going to manage. We are virtually living on the poverty line". Pure tension and anxiety caused stomach pains and which woke me up in the early morning. But I realised I was not alone when I saw a cartoon in one of the papers in which a father was speaking to his son, who was in his mid-thirties – exactly my age – saying "If you don't have a mortgage, overdraft and peptic ulcer at your age, then you are a failure in your life!"

Early 1975 I was preoccupied with the decision I had to make about my job. A move to Norwich would be a tremendous hassle for me: what would I do with my house?; what about the children's school?; and I didn't have a car, which would be essential for this job in Norwich, and I hadn't even passed the driving test.

Meanwhile, a consultant job was advertised at the nearby Haroldwood Hospital in Romford. When I went to the hospital it did not appeal to me at all. There had been no consultant in post for more than three years and it would be an uphill task to build the Department. Still, I decided to apply in consultation with my mentor Dr Michael Mason, in order to avoid the Norwich half of my existing job.

There were problems at home too. Hashi was young, not very educated, and always tired with the household chores and children. In February, it was our eighth wedding anniversary. I bought a Parker ballpoint pen and a few drinks to celebrate, but there was no enthusiasm from Hashi, still shabbily dressed, and with no zest for life, so the evening passed just like any others. I wrote on 18th February "Eight years of my life has passed with Hashi, perhaps the rest will also pass like this, unfulfilled and un-contented".

In April, I got a letter from my brother's son Tulu, demanding money to buy land for a house. In my diary I wrote: "The situation is that I am in debt so how can I give money to others? No one at home would realise that I am in fact on the poverty line and haven't any money at all. How long will I be able to undergo such strain, before I give in? I feel my whole life will be spent in this way. I never had enough money, never been able to do whatever I wanted to do or buy whatever I wanted to buy. From student life onwards, the same problem – money, money and money – the lack of it."

I took two weeks off work but money was so short that I could not even go to nice places in London with the kids.

My work as a Senior Registrar at the London Hospital was going well. I was established with some authority over junior doctors and ancillary staff within the department. But I was still thinking about how to avoid going to Norwich, by getting a job as a consultant before my term ended.

A job was advertised in the London Borough of Newham. It was not a very good area or a good job but for me anything would do. I applied for it, appeared in the interview and did not get it. On the panel my consultants were there, amongst others. I was told my interview was not good enough, but I know the real reason was that there was a white local candidate.

I went on to appear at three interviews for a consultant's job and in all of them local white candidates were appointed and at least in two of them the appointee was not of a better calibre than myself. I also took a driving test three times and failed.

And meanwhile bigger things were happening in my home country. 1975 saw the coup in Bangladesh, where the leader of the Bangladesh movement Sheikh Mujibur Rahman, was killed along with his whole family. I heard the news at the hospital from a Sudanese doctor, and later got the details from the broadcast news. I felt sad about Sheikh Mujibur Rahman who sacrificed so much for the people of East Pakistan and now in independent Bangladesh was killed by his own people. Very tragic indeed.

15

East Anglia

I n the autumn of 1975 I had to go to Norwich for my job. It was heartbreaking for all of us. Since we had come to England we had always been around the East End of London with a circle of friends and acquaintances, and to move to an entirely new area in a totally different part of the country was uncomfortable for us and traumatic for the children.

We hired a van and left for Norwich in the morning. Our house was let to an Iranian doctor and his wife, who would move in a few days later. I was so glad that I found this doctor in the London Hospital who agreed to move in at short notice. I could not afford to leave it unlet, because the mortgage payment and the rent of the house I was moving to in Norwich would have been too much for me.

At Norwich, I was impressed with the house I was given. It was a semi-detached, three-bedroom house in a quiet cul-de-sac. The rooms were spacious, and kept clean and tidy. The only problem was the heating. It was coal fired central heating and the first evening there I was unable to work it out. The house was very cold and with small children I was in real trouble, because night was approaching. In desperation, I asked a neighbour who kindly spent nearly an hour and managed to get the heating started. I was so relieved and thanked him from the bottom of my heart.

So my life started in East Anglia, a nice part of the country, but with no Asian inhabitants, no Asian shops and where the people generally kept aloof. I did not yet have a car, so I used taxis to go to the various hospitals and the hospital authorities reimbursed it.

In the first week of November 1975, there was yet another coup in Bangladesh and this time the coup leader was Brigadier Khaled Musharraf, a man I knew well from my student days In Chittagong. It was he with whom I had my first sip of beer in the Cantonment. He remained the President for two to three days and was killed by yet another coup and Mr Ziaur Rahman became President.

So I settled in Norwich and my son went to the local school. He was the only Asian and there were racial taunts at school, which I reported to the headmistress. In December I wrote in my diary "I feel I am doing the wrong thing for the children to bring them up in this society".

But I had no other option but to stay put in Norwich, where at least I had a secure job as a Senior Registrar. I soon bought a car, my first in this country. It was a Ford Escort 1300, a good car and brand new. Sajal was excited to see it and we all enjoyed driving down the quiet country roads in East Anglia. My clinical work meant travelling all over East Anglia from the main base at Norwich, to Aylsham, Great Yarmouth and Kings Lynn on different days for outpatient clinics. I also tried to do some clinical research so that I had some published papers to my name. They also enabled me to attend conferences including the International League Against Rheumatism (ILAR) meeting held in San Francisco, at the very best hotel in San Francisco. For the first time I realised how the rich people lived in luxurious hotels. On one hand I enjoyed the trappings of the rich and famous, on the other hand I felt unhappy at the waste, with which I was not used to.

It was here on one evening I met my former boss and mentor Dr Michael Mason, for the last time. It was in the hotel foyer, and he was surrounded by many doctors. I went to pay my respects, and he immediately said "Now I have to get you out of Norwich" – which meant that I need to get a job as a consultant, and of course he would be my referee. But that night he had a massive heart attack and died. When I heard the news at breakfast table in the hotel, I was simply stunned.

The conference lasted for a week and I read my paper, simultaneously translated into Spanish and French languages, in front of a huge gathering. At the end, I felt proud of myself and I wrote a long letter to my father. He was in his village in Bangladesh and I was almost at on the top of the world, but I remembered him and paid respect to him, for all this success was due to his sacrifice. He never knew where in the world San Francisco was, but I felt it was my duty to remember him and I felt pleased about expressing myself to him.

Following the meeting, I visited a few other places in the United States, including Houston to visit an old college friend. It was the 4th July, American Independence Day and they looked after me well. From there I went to Disneyland and phoned my wife and said that this was the place where we should take our children.

After two weeks in the United States I returned to England and to Norwich, where the consultants and other staff were very appreciative of the fact that I had presented a paper at ILAR.

In the autumn of 1977, there was a dinner of local doctors in Norwich, a huge gathering. My boss invited me to be his guest and it was necessary to wear a dinner jacket so I bought one from the local Burtons and looked smart. The consultant asked me and my wife to go to his house for a drink, and then to this hotel for dinner.

I felt proud wearing my first dinner jacket, with my new car and wife beside me. The babysitter was looking after the boys. At the consultant's house, we had a few drinks and then he asked me to follow his car to the hotel.

I was a new driver, excited about the first ever dinner, wearing a dinner jacket and perhaps having had a few drinks. At a crossroads he crossed and I followed him, without looking properly and a car hit me from the right side. It was purely my fault. Fortunately none of us was injured, but the car was severely damaged, though driveable. I was totally shaken, but I made it to the dinner and managed to enjoy it.

The following morning, I saw the extent of the damage to my car. When my youngest son Faisal, then three years old, saw the damage he blamed it on his brother, saying that he had hit it with a hammer...

The Iranian doctor who was renting my house in Gants Hill gave notice that he was going back to Iran. Now I had a new problem – how and where to get new tenants. It was advertised locally and the only response we got was from a group of Sri Lankan students. I had no option but to let it to them. There were three of them, and I made one of them responsible for collecting and sending me the rent since I could not afford to miss even one month's money. They did pay regularly although the house and garden were not at all maintained.

I was desperate to get a consultant's job, but there was none. Whenever there were any advertisements it seemed to have been fixed for the local candidate, and so there was no point in applying. Even then, I needed to apply to show that I was trying my best to secure a job. I got a number of interviews but I was not successful. In Doncaster, for example, I was turned down for the job but they appointed a local white candidate who had only one year of Senior Registrar experience.

I was totally disheartened and told myself and my wife that I would never get a job as long as even an English dog applied. The date was fast approaching when my two-year tenure would expire. In desperation, I applied for jobs in the Middle East and got an offer from Iran, but decided not to accept it.

I received a letter from my father that a piece of land had been procured for my brother in Kushtia and I had to provide money to purchase it, because he and his wife and their many children were living in rented accommodation. We knew he needed a roof over his head, but he did not have a penny and his in-laws, though financially better-off, never thought of helping him out. So it fell on my father and me to find money and I was told to find around £300. This was quite a lot of money in those days, and the money was needed immediately. I never had such cash.

I heard that an old school friend, a high ranking officer in Bangladesh, was coming to England and I wrote to him asking him to give the cash to my brother and I would pay him the equivalent money in pounds sterling. With great difficulty I managed to raise the money to pay him when he arrived.

Then another financial crisis arose when the students renting my house in Gants Hill gave notice that they would be leaving. Now I had to find another tenant, and quickly. If I did not find one within a month, I would fall behind on my mortgage payments.

So all these problems hung over my head like the Sword of Damocles and there was no one to share them with. My wife was young and not highly qualified; she could only listen to my concerns but could give no advice or suggestions for the future. It was all mine to deal with, and mine alone. Nobody at home had an inkling of what I was going through and none of my friends and colleagues here realised how much stress I was under.

My two years were up at Norwich and it was time to move on. It was the turn of my successor at the London Hospital to take up the Norwich post but I asked him to stay there until I got a job, but there was no reason why he should and so he came to Norwich. Now I was in a worse situation, although I was told by the local consultants that there was a need for two Senior Registrars and I could also be on the payroll until I got a job. But it was an uncomfortable situation, for there were two Senior Registrars for one post. I gave up the ward responsibilities to him and did some outpatients works only.

The students in my house left and the house was empty. Wherever I looked the situation was desperate. There seemed to be no light at the end of this long tunnel. I made frantic phone calls to London, to various friends and acquaintances and managed to find a Bangladeshi man who would rent. I came down to London and handed him the key, and he had to pay the rent monthly by cheque. There was no written tenancy agreement and I trusted him as the relation of a doctor friend of mine.

My parents were now very old. My father, over ninety, kept on writing about wanting to see his grandchildren. My parents-in-law also had not seen my eldest son, now nine years old, since he was a baby and they had never seen my second son, now aged four. From all of them, there was this pressure to go home, at least for the sake of the grandchildren, since my eldest son was the first grandchild of my parents-in-law.

The financial situation was such that it was not possible for the whole family to travel together. But if we delayed it another year, my eldest son would have to pay full fare. So it was with great reluctance that I decided that I should send my wife and two children home, to see their maternal and paternal grandparents. It was a wise decision; otherwise my father would not have been able to see them, for he died in March 1979, less than two years after their visit.

So in December 1977 they all went to Bangladesh. I drove them in my Ford Escort to Heathrow Airport. My youngest, Faisal, then four years old, was looking so smart in a corduroy suit. Apart from the air fares, it was always very difficult financially when we embarked on a Bangladesh trip, because relatives near and far all expected presents. So I was totally exhausted in finding the air fare and present money for the trip.

When the New Year started in January 1978, I was alone in my room in Norwich, cold, snowy and gloomy. Bangladesh was in the news because the British Prime Minister; Jim Callaghan, was visiting Dhaka.

On my own at home I was contemplating the future. A consultant job was advertised in Bournemouth and I went to find out about the job and meet the consultant-in-charge. He was a nice man, and at the end of the tour of the hospital, he said "Lots of local candidates are interested". I knew what that meant, so did not apply. There were one or two further jobs advertised and the situation was the same. There was always "the local candidate". I wrote in my diary at the time, "So after 10 years in this country – no hope of getting the consultant job – so what would one expect of the next generation?"

This was the end of January 1978 and the family was still in Bangladesh. On the 26th I got a letter from Bangladesh which I thought was from my wife, but in fact it was from a Mr Chowdhury from Dhaka, a head clerk in the Health Secretariat and responsible for screening and forwarding applications for going abroad. He had been responsible for alerting me to the British Council scholarship that brought me to England to study Physical Medicine, and helping me fill in all the forms. The day I left for England, I saw him personally at his house, gave him some sweetmeats and expressed my deep indebtedness to him.

Now when I opened the letter, ten years to the day since I arrived in England, I found that he needed some money for the wedding of his daughter. I wrote in my diary "The whole of Bangladesh demands money from me!" It was because of lack of money that I could not accompany my wife and young family to Bangladesh, and was just eking out an existence – now there were still more demands. But Mr Chowdhury was such a nice man I could not ignore him and did send him some cash to help him out.

After nearly two months, my wife and two boys returned from Bangladesh. The boys looked tanned, spoke fluent Bangla, and the young one was looking smart and even had difficulty in recognising me. The weather was cold, typical of East Anglia, and the boys were excited to see snowflakes.

My worries about a job were still hanging over my head. I felt I had made a mistake of not accepting offers to go to Canada or the USA. Apart from the job worries and lack of friends in Norwich, we were settling in there. We found a good butcher who was happy to supply exotic meat such as goat and lamb, which we slaughtered ourselves in the Halal way.

The semi-detached house we were staying in Norwich belonged to the hospital. Next door lived a childless couple who worked in a bakery. They complained a number of times that their sleep was disturbed because of our children's noise. There may be some truth in that, but in a semi and with small children, some noise was inevitable. The man was racist, refused to have a civilised conversation at any time and even in that cul-de-sac, he and his wife would cross the road to avoid encountering us. It did not bother me that much, but the most disturbing aspect was the nuisance telephone calls at odd times of the night. I found out it was him, for it coincided with night duties at the bakery. I reported it to British Telecom, who helped to screen the calls. Eventually, the people moved away and a very nice young couple moved in, with no complaints.

Spring arrived and I was still looking for jobs. Meanwhile, I decided to do some locum consultant work elsewhere. The hospital was happy because they would not have to pay two Senior Registrars. I took a consultant geriatrics job in Worksop, which gave me some confidence and also the money was a bit more than the Senior Registrar.

The Bangladeshi man who rented my house in Gants Hill had been paying rent regularly but one day he gave notice and paid me the last month's rent by cheque. I remember the amount. It was £109.00, which was a lot of money in those days, especially for me, and I paid the cheque into my building society account. About a month or so later I got a letter from the building society saying that the cheque had bounced. I could not get hold of the man, and I was in financial turmoil again. I wrote to the manager of the building society and asked why they took so long to inform me. Their reply was non-committal and they would not accept any blame. Then something happened which could be called a miracle or a coincidence.

A middle-aged lady was admitted under me at the hospital. She was not married and had no relations locally. One day I saw a young man at her bedside who turned out to be the lady's nephew. He told me he had come to see her from Gants Hill. When I asked him what he did he said that he was the manager of the local building society. Then I realised he was the man I had been writing to about the bounced cheque. I explained to him what had happened and within a week he was kind enough to credit £109.00 to my account.

Meanwhile a job was advertised at Hemel Hempstead and St. Albans. I said to myself that if I had failed to get the job in Doncaster, and was not even short-listed for jobs in Bournemouth, Gloucester and Burnley, what chance did I have to get a job at sought-after places like Hemel Hempstead and St. Albans? It would be ideal for me, but by now I had lost all confidence and was not at all sure whether I would ever get a consultant's job.

16

At the top of the tree

The job in Hemel Hempstead and St. Albans was advertised in April 1978 and the job description said that the main hospital would be Hemel Hempstead, with a few sessions at St. Albans and Garston Manor Rehabilitation Centre. There was no regular consultant at Hemel Hempstead, as he retired some five years ago due to ill health, and the work was being done by locum consultants. Both at St. Albans and at Garston Manor there were consultants and it is mandatory that intending applicants visit the hospitals and talk to the other consultants in these posts. I made an appointment to see Dr Beatty, the consultant at St. Albans, and on the same day to see Dr Mattingly at Garston Manor. I drove all the way from Norwich to St. Albans, the first time I had been there.

Dr Beatty was a perfect gentleman, soft-spoken, gentle with human touch on every question and conversation. I asked him whether there was anybody else interested in this post. He said no one in particular, but like me there were a few candidates showing interest. I found him very sympathetic to my plight that I was now a 'time expired' Senior Registrar through no fault of my own.

I then went to Hemel Hempstead and was totally depressed with the hospital where I would be working if I should get the job. The department was based in war-time prefab accommodation which was falling to pieces. A physiotherapist kindly showed me around. I needed the job, so no matter what the situation of the hospital and department is, I would accept it if it was offered to me.

From Hemel Hempstead Hospital I went to Garston Manor Rehabilitation Centre and met Dr Mattingly. I had known him before, having attended a lecture delivered by him when I was preparing for my Diploma in Physical Medicine Exam. He was a nice man, tall, upright with a moustache, more like a military officer than an NHS consultant. In fact, he was a Colonel in the Territorial Army. Like Dr Beatty he was kind and compassionate. We talked about a paper I had published in the professional journal, on a subject he was interested in. As I was leaving, Dr Mattingly advised me that the job was not up to scratch, but that I shouldn't demand too many things at the interview. If I was offered the job I should just accept it and then try to improve it. If I demanded a Senior House Officer and other staff which a consultant should have, the panel might consider me too demanding. He could not have been more right, but I did not care about anything, apart from the job, a consultant job.

As I was driving back to Norwich, I had a feeling that I might get this job – providing there were no local graduates. Both Drs Beatty and Mattingly were very nice to me and I felt they were impressed with me. Both of them were at the Advisory Panel

On the day of the interview I found that there were three candidates. One was local, with an English-sounding name, then another fellow Bangladeshi and me. My heart sank, on seeing the name of the local candidate; because my surname starts with 'W' my turn was at 3 p.m. The first candidate was the local one; his surname starts with a 'B'. I and the fellow Bangladeshi were in a waiting room. His time was at 2.30 p.m. For whatever reason, the local candidate never appeared, neither withdrew nor informed the Regional Health Authority. It was my good fortune, for I knew and was confident that if the competition was amongst the overseas qualified candidates, I would succeed. Much later I learned that the English-sounding candidate was in fact Irish and got a consultant job in the Republic of Ireland.

At my interview there were ten people on the panel. Apart from Drs Beatty and Mattingly, there was another rheumatologist, whom I vaguely knew. Lots of questions were asked and I thought I answered them quite well. There was one panellist, whom I did not know who asked me "Why do you want this job in a department which is so decrepit?"

My answer was frank. I told the panellist that "I needed a job somewhere, and would accept the challenge to build the department to a national standard". I thought that I had done well.

The usual practice was to tell the successful candidate straight away. So after the interview there was a half hour wait. We two Bangladeshis were waiting with unbearable apprehension. Then a lady came to the room and called my name. I was so delighted that I was lost for words. The other Bangladeshi friend congratulated me on my success. He later got a consultant job in Durham and we remained life-long friends.

In those days, there were no mobile phones, so from the public telephone I phoned my wife to give her the good news. Following the interview, I went to Avery Gardens to see the condition of my East London house, and then returned to Norwich. On that night, my son Sajal was not at home, because he had gone to Snowdonia with the school for a week. I thanked Allah the Almighty for this job, and that all my hard work from the schooldays to post-graduate studies in the UK had ultimately borne fruit.

The following day, I told the good news to the consultants, fellow junior doctors and the staff. All of them congratulated me.

Although the Advisory Panel had recommended me for the job, it had to be ratified by the Regional Health Authority. Though it was a mere formality, until that meeting I wouldn't get the official letter of confirmation and couldn't give in my notice.

I got the letter of confirmation at the end of May and was delighted that the Regional Health Authority agreed to give me two salary increments at the start of the job. This was because of my age – I was 41. Most of the local graduates got into my position in their mid-thirties.

I gave my notice to leave Norwich and East Anglia in mid-July to take up my new post as consultant as from 15th September '78. Though I visited and worked in almost all the hospitals in East Anglia, when the time came for me to leave, there was no farewell do. I had been there for two and a half years and had worked hard. I had seen other registrars and SHO's leave and some sort of farewell was arranged. I said goodbye to each hospital on different days, but not a word about my leaving. I felt sad and unwanted. My only conclusion was that nobody liked me during my stay there, which I think percolated from the top downwards.

Still it did not matter to me; I was delighted that I was moving back to my own house and the area that I was familiar with.

Back at Gants Hill, in our own home, the house and garden were in a total mess. The students never cleaned the floor of the kitchen, carpets or the bathrooms. The garden was totally out of control. Still I was in good heart. I now had a permanent job and these things were trivial in comparison.

It was the height of summer and I travelled to St. Albans, to the hospital again, and met Dr Beatty, who introduced me to various staff within the Department and told me about the good schools in the area and the town we should live in.

I also took the opportunity to visit a few estate agents and enquired about the houses in and around the city. I was extremely surprised to see the prices. They were far beyond my budget. I was going to have to modify my ambitions.

The 15th September 1978 was a memorable day for me, when I became a consultant rheumatologist. It was a Friday. I chose that day as an auspicious day for us Muslims. Summer had passed very quickly and I hadn't yet been able to find a house in the area. So I drove to and from work from my house in Gants Hill.

I wrote in my diary on that day "This is my new job – Pray to Allah that I succeed here".

My real work started the following Monday. I already knew what I was in for. The clinical work was enjoyable, but there was no supporting medical or secretarial help. I had no junior doctor, no secretary, not even proper note paper to write the patient's history and findings. So here started my uphill task to build a department. I never had a place which I could call my own, where I could sit and do the paperwork.

At my first medical staff committee meeting with the fellow consultant there was a sherry party to welcome me. The fellow consultants were sympathetic to my plight, that I had nothing at all that I could call a Department. Still, I knew that I was fortunate enough to have a job and it was only a matter of time before I would get somewhere. Meanwhile I had tremendous burdens and extreme mental stress on me, from various fronts:

My children's education, for example: I had two boys of school age. The youngest could go to a state primary school, but the eldest one was turning eleven, and we wanted him to go to a good secondary school. Like all parents of Asian origin, it was our primary goal to give the children a better education, and everything else in life took a back seat. So in spite of our precarious financial situation, we decided to send my eldest son to a public school. Dr Beatty suggested St. Albans School and we decided that Sajal should sit the Entrance Exam. He was extremely bright and passed the exam without any problems.

Although he was offered a place, the school was nearly 25 miles from Gants Hill. I had been desperately looking for houses to buy, but nothing suitable was available. Rented accommodation was not possible for financial reasons. So I persuaded the headmaster of the St Albans Boys School to accept that Sajal would be travelling with me from Gants Hill, until we found a house nearby.

The last months of 1978 were a tremendous strain, with no new house in sight and too much travelling back and forth. Some days our commute took over two hours, due to traffic, fog and wintry conditions.

My brother-in-law, Dr Ahsan, was with us, which helped us and the children very much. He sat the qualifying exams unsuccessfully many times, and eventually decided to give up and go to Nigeria. If he had stayed with us in England his life and as well as perhaps ours, would have been much enlightened. Perhaps my two boys would have got affection from people other than parents. Two decades later, he became a perennially unemployed doctor in Bangladesh with great financial difficulty to make ends meet and we remained in England without any close relatives nearby.

But there was nothing I could do to change his mind, and I felt really sad for him. It was with so much enthusiasm that we greeted him at the airport nine months ago and now we had to say goodbye to him at Heathrow.

A great man dies

On Sunday 25th February 1979 at four a.m. I was woken up with a telephone call from Bangladesh, but it cut out. Later that day I got a telegram which simply said "Father serious, come quickly". I had dreaded this news all my life. My father was very old and usually got ill every winter, but I never thought that I would lose him. Later that day I booked a trunk-call to Kushtia and spoke to my nephew Ilias. He wanted me to go home as quickly as possible, for my father was now bed-bound.

I was always close to my father, perhaps part of Eastern culture, particularly among the Muslims. I cannot explain that bond. It is not that he gave me lots of toys or took me to football matches or other social gatherings, but from the age of four or five when I became conscious of my surroundings, I had tremendous respect and affection for him. I used to be restless if he came home late. I could not sleep if he was away for any reason. I thought my life was not worth living without my father.

I am the youngest of six siblings and when I was born, my father must have been in his late forties or early fifties. I was only three months old when the unfortunate attempt on his life occurred and I only knew about it when I was older. Both my parents exhausted themselves totally in bringing me up, initially with their physical and psychological support for the repeated illnesses I used to suffer and later spending all their money on sending me to medical school.

One day, when I was five or six, my father felt unwell. A local person with some knowledge about health immediately said he had "pox".

He was right – it was chicken pox. I had no idea about the difference between smallpox and chicken pox, all I knew was that it was "pox", which might threaten his life. I was inconsolable. In fact, he got better within a week and village customs in those days dictated that the god who saved him from 'pox' had to be thanked. Among other things, "ripe bananas" would be required. I went far away to a market to get the bananas for him so that the "god would not send the pox" again to attack my father.

As I grew older and went to school, I always told him what was happening at school and how I was doing. He would sit or lie nearby when I was studying. There was no table or chairs. I would read and write sitting on the mat and he would listen. When at primary school he would help me with maths and Bengali spellings, but was totally illiterate in English.

My father was a wise and intelligent man. If he had had a secondary education, he would have done well in life. In conversation with him while I was at medical school, he would understand the complexities of medical studies and other problems, both financial and social. While I was the Student Union President, which involved some amount of student politics, the Military government of Ayub Khan sent a letter to my father telling him that I was involved in politics and neglecting my studies. My father had so much confidence in me, that he ignored the letter. He was right. I never took part in any anti-state activities.

While still at home, I would always do my homework and then do some housework, such as looking after the horse and procuring food for the goats, watering the vegetables and tender tobacco plants. All these I did with the utmost efficiency. My father would praise me in general terms; and give examples of great men. He would very often say "the lotus grows in cow dung", which meant that though our surroundings were poor if I had high ambitions I could go far. How right he was. I never thought I would be a doctor, but I did dream of doing something better in life. In our family my eldest brother was the strong-man, not only physically strong and handsome, but also looking after the land which grew the cash crop and rice. My father was the head of the family, looking after our welfare and planning and budgeting with the meagre cash he had at his disposal.

At the age of fourteen, when I had the dreadful experiences I have described while staying my brother in Kushtia, my father was well aware of the situation there. He knew I was not being well looked after, and that I didn't get enough food, but being wise and patient he tolerated it and asked me to be tolerant. How right he was. If I had rebelled and left my brother's house and joined the army as I had intended to do, I would not have been able to go for higher education. Although those five years of my life broke my confidence as a man, my education did not suffer and I was able to become a doctor.

I remember my father's sacrifice when I fell ill with typhoid in the first year of college life. I was at death's door again, and it was with my father's devotion and sacrifice that I pulled through. He went to all the doctors to seek advice about me. He would walk mile after mile to get the medicine, diet and other nutrients. Money was always in short supply but it did not matter – he would spend enormous sums to get the latest medicine for me. I survived but It took nearly a year before I was able to resume my studies. While I was at Kushtia, he would come from time to time on other business and I would be happy and cheerful, and go with him to the shops for condiments to take home, and see him bargaining with the shopkeeper. I would come across one or two friends from the college and would tell them that he was my father. He always used to carry a home-made bamboo staff in his hand.

Though he was very affectionate towards me, at the same time he was very strict about education and study. He would not tolerate any slacking or idleness. Just one example: it was summer and I went home on leave from Kushtia. I would stay at home to the very last day, for I hated returning to Kushtia to my brother's place. So on the appointed day of departure, there was huge rainfall and the river, my favourite place, became swollen. We all knew this was the day to catch fish, almost certainly there would be plenty. My eldest brother and my mother thought that I should stay one or two days to enjoy the harvest of abundant fish and I agreed with them. My father would have none of it. Nobody could disagree with him and I left home wiping my tears. As I came near the river bank, I looked helplessly at the swollen river and said "Goodbye" to it. But my father was so right in his judgement although I was unhappy and tearful at the time.

When I completed my 'A' levels with relatively good results, the decision had to be taken for my higher studies. I myself had an open mind but like my other friends I quite wanted to go to university and get a degree. As I have related, I went to medical school instead, but I must mention here that it was my father who was the main instigator and my brother joined in. Though my father was keen that I become a doctor, I was apprehensive about how they were going to support me. But his personality was such that once he pronounced something and decisions were taken, it was unlikely that my two brothers would veto it. They had to abide by his decision. Now, when I look back and compare myself with those friends who went to university and studied general subjects I realise how fortunate I am. All the credit for that goes to my father.

When I went to medical school in Chittagong, which was far from home, my father was already in his mid-sixties. Friends and neighbours suggested that it was unlikely that he would see me qualify as a doctor. Such negative comments and ill-considered remarks were very common in our part of the world. At medical school I remained worried about my father for two reasons. One was money. I knew how very difficult it was for him to get his hands on the hard cash to send to me each month. I well knew the sources of his meagre income. It must have been a terrible strain on him. My other worry was his health. So I remained anxious for his letters. Every night when I went to bed and turned out the light, I always prayed to Allah the Almighty that my father would remain in good health and that I could repay some of my debt to him after I qualified as a doctor. Any delay in his letters and the resultant tension and anxiety would be apparent to a few of my closest friends. They would comment "Don't you think we have fathers too?"

My happiest time with him was when I used to return home after six months or a year from medical school. In his naïve way he would ask me about the dissection of human bodies and other activities, and I would willingly tell him all about it. He was also very interested in the other boys and how well-to-do their parents were. Being far from home, I felt that my ties with my father became stronger.

When in my third year of study there were plans to marry me off with a rich man's daughter, I refused, and my father was understanding and never raised the subject. He had enormous trust in me, and I never betrayed that trust.

When I qualified as a doctor in 1963 there was jubilation all round and my father slaughtered two goats and invited relations, neighbours and friends to join in.

When I returned to Chittagong for the house physician's job, I found myself unemployed, because of a country-wide strike. I was in no position to support myself and left Chittagong for a private hospital. When I got my first month's salary – the first thing I did was to send him a money order. I was thankful to Allah that I was able to do that.

Every winter my father's peptic ulcer got worse. In retrospect I think he was suffering from helicobacter Infection due to poor drinking water at the village. However, while I was doing the house officer job at the private hospital, I got news that my father was seriously ill. I immediately left for the village, taking a short cut, which involved crossing the mighty Padma in a small boat. I did not care; I was young and full of confidence.

When I reached home I found him ill and dehydrated. The customary antacids were not helping him and I decided to take him to my hospital. The journey was bad as there were no motor vehicles in those days. From our home the bullock cart took nearly eight hours to cover the distance of twenty miles to reach the nearest railway station. All the way he was in pain, sick and wanted to return home. Investigations at the hospital did not show anything in his stomach, and he recovered quickly with nursing care and a balanced diet. He looked happy and cheerful and wanted to return home. Once again I took a few days leave and took him back home healthy and rejuvenated. He was full of praise for me at the way he had been looked after at the hospital. I was so pleased, that I had been able to do something for him.

During this time I was thinking about my future, as to what direction I should proceed for my career. One option was to join the Pakistan Army Medical Corps. This was lucrative because the pay scale was double compared to the civilian health service. But it would be difficult to go on to further studies and here would be much less chance of going abroad.

Still I thought it was worth considering, so when recruitment began I applied. There were twelve of us. There was a strict selection procedure and medical examination. Six were selected and I was one of them. I was delighted. I looked forward to having more money, a disciplined life, and being posted in faraway places in West Pakistan, where I could meet my old friends.

When I broke this news to my father, he was vehemently opposed to it, and there was no way I could overrule him. So I was the only one of the six selected who did not join. In retrospect, I know how wise he was and what a disaster it would have been if I had joined the Army. Within five years Pakistan was broken, Bangladesh was created and the other five doctors were in the POW camp in Pakistan, while I was already in England with my family and preparing for my MRCP Exam. How right he was and I remain infinitely grateful for his veto, for not joining the Army.

Even when the time came for my marriage, he leaned heavily on the side of the girl and the family to whom I got married. Of course, it was an arranged marriage as is the custom but being more modern than many in our society my parents gave me a free hand to find a suitable bride. But when I was nearing 30 and still unmarried, my parents got worried. But then I found my beautiful bride in Kushtia, and my father supported my choice, happy that would have a relation at the district town where he could visit them and be entertained.

In Eastern culture when a marriage takes place, it is in some sense a marriage between the families as well. Sometimes, as in my case, there is a strong and binding friendship through the rest of their lives. My father, though much older than my father-in-law, became very friendly with him. Indeed my father was seen as an elder brother and respected and welcomed as such. I am glad that in his old age he was close to my in-laws, particularly when we are abroad. It was my father-in-law who made that trunk call at four a.m. on that fateful Sunday.

I made up my mind to travel to Bangladesh to be at his bedside for a man who meant everything to me. Although I was married and had my own family, my love and affection for him was undiminished. My respect and reverence to that old man in a remote village in rural Bangladesh pulled me like a magnet.

I reached Dhaka and was met by my brothers-in-law Kafi and Ranju, both students at the university. It was my first trip to Dhaka in eleven years.

In Dhaka, my relatives knew that my father was ill, but no one could tell me the latest news. In those days, there was no telephone link and the only way to find out the news was by letter or through word of mouth.

The following day I started for Kushtia, with one of my brothers-in-law. The old ways of transport had changed a bit. There was no need to travel by steamer because the river had dried up. Instead, we crossed the Meghna river by ferry and then had to take a train from Goalundo Ghat to Kushtia. At Goalundo Ghat I bumped into a village friend, Aftab. He was the same age as me, and went into the Pakistan army in the same year as I went to medical school. He was a very honest and sincere man, and an ordinary soldier in the artillery. While he was in the Army and I was at the medical school, we kept in contact and I must have given him my photograph. During the war with India in 1965 he was posted to the front, where he happened to meet a doctor friend of mine, an officer. When this man found that Aftab was from East Pakistan and from the Kushtia district, he asked whether he knew me! To my friend's surprise, Aftab took out a photograph from his dirty artillery uniform, which happened to be of me. Like the five doctor-colleagues who ended up in a POW camp, Aftab was also a POW and was released after the cessation of hostilities. Now he told me that my father was alive yesterday, when he left the village.

I reached Kushtia in the evening and my brother said that father was still alive that morning, but he could not be sure what had happened later in the day. I decided to stay overnight with my brother and start for the village early the next day. I left on the first bus which went as far as a place called Pragpur, two miles from my village, and from there I would have to walk.

When we reached Pragpur, it was nearly midday. Though it was March and the beginning of spring in England, over there it was scorching dry heat. As we walked towards our village, passers-by knew who we were and why we were going there. One or two said "Walk faster, if you want to see him alive!" We had no umbrella for protection from the sun and the temperature must have been over 30°C.

Finally we reached home and I had the first glimpse of my father, lying on his favourite bed in that big house roofed with corrugated iron. The whole room was like a furnace. I embraced him firmly and told him I was with him. He just opened his eyes and said "The boys are in good health?", meaning my two sons. His expression told me he was at least pleased that I was at his side at his very last moment of life.

I could see that he was very uncomfortable, due to the extreme heat, surrounded by well-wishers, relations and neighbours. The numbers grew with my arrival.

I saw that he was moved to another room in a thatch-roofed house, which was cooler. I asked people not to obstruct the airflow. I also made sure that at least one or two people would constantly fan him with a hand-held fan. I had some grape juice that I had brought for him from England, and asked him to drink. He took a few sips and closed his eyes. He was semi-conscious and in some sort of physical discomfort but could not tell what it was. The day passed and in the afternoon there was a trace of consciousness when he opened his eyes and asked me again when I had arrived from London and how were the children. I never left his side during the whole night.

The following day – the 6th March 1979 – will forever be written in my memory, the day I lost my father. The day which I had dreaded so much from my early childhood had arrived.

My father tossed and turned the whole day with all-over discomfort. My brother-in-law said that he had not passed a motion which might be bothering him. I tried and succeeded in doing a rectal evacuation with finger and he seemed more comfortable after that.

However, from the afternoon onwards his condition started deteriorating. As the evening wore on, his breathing became shallow. He could not raise an arm as he was able to do during the day and his pulse became irregular and feeble. He was in shock and the end was not far. He opened his eyes and his last words were "You three brothers live in peace and amicably together". Then he closed his eyes. I could not feel his pulse anywhere, and when I put my stethoscope on his chest, his heart was still beating, but very slowly, may be 20 or 30 beats per minute. Then he opened his eyes widely, very widely, with the pupils dilated. Some sort of neurological disconnection was taking place in the brain, and the village folk said that "his soul left through his eyes". There were no heart sounds now and I closed his eyes. The time was 11.30 p.m. on Tuesday 6th March 1979.

That night as religion and custom dictated, the women started wailing loudly, but I shouted at them to stop. People surrounding the body started reading the Quran. The whole night we all were awake, praying, reciting the Quran and making plans to bury him in the morning, sending news to far and wide about the burial.

Whenever I land in Bangladesh from abroad and until I re-embark, all the expenses are mine. I volunteer it, knowing that my brothers and relations are not financially well off. But when it came to the death of my father and head of the family I expected my brothers and relations to come forward even before I said anything. It did not happen. The following morning, when money was needed for buying a simple shroud, no one offered to pay. I did not have any cash with me, because there had been no time to change my traveller's cheques in Dhaka, the only place I could have done it. There was a crowd of people inside and outside the house and I spotted my friend Aftab. I asked him to come forward and whispered in his ears that I needed some cash. Within a few minutes he returned and handed over some cash, enough to buy all necessary articles including the shroud. So my father was buried in a shroud bought with borrowed money. This I will never forget. Of course, within the next few days I was able to repay Aftab.

A grave was dug in the family plot and my brother and I lowered his tiny, thin body into the grave. It was covered over and the necessary prayers were said by the local Imam. After that the huge crowd gradually dispersed.

So ended an era. I stayed behind in the village and managed to build a brick-built tomb with his name inscribed. It said he died at the age of 97, which I do not think is true. Much later I calculated his age, because he used to say that he was five years old when the big earthquake happened, and that was in 1897 so he was probably born in 1892, which made him 89 years old, a great age in a poor, underdeveloped country like Bangladesh.

After staying for a month I returned to England at the beginning of April.

18

Under attack

B y the middle of 1979 I still had not been able to find a suitable house in a reasonably good area. Nor had a buyer come forward for my house in Gants Hills.

Meanwhile my son, Sajal, sat the entrance exams for a number of schools, including two public schools and one good grammar school. He passed all of them, but our intention was to move to St. Albans and send him to secondary education here. So he sat yet another entrance exam at St. Albans School and passed.

Finally, I found a house which we liked and which I could afford in St Albans. It was a three-bedroom house situated on a main road. I liked the garden and the house was brick-built in the early thirties. I decided to buy this house, put down a deposit and applied for a mortgage, even though my own house was not yet sold, though at last we had a prospective buyer. I took a bridging loan for three months, and my employer paid the interest. In those days you could only get a mortgage up two and a half times your salary and with the help of a friendly Building Society Manager; I managed to get the loan.

We moved to our new house in September 1979. There were no carpets or furniture but slowly we managed to furnish it. The outstanding problem was the sale of my Essex house. If I couldn't sell within three months, how could I pay the interest on the mortgages of two houses, pay the school fees, and maintain my family on a single income? The financial worry was such that I could not sleep at night.

Ectopic heart beats became frequent and for no apparent reason I would start shivering. On two occasions, I had to call my GP because of it, but I know it was nothing but the anxiety of maintaining two houses and also running an under-resourced department. As a newly appointed consultant I was in demand to give talks at the lunch-time grand rounds, in my hospital and surrounding hospitals. I could not avoid this public speaking, but it added to my anxiety, and I could not really share it all with my wife.

1980 started with another baby on the way. World politics was also in turmoil, with the Soviet Union invading Afghanistan and American hostages being taken in Iran. The Cold War was at its peak and the clock seemed to be ticking towards nuclear confrontation.

When my wife went for a dental appointment and her dental x-rays were taken, she did not tell the dentist that she was pregnant. He was upset when she told him afterwards and this made her anxious about the consequences. Here was another worry. I spoke to my radiology consultant colleague, who assured me that dental x-rays would not cause any problem so long as there was no radiation to the pelvic area. But the doubt and anxiety continued throughout Hashi's pregnancy and she could not enjoy it.

Although we were in our new house and the children were settled at their respective schools, financial difficulties remain. Each month my bank account would be in the red, no matter how hard I tried. The house needed re-wiring for electricity, woodworm treatment was required, carpets, curtains and so many other things were also needed. Also, the house was exposed to the main road, because the wooden fence had rotted a long time ago and it looked dilapidated. I decided to get a brick wall built. A GP friend found an Indian builder, who erected a wall with an iron gate which gave some security and privacy to the front garden. It was a big garden and needed some attention, particularly the grass. I had a small electric mower but it was not enough. I had no money to buy a petrol mower and did not want to borrow any more, because I still owed nearly £5,000 to the bank for various expenses incurred after moving house. At this point, a letter came from my brother in Kushtia demanding money that was needed for his daughter's wedding. Nobody back home would believe a word about my financial situation here in

England. All of them assumed that as a consultant I was terribly well off and could afford anything and everything. However, whenever any demand for money came from any quarter, there was no way I could refuse. So once again I had to borrow money from the bank and sent £115 to my brother – which was quite a large sum in 1980.

There were a few surprises. In April 1980 we got a telephone call from the Prime Minister of Bangladesh, Mr Shah Azizur Rahman, who was visiting England. He was close to my father-in-law's family and we invited them to dinner that night. The house was full of people, including Security Police.

Hashi went into hospital on the 10th June 1980 and the obstetrician decided to keep her in due to raised blood pressure, as had happened in previous pregnancies. Being a consultant's wife she was given preferential treatment, with a private room of her own and the consultant herself looking after her. At that stage we did not know whether the baby was a girl or a boy. She stayed in the hospital for three days and it was decided to have a caesarean section rather than prolonging it.

It was Friday – an auspicious day in the Muslim calendar. The date was 13th June. A beautiful baby girl was born at 7.55 pm. She weighed 8lb 2oz. Remembering the fuss over the dental x-rays, as soon as Hashi recovered from the anaesthesia she asked "Does the baby have all her limbs?"

That night I wrote in my diary "Pray to Allah that the baby keeps on well, grows up nicely in this hostile world, may she be intelligent and religious and keep up the good name of the family". That evening, I took my two boys to the hospital to see their sister, who was fast asleep. The boys were excited to see her, and touched her small tender fingers. The following morning, all three of us went to St. Albans City market and bought the largest card available. We all signed it and with a bouquet of flowers went to the hospital. We decided to call her Julekha Rita Wajed. Her middle name was due to the excellent care we received from the gynaecologist who was pleased when we told her about it.

Hashi was still in pain from the section, so she had to stay at the hospital until the 21st June, when Sajal, Faisal and I went to the hospital and brought my little daughter home. We were all very very happy – now the family was complete.

Despite our poor finances, we gradually furnished the house. I managed to buy a petrol driven lawn mower and kept the grass neat and tidy. The garden looked beautiful. The previous owner must have been a keen gardener who had a large vegetable plot and I managed to plant some vegetables of our own. The two boys also joined me and wanted a separate plot of their own, although mysteriously nothing grew there.

We had very good neighbours. On our right, there was a childless couple, extremely nice and helpful. On our left, there was another couple, middle-aged, whose children had grown up and left home. So neither of the neighbours had children to play in the garden, and when my two boys arrived, the garden was full of activities with football, tennis, badminton and general children's noise. Both neighbours would lean on the fence and talk to the children and to us. Julekha was only a few months old. We also had a neighbour at the back, whom I would see working in his garden and who turned out later to be Polish. He must have been retired, but I wondered how he managed to buy a house in that expensive road. He looked like a working-class man.

However, one day I found him at the hospital as my patient. I discovered that he had been employed as an engineer by British Rail in London. When the M1 was being built, his house in North London was in the way and was given compensation and transferred to St. Albans. With his compensation money he managed to buy his house in a good area of St Albans.

He had a badly affected arthritic hip which needed an operation and I referred him to my orthopaedic colleague, and discharged him from my care. I continued to see him in the garden, limping and working. One day I called him over the fence and asked about his operation. He said there was a two- year waiting list and he could not bear to wait that long because of the pain. He would rather sell his house to pay for a private operation, unless I could help. I spoke to my orthopaedic colleague, who kindly brought the date forward, and the man had a successful hip replacement. He remained grateful to me for a long time and continued to send me Christmas cards after he had moved away.

So life was settling down and I just paid my son's autumn term school fees. He had had a good school report and we were pleased with his progress.

Everyday life threw up occasional memorable incidents. One day in mid-December our colour television packed up. We had had it since Norwich and it had been moved between our various homes since then. I contacted a TV repair man via an address in the local newspaper. The following day a man with an unmarked van came and fiddled with the set and told us that it had to be taken to a workshop in the nearby town of Radlett. I readily agreed but asked him to give an estimate before going ahead with the repair. Later it turned out that this man's only job was the collection of TV sets from people's homes and the repairer was somebody different.

After the TV set was taken, we heard nothing and I got suspicious. I rang them to find out and was told the set was ready and the cost was £50. I was very surprised with that exorbitant charge. Nevertheless, we needed the TV set as Christmas was near and I went to collect it with a friend of mine who had an estate car.

At the repair shop I protested as to why the repair was carried out without informing me, despite my request to do so and the man became extremely violent and started shouting and swearing. My friend and I were astounded. My feeling was that if I uttered another word he would have physically assaulted me. My friend suggested that I pay the money and get out.

The following day I phoned the local newspaper and explained what had happened. To my surprise I was told that I was not the first person to be treated like that and they had had numerous complaints about this man, but they could not do anything apart from stopping advertising his services, which I was happy to learn that they did.

A few years later I read in the same local newspaper that the man had been arrested for some offence and his daughter had been killed in a road accident. The TV set did not work properly and I had to buy a new one within a few months.

We had a set of coffee tables bought locally, with a map of the world on the top covered by glass. Somehow the glass top over one of the tables cracked and so I took it to the shop where I bought it and asked them to replace the glass top. I was given an estimate with which I agreed. It was repaired and I collected it on Friday afternoon on my way home from the hospital. The table was nicely wrapped up and I did not feel the need to unwrap it. I came home and opened it, only to find that the glass top was broken. It could not have happened during the journey from the shop to my home so it must have happened before it was handed to me. The following day when I took it back, the manager refused to believe my side of the story. He was convinced I had broken it either during transport or at home. His name was Mr Pigg and frankly he behaved as such. Later I wrote to their head office and was supplied with a brand-new coffee table. Mr Pigg left the shop, which itself went out of business a few years later.

At various points in my early years in the UK, as I have mentioned, there were obvious overtones of racism in the society I lived and worked in. In the summer of 1981 there were actual race riots in various places in England, including London. All of the immigrant populace were rather frightened, in London, Birmingham and other places, and the National Front was making life extremely difficult for us. There was wide coverage in the media, both nationally and internationally and my brother wrote from Bangladesh to suggest that we return to Bangladesh. He had seen first-hand how communal riots take their toll, in Calcutta in 1946, between Hindus and Muslims. Even in St. Albans, a peaceful area, we saw some disturbances.

Even doctors were not immune. Whatever may have been the underlying cause, it frightened us educated people living and working in the UK. There was daily news of physical attacks on Asian restaurant workers, labourers and ordinary peaceful citizens. They were organised by the National Front and anti-immigrant utterances by the newly elected Prime Minister, Mrs Thatcher, didn't help the situation. Like me, most of my doctor friends rarely risked walking alone and in the dark on the streets of London. Most of us had cars, but even then we did not escape racist attacks. I heard from various doctor friends in London, Nottinghamshire and Durham that there had been attacks on their properties with windows broken, or the front doors smashed. This was the time when all of us first generation immigrants were on tenterhooks as to what was going to happen.

These were mainly minor things but they had a negative effect on me, just like the time a patient refused to be examined by me at Whipps Cross Hospital. A decade or so after that event, I was still not settled in my mind about whether to stay in this country, as I was always apprehensive about my children and what sort of environment they are facing at school. Though my eldest son was in private school, he was not immune from racial taunts in the playground. One day I went to my usual work at the hospital and even within the hospital compound at St. Albans, and a scruffy-looking young man shouted at me "Go back where you came from!"

But I still did not take it seriously until I got a direct attack on my property.

We must have caught the eyes of a racist living in the council houses nearby, because we were the only Asian family in the road. We had friends visiting us and they were usually Asians. After moving in, we built a brick wall in the front garden with a cast iron gate. Also I bought a new Japanese executive car. All of these must have caused a certain amount of envy.

During one autumn weekend, my whole family went to London to visit a friend. When we returned home we were shocked to find several acts of vandalism: one of our windows had been broken with a brick, the brand new brick wall had been daubed with the National Front insignia in red paint, and there was a telephone kiosk just opposite our house which had also been vandalised and ' NF' and a swastika painted on it.

What could I do? I was in total shock, particularly for my young family and the effect it would have on their minds. I phoned a Muslim GP friend who told me to inform the police, which I did. The police officer came very quickly and was a great help. He was a sergeant and told me that he had a pretty good idea who was responsible. He said there was a National Front member who lived in a council house nearby, but without any evidence the police could not do anything. He assured me that the police would keep a watch on my house.

Against the wish of my wife, I told the local newspaper and gave a statement. It made a front-line story with the photograph of the house and the telephone kiosk opposite. Now everybody knew, both at my hospital and by the neighbours. One consultant colleague who was Jewish telephoned me to commiserate. Apart from that, not a word from anybody, though everyone knew it was me. One or two Asian colleagues suggested I should sell the house and move to an exclusive area. I did not have enough money to consider that option.

So we stayed put and the regular attacks on my property continued. I lost count of the number of times someone removed the top of the gate pillars, or took away the iron gates and dumped them half a mile away. On one occasion, one gate was found by the police who bought it back to us and we secured it with a special pin so it couldn't be lifted so easily. These attacks on my property continued unabated for well over ten years or more, and only lessened from the early 1990s. I think the last attack on the property was sometime in 1996.

There were many occasions when we were called 'Pakis' – on the roads, in the park and in car parks. These remarks and racist taunts also affected children at school, though to a lesser extent at public school where I managed to send mine.

One day in the mid 1980s my two sons were playing in the back garden which backed onto the back garden of the house from another road. Two girls from that house were also playing in the back garden opposite. I was inside the house and was watching them play. Suddenly I heard the girls call my sons 'Pakis'. My eldest son immediately told the youngest one "not to tell this to daddy" and both of them started throwing stones at the girls. That was the end of the matter, but I immediately realised how hurt the boys felt when they decided it should not be brought to the notice of their dad.

We have been fortunate with the neighbours on both sides, and over the road. It was thanks to their support, help and sympathetic consideration to these attacks that we decided to stay in our house. We remain good friends and we always let them know if we go away, giving one of them a key to keep an eye on things.

By 1982 I had been a consultant for four years and had gradually established myself. I also had a reasonably good private practice which gave me financial solvency, particularly the mortgage and the school fees.

In mid-1982, hostilities broke out with Argentina, which culminated in the Falklands War and the defeat and surrender of the Argentinean Army. In that war my support, like many of my friends, was neutral. Though I had been in the UK well over fourteen years and my children were born here, we still could not support England in any football or cricket games. No matter who played England, I always supported the opponent; I did not feel the English community accepted us as equals.

Also, the racial attacks, both directly and indirectly, and comments from Conservative politicians always made me uncomfortable and I could not accept England as my home. It was at this time that I met a friend who had emigrated to the United States in 1973, the time I was also thinking of leaving this country, who told me that he felt like an American and would fight for America if the necessity arose. I was surprised by his comments. He explained that he had lived in England before he decided to leave for the States and could compare life on both sides of the Atlantic, and his considered view was that America had accepted him as one of her own and there was no reason why he should not call himself an American. But I could not call myself British. Still, when the Falkland War broke out, I found myself either neutral or even supporting England. The main reason perhaps was that it was a just war and Argentina started it.

In January 1983, I decided to go to Bangladesh. This would be my third visit since I came to England and my first visit since my father died. I spent nearly a month, mainly in Kushtia at my in-law's house and also my village home in Dharmadaha. As usual, the visit was emotional and physically exhausting. Emotional because wherever I looked there were inescapable signs of poverty, in the nation, which was called a "bottomless pit", by Henry Kissinger, the American Secretary of State, but also in my own family. At Kushtia, though my brother had a roof over his head, thanks to my father and my earlier contributions, but all his children, as many as nine, were young, ill-fed, and ill-dressed but at least extremely well-behaved. This was what happened when there was no family planning. There were occasions when proper medical treatment could not be given when any of them was ill. My brother had a meagre income as a legal practitioner and poverty was evident wherever I looked.

In my village, my mother was now old, infirm, and just about managed to walk. Old age and ill-health made her almost bed-ridden. As a specialist, I knew what her physical problems were, but in her remote village, devoid of any facilities, I could not provide her with any help. I wished that I could take her to England. Also in Dharmadaha, my elder brother's children were not in any gainful employment. There was discord among my cousins, and both my brothers looked to me to give money to help their children to become established. My eldest brother wanted me to provide money for buying a mechanised plough and water pump, and the elder brother wanted me to provide cash for the upkeep of his family, just to keep his head above water.

My sisters were also in need of money, but none of them expressed it as such, but one of my sister's sons had a severe chest problem, which I could not ignore. The chest x-ray showed he had a serious, and potentially fatal, condition called bronchiectasis. I bought him to Dhaka and consulted the only chest surgeon there, who happened to be a good friend of mine. He was pleased to see me after he left England some five years ago. He invited me to his house for a lavish supper and also asked me to see a difficult medical patient for him, who happened to be his friend's wife. I arranged the admission of my sister's son to the hospital for a major operation, and then left for England. But the young man changed his mind about the operation, for there was nobody in Dhaka to look after him before or after the operation, or provide the necessary blood for transfusion or medication. My sister's family was so poor that they didn't even have money to travel to Dhaka, let alone stay there and look after him at the hospital. The result was this boy discharged himself from the hospital, returned to his village home, and – as I expected – died a few years later.

So that was my trip to Bangladesh in 1983. I was pleased to be back and meet my family here in England.

PART III
TOWARDS THE FALL

Happy family, with Faisal on right

19

Trials and tribulations

The opportunity arrived for me to visit Moscow in the summer of 1983, on the occasion of the European League Against Rheumatism (EULAR) meeting. This takes place every four years in various European cities and this time it was Moscow's turn.

Growing up in an underdeveloped country like Pakistan, I always had a romantic notion about communism and the communist countries. Although Pakistan was a staunch American ally and all the information about America and Britain was available from their respective Embassies, there was also some communist propaganda and lots of leaflets were distributed among the students. It was those communist leaflets that drew more attention to the young and vulnerable minds. Lots of talented youngsters ruined their lives by being brainwashed at the lure of communism, particularly Marxism.

I never got involved in any active participation with communism, for I was too poor, and too busy doing something about my future career. But in my mind's eye I always compared the USSR with the USA, as a super-power. During the Suez crisis, when I was only 18 and was preparing for my 'A' levels, we took much pleasure when the Soviet Union threatened to send forces to Suez. After I qualified as a doctor, our admiration for the Soviet Union was further enhanced, when a spy plane from the US was shot down and Sputnik was sent into outer space.

I had been able to visit the United States in 1977 and was amazed at the freedom of the people and their opulence. Though there were poor people, overall my impression of the USA was that of a country well-advanced in every aspect.

So when my invitation came to visit Moscow, I was delighted to get the chance to compare Russia with England and the U.S.A.

My hopes were somewhat dashed, when I went to get a visa at the Soviet Embassy. I was surprised that my visa allowed me to visit only Moscow. I would not be allowed to go outside the city metropolis and there was no question of me visiting other cities like Stalingrad or Tashkent. Separate visas would be required and almost certainly none would be granted.

My view of the USSR and the romanticism I has felt further eroded at the airport. There were so many obstacles and so much waiting. Finally, I arrived at the Immigration Desk. The officer was in full military uniform. He was an extremely serious-looking man, with no hint of a smile. I handed over my British passport and he looked at it for a full two minutes and then stared at me fixedly for another full two or three minutes. He made me feel like a criminal. He was still not satisfied and picked up the phone and spoke to someone. Eventually, my passport was stamped and I was allowed to enter. Later I learned that this was the case with all the passengers, particularly those of us who were of Asian origin and held a British passport.

We were taken to the Europa hotel on the bank of the Moskva River. At the reception, everybody was serious, no smiles, and no thankyous. We were given a badge which had to be worn at all times or the guard at the door would not allow us in. The following day when I registered with the Conference, I was given another badge for the entrance to the Conference venue. So I had to wear two badges all of the time, one to enter the hotel and the other to enter the Conference centre. If one was lost, then there was trouble.

There was another doctor from Bangladesh, and we shared a room to minimise the cost. This was a great mistake, and since then I have vowed never to share a room with anybody. I could never have realised that snoring could be so loud and so disturbing. It was so unbearable that I resorted to lying in the hallway. I will never forget those six or seven nights of absolute hell due to the incessant snoring of this doctor friend.

While in Moscow, a Bangladeshi man, a friend of my brother-in-law, came all the way from the Ukraine, where he was a postgraduate, to see me. He spoke fluent Russian and with him I explored some of the Kremlin and the shopping malls. There was nothing to buy and in the shops, all there was to see were samples. If you wanted to buy something, it had to be delivered from inside so there was no way one to inspect the item you were buying. At times, the queues for ordinary items like bread and fruit were so long that it was simply unbelievable.

While walking with him along the river in the splendid summer afternoon, I noticed that there was not a single bench to sit on. Not even for old and infirm people (though I did not see any disabled people or people in wheelchairs). I asked the young man who was accompanying me why there was no place to sit and he told me it was the policy of the Communist Party and the Government that the ordinary people should not get too comfortable. Also if they sat together, there would be conspiracy against the Government He also told me that all the rooms we were in at the hotel were bugged. Even if we spoke in Bengali, there were Bengali speaking listeners who would monitor every conversation. He himself was under more scrutiny than others because he was a foreigner who spoke fluent Russian.

On a Friday while I was there, another doctor from Pakistan, a very religious man, asked me if I would be interested in going for Friday Prayer. I readily agreed, but none of us knew whether there were any mosques, because religion was totally forbidden in the USSR. However, he had found out about a small mosque somewhere in Moscow, set up at the instigation of the Muslim countries, particularly for the Muslim athletes who had attended the Moscow Olympics a year earlier.

We hired a taxi and asked him to take us to the mosque. He was driving an old banger, and had no idea where to go. He drove around and would stop and ask his fellow taxi drivers for directions. It was fast approaching midday and prayer time and we were nowhere near the mosque. Eventually, he drove us to a very poor suburb of Moscow and pointed out a dilapidated building. We left the taxi and walked towards it.

I was simply overwhelmed with the poverty. It was no different from an underdeveloped country like Bangladesh. The alleyway leading to the mosque was lined with elderly men and women, leaning on walking sticks and begging for money. I was astonished. I was brought up with the notion that nobody in communist countries was hungry. Everybody had shelter and food. How wrong that propaganda was.

At the mosque we wanted to use the bath to carry out the customary ablutions, but the state of the bathrooms was indescribable.

Once we were inside the mosque we found some local Muslims, most of them old. There were hardly any young local Muslims. I was told later, that these people were born before the Revolution and clandestinely practiced Islam though after the Olympics they were a bit more open. We were invited to move forward to the first or second row. They obviously realised we were foreigners and young. We both moved into the front row and found other people from Asian countries. After the prayers, I became friendly with a Bangladeshi diplomat called Mr Rahman, who kindly gave us a lift back to our hotel. On our way to the hotel, he told us that the religion was still forbidden for the locals. There were no prayer beads, and so people were using date seeds. Foreigners were forbidden from presenting copies of the Quran to locals. All in all, it left me with the impression that some people are still able to practise Islam in those difficult circumstances. Looking back, I am glad that I made the effort to go to that Friday Prayer, which will remain imprinted in my memory.

On the penultimate day of our stay in Moscow, we had a guided tour. An American in the group wore shorts, which he thought was appropriate for summer excursions, but he was not allowed on the coach. An argument followed, in two languages, and he was left behind.

The guided tour took us to the Kremlin and we were given the opportunity to stand on the Podium from where the Soviet politbureau would watch the military parades in Red Square, something I had seen many times on TV. Also we were taken to various museums, where the wealth and artefacts of the Tsarist regime were displayed

We were also taken to the outskirts of Moscow where there were huge tank barriers made of metal bars which marked the spot where the Germans were stopped in their advance to Moscow during the Second World War.

We left Moscow after a week and at the airport all of us again were subjected to rigorous checks at every level. Finally, I was allowed to go to the departure lounge, where I met my fellow medics. But none of us talked much or exchanged greetings. Everyone was sombre and our experience over the past week was that the Soviet Union was a vast prison, where there was no freedom and every step was being watched. We were told that even conversations in the plane may be monitored when it was over the Soviet Union, which is why there was spontaneous clapping and cheering from all the passengers when the pilot announced that we had left Soviet airspace.

My romantic view of communism disappeared with my visit to Moscow. In my opinion, the USSR had only maintained its military superiority with the West at the cost of the health and welfare of the ordinary people. Basically, the USSR was seen as a super-power, only because of her military prowess. Once that was removed it was a third world country.

In 1984 I consolidated my position as a consultant at the hospital, had a new colleague, and private practice was beginning to pick up. But my anxieties continued unabated due to pressure at work, intermittent racial attacks on the property, the future of my children's education and sometimes the lack of intellectual support from my wife.

But there was good news in 1984 when Sajal took his 'O' Levels and secured 'A' grades in eleven subjects. I prayed to Allah the Almighty for His mercy and asked Him to give my Sajal a long and happy life and continued success in future examinations.

The news from my family in Bangladesh was not so good. 'Family' in western countries usually refers to the 'nuclear' family, which consists of husband, wife and children. But in Eastern culture, particularly in the Indian sub-continent, 'family' means the extended family, including parents, grandparents – if they are still alive – and brothers with their children, sometimes living in a common ancestral home with the father as the head of the family. Also, if the daughters married and moved out, they were still considered as part of the family, and as often is the case, they lived in the same village or within a reasonable distance, so in any crisis in the family, they all came to each other's assistance.

My elder sister got married in 1942, when I was only five years old. My brother-in-law was an influential man in his village, which was only five miles from ours, and he had grown-up children, three boys and three girls. He was the chairman of the local Union Council, and so he got involved in village politics. As in any political context, there were people who supported him and others who would opposed him.

On April 20th 1985, I got a phone call from my father-in-law, who said that there had been an attempt on the life of my brother-in-law, but he had survived. As a result, in revenge, his supporters had gone on the warpath, killing three people.

The authorities accused my brother-in-law, his two sons, who were both married with young children, and my elder brother's third son. My father-in-law said that on hearing this my mother suffered a stroke and was lying helpless in the village home.

It was terrible news, and I felt helpless at this family crisis.

Later when I received a letter from my nephew, I heard the facts:-

In April, the weather is hot with a dry heat before the arrival of the monsoon rain and tempers can rise. The situation in my brother-in-law's village had been gradually deteriorating, with the rival parties each hurling accusations at the other. My brother-in-law had a sense of some impending danger.

One day, while he was travelling from one village to another on his motorbike, with a bodyguard on the pillion, the opposition party hired a group of men to assassinate him. As he was riding past a narrow road, someone from the side threw a spear aimed at his chest. It missed his chest but pierced the arm muscle of the right forearm. He fell off the motorbike, bleeding profusely from the injured arm. His bodyguard, who was uninjured, saw that two or three assailants were coming towards my brother-in-law and one had a dagger in his hand to finish him off.

The bodyguard picked up the blood-stained spear from the ground and stood guard, saying "I will certainly die, but want to kill all of you before that". The assailants hesitated. People gathered, and there was pandemonium. My brother-in-law was brought home, still bleeding, and it was decided that he should be transferred to the nearby hospital. He was conscious and before he left for the hospital, he apparently said: "I want to see the dead bodies of those three people". This was taken as an order, and was the root cause of the accusation of murder against him, which led to him suffering immensely. This 'order' was followed to the letter. Hundreds of people took part in a search for the three men, but the main pursuers were my sister's two sons, and my nephew.

The three assailants were caught at the Indian border, beaten mercilessly and barely conscious when they were brought to my brother-in-law's house. I later heard that the men begged for water but nobody complied with their request. The whole village was on the warpath and their blood was boiling for revenge. The three men died of their injuries and my brother-in-law was the focus of police action. The police were corrupt with bribes were paid from both sides, but the fact remained that there had been three murders and something had to be done.

My mother remained critically ill, unable to get up from her bed, although she was now able to speak and communicate. When I was told all this, I was in a dilemma. Should I visit home, at least to see my mother?

I already had a plan to visit Australia for a week in May for the International League Against Rheumatism (ILAR) meeting. When I received the terrible news of the family crisis and my mother's stroke, I investigated visiting Bangladesh en route for a week or so, and I arranged to do it with a stopover in Bombay and then taking a Bangladesh Biman flight to Dhaka.

The Bombay stopover was an experience. During my time as a student, I had heard so much about Bombay, the nerve centre of Indian cinema. We were brought up with Bombay films and songs, and the actors and actresses were household names in the fifties and sixties. In my school days, there were a few pupils who stole money from their wealthy parents and took a trip to Bombay, which was nearly 2,500 miles away. Some of them would boast of seeing the most famous film actresses. Also in undivided India, Bombay was the only sea-port from where the pilgrimage to Mecca would start. So, though Bombay was far from home, one way or the other it was quite familiar to me.

But my first visit to Bombay came when I was nearly fifty years old and had already lived in England for over sixteen years, and had visited most of the European capitals. In fact, it was a bit of an anti-climax.

It turned out that I would have to spend at least twenty-four hours in Bombay, and a friend of mine suggested that I stay with his brother. In the scorching Bombay heat I was driven to the friend's flat on the coast of the Arabian Sea. It was a good half hour drive, and on my way I could not help noticing that the slums on both sides of the road were no different from those which I had been used to seeing in Dhaka.

My hosts were well-to-do people, running a restaurant business and had a flat on the eighth floor of a nice apartment building. They tried to make me as comfortable as possible and provided me with the only air-conditioned room, to catch up with some sleep. Though I was jet-lagged I couldn't sleep, so I decided to go out for a bit. I was taken around in a friend's car and driven to the most elegant parts of Bombay, including a famous road where film actors lived, and also to the beach, where I saw a beautiful sunset over the Arabian Sea. But the famous roads and beaches which I had envisaged as a youth did not impress me at all, for I had now seen much better places elsewhere.

Night approached. It was a moonlit night and just happened to be the night of a lunar eclipse. There were people praying to the gods, and to my amazement I found that all the cooked food in the household was being distributed to beggars. I was told that Hindu custom dictates that during a lunar eclipse all cooked food has to be thrown away or given to others, because it would be "unclean" and may be "harmful" on eating.

After my twenty-four hour stopover in Bombay I flew on to Dhaka. My brother-in-law Kafi was there to meet me. The temperature in Dhaka was a bit cooler than Bombay, but it was still 34°C. I stayed with my sister-in-law, whose husband was an engineer, and caught up on my sleep. The following day, I was invited to Kafi's flat and met his wife, Daisy, for the first time. From the very first meeting, I could see that Kafi had been lucky to find such a nice girl, and I still have that view thirty years later.

The following day I started my journey to Kushtia and on to my village, reaching home at mid-day. I wrote in my diary: "I saw my mother lying curled up – a small pathetic figure – for whom I have travelled half-way round the world. She was conscious and was aware of my presence and started crying."

She was lying on a mat on the bare floor, being nursed by my elder sister, who herself was old and in poor health. She had no knowledge of nursing or experience of looking after someone. I felt bad in because I was helpless at providing any sort of medical or nursing assistance to my mother in her dying days. I knew she was bed-bound, so I had carried a bed-pan all the way from England, but it was no use, she was not able to sit on it. So she virtually passed motions where she lay, to be cleared away by my sister with her bare hands. I told myself that it would be better for her to die, rather than suffer this indignity.

Also, the whole atmosphere of the house was depressing, because of the murder charge hanging over the head of my nephew, who had absconded from the police. My eldest sister was not able to look after my mother, because her husband and two sons had also absconded.

I stayed in the village for three days and with the help of my sister, I tried to do as much nursing as possible. My mother was aware of her surroundings and could say a few words with difficulty.

When it came time to leave, I knew – and so did my mother – that this would be the last time I saw her. I kissed her so many times and touched her feet so many times, then with tears rolling down my cheeks, I said goodbye. It was such a sad occasion. My parents had made so many sacrifices to make me a doctor and this was the last time I was going to see my mother. That night I stayed at my in-law's house and prayed to Allah the Almighty that my mother would die peacefully, with dignity, pride and decency.

I stayed in Kushtia for a day or two, and even there I had to face demands for money from everywhere. The patients from the village started knocking on the door of my in-law's house for consultations. My brother was unwell, and I had to take him to a doctor, where his cardiogram showed ischaemic changes.

I returned to Dhaka to resume my journey to Australia via Bombay. That night in Dhaka I said to myself that though this journey was physically demanding, mentally I had found peace inside. I felt that the journey was worthwhile and I felt much better deep inside me.

In Dhaka, as in the village and at Kushtia, I found signs of poverty everywhere, particularly with my eldest brother's son, Idris, whose study I was supporting. He was in a pathetic situation with his wife and family, without even enough money to feed his children. There was nothing I could do. He had brought all these sufferings on himself. He never took advantage of the financial assistance and other help he was fortunate enough to get from me. I wondered whether it would be better for him to leave Dhaka and stay in the village and eke out an existence by ploughing the land. This he did, and in fact did well in later years, but as his nature was and still is ill-tempered, he never gets on well with any member of the family.

Also in Dhaka my elder brother's two sons had managed to get low paying jobs and both of them lived in a small ground floor flat in much poverty.

On 17th May 1985, I boarded the flight to Sydney and found that nearly a quarter of the plane was full of doctors in my speciality, to attend the same Conference. The Conference was officially opened by the Governor-General of Australia, and over the next week I mixed business with pleasure, meeting new colleagues from other countries, and seeing something of the country and its flora and fauna, a marked change either from my own homeland or the U.K. where I had spent most of the previous two decades.

I travelled back via Singapore, which struck me as an enclave for rich tourists who were isolated from any real Asian community while they moved between luxury hotels in air-conditioned coaches. To escape, I visited an area called "Little India," inhabited mainly by Tamils from South India and Sri-Lanka. I enjoyed my first Indian rice and curry since leaving Bangladesh. While I was there, I heard the terrible news of a devastating cyclone that had hit the coastal areas of Bangladesh. This was the main news on all the channels, showing film of the suffering of the people from the affected area. I knew fully well the devastation such cyclones can cause, for I saw it with my own eyes as a medical student in 1960 and 1962.

This news dominated my thoughts during the following days, when I flew home and got back to work at the hospital. I continued to get letters from my nephew in the village, saying that my mother was still lying as I had left her, able to eat and drink, but unable to get up from her bed. I could easily imagine the situation, particularly since she was still without nursing care. Eventually, I learned that a regular maid-servant had been found to nurse her.

My other anxiety was the murder case. My brother-in-law, his two sons and my nephew had decided to surrender to the police, and the case was referred to the Military Tribunal in the nearby Jessore Cantonment. This was very disappointing news because the Military Court was unlikely to analyse the background of the case and there was no jury as there would be in the Civil Court. My relatives were locked up in police custody pending the outcome of the trial.

So all of us, in England and back in Bangladesh, were in great distress over those two events. My sister's family was in extreme financial need because their menfolk were in jail. I had to send money for the day-to-day family expenses, while I continued to send money for the upkeep of my mother.

Finally, on 28th November 1985 I heard from my brother in Kushtia that my mother had died on the 19th November. In a way, I felt it was a happy release for her, but in other ways I felt a sense of terrible loss. From that day onwards I was an orphan. My mother had sacrificed her life for the children, especially for me, right from my birth until I became a graduate. This sacrifice was only possible in Eastern cultures and by Asian mothers. I could not repay even 1% of what she did for me. So all I could do was pray to the Almighty that her soul rested in peace and that I would meet her someday on the Day of Judgement, and I was consoled by the Imam of the local mosque, who came a number of times to my house to read the Holy Quran and pray to Allah for the departed soul of my mother.

I continued to get letters every week about the murder case. Four close family members were locked up in Jessore Jail and the hearing started at the Military Court. There were Defence Counsel appointed and lots of money paid. After all the deliberations and the hearing, the judgement would be delivered sometime in December. I had a few friends in the Army, mainly doctors, and in desperation I phoned them, but nothing happened.

The punishment for first degree murder was death by hanging, and I was worried for the lives of my relatives if they were found guilty. What would happen to the family? I was on tenterhooks.

Finally, a letter came which I knew would contain the result of the Military Tribunal. I asked my wife to open it. We were relieved to learn that their lives had been spared, but they were sentenced to between 20 and 30 years in prison. At least they were alive.

In fact, they served their sentences for three years, and then, after a change in Government there was a general amnesty for those who had been tried and found guilty at the Military Court because the trials may not have been fair. As I write thirty years later, all of them are alive and well, with my brother-in-law being in his early eighties.

20

The joy and pain of children

We at least had good news on the home front. Sajal was doing well in his studies and was expected to go to a good university. He wanted to study medicine and had already got offers from two very good medical schools in London, but he also sat the entrance exam to study natural sciences in Cambridge, at Gonville and Caius College. Despite very tough competition, he was accepted and we were absolutely delighted when we got the news that he had got in. We thanked the Almighty for His infinite mercy, for it was beyond my wildest dreams that my son would study in a world-famous university such as Cambridge. We shared the good news with local friends, but much later we learned that it is better to keep good news within the family, because not everybody is happy to hear it.

My son Faisal had not been very studious at school, and did not like hard work. Nevertheless, when the time came to take the admission test for the secondary education to the local private school, he did well enough to get an offer, but we also asked him to sit the entrance exam at the nearby Berkhampsted School as well. To our surprise, he not only did well, but was offered a scholarship. This would help a lot with tuition fees.

We could not believe our luck. Our friends and neighbours were all pleasantly surprised. Berkhampsted was fourteen miles from where we lived, so we promised the Headmaster that we would move house to Berkhampsted, another sought-after residential town.

1986 started with very high hopes, with one son going to Cambridge and the other with a scholarship to a good public school. In the spring, I got a glimpse of 'the lives of the rich and famous' when I was invited to a seminar in Monte Carlo. Helicopter flight from the airport, four days in a luxury hotel, within touching distance of houses and apartments owned by actors, tennis player and other celebrities, and a glimpse of a luxury yacht in the harbour, belonging to King Fahd of Saudi Arabia. We visited the Monte Carlo casino, and I saw the surroundings and atmosphere where people gamble and loose tens of thousands of dollars.

This trip reminded me of my own ongoing financial problems and I wrote in my diary on 20th March 1986: "I have the best food, best accommodation and best company, yet I cannot relax, and feel restless, why? Maybe it is my upbringing, maybe I will never be able to enjoy life, which is not surprising, for the company I am in are all upper middle class, talking about their skiing holidays, and here am I, not even able to take my family on holiday in Europe."

A memorable day occurred in October when we took my eldest son Sajal to Cambridge. This would be his first step on his own in the outside world, and for us the beginning of 'Empty Nest Syndrome'.

When my colleagues at the hospital heard that my son had got into Cambridge, some of them, who had children of the same age commented that "I would have wanted my son to go there more than winning the lottery!"

On 5th October 1986, we packed my VW Passat Estate Car with all sorts of things Sajal wanted to take to Cambridge. Apart from pots and pans and books, he had a large Eastern musical instrument, called a "Behala" bought from Bangladesh. He never had any lessons on it, but he took it to impress his fellow students.

As we left him standing in the forecourt of the college, I was full of joy and still remember his face, smiling and waving at us. As I reversed the car, I found that Hashi had tears rolling down her cheeks. They were tears of joy. In the back of the car were Faisal and Julekha, both were sad, and speechless at his departure. I wrote in my diary on that night "I saw Sajal standing and waving from the forecourt of Harvey Court – his first day at the college, independent, free from parental control. It is the beginning of his independent life – a life I hope and pray to Allah that becomes smooth and free from struggle".

We went to see Sajal three weeks later and he was full of hope after his first few days. His mother cooked lots of food to keep him going. We found him physically well, but not very cheerful, perhaps because of pressure of work, the new surroundings or even his unhappiness in sharing a room.

At home I was struggling to sell my house in St. Albans and trying to find one in Berkhampsted, where Faisal was studying. Though the distance from home was only fourteen miles, it took a long time to drive him there and so almost every day he would be late and I would suffer from anxiety in getting him to school. But by the end of 1986, in spite of the various ups and downs, I felt I had could say to myself that I had reached the top of the tree, the tree that I had been climbing ever since my first faltering steps across the threshold of the medical school in Chittagong. Looking back, I think I was right, but I certainly wasn't prepared for the fall that followed.

The year 1987 started well – full of hope and expectation about the children's education. After all, in an Asian family the children's education takes priority over everything else, and we were prepared not only to forgo the holidays and other luxuries of modern living, but if necessary we would economise on essentials. That is what happened with my education, when my parents were completely exhausted by bearing the expenses of my university education.

So at the beginning of 1987 I was so happy that I had a son at Cambridge and another at a good school. My only daughter, the apple of everyone's eye, was at the local primary school, well settled, not only in her studies but in music as well. I had been a consultant for nearly eight years, and private practice had picked up well enough to pay for the children's education.

There were some lingering anxieties. There were my sister's family's problems, with me having to supply the missing family income, as well as lawyers' fees to deal with the ongoing problems of my brother-in-law and his sons. And it turned out that my sister and my brother needed cataract operations.

Taking my cue from the way things were done in Bangladesh, where friends, old acquaintances, and even people one barely knew could be corralled into fast-tracking personal problems, I tried to get the help of the head of the army in Bangladesh to intervene in my brother-in-law's situation, to no avail. I even thought I'd see if such things worked in England and I approached my local MP, who was actually very kind and sympathetic and who raised the question with the Foreign Minister to see if he could get the Prime Minister, Margaret Thatcher, to raise the issue informally with the Bangladeshi President, General Ershad, at the forthcoming Commonwealth Conference. Perhaps not surprisingly, that got me nowhere. In the end, with the change of the Government, my relatives were released after serving a couple of years.

I was still trying to find a house nearer to Faisal's school in Berkhampsted, to avoid the complexities of a commute when he started at 8 a.m. and I started at 9.30. I would knock on the doors of every estate agent in Berkhampsted, seeking any new property that might have come on the market overnight. This was during the period of Mrs Thatcher's premiership, where everybody was being encouraged to own his own house, and as a result property prices were at their peak.

Then, one morning, after I visited a prominent estate agent, I found a new employee, a young girl. By now of course, the manager and the older employee knew my face and requirements. When I asked about any new properties, she admitted that one had come up last night, but the details had not been printed. From her, I found out the location and description and it sounded perfect. It was the type of accommodation we had been looking for over the past year. I immediately went to see the house from outside. It was in a private road, virtually walking distance to the school. What's more, the house was empty because the landlady had become old and frail and been sent to a nursing home. Her grownup children lived elsewhere, and the sole agency had been given to the estate agents. I phoned my wife and we saw the house that morning and both of us immediately fell in love with it. I offered the asking price over the telephone and promised to send a cheque the following morning as a deposit. That night, we were so excited. There was no chain involved and my house was also under offer, so the situation was perfect.

The following morning, after dropping my son at his school, with cheque book in hand I went to the estate agent. This time the manager was sitting in his office, which was out of earshot of the other employees. By now he knew me well and had even attended my department at the hospital for treatment for his knee. I explained to him that after waiting so long we had found the house we had been looking for. "I agreed it with your colleague and have a cheque for the deposit", I said. He did not look very enthusiastic, and said something incomprehensible. He wouldn't accept my cheque and offered the lame excuse that the property had just come on to the market and he would wait a bit longer. I tried to point out that I was paying the asking price, so why wait?

But there was nothing I could do and we were very disappointed. That night, I spoke to a friend of mine, who had been helpful all along with various advice. He suggested that I offer another £5,000, which was a lot of money in those days. The following morning, I went to his office and offered £5,000 more, and virtually begged him to sell the house to me. He gave a wry smile and said "Sorry doctor, someone came up with cash and the house has been sold!"

I suspected that this was a downright lie. I was sure that he never wanted to sell the house in a most sought-after location in a private road to an Asian. My assumption turned out to be true. At the hospital, I asked my English secretary to phone the estate agent about the property and she was told that the house was still on the market. My suspicion was now confirmed. I felt sad and dejected but could not do anything. Would it have helped if I complained to the Race Relations Board about this racial discrimination? Perhaps not. However, I did write a letter to the managing director of the company, who did not apologise about what had happened, but instead offered me another property in another part of the town which I rejected. I had never had a high regard for estate agents, but this episode caused me to put them at the bottom of the scale of professional ethical behaviour.

After this betrayal by this particular estate agent, I lost interest in looking for houses in and around the Berkhampsted area. We had been managing for over a year and somehow I got resigned to the journeys. We discovered a short cut and a less congested route to the school, and I would take Faisal in the morning and my wife would pick him up in the afternoon. The time of this school run coincided with my daughter's school finishing time, but fortunately there was help at hand. My daughter had a friend, Tanya, whose mother, a very caring Australian, kindly volunteered to pick her up from the school gate and both of the girls would play for an hour or so, before my wife collected her. Some days Jukekha would have supper with Tanya and over the weekend, she would spend the whole day and play in our large back garden. This arrangement was working well and also we thought after a few years Faisal would be able to drive himself to school when he becomes sixteen.

After we withdrew my house from the market, we thought of building an extension to our house on land which had useful space at the side of the house.

With the help of a friend, we found an architect who drew up the plans, but was not available to supervise the work of the builders. Being extremely naïve, we paid their fees and the drawing was submitted for local authority planning permission. There was no problem in getting the permission and now we were looking for builders. This is where we were to make a mistake which we regretted very much and which taught us a harsh lesson about hiring builders.

The behaviour of the estate agents, getting ready for the house extension, pressure at work and running a department, the situation back at home in Bangladesh, all the while having to deal with the situation on my own, was taking its toll on my system, but we could still cope. But the next event was unbearable.

On November 24th 1987, I got a letter from the school to say that Faisal had been suspended from school for a week for shoplifting. The headmaster had announced it in assembly, mentioning that three boys were involved and Faisal was one of them.

This was devastating news. We went to see the headmaster who gave me the details of the articles stolen and the shop. My wife and I visited the shop, which happened to be an Asian corner shop and the owner told us how Faisal stole a magazine. He had also stolen a student's fountain pen. We were extremely disappointed in him, and I was also worried that, after all this trouble to keep him at that school in spite of the arduous commute, if he was in school's bad books perhaps his scholarship would be suspended. But we also thought Faisal could change, after an admonition from the headmaster and with us promising to control him strictly, but it was not to be. Faisal went to school after a week's suspension and we thought he had learned his lesson, but we were wrong.

Berkhampsted School had some boarders, so the day boys were also required to attend the school on Saturdays. This was mainly for sports. My wife dropped Faisal at school and at around 10 a.m. I was about to go out to do the usual Saturday chores. It was only three weeks after we had got the letter from the headmaster about his suspension. The telephone rang and it was the headmaster, who wanted to see me immediately.

My daughter Julekha, seven at the time, was at home and so the three of us set off for Berkhampsted, not knowing what to expect. All we knew was that something very serious has happened to Faisal, otherwise we would not have been summoned to see the headmaster. Lots of thoughts crossed our minds as we wondered what else Faisal might have done.

At the school, I decided to leave Hashi and Julekha in the car and go alone to find out what the headmaster wanted to say.

The headmaster, Mr Driver, was a tall handsome man in early fifties, originally from South Africa, but he had to leave the country because of his anti-apartheid views. On a previous and happier occasion, I mentioned the name of my mentor Professor Harry Currey, also from South Africa, whose father used to be a headmaster in one of the best public schools. He recognised him immediately.

The headmaster's study was as dignified as you would expect from an old and rich public school, whose alumnae included the novelist Graham Greene and Robin Knox-Johnston. The headmaster was sitting behind his oak-panelled desk with a leather top. His face was sombre and in the corner my son Faisal was sitting in his school uniform, with his head down, almost like a sacrificial lamb.

Without much preamble, the headmaster came straight to the point. He said Faisal had been caught red-handed shoplifting again, despite the warning and suspension after the first time, and so, he said, he would have no alternative but to expel him from the school. I just opened my mouth to beg him to reconsider, but before I could say anything, he said, "I am sorry doctor, I have made the decision, Faisal is expelled – take him home".

I thought the earth had moved from under my feet. I did not know what to say or what to do. I thanked the headmaster and left the room with Faisal. The whole conversation took less than ten minutes.

In the car park, my wife was waiting on tenterhooks. I sat in the car in the driver's seat and broke down in front of my wife and two children. Hashi wanted to know what had happened and I simply said that Faisal had been expelled from the school, for shoplifting again. She too broke down.

While we were still in the car park, it was time for the school to break up. There were 750 boys, most of them in school uniform and some sixth formers in blazers or in their new suits. We watched from inside the car: all of them were happy, laughing, sharing sweets amongst themselves and the school forecourt was nearly full. I said to myself that out of all those 750 students, it was only my son who had been expelled; he would never again join them at this school.

We set off for home, without a single word spoken during our journey. My daughter realised something serious had happened with Faisal.

We had an invitation to a house with some local friends and we could not cancel it. My wife and I attended it, but hardly communicated with any other guests. They must have guessed that there was something wrong, but this was something we could not disclose to anybody.

The following week, I got a telephone call from Mr Driver who said he was sorry about the action he had taken, but I understood his point of view. By expelling Faisal, he had set an example so that no one else would dare to do this. After all, he had to maintain school discipline. He also told me that Faisal had potential and would do well if he got back on track. He advised me to approach the headmaster of St. Albans School, where Faisal had also passed the entrance exam, and where his elder brother went, and he kindly agreed to put in a word with the headmaster. He also advised me that Faisal should see a child psychologist.

It was now the second half of December and people were in a holiday mood with the approach of Christmas. I contacted Hertfordshire County Council for a child psychologist's help and was told there was a three-month waiting list. So I contacted one of my psychiatrist colleagues at the hospital who offered to help. She was about to retire and specialised in adolescent psychiatry. She agreed to see Faisal at her home in North London, and so I had to take him to her house every week for a few weeks, especially during the Christmas holidays. I never wanted to know, neither would she tell me, what led Faisal to do the shoplifting and steal another student's fountain pen.

Before the schools closed for the Christmas holiday, I made an appointment to see the headmaster of the St. Albans School. I explained to him that I wanted my son Faisal to be admitted to this school, for which he had passed the entrance exam. I said that we were finding it difficult to take him all the way to Berkhampsted, and we would rather him be at this school, which is in my own town and where his brother went. The headmaster readily agreed, then he said "Of course, he had a bit of trouble at Berkhampsted School, didn't he?" Obviously, he knew what had happened there. Mr Driver had spoken to him in detail. But we were relieved that Faisal would start in a new school in the New Year, and in new surroundings, which we were sure would be a turning point in his life. We had such high hopes, but we were wrong.

Meanwhile, the extension work on the house started in October 1987 and the agreement was that all the works would be completed before Christmas. This was a big extension on both sides, with two storeys, as big as building another house. The builders started the works well, particularly at the ground level, but as the brickwork rose, there were many irregularities and total mismanagement. Some days one or two bricklayers would come, then nobody for a week, then a completely new batch of bricklayers would come, and pile on a few more bricks. By the time Christmas arrived, the house was in a total mess and the job was not even half done. I made numerous telephone calls, and often confronted them openly, but they knew full well that I was a novice client and there was no penalty clause in the agreement, and no supervision by the architect. They did the work at their own pace and paid not the slightest attention to the inconvenience they were causing with the bricks, mortar, iron rods and other building materials strewn all over the place. One evening my wife fell down, stumbling on some of the building material, and cutting her knees. Protests to the builder and even a threat of legal action did not seem to make a difference.

The building works stretched to the end of March 1988, by which time I became mentally and physically exhausted. A heartbeat with extra beats caused great discomfort, but investigations suggested that it could all be put down to extreme anxiety. Also at this time, my peptic ulcer flared up and I had to depend on medication to suppress it.

However, there was encouraging news for Faisal at St. Albans. He started well, settled in his new environment and we were extremely pleased with the first term results. He got commendations for his marks in art subjects. We were much relieved and thanked Allah for His infinite mercy for bringing Faisal back on to the right path. But as events turned out, we spoke too soon.

At the end of March when the final bill from the builders came, I was shocked. I had already paid two instalments before, but when the invoice came for the final instalment it was for £7,500, far more than I had expected. He had charged 10% on every fitment such as windows, doors etc. etc., though I paid separately for them. On the day I received this invoice, I could not sleep that night. I spoke to a few friends but no good advice was forthcoming. I decided to confront the builder myself and went to his office with the invoice in my hand and simply blew my top. I raised my voice, shouted and demanded that it should be reduced. The builder was quiet, not saying a single word, and he listened with total calmness.

I realised my mistake. If I had been calm and talked to him rationally and requested him to look at the invoice again to see whether there was any room for improvement, I am sure he would have considered. I phoned a barrister friend of mine, who also advised me to pay up. I said "After all my shouting and raised voice, I still have to pay the full amount. I'm sure the builder will laugh." My friend said "You would not hear it". So ended the episode with the builder.

My eldest son, Sajal, did very well in his first-year exam at Cambridge. He got a First, and his second-year result was due in June. We were all expecting that he would again get a First, but he was disappointed and so were we that he only got a Second. This was not unusual at his stage, for he had slackened in his studies and may have been socialising a bit more. Still he got a 2:1, with which we were pleased, though he had the potential for more.

(21)

Friends and neighbours

We were now quite happy and settled, because the builders had left, the house looked impressive with five bedrooms, three bathrooms, and utility rooms, all new and spacious. I was very busy doing the internal decorations myself, as I had no more cash to employ an interior decorator.

In November, I got a telephone call from a friend telling me that a man called Ali Imam had died in Maidstone. Ali Imam was a school friend and I had not met him for over 35 years and did not even know that he was in England. He had had a pathetic death and his body lay in a hospital mortuary for over a month, because he had no relations or Muslim friends who could bury him in the Islamic tradition.

I later learned that he came to England, and remained single. He had always been a quiet type. He did some sort of official job in Maidstone and had a few English friends and colleagues, who met him at the weekend at the local pub. When he died of an undisclosed illness, the local friends did not know what to do. They did not know about his origins, or home address and he had no local Bangladeshi friends. The friend who telephoned me had sent him an invitation card to attend his daughter's birthday. The letter remained in his hallway for a month. Finally, one of his friends picked it up and found the telephone number and he was told the sad story of his death nearly a month before.

I had a doctor friend in that area, and with his help a funeral was arranged and the local Imam performed the ceremony in a village church.

There were lots of English people, mostly his friends and colleagues, and for their benefit I said a few words. He was buried in a Christian cemetery, where he still lies.

I wrote to my brother in Kushtia about this episode. He knew Ali Imam's father who had wondered why he had not written to him for such a long time and, more importantly, why he had stopped the remittances. His father wrote to me and I explained what had happened. He was relieved that his son had at least been buried in the Islamic way and was grateful to me. Ali Imam had a house in that area, which was sold by a local estate agent and the proceeds were sent to his father in Bangladesh. As is often the case, the parents and brothers are almost always interested in the remittances rather than the way that the money was earned abroad. His father never realised how sad Ali Imam's life had been in England, on his own, without any wife or family. The father was happy so long as he was getting his hard-earned money. I am sorry to say that this is the attitude of most relatives, who think that the money is like autumn leaves in Western Europe and America.

About this time, our neighbours with grownup children decided to sell their house and move to a bungalow at the other end of the town. Their house was on the market and a young couple moved in. The man looked as if he was of Middle-Eastern origin, and I thought he might be Arab or Turkish. His wife was English. After a few weeks or months, over the fence at the back garden, we spoke. It transpired he was a Jewish man from Scotland. I couldn't fathom the exact nature of his work, but he was in some sort of teaching. His wife did not work and was at home most of the time.

It must have been in the middle of 1987 when I was in turmoil with Faisal and the extension of the house, that my wife looking from upstairs noticed that the man – let us call him John –was on his patio looking very upset and seemed to be looking anxiously at our house to attract attention. I went to enquire, and he said his wife – whom I'll call Jane – was unwell and could I help? He knew that I was a doctor. I went inside their house and Jane was in the drawing room, extremely breathless and spitting blood and very tense and anxious. She was somewhat relieved to see me, but her eyes were fixed on John and she told him "I don't want to lose you, John". I did not know what she meant.

Anyhow, it transpired that she was three months pregnant, had not been to any anti-natal clinics and had a history of a heart murmur. In answer to a query from me, she said had had rheumatic fever as a child. I immediately knew that she must have a tight mitral stenosis, a narrowing of one of the valves of the heart, which had caused pulmonary hypertension, hence the breathlessness and coughing of blood. I phoned her GP who arrived shortly, while I was waiting and comforting her. The doctor, whom I knew very well, agreed with me and after formal examination, it was decided that she should be sent to hospital immediately. The ambulance came and whisked her away to the A&E Department of the local hospital.

I continued to monitor her progress. She was transferred to the cardiology unit at the Hammersmith Hospital in London where she had surgery. She felt well and there was no danger to her or her unborn baby.

This was the time when the extension work of my house was in full swing. My long driveway looked like a builder's yard. There was an overflowing skip, and hardly any place to keep two cars. Mine was a VW Passat Estate, a pretty big car and my wife's was a Ford Fiesta. So I asked John whether we could park at least one car in his driveway, because he had an enormous place and only one car. He readily agreed and I parked my car in their driveway while Jane was at the hospital.

After about ten days or so, Jane returned home. I was naturally happy and wanted to know how she was doing and what happened at the hospital. When I went to see her, though she was physically well, her body language suggested that my presence was not welcome. Whatever question I asked, she answered in monosyllables. I could not understand the reason. She never thanked me for the help I offered before she went to hospital.

I left her house and told my wife what had happened. She immediately said that it was because of my car parked in their driveway. But I hadn't thought that it was causing any inconvenience and I not convinced that this was the reason. But my wife's assumption proved right the next day. On my return from the hospital, when I tried to park the car in their driveway it was blocked by his car, which was parked in such a way that I could not even enter, though he well knew I would be back in the evening to park my car as I had done previously. I understood this, and had to park my car on the grass verge by the road.

Their bad neighbourliness continued when my fence fell down in the strong wind. Jane would not allow the workers to cross on to their land, while my previous neighbours had been perfectly happy to allow this. There were other sources of irritation too, relating to fences and plants and the border between, and there ended up being virtually no communication between us. I felt very bad about it, but nothing could be done.

On top of this, John was some sort of musician of oriental music. Over the weekends when we relaxed on the patio or invite guests, our enjoyment would be spoiled by his music. Some days he would invite many other friends and would bang on drums, cymbals and other instruments. Life became intolerable. English people have lots of patience, and the neighbour on the other side did not bother to protest. I did once or twice but it did not matter.

Fortunately, the man inherited some money which allowed him and his wife to sell their house and move to a bigger one. We were very relieved. We bumped into them once or twice, but avoided exchanging glances.

Many people with young children would go away on holiday to France, Spain and other parts of Europe, but I could not manage it in the seventies or eighties. The money was so tight. This was the case with my fellow Bangladeshi friends as well, who were in the same sort of situation. My English colleagues in a similar age group sometimes saved money by going to Europe in a caravan for two or three weeks but I never had the courage to do so. I had never driven on the continent, and I wasn't brave enough to start.

Sometime in the late 1980's, we decided to go to the West Country on a self-catering holiday with a friend. We found a house to rent right on the coast.

My friend had a son, slightly younger than my son Faisal. We were all sitting on the shingly beach, soaking up the sunshine and enjoying the warmth of the pebbles. My daughter was making a sandcastle, and Faisal and my friend's son were in the water. Faisal knew how to swim, but the other boy didn't. I was keeping an eye on them. I saw a piece of wood floating, and both of them went to catch it. Faisal managed to get hold of it but I did not see the other boy. Suddenly I saw his face popping up and down in the water in great distress. I was fully clothed and but ran straight into the water and got hold of the boy, by which time he had swallowed some seawater and started being sick, but he soon recovered. If I had not been keeping an eye on the boys playing, I am quite sure the other boy would have drowned.

The boy's mother did not say anything, or offer any words of thanks to me, but was very cross with her husband, saying: "What were you doing while your son was in the water?" The poor husband didn't have an answer. Saving that boy's life assumed an ironic significance later.

Though Faisal had settled in to his new school and did well in his first term, he began to slip back. He was doing just enough work to keep the daily routine going, but not the sort of work that would be required for his GCSEs. On top of that he was seen in the company of a group of boys, smoking God knows what. The police caught them, and all the boys gave false names and addresses to the police except Faisal. The police came to our home and cautioned him and us. We kept an extra watch on him, and did not notice anything untoward, though we got a report from his form tutor that he smoked when he went on a school outing in Wales.

We knew from Sajal's experience how much effort was required to get good grades, but Faisal would not study at all. In his waking hours he would daydream, and often he would just sleep and sleep. We became concerned about his grades for the forthcoming GCSEs, but he was not at all bothered. What was going through his mind only God knew.

Sajal, meanwhile, got a First in his final year at Cambridge and was pleased that not only did he get a good grade, but also got a graduate place at St. John's College, Oxford. It was a great achievement for him to study at both Cambridge and Oxford. We were really proud of him.

His graduation ceremony was at midday in the gorgeous setting of the Senate Hall. We took our seats and when his name was called out and my son went to collect his certificate from the Vice-Chancellor, I had a lump in my throat. My son was now a graduate from this world-famous university with a double First. I was so proud, and overwhelmed with a pleasure that was beyond words. My parents had not even known where Cambridge was and what it was all about, and I myself went to an unknown medical school and had the good fortune to come to England. And here was my son, a Cambridge graduate. It seemed that all our hard work, sacrifices, sufferings and economic hardship has borne fruits. We felt it was all worthwhile.

After the ceremony, on a clear summer day, all the parents gathered for informal talks in the grounds of the Senate House. I was in my best suit and my wife was in her best sari. We talked to other parents and in some cases grandparents, almost all of them white English. There were many in the grounds who had been three generations at Cambridge and in the same College, Gonville & Caius. There was an American couple whose surname was Grant and it turns out they were direct descendants of Ulysses S. Grant, the American general and the 18th President of the United States of America. People were enjoying the sandwiches and champagne provided by the University. But my wife remained subdued and did not seem to be enjoying herself at this proud moment of our life. When I asked her why, she replied "Would my Faisal be able to come here?" I was cross with her and told her in Bangla: "God damn it, enjoy your day here today and think about Faisal later".

After the ceremony, we left Cambridge just before sunset, with the car full of articles from our son's room which had been collected over the past three years. We returned home with the good memory of Cambridge which still lingers on.

At the hospital, my work situation was more or less stabilised and I had now been in the post for over twelve years. I was involved in several activities above and beyond my duty as a consultant, including being the Chairman of the Hospital Ethics Committee, a responsible job for the approval of any research projects and drug trials.

There was a system in the NHS where doctors got what were called Merit Awards. These were very valuable, a recognition of merit by permanent increases in salary. But the system was confidential – no one knew who had received an award and who hadn't. Any individual could apply for an award and I received an invitation to do so.

I felt I deserved an award and so I applied. But two other consultants, both white, got awards and not me. When I brought it to the attention of the hospital representative for such recommendations, I was told that I had narrowly missed it and would be considered next year. So then I reapplied. The old representative was now retired and there was a new person. I saw her and made the point that I deserved an award this year but she was thoroughly dismissive and quite unpleasant. I did not get it that year and in fact I never did get the merit 'C' award, which I felt I deserved.

I led a campaign against the confidentiality of the Merit Award system and spoke out at the Medical Staff Committee meetings, knowing full well that I had missed my chance. It was largely due to my effort that the whole list was published and it was no surprise to discover that none of the holders of the awards had qualified overseas. This seemed blatant racial prejudice against doctors from Asian backgrounds. By now, I had published a few letters to various medical journals about the injustice being done to overseas doctors. There were a few other colleagues in a similar position to mine, but they took a laid-back attitude and resigned themselves to the fact that they would not get an award, and instead they concentrated on private practice.

In August, we got Faisal's GSCE results. They were worse than we expected. He did not get a single 'A' grade in any subject, managed to get a few B's, and the rest were C's and even some D's. It was devastating news for all of us, though not unexpected. Only a few years back, my eldest son got all 'A's in 10 or so subjects. What a contrast. They even both went to the same school. We found out that a few of our friends' sons from state schools did far better than Faisal. There was nothing we could do and a pall of gloom fell on the household. It was much harder for Hashi, because I was busy at work but she was at home all the time looking after the children. She felt that this failure was hers as well.

Faisal started his 'A' level course, not being sure what subject he would study or what career he would aim for. He chose some arts subjects and stayed at the same school, with its hefty tuition fees. Removing him from the public school to a state school was possible, but we thought it would be unfair and would make him take the blame and not us for his future.

I got an invitation to go to a conference in Dubrovnik, then in Yugoslavia, now in Slovenia. The plane journey was fine, but the landing was very rough. It was night and there was a high wind. When we landed, we thanked Allah for His infinite mercy.

One day. three of us attending the conference decided to go up a mountain called Sardj by cable-car. At the top the view was breathtaking. You could see the beautiful city of Dubrovnik with its zigzag road, and beyond that the blue Adriatic Sea. The three of us enjoyed the scenery, and had lunch there. Now, as we were thinking of going down, the wind became gale force and we were told that the cable-car would not operate until the wind died down. No one knew how long this would take, and since we could see the town just below us and since all of us were able bodied people, why not walk down? In theory, it was a sensible idea, but in practice it turned out to be a disaster. We started walking down the hill, on a narrow footpath, through rows and rows of pine trees. Soon we got lost. We could neither see the hill from which we started, nor could we see the town any more. We had no option but to keep on walking down the hill. We also realised that there were no houses nearby and no one else following us or in front of us. We did not panic, because it was still daylight. All we knew was that we were going downhill and it was now more or less level ground. We suddenly came across a small car parked in the bush with a man and a woman in warm embrace, suggesting that human habitation was not far. We kept on walking, until we had walked for at least two hours. We came across a farm house with some horses in the yard. At the gate, we explained to a bemused man why three Asian men were standing in front of him out of breath. He spoke good English and told us we were miles away from our destination, and we had walked down the wrong side of the hill, away from the town and the sea. He was very kind, and when he heard that we were all doctors and had to attend a dinner at 6 p.m., he gave us a lift to our hotel and we thanked him profusely and learnt a lesson not to stray off the beaten track in unknown places.

In September while in the shower my wife noticed a lump in her breast and told me about it. I examined her and indeed there was a lump measuring about two inches by one inch. It was firm and mobile. We knew what it could be and tried to console each other that night, which was pretty sleepless for both of us. The children slept in their adjacent rooms, oblivious to what was happening to their parents.

In the morning, I contacted my surgical colleague, a very good friend of mine. On the same morning, he saw her and confirmed my diagnosis.

He immediately called a radiology colleague, also a family friend of ours. Both mammogram and ultra-sound scans were performed that afternoon and the two doctors confirmed that the lump looked benign. We were reassured and thanked Allah the Almighty for the good news so far. Nevertheless, it was decided that a confirmatory test should be done with a needle biopsy, three days later. Another colleague examined the sample and telephoned me to confirm that the lump was benign, though my surgical friend suggested that it would still be advisable to get the lump excised. We readily agreed, and he did the operation the following week.

I gave some presents to all my colleagues for their help and kindness, and by the grace of God, there have been no recurrences.

In our road, we were still the only Asian family and had now lived there for ten years. My daughter was born here and the last racial harassment we experienced had been in 1983 and we thought we had seen the back of it, but we were wrong.

One morning in October I found that all the pillar tops from the front wall had been removed and taken away. I was horrified. The memory of the last racial attack on the property flooded back. I thought that whoever had done it had been watching us and under the cover of darkness attacked my property like a coward. I knew there was no point in informing the police or the press. But we had just extended the house and decided that no matter what happened we would stay put.

I became anxious again, with disturbed sleep at night and the return of my ectopic heartbeats. I bought some more tops for the pillars, including some extra ones, suspecting that they would be needed in the future. Before we had even replaced the pillar tops, someone, probably the same person, uprooted my newly planted conifers. These incidents affected not only me, but also the children. Sajal was mature and at university, Julekha was still young, but it was Faisal who took it very badly. At school, he talked it over with his fellow students and with some teachers, who lent a sympathetic ear. He also asked me to install a security light. I am sure these incidents must have caused turmoil in his mind, particularly when he was not as much dedicated to his studies as we hoped. His anger at the time must have influenced his subsequent actions.

We now had to decide which school my daughter Julekha would go to. We visited St. Albans Girls School, a very good public school, but also went to see Haberdasher's Girls School. Julekha sat the entrance exam for both schools, and we decided that she should go to the local one, which was virtually walking distance from home and she was very happy there.

Worries at home and abroad

1989 was a year of national and international events which would have profound implications for the future. It was the year when the Berlin Wall fell and the year which saw the beginning of the collapse of the Warsaw Pact countries. Both East and West Germany were unified and once again became one Germany, with reunited Berlin as the capital.

Also in 1989, Saddam Hussein invaded Kuwait for the sake of its oil revenue. There was international outrage which sowed the seeds of further conflict in the Middle East, starting with the first Gulf War, then the second Gulf War. In this year I appointed Dr Kola, a Kurd, as my assistant in the Department, and it was from him that I learned so much about the sufferings and subjugation of the Kurdish people and how they had done well in that conflict and are now more or less autonomous.

In the UK, Margaret Thatcher's power came to an end after ten years or so. She had been a towering figure in British politics for twelve years and won the war with Argentina, and now she had to leave ignominiously.

In Bangladesh, the rule of President Ershad came to an end, providing some hope for the possible future release of my relations from Jessore Jail.

1990 started with Sajal beginning his clinical years at Oxford, and my daughter showing early promise at school and in her music. In fact, she was so good at the violin that she managed to secure first place twice in a Hertford County Council competition. We were so proud of her, and her mother displayed the medals to her friends. Julekha continued with her violin practice until she too went to medical school, where she was a leader of the University Orchestra.

But there was disheartening news. My relations were still incarcerated in Jessore Jail, and all attempts to free them, and all the bribes in various places, were to no avail. Pleas for money kept on coming from relatives, which I had to provide with the best of my ability.

But the main discontent and unhappiness within the family was with Faisal. We could not get anywhere with him. He was not at all interested in studying. In fact, I would have been glad if he had taken an interest in *anything*. No sports, no games, no friends and no study, not even the enjoyment of reading novels. We went to the school Open Day where the teachers tried to paint a rosy picture of him, but we knew how bad he was. Very often at home, there would be harsh words with his mother. At heart, he was good, kind and compassionate. He would always ask his mother whether she would like a cup of tea and she would get annoyed, and would ask him to go to his room to study. He would be silent and would not protest.

I wrote in my diary on 28th February 1990: "... the way Faisal is behaving, it seems his future is bleak. Once again there was an argument this evening – he does not understand how lucky he is ... when he realises it, it may be too late".

In 1991, after the change of the government in Bangladesh, our relations were all released from jail and I was overwhelmed with this good news. Also this year, Sajal qualified as a doctor from Oxford, though he was disappointed not to get a house job there, and had to be content with his first surgical job in Birmingham. We were pleased with Julekha. She not only qualified to get in to St Albans Girls School, but continued to do well with the violin and took up piano lessons as well.

My private practice picked up and I was comfortably well off in maintaining the household expenses and school fees for two, now that Sajal was earning money to support himself.

But the big problem continued to be Faisal. He showed no motivation or enthusiasm for his studies. He would sit alone all the time as if he was dreaming. We knew how much study was required for 'A' level subjects, and the way he was behaving worried us and I simply did not know how to handle it. We all thought that there would be a turning point for him, but it never arrived, and in fact, the situation was going from bad to worse.

I had a friend who was a psychotherapist and he agreed to see Faisal at his office in London. Faisal's appointment was in the afternoon but he did not return home until late at night. We were worried about what might have happened but he eventually returned at 10 p.m. still unhappy. He did not tell us why he was late, but he had seen he psychotherapist. The following day, I telephoned this friend who said there was no serious psychological problem, and advised Faisal to read some books.

We now know that Faisal was getting more deeply involved in religion and Islam and getting much comfort from this. He was being indoctrinated by certain groups and although we are Muslim we do not adhere to it strictly, but Faisal started praying the requisite five times a day and he talked and argued with us about religion. Sometimes he would be on one side of the argument and the entire rest of the family on the other side. We knew that he was not studying at all and very much doubted whether he would get into a university.

In the summer of 1991, I was proud to be elected a Fellow of the Royal College of Physicians of London, and attended the gorgeous ceremony at the College in Regents Park. This was watched from the gallery by lots of guests including my wife and many other friends and colleagues from home and abroad.

Also this year I went to Budapest to take part in another EULAR meeting. We stayed there for seven days, and on one day went to visit Lake Balaton. On our way there by coach, we stopped for lunch and I found a statue of Rabindranath Tagore, the Nobel Prize-winning poet of Bengal, and underneath a verse written in Bengali. I was familiar with that poem, written to praise the Emperor Shah Jahan for the building of the Taj Mahal. It turned out that Tagore had been to this place in 1926 to convalesce.

While in Budapest, I kept in touch with Hashi at home. When I phoned she told me Faisal had failed his driving test. I wrote in my diary – "the boy is not becoming successful in any sphere of life, yet he is trying".

What Faisal was trying to achieve only he knew, but as far as we could fathom, he was always dreaming and thinking. His mind was always elsewhere.

On my return from Budapest over the weekend, I was very surprised when my wife said she had seen Faisal's school report and she was pleased with every teacher's comments and expected good grades in the forthcoming 'A' levels.

I looked at the report and immediately recognised that it was in Faisal's own handwriting. He had used different ink and pens, and also tried to use different styles of writing. He also copied the signatures of all the teachers, including that of the head teacher. I immediately asked him to give me the real report but he remained silent. I eventually saw the actual report, which was not at all favourable as I might have expected.

So what made Faisal go to such lengths as to fake his own school report, knowing full well that he had been expelled from a school only three years ago? I do not know. Faisal's lack of progress and questions about his future were the only things my wife and I talked about at home. One good thing in Faisal's real school report was praise from the headmaster about a speech he gave in front of the whole school and the teachers about Islam. Obviously he had been studying Islam a lot and was more interested in religion and Islamic studies than in his usual class studies. The headmaster was pleased with his style of speaking and the content of his talk. It turned out later that he had a circle of Islamic friends in St. Albans and nearby Luton, although very few of them ventured to come to our house. However, when they did come, they looked humble and sometimes would pray together in his room.

On the occasion of Sajal's graduation as a doctor, as with similar successes in the lives of our children, it was customary to invite friends and give 'Milad', which essentially means thanking Allah for the successes, saying some prayers and having nice food.

We arranged such a 'Milad' for Sajal but Faisal was against it because he felt that the true Islamic faith does not approve such things. He was correct in terms of strict Islam, but there is a tradition that allows that it be done, as my father did when I qualified as a doctor, and so Faisal was overruled.

On the day the guests arrived, we needed all the help we could get but Faisal was in his room, and reluctant to come out and help us with the arrangements. I did not know at the time, but my wife told me later that

Sajal, in whose honour it was being done, was rude to Faisal and even manhandled him. Faisal never protested and kept quiet and dignified. When I heard this, it bought tears to my eyes. For Faisal might not be doing well in his studies and may have been in lots of mischief, but I had never been rude to him, let alone used violence. I felt very sad and apologised to him for Sajal's behaviour.

At the end of 1991, Hashi, Julekha and I set off on a visit to Bangladesh. It was a bitterly cold and frosty night. Though we were happy that we were going to Bangladesh as a family, we were very concerned about Faisal, who would be staying at home on his own. He was now over eighteen years old, and so an adult, and he said he could look after himself. We knew he would be relieved that he would be on his own, and could have his friends at the house. Indeed, after we returned one of our neighbours said that one day a bearded man in Muslim dress had knocked on their door by mistake, and other neighbours had also noticed strange young men visiting our house. Those were the days before the 9/11 attacks. Now such a house would be put under surveillance.

When we reached Dhaka, my nephew had arranged a hotel for us. It turned out to be a hotel for local people and not long ago, a man had been murdered in one of the rooms and it was big news in the national newspapers. Hashi and Julekha had heard about this and were frightened, and had decided to stay awake all night. The next day we moved into a better hotel.

The journey from Dhaka to Kushtia started well in a luxury coach for about sixty miles to Aricha Ghat. The plan was to cross the Meghna river by ferry and on the other side we would take the train to Kushtia arriving by three or four pm.

After crossing the river, we were told that there was no train because of a derailment somewhere along the line. What were we to do? We in the middle of our journey. We didn't know whether there would be any trains at all, and it was also impossible to return to Dhaka. Fortunately, we had two young relatives with us, my nephew and youngest brother-in-law, both of them young college students. Their presence was a godsend. There were suggestions that we find a scooter taxi, but every marooned passenger had the same idea. Nevertheless, those two young men somehow managed to get two such ramshackle "taxis" and loaded our suitcases into them. We had to reach a railway station called Rajbari, half way between Kushtia and Goalundo Ghat. Julekha, Hashi and I were in one taxi, and the two young men and the luggage were in another. We had to travel about twenty miles, on a single-track road. I held Julekha tightly, fearful that at any moment the flimsy thing might overturn because of the heavy load, or we might end up dead in a head-on collision with heavily loaded trucks coming from the opposite direction. I really thought that this might be the end for all of us. However, God saved us and we reached Rajbari station by 5 p.m.

I was very familiar with Rajbari station, from my days at medical school, when I travelled by train through the station. It was built by the British and had its glory during the British Raj but now it was decaying all around. When we arrived, there was barely even standing room on the station platform. It was full of passengers who were eagerly waiting for any news of the trains. We had great difficulty in holding on to our luggage. Our two young men cordoned off a bit of platform for us to sit on our suitcases. We missed our lunch and did not use the toilet facilities. Julekha was bearing it well. (Every now and then, these days, when I am stuck in a traffic jam in England, I remind Julekha of "Rajbari".) The situation couldn't get any worse. The station did have toilets, but they overflowing with urine and faeces and it was not possible to use them. I noticed a railway police station, and thought they at least must have a clean toilet for the ladies to use. They were sympathetic and allowed us to use their toilets, which were equally filthy, but we had no option.

At the station, as we waited hungry and thirsty, our western clothes and luggage attracted attention and everybody was staring at us. It was very uncomfortable, particularly for Hashi and Julekha. I don't remember when the train came, but we managed to get tickets for first-class carriages and reached Kushtia at 9.30 p.m. It was already dark and everybody was anxious about what had happened to us. We reached my father-in-law's house totally exhausted. It had taken more than twelve hours to reach Kushtia. This was an experience Julekha will never forget.

She was eleven years old, intelligent and inquisitive and she was looking forward to finding out about everything in Bangladesh – the trees, the crops in the fields and the animals and birds. I had already told her a lot about it.

We stayed at Kushtia for three days and with the care and hospitality of our relations we recovered from the ordeal of the journey from Dhaka. While we were there I took Julekha to the shrine of the famous folk singer called Lalan Fakir. He was a mystic and had written many songs, which are still extremely popular among Bengalis on both sides of the border.

The final stage was the journey to our village home in Dharmadaha. Even in late 1991, there was no organised transport. There was a so-called public bus service, which was overcrowded at all times, and it was impossible to get on. Julekha was surprised to see as many people on top of the bus as inside. I, of course, knew those buses well from my time as a student. They would all have been condemned by western standards, but people had no option but to board them. There was no control over the number of passengers the bus could accommodate. As a result, there were people inside, on the roof and hanging off the sides. From a distance it looked like a rectangular object coated with people. The roads were bad, accidents happened and people died. But who cared? Life is cheap in Bangladesh.

Many years later a distant relative of my wife was staying at our home in England for a few days, on his way to Canada. It turned out he was a bus owner. I asked him what happened if an accident occurred and people were injured or died. He said that if a person dies, the situation is simple, the bus owner pays a fixed fine of 4,000 Taka – about £40 – and that is the end of the matter. And that money goes to the police and perhaps stays there. No compensation goes the relatives of the victim. According to him, the problem is more complex if the person survives and stays in hospital. You have to provide for his treatment and medical expenses which may run into double the figure of the death.

However, for us, we had no intention of boarding those death traps. Someone promised to lend his car, but there was no driver. Luckily, an old friend of mine had a small Japanese car with a reconditioned engine and he gave us a lift to our village, which took only an hour and a half, a distance of 36 miles.

At the village, the first thing I did was to visit my parents' grave with Julekha. This was the first time I had visited my mother's grave. Both my parents were buried side-by-side in the family plot. The graves were brick-built and painted white, a rare scene in rural Bangladesh. Only the well-to-do can manage to supply a brick-built grave. I offered prayers for the souls of my parents and told Julekha that this was the place where it all began. These were the two people who sacrificed so much, and it was because of them that I was a doctor and had been able to establish myself in England.

We arrived home in England on New Year's Day, 1992. Julekha kept repeating "It is so peaceful here, dad". I entirely agreed with her and I always felt myself at peace whenever I arrived back from Bangladesh. No honking of the motor vehicles, no loud music on the loudspeakers, nobody disturbs you at odd hours of the day or night. No wonder Julekha felt the same. During this time, Sajal was on his elective year in Japan and he too arrived home during the first week of January. I thanked Allah in a Friday prayer, that all of us from various parts of the world had arrived home safely.

It was at this time that Hashi and I decided to do something for the Bangladeshi community in my own town of St. Albans. They are mainly Sylheti, from a city in the north of Bangladesh, and illiterate. The children speak Sylheti at home and learn to speak, read and write English at school. We thought it would be a good idea if we could open a Bangla school, and teach the young boys and girls basic Bangla (or Bengali). With the help of two non-Sylheti Bangladeshis we formed a committee and called the project "Bangladesh Progati Samity". We also got help from the St. Albans City Council with some finance. We hired a school on Sundays and started the school. We had a very good response from the parents, who started sending their children to our school in droves. It was officially inaugurated by the local MP and the High Commissioner for the People's Republic of Bangladesh. It was a wonderful occasion and I gave a keynote speech which was well-received and widely reported in the local papers.

Then the problems started. A group of Sylheti Bangladeshis assumed that there must be some financial gain for us, otherwise why would we spend so much time teaching Bangla to their children? What interest did we have? There was a group who went door-to-door to tell parents not to send their children to the Bangla School. Despite this campaign, the school continued to do well, and we started getting further funds from the Hertford County Educational Council, though it eventually closed down when I had other preoccupations.

In July 1992, we were proud that that Sajal qualified as a doctor from Oxford University, twenty-seven years after I had qualified, and it was a day that still remains in my memory like a bright star. Sajal had been a brilliant student and God gave him an unusual talent.

All of us went to Oxford for the ceremony. Faisal was in his best suit, and so was I. My wife and Julekha were similarly well-dressed. By this time, we knew that Faisal's 'A' level results would be bad and therefore there was no chance of him getting into Oxford or Cambridge.

At the ceremony, we were introduced to Sajal's tutor, who was very happy to see us as a family and pointed towards Faisal, saying "It will be his turn next!" We wished he had been right.

Although Sajal had qualified as a doctor and spent several years at Cambridge and Oxford, he had not yet come across a girl he wanted to marry. We did not put any restrictions on him with regards to race, religion or creed, and although he had female friends, there were none he could call a girlfriend. So, in Bengali fashion, we had been looking for a suitable bride for him, perhaps a doctor with a similar background. There were quite a few young women among our friends and acquaintances whom we introduced to Sajal directly or indirectly. But it did not work out. I do not regret it and it was all for the best. I do not think I could have had a nicer daughter-in-law than the woman Sajal eventually married.

Faisal's 'A' level results were bad and he decided to re-take them with the hope that the grades would be better. But his mind was not on his studies and, because we had such high expectations he just could not meet, he turned to religion. As expected, his re-take results were not up to the mark and one by one he was rejected by most universities. But he was lucky because in this year many polytechnics were upgraded to universities and after a number of applications Faisal eventually got a place at Greenwich University to study law.

We were very happy that he had got into a university and began to believe that this might be the turning point in his life. We thought that when he was away from home he would have his circle of friends, enjoy university life and will be a good lawyer one day, because his speaking abilities were excellent.

We happily took him to his university accommodation, paid his tuition fees, and looked forward to Faisal having the same sort of enjoyable and successful university life as Sajal's. But our calculations were wrong. He was not at all interested in studying, which we learned after the end of the first year. He did not attend any of the lectures, did not do any course work and fell behind. When I talked to his tutor, he told me that since Faisal was an adult, he would speak to him, rather than us. Whenever we visited him at his hostel, we found him lifeless, virtually on his own, no friends, no relaxation and no sporting activities. His mind was elsewhere and I felt that there was something seriously wrong. When he came home, there would be telephone calls from people who were not students, there would be coded talk in low voices, there were talks of buying and selling books, and so on.

One year passed, and his results was abysmal. He had not passed in a single subject. I collected him from his hostel and was not able to speak a single word to him. What could I say? I knew very well he was not studying at all.

At home after we had all settled down, I talked to him about his future. What would he like to do? The options were: to leave university early, and he would then be a school leaver and not a graduate, or if he so wished he could try again. He decided to try again. This meant he would be living in rented accommodation, and I would have to bear all the expenses, including tuition fees. Once again, we thought it would be yet another turning point in his life. Once again, we were wrong. It was becoming clear that the old English proverb applied in this case: we could take our horse to water but could not make him drink.

Sajal got a good job in London and we managed to buy a flat for him in St. John's Wood. Julekha was happy at school with her study, music and games. We took her to Disneyland in Paris and stayed there for a week, which was thoroughly enjoyable. We still continued to look for a suitable wife for Sajal and saw at least three in 1993, but none were suitable in one way or another.

At that time, quite a lot of changes were taking place within the NHS. There had been a major reorganisation. Health Secretary Kenneth Clarke under Mrs Thatcher introduced so-called market-economy and competition between hospitals for patients. GPs were holding the purse-strings and they became all powerful. Not all the changes were helpful to me, as a specialist in a non-essential subject. The success of a department was being measured by how many referrals we had from GPs. The whole hospital was divided into several directorates, with one director for each and a business manager. The changes left me feeling helpless. New consultants were more in tune with the changes and they became the directors, in my case in the directorate of medicine. These young consultants questioned the validity of my helping at the Outpatient Department. My referrals fell dramatically because GP's were now sending patients directly to the physiotherapists and bypassing me. I could not stand my ground and had to lose some clinical assistant sessions. I was even concerned about my own job, because of the fall in the referrals. I did not get any help from any other colleagues. All this stress and strain caused more physical problems, like ectopic beats, night sweats, and digestive problems. Stress continued both at home and at work.

Internationally the Muslims of Bosnia and Palestine were being massacred on a daily basis. In fact everywhere I looked I found the news and the situations depressed me.

Faisal restarted his university studies at Greenwich, and once again there was no progress. He never concentrated at all, and never attended his classes; instead, as we found out later, he travelled up and down the country with an Islamist Group, giving lectures in the mosques, and taking part in meetings for the help of Bosnian Muslims. At home, we would very often get in an argument with him. The main thrust as far as he was concerned was religion. His view was that Islam was "central to everything", and studying, family life, and personal relations were secondary. I could not convince him that at his age studying and building his career was more important than religion, which he could practice all his life, but once he missed the boat it would not be possible to catch it again to build a career. We did not succeed in convincing him. He grew a long beard, prayed five times a day, and was meticulous about eating halal food, which we had to obtain especially for him.

In the summer of 1994 I decided that Hashi should go to Bangladesh with Sajal and Faisal. Sajal was now a doctor and earning money and Faisal was − at least theoretically −a university student, though we knew he was not doing well. Faisal was by now an Islamist with a long beard and wearing Islamic dress. In my village, the people were simply mesmerised with his behaviour, and his deep devotion to regular prayer.

He would take the hand of my elderly brother and they would walk together to the mosque. Ordinary, illiterate and deeply religious village folk were simply amazed that this young man, born and brought up in England, was one of them

We had bought a video camera, which the brothers took to Bangladesh and took many pictures of the village, of the lush green paddy fields and of the swollen rivers in rainy season. They thoroughly enjoyed their trip to Bangladesh, whereas here in England, Julekha and I managed to look after ourselves.

My problems at the hospital continued, my referrals continued to fall, and a colleague whom I appointed to get strength and fight for our corner did not materialise.

In the autumn of 1995, Faisal's results came and as expected, he had not passed in a single subject. This was the second successive year that he failed to pass. The University had no option but to expel him. His education was over. We had to accept that he was not going to graduate in any subject. It was a severe blow to us, though we had been expecting it. I tried to analyse what had gone wrong with him. He was an intelligent boy, and had managed to get a scholarship to a public school. At home, he had everything he needed, including the attentions of a full-time housewife mother. Still he could not graduate in any subject, from any university in the country.

In the summer of 1995, we extended the house further. This time it was supervised by an architect, who is a friend and neighbour. The building of another room, porch and conservatory went on smoothly and it was nearly complete by the autumn. We were pleased with it. Life was going well, apart from with Faisal, who was at home doing nothing, looking for odd jobs and involved in his religious works.

The Bosnian War was in full swing, and we were all upset at the suffering of the Muslims at the hands of the Serbs. While we discussed the war amongst ourselves, Faisal became involved in raising funds for the victims of the war. He and his friends arranged car boot sales, and collected clothing and other articles to raise funds. He also came into contact with a few Bosnian refugees and helped them settle down in their rented accommodation. I overheard that he might even join the fighting in Bosnia.

During the Bosnian war, the West stood by while the ethnic cleansing of the Muslim population went on unabated. We all got used to the wholesale murder of entire families and the destruction of mosques. It was a heart-rending sight. I had never realised that there was so many Muslims in Europe. In November, we heard the terrible news of the assassination of Itzhak Rabin, the Israeli Prime Minister, by a Jewish extremist. I felt sad, but thought that there might now be the possibility of peace with the Palestinians. I was encouraged to see the Arab leaders, including Yasser Arafat, attending the funeral service of Rabin. I had high hopes that at last there would be peace between these two people, but nothing happened.

We never managed to find a bride for Sajal, though there were at least two close encounters. At this time, he was working as an SHO in Southend and became friendly with an English girl called Rachel who was his House Officer. Sajal liked her and brought her to meet us on his 28th birthday in December. We liked Rachel and hoped that the relationship would develop. That night, we went as a family to a Pakistani restaurant to get to know Rachel. It turned out that the owner of the restaurant was a patient of mine and insisted that the whole meal would be free. I could not agree, but accepted part of the meal as a gift.

It turned out that 1995 had been a crucial year in many aspects, and looking back, in the light of later events, it was the happiest year of my life. At the beginning of my 1996 diary I wrote "I pray to Allah for His infinite mercy on the welfare of the family. Sajal will sit for the Final FRCS and Julekha will sit her GCSEs, and I pray to Him for their success. I pray to Him for the guidance of Faisal, for he is wandering aimlessly."

Enter Aliyya

January 1996 was the month of Ramadan, and I fasted just for a few days, unlike Faisal who followed every single requirement of Islam for the whole month. Faisal had been doing a few odd jobs here and there, but his main focus was on religion and prayers, preaching Islam whenever the opportunity arose, including visiting the local prison every Sunday to give a talk to the Muslim inmates. He was young and articulate and the prisoners appreciated it very much. Also, he would set up a stall on market day on a Saturday in front of the local Barclays Bank in St. Albans with various books and literature on Islam. Almost every Saturday we used to go to the market, and would see him distributing leaflets and books to the local people. These were the days long before 9/11, but still people would frown at the bookstall distributing Islamic literature. In fact, the books he used to distribute free of charge were a moderate form of literature, not the extremist type other groups like Al-Muhajiroun would distribute in other cities.

One day I confronted Faisal about the book stall and why he was doing it, virtually on his own, when there were so many Muslims in St. Albans. His answer was "Somebody has to do it, to save Islam". He totally disagreed with the literature and philosophy of Islamic extremists. At least once a week there would be a "Brothers Week" where other like-minded young men would gather in someone's house and Faisal would be the main speaker. Also, there would be a "Sisters Week" where he would give a talk to Muslim women and girls wearing total Islamic dress covering all parts of the body except the eyes.

Sajal bought a flat in St. John's Wood, London, and we helped him furnish it. Julekha was doing very well in her school and we were confident that she would continue to do well.

In the spring of 1996, Faisal told us that he had found a girl, a Muslim convert, who was interested in him. This seemed unlikely to be serious since he was unemployed with no career prospects, but we were prepared to be surprised.

Sajal was busy with his final FRCS Exam and was unhappy with his job in Oxford. Very often he would come home and vent his anger at his mother. I would hear about it later and would try to understand what exactly was happening and how it could be remedied. Complete job satisfaction is rare, and certainly in my case I made the most of my opportunities to make a good living. At that time Sajal was doing neurosurgery and I suggested that he should change to something else. But in fact he was never dedicated to any one branch of surgery, like some people who develop their professional interest in their student life.

On 15th May 1996, Sajal passed his final FRCS and became a Fellow of the Royal College of Surgeons, a great achievement. He passed it on his first attempt, which was really great news, and we felt extremely proud

Also on that day I felt happy for another reason. This was the day that Faisal's female friend, a girl called Aliyya, came to our house with a bunch of white daffodils. She looked absolutely gorgeous, in her Islamic attire. She was tall, blonde, with blue eyes and a lovely voice. She was apparently overwhelmed with Faisal's speech at one of the Sisters Meetings, and was attracted to him for his knowledge of Islam. In fact, she wanted to marry him. We hardly knew her, and had only seen her once, yet, astonishingly, she wanted to marry my Faisal, an unemployed young man of 22 and she just over 18. She told us in her articulate and public school accent, that she was the daughter of a physics teacher at the local public school, where my two sons went. So I immediately recognised who her father was. She had another sister who also went to the same girl's public school as Julekha. The family was perfect. She said that she converted to Islam after reading about it.

Events were moving fast. Two days later Aliyya again came to our house and had lunch with us. We found nothing to say against her. The following day, her parents came, obviously at the instigation of their daughter, and said they had no objection, and indeed, they would be happy if Faisal married her. I pointed out that Faisal had no apparent prospects, and that he was not even a graduate, but still this intelligent, beautiful eighteen-year old wanted to marry him and her parents agreed.

Meanwhile, a few of Faisal's Islamic friends came along and urged us to agree to the marriage. I hesitated, and asked: why marry? Why not get engaged and stay together for a little longer. No, they said, it was not permissible in Islam. No cohabitation outside marriage. My wife and I mulled it over for a while and in the end, we gave in.

That was the greatest mistake of our lives. I still firmly believe that, if this girl, who had a chequered past even by the age of 18, did not come into our family as our beloved daughter-in-law, my Faisal might have been alive today.

We said to ourselves that we had been looking for a suitable bride for my eldest son for over five years and nothing happened, even though he was tall, handsome and an Oxford graduate, and here we are, a beautiful, intelligent girl from a good family begging to marry Faisal, so on what grounds should we refuse? She was a devout Muslim and her recitation of the Holy Quran was like music, so we could not see any argument for rejecting her. Everybody that we knew from Faisal's circle of friends and their parents were all begging us to agree. We discovered that this girl had a shady past, but we turned a blind eye, thinking that she was a reformed character, a devout Muslim, and would be unlikely to revert to her old self. How mistaken we were.

So on 23rd May 1996 we agreed that Faisal and Aliyya could get married. Aliyya and her family were delighted.

My wife, a happy-go-lucky and fun-loving person, liked Aliyya enormously and straight away she took her to Luton and bought £200-worth of jewellery and dresses. After all, she was going to be our first daughter-in-law. That night I wrote in my diary: "To us it all seems unreal! Things are moving so fast, that we cannot take it all in! It is all Allah's wish and we Pray to Him for the successful outcome."

Once we gave our consent for the marriage, there was strong pressure from the girl and her parents to fix a date for the wedding. It seemed to us that we had no control over events; we were simply being carried away by a strong current.

A week after these tumultuous events, I set off on a trip to another conference, this time in Reykjavik in Iceland. On our drive from the airport to the hotel, I was surprised to see the barren landscape. There were no trees or vegetation, just dry rocks like a lunar landscape. We were told it was a new island, of volcanic origin and it would take many thousands of years for vegetation to grow – if any could take root at all in the arctic conditions. The hotel was peaceful, and the roads were quiet, with not very many people around. When I went to bed at midnight, there was still blazing sunshine and I had to draw the curtains to make the room dark. The following day, a colleague and I went to see a football match between Macedonia and Iceland. I did not realise it would be that cold, even though the sun was shining. I was shivering and had to borrow a coat from the coach driver. The stadium was small and Iceland was defeated.

Then we went for an enjoyable meal in a very good restaurant. The setting was excellent, at the top of a multi-storey building, and the whole restaurant was revolving, so as we sat the horizon would change. The food was extremely interesting, raw meat and vegetables served on a hot rock, which cooked as you cut a piece to eat.

After the conference, we had time to look around the rest of the island with a few friends. This included a visit the Langaker Glacier, at the centre of Iceland. It took us two and a half hours in a specially adapted four-wheeler to reach the top, a breathtaking sight and experience. We changed into special clothes provided by the organisers and then got on to snowmobiles. I drove one of them as fast as I could in the undisturbed snow. It was so silent, so peaceful and calm, as if there was no worry or stress anywhere in the world.

On our last day in Iceland we went to visit the Blue Lagoon, a naturally occurring hot spring with geysers erupting every few minutes. It has been converted into a health resort where people submerge themselves in hot mud which is supposed to have some soothing effect on the body.

When I got home from Iceland, bringing presents for all members of the family, including my future daughter-in-law, Aliyya, I found that the wedding date had already been fixed for 5th July 1996. 'Fast work!' I thought.

Our plan was to have a simple ceremony at home in the Islamic way, followed by the official wedding at the Registry Office. Both Faisal and Aliyya and her family were extremely keen to get the whole thing over and done with. In mid-June, my wife and I and Aliyya and her parents went to Green Street in the East End of London and chose an expensive wedding dress for Aliyya. It was imported from India, bright red with beautiful handwork. She looked absolutely fabulous when she wore it. We also bought Islamic wedding clothes for Faisal and matching jewellery of pure gold for Aliyya. After the shopping, all five of us had a good meal in one of the Indian restaurants and returned home tired and exhausted but happy.

Before the actual wedding day, Aliyya's parents came very many times to find out how the preparations were going and offered help. I felt Faisal was so lucky to be linked to such a good family. The Islamic part of the ceremony would take place at our house with the Imam of the local mosque performing the ceremony.

On the wedding day, my house was full of guests, young and old, male and female of all races and religion. It was a beautiful summer day and Aliyya and Faisal both looked beautiful. Immediately after the wedding, Faisal and Aliyya went away to Edinburgh on their honeymoon. I drove them to Luton Airport and felt extremely happy.

While they were on honeymoon in Scotland, my wife and I went to North Wales for a few nights to attend a college reunion. When we returned, we expected the newly-weds to be at home, but they weren't. We found a note addressed to Faisal by Aliyya which worried us. There had been some argument between them, and the note was an apology to Faisal. Doubts about the mentality of the girl had begun on the wedding day, when the house was full of guests, all of them wanting to see the bride and bridegroom walking in the garden in their wedding clothes. But instead Aliyya went upstairs to the bedroom, complaining of headache. Now this note of apology for some quarrel, only ten days after the wedding. But we were relieved to see them happy on their return home that night.

The couple stayed in our house, and Aliyya's parents, particularly her father, David, came almost every day without any notice, or would telephone to see how their daughter was doing, and ask whether she was looking after herself. Perhaps he was worried about the instability which led her suddenly to change religion and embrace Islam. I became friendly with her father, a soft-spoken, mild-mannered, amiable character. He would bemoan the fact that his daughter, whom he still called by her English name, broke up with a boy called Thomas from a well-to-do family. He was also very ambitious for his daughter to continue her studies at university. I was not interested to hear about his daughter's previous relationships and felt offended. It is not in our culture to have relationships before marriage, and my son Faisal was an honest, sincere boy and a virgin. Still, we wanted to turn a blind eye to her past, when she had had many relationships with other men. She was only 18 when the wedding took place, but her relationships with men started much earlier. This was also the case with her younger sister. But we still felt that she was a reformed character and was now a devout Muslim, so we were prepared to forgive and forget.

The summer of '96 was gorgeous. I turned 59 in July and Sajal and I went to Lords Cricket Ground to see Pakistan play England. Sajal was unhappy with his work in Oxford and left that job and came to London. His friendship with Rachel was crystallizing and was leading towards engagement. Julekha was very happy at school and enjoying her study and music. Everything looked happy and cheerful, particularly as Sajal got a job with the South-east Thames Region, which would be for the next six years, taking me to my retirement.

Despite the fact that there was still tension at work, particularly with my own departmental colleagues, and disappointment at not getting a merit award, I got immense satisfaction when I came home to be with the family. Though Faisal did not live up to our expectations, he had married a beautiful girl and she did reasonably well in her 'A' level exams and was trying to find a place at university.

Aliyya got a place at Leeds in Arabic Studies and by a stroke of luck Faisal was also offered a place for the same course. Obviously, we were all happy with this, but I had wondered whether Faisal would be able to stick with it. Still, I felt that this could be yet another turning point in his life and perhaps, now that he had a wife, the situation would be different.

Following their wedding and honeymoon, they were staying in our house. We did everything to make Aliyya happy, especially my wife, who loved this girl so much that she spoilt her. But we got little in return. She would be moody, unpredictable and often raise her voice. We ignored it, thinking she was young and would change in due course. We were wrong.

Aliyya's father managed to find accommodation for both of them in a run-down area of Leeds, and we agreed to share the expenses fifty-fifty. In September, they left for Leeds to start their studies and I prayed to Allah for their well-being.

In October I attended a EULAR meeting in Madrid. I took the opportunity to visit Cordoba, the seat of Muslim power for 800 years. The famous mosque is now a church, a magnificent building which could hold 10,000 people at one time. I remember reading an essay as a schoolboy, entitled "Islam in Spain", the first line of which said "Islam in Spain offers us a melancholy contrast". I did not understand it as a boy, but later I found how successful and advanced a society Spain was at the time of the Moors.

After my return, I went to Leeds, with Julekha and Aliyya's sister Liz, the same age, to see how Aliyya and Faisal were settling down. I was not very happy with their accommodation but I told myself that we had lived in even worse accommodation than this in the East End of London. Liz and Julekha stayed, but we returned home.

Julekha returned after three days and paid glowing tribute to the way Faisal looked after her. The only thing she said was that he was not eating much and it seemed he had lost some weight, which we too had noticed. We warned Aliyya that she should take extra care of Faisal, who was not physically strong. He was 23 years old on 24th October, and he had already forbidden us to send birthday cards or present, for it would be "unIslamic".

On 27th October 1996, I wrote in my diary "Rachel is probably going to marry Sajal against the wishes of her parents. I believe in Providence". The following month, we were thrilled at Julekha's GCSE results; she got 9 A's and 1 B. Such an excellent result mean that she could go on to higher studies.

As if life could not get any better, we suddenly got a telephone call from Aliyya telling us that she was pregnant. This was excellent news, and it meant that I was going to be a grandfather. It was a wonderful feeling.

I had stopped worrying about what was going to happen to the couple's careers, and I wrote "Everything in Faisal's life had been unpredictable, so this was one of them – where it will end, only Allah knows".

Faisal and Aliyya came home for the Xmas break, and Aliyya looked beautiful in her early pregnancy. As soon as she entered the house, I kissed her on the cheek. This was the first time I had kissed her, as I was so very happy.

Though there were still problems with the situation at work. and in fact I had been looking forward to my retirement, as a family man I was quite contented. I also felt I had truly integrated with British society, socially and culturally. We were quite friendly with all the neighbours and a few other English people in our road. Most of my daughter's friends at school were English. It was a pleasant scene in our back garden whenever my daughter's birthday was due in mid-June. All the white girls would be playing and dancing and my Julekha was the only Asian. I thought integration with the local community was further cemented by Faisal's wedding and the forthcoming next generation. I was looking forward to seeing what my grandchild would look like. Aliyya was so beautiful and Faisal was handsome, and whether it was a boy or a girl, surely he or she would be attractive.

Also, Sajal's friendship with Rachel was deepening and she too was from a good family and I hoped they would get married soon. So my wife and I were full of hope. Life was rosy on all sides. We had many friends both locally and throughout the country and there was hardly a weekend that we were free. Also, Faisal's in-laws who were very friendly people would visit us almost daily. This was how 1996 came to an end.

The story of 1997 – the year I was 60 – is the story of how I died in spirit, if not in health. 1997 would be the year I fell from the top of the tree, which I thought I had climbed all the way up from the lower branches, as I used to as a boy. One day when I had been trying to grab the ripest mango, I had slipped and fallen, breaking my arm. The events of 1997 were to produce a similar precipitate fall, breaking my heart and, in fact, my whole life.

A loss beyond all losses...

How I was inspired to keep a daily diary I do not know, but this has been a habit since my days at medical school. As a child, maybe when I was 8 or 9 years old, I went with a group of my friends to a part of the village which was inhabited mainly by the Hindu community. It was round about 1948, the year of turmoil in the whole of the Indian subcontinent. The country was divided into two separate states and by the skin of our teeth we became part of Pakistan. The very rivulet we used to cross every day became an International boundary.

The Hindu population were educated and cultured and knew exactly what was happening, while the Muslim community was largely from an illiterate, peasant background and most of them did not know or even care whether the country got independence or not. I even heard people openly criticising the idea of independence: according to them, the British Raj was best. In their estimation, the King of England and his descendants were fit to run the country and no one else. Most of the Hindu community, when they realised that they had become part of the Muslim state of Pakistan, prepared to leave their homeland for mainly Hindu India. Sifting through the discarded and abandoned papers, I came across a handwritten diary of a Hindu man whom we knew as a respected village elder. Other people would have burned their unwanted papers and books, but Hindus would not burn any paper, and particularly books, because they believed that books are sacred and if they were burned, or even touched your feet, the god Saraswati, the god of learning, would be unhappy. So the papers, journals, and that diary I found, were abandoned. This may have planted in me the idea of keeping a diary.

The diary I kept for ten years from my time in medical school to coming to the UK was among papers which were looted and burnt during the Civil War in 1971, which led to the creation of Bangladesh.

But from that time on, I have kept a daily diary which has become such a habit that I feel uncomfortable when I miss a day. My wife has never commented about it but my children sometimes ask what the point is of an ordinary person like me keeping a diary. Perhaps they are right to be dubious, but I feel happy that I can account for whatever happened in my life, this day, say, 25 years ago, 20 years ago, 15 or 5 years ago

When I start writing in a New Year, the first page is always the same, invariably devoted to God Almighty, for I have always prayed to Him for the health and happiness of my family. The first page of my diary for 1997 was no different and it began:

> "In the name of Allah the Almighty I begin to write the diary of 1997. I pray to Allah that in the forthcoming year, we all remain in good health and have peace of mind. Pray to Him for the good health and happiness of myself and my wife who intends to visit Bangladesh this year. I Pray to Him that Sajal gets a suitable bride and gets married. I Pray to Him that Faisal becomes the father of a healthy child and our first grandchild. I Pray to Allah that Julekha remains in good health and spirits and continues her preparation for her 'A' levels. I Pray to Him that the relations in Bangladesh remain in good health. The New Year started with extreme cold and the temperature was below freezing. There was unmelted snow and ice with short and dark days. It is not a good sight especially when one is not well with flu and back pain."

Those were the words of the first day of 1997. Now, when I am writing this memoir it looks strange, unreal and like a bad dream. Not for a moment could I have imagined what lay ahead. In January, we were a happy and contented family, but at the end of the year the family was in complete ruin. So much pain, so much suffering, so much human misery, that I still feel it is unreal.

In this chapter, so important to my life, I use some of my diary entries to convey the immediacy of the events and the vividness of my feelings as they unfolded.

4th January, Saturday - "We are thinking about Aliyya and Faisal. From what I hear from Hashi I don't know what the future holds. It seems Aliyya is irresponsible, downright rude, devoid of any compassion and feeling for others. I hope she improves as the time goes by".

17th January, Friday – "This afternoon Hashi, Aliyya, and her sister came to my office and had her pelvic scan. There is a foetus. I spoke to the gynaecologist – it is there! I am a grandfather!"

25th January, Saturday – "All the expectation of having a grandchild is gone tonight, when Aliyya was admitted to the hospital with a miscarriage. She is immature and boasted about her pregnancy even when it was not well established".

When Aliyya missed a period and a urine test and scan showed she was pregnant, we were all delighted. She had the symptoms of early pregnancy and could not continue with her studies, so she came home and stayed with her parents and occasionally visited us. On the day she had a miscarriage, she came to our house and at lunch met other friends who were also young mothers. One of them commented on the fact that Aliyya had gained some weight and her tummy was already bulging. This was true and she should have appreciated it. Instead she took it offence and went home to her parents. Her mother was disabled but had been a midwife. What happened there we do not know, but she might have assumed that the weight gain was not due to pregnancy but to lack of exercise and a high calorie diet.

Aliyya decided to do vigorous exercises, and the result was that she started bleeding and ended up miscarrying. This was a terrible blow to us. We had built up so much hope and liked to say to each other things like: if it is a girl, how nice she will look, because the children of mixed marriages are all very attractive and beautiful. In my view, one night's unwise behaviour could have led to the miscarriage, and all our hopes were dashed.

8th February – *"Today is 'Id-ul-Fitr' (a most auspicious festival day in the Islamic calendar – which marks the end of the monthly fast of Ramadan). Sajal and Faisal are both away – I hope we can celebrate it together next year."*

14th February – *"Iron gate from the house was removed, this sort of racist attack did not happen for a long time ..."*

I got the gate back.

16th February – *"Once again the iron gate had been removed and abandoned a few hundred yards away. Julekha was leaving for Germany with her school orchestra – She was upset about it".*

The racial attack on the property returned with a vengeance.

28th February – *"Rachel's parents came and had supper with us. They are committed Christians and not happy about their daughter's wedding to my son. From my point I have no objection, provided Sajal and Rachel are happy".*

1st March – *"Once again the iron gate has been stolen by vandals – this is the third time within a month. Someone is doing it deliberately and this is the price I have to pay for staying in this country".*

9th March – *"Sajal and Rachel got engaged today. We hope and Pray to Allah that their life together becomes a successful one. I do believe in Providence.".*

27th March – Hashi complained about abdominal pain and on examination I found a mass in the right upper quadrant. It frightened me. I asked her to see her GP. The GP has referred her to Mr Sagor, a consulltant surgeon.

1st April – *"Tonight as I write this diary, I am at peace with myself, for by the grace of the Almighty, Hashi's abdominal ultra-sound revealed a huge gallstone – so big that my radiology colleague had not seen such a big one. It was such a relief and I thanked Allah a million times – who answered my Prayers. She later saw Mr Sagor who wants to operate as soon as possible."*

5th April – *"I could not sleep well last night. Woke up at 6 am and went to the BUPA hospital at 7 am – where I found Hashi very tense. She calmed down when the Pre-med was given. She had a very successful operation and a huge stone was removed".*

8th April – *"Life is full of drama and surprise. One was enacted today! In the evening, Julekha alerted me of the sound of the opening of the garage doors. I rushed outside and became face-to-face with two young white youths who were trying to steal two bicycles in the garage. I nearly got hold of one of them. Faisal chased them across the road, in the process got hurt in the shin."*

20th April – *"Early in the morning I took Faisal and Aliyya to Leeds. I got there in three hours. Faisal showed me around his department. I am so pleased with Faisal's performance though lots to be desired from Aliyya. I returned home safely."*

4th May – *"Hashi and I went to London to the St. James' Court Hotel for organising the reception of Sajal and Rachel's wedding."*

11th May – *"Hashi, Sajal and Rachel went to Green Street in East London for wedding dress shopping. We bought a necklace for Rachel."*

23rd May – *"No end of Faisal saga. He has come home to study but his attitude to studying has not changed and I very much doubt whether he will make it. Aliyya is serious about her study – she will make it, but what about Faisal? If he falls behind, then he will feel inferior to Aliyya."*

16th June – *"Went to St. James' Court Hotel and paid a deposit of £1,000 for Sajal's wedding reception in September."*

19th June – *"Aliyya and David brought all their household belongings and stored them in my garage. I helped unloading them."*

20th June – *"Faisal is staying with his in-law's – No hope of getting through his exams."*

23rd June – "Today, all the members of the family, except Julekha, are at home. Rachel is staying with us – getting ready for her Part I MRCP Exam."

26th June – "Good news! Both Faisal and Aliyya have passed their First Year exams."

30th June – "Because I had no work in the morning, I went to Green Street in London and ordered the invitation cards for Sajal's wedding."

1st July – "Already half of this year has gone. It was a sunny day today. No patients on the ward so came home early and did some gardening."

5th July – "Went to Austin Reed in London and met up with Sajal to order made-to-measure suits for his wedding, one for him and another for me."

17th July – "Despite a heavy schedule, I came home at 6.30 pm. At home I found Faisal lying on the settee – not very well. Hashi asked him to go and see the GP. Both of them went to Faisal's in-laws' house.

Got a frantic telephone call at 7 pm. Faisal not well. We went to see him, running temperature, blocked nose and flu symptoms. Everybody got uptight. I went to see him twice."

18th July 1997 – "TOO PAINFUL TO WRITE ON THIS PAGE AND NEXT PAGES.

THIS IS THE DARKEST DAY OF MY LIFE. FOR ON THIS DAY, SUPPOSED TO BE MY 60TH BIRTHDAY, I LOST MY BELOVED SON, FAISAL, A VICTIM OF MENINGOCOCCAL SEPTICAEMIA. I WILL NEVER, NEVER, EVER FORGET THIS DAY TILL MY LAST BREATH IN THIS WORLD."

My diary for 1997 remains blank from the 18th July until the 6th August. I couldn't write anything, let alone my diary. I did not consider myself a human being on those days; I did not know how the glorious summer days passed. I have lost the most precious thing in my life – my son.

It is no exaggeration to say that there was no hurdle that I would not have crossed for the sake of my son, Faisal. If someone had asked me to cross the Pacific Ocean alone in a boat I would have done so. If someone had said go to the top of Mount Everest to find him, I would have done so. In other words I would have given my life for my Faisal.

In the Indian subcontinent there is a story which is told to every student:

When Humayun, the only son of Babur the Lion, the founder of the Mogul Empire, became ill and the Hakims and physicians gave up hope for his life, Babur, realising that with the death of Humayun there would be no descendant to rule the Moghul Empire, prayed to Allah the Almighty, holding the corner of his bed. He prayed that the life of Humayun would be spared and his own should be taken instead. His prayer was granted. Babur started feeling unwell and Humayun started to improve. Ultimately Humayun survived and Babur died. Humayun went on to become a famous king and became even more famous by being the father of another Moghul Emperor, Akbar The Great.

I simply narrate this story, because if I had been given the opportunity and option, I would have taken the role of Babur with Faisal as Humayun.

Until the night of the 17th July 1997, we were a happy family. Against all the odds we had made it. I managed to hold on to the consultant's job, despite many changes within the NHS. It is true that there were disappointments, such as not getting a merit award, but when I came home to the family each night I felt happy and contented.

18th July is a memorable day for me, for it is my birthday. The 18th July 1997 would have been more memorable because it would have been my 60th birthday. It was a Friday and it was already planned that I would not have a clinic in the afternoon. Instead, after lunch and Friday prayer, my wife and I would go to a nice hotel in Surrey, where there was going to be a meeting of alumni of my medical schools. The reunion was on Saturday and Sunday, where as many as 75 doctors and their families would attend. Our plan was to go there one day early to celebrate my birthday. I had been to this hotel before, which was situated in a wood with a lake outside. I had planned to spend the evening quietly with my wife, while Julekha was in Prague with her school orchestra, Faisal was with Aliyya at his in-laws and Sajal, my elder son was in his London flat. Everything was so well organised.

I now need to expand the spare, stark words of that last diary entry:

On the 17th July – the day before this planned weekend trip – I was exceptionally busy at the hospital, but when I returned home at 6.30 p.m. I found Faisal lying on the settee, with Aliyya sitting by his side. My wife had already asked him to visit his GP, who had seen him half an hour earlier. Faisal was told that there was a bit of 'flu around and he would be all right the following day. My wife told me she had been worried about meningitis and was glad the doctor had cleared Faisal, so now we could go on our trip to the hotel tomorrow in peace. I agreed with her.

Soon afterwards Faisal said he was feeling better and said to Aliyya "Let's go home", meaning his in-laws' house. Aliyya's parents were on holiday for a week from the 12th, so the house was empty apart from Aliyya's 90-year-old grandfather.

At 7 p.m. we received a telephone call from Aliyya saying that Faisal was having difficulty breathing. She was panic-stricken. We were about to have our supper. We immediately drove to their house which was less than a mile and a half away. It took only five minutes but all the time I was thinking, wondering what this difficulty in breathing could be due to. The only serious problem I could think of which could be life threatening is epiglottitis, which is the inflammation of the epiglottis, the valve between the air entry to the windpipe and entry of food to the gullet. Epiglottitis in adults and children can be fatal in a very short time.

We reached their house, anxious as to what we would see. In the upstairs bedroom there was hardly a place to set your feet, with clothes scattered everywhere, bottles of liquid for cleaning contact lenses, books, and so on. It looked disorganised and unhygienic, but this was not our house and telling the young couple what to do was counter-productive, so we had given up doing so a long time ago. We found Faisal lying on his back, but not in a great deal of distress. His nose was blocked, but he could breathe easily and effortlessly through his mouth. There was a mild temperature, and so I thought it might be 'flu. But suspecting that meningitis was also a possibility, I asked him if he had any headache, neck stiffness or aversion to looking towards the light. He said no and I was reassured. Aliyya kept on telling us it was 'flu, because she had had it a few days ago, all the members of her family had had it, and the doctor herself diagnosed it. Even then my wife, with her mother's instinct, felt all was not well. Faisal did not look well. Usually he was a strong individual, so why did he look so ill with just a slight fever and so-called 'flu? She suggested to Aliyya that we had better take Faisal to our own home. Aliyya was short with us and said: "What can't I do here, that you would be doing at your home?" There was no answer to this question. I pleaded with her that there was no one at home except herself and very old grandfather. She would not budge and Faisal wanted to stay.

We came back to our house, feeling uneasy. The food was cold and I did not feel like warming it up. We finished our meal and continued to think about Faisal. At times I told myself "You are overreacting and making a mountain out of a molehill".

I decided to go and visit him again at 10 p.m. My wife could not come with me, because one of our friends was coming and would be accompanied by a famous film actress from Bangladesh. Hashi asked me to go and see Faisal, and to ring her if anything was wrong. I thought of taking some antibiotics with me, but never did.

When I arrived at the house, I went straight upstairs and found Faisal lying face down with his whole back exposed. His thin, skinny body, which is rather like mine, was in full view. There was no one at home. I asked Faisal how he was and he said he was feeling a bit better and felt like sleeping. His breathing was fine. I had a thermometer with me and his temperature was 38.1°C, a little above normal. By this time Aliyya had arrived. She had been to pick her sister up from somewhere. Everything seemed fine, except that when I felt Faisal's pulse there was a rapid heartbeat, which was unexpected with the temperature he had. I paused for a moment and thought why? I once again dismissed it as 'flu. Also, although I was a doctor, I specialised in other conditions, and was not aware that there is a condition called meningococcal septicaemia, or blood poisoning, which can happen quite differently and separately from the signs and symptoms of meningitis. The signs and symptoms of meningitis are well documented and highlighted by the Government, but septicaemia is less well publicised but more dangerous, and had I known this, perhaps my son would have been alive today.

I left him around 10.30 p.m. and left behind the thermometer, some Panadol and my doctor's emergency telephone number. I instructed Aliyya to contact us at any time if she should feel Faisal's condition had deteriorated or noticed anything abnormal. That was the last time I saw my son alive.

The next paragraphs and pages were very painful for me to write. Each time I put my pen to paper, I hesitated. I left off for days and weeks and then tried again. The incident was years ago, but to me it is as if it were yesterday. The pain is just as bad, and the wound as fresh. Whenever I tried to write about the events of the 18th July 1997, my hand trembled and my eyes filled with tears. I became emotional and considered myself not to be a normal human being.

Still I knew I had to write the account of that fateful day, the day that stole sunlight from my life and also from the lives of my family. My wife, who had normally a bubbly character, friendly and fun-loving, had become a mental wreck. She had no contact with our old friends and only a few close relations abroad kept her going. Sajal was busy, keeping himself occupied with work, but inside he was so traumatised at the loss of his only brother and support in this country. My daughter, Julekha, was only 17 at the time, a very happy child, born and bought up as English, good at studies, sports, and music and she had everything in life and was looking forward to her university education. She had decided on Manchester because it would not have been far from Leeds University where Faisal and Aliyya were students. Then this sudden blow shattered her life. She continued her studies, but underneath she was traumatised.

But to return to that fateful day.

In the morning, at around 7.30 a.m., we were woken by a frantic telephone call from Aliyya telling us that Faisal was very unwell. We never had time to think but jumped into the car and drove over to their house.

When we reached there, I found Faisal hardly able to talk coherently, with a definite rash on his body. Without checking his pulse or recording his temperature, I knew he was ill, but not so ill that he was at death's door. I guessed that there was some sort of infection which could be put right with hospital admission and appropriate antibiotics and re-hydration. I dialled 999 for an ambulance. The ambulance arrived within three to five minutes and the paramedics put him into the back of the ambulance. I noticed they wore rubber gloves and one of them recorded his blood pressure. The ambulance drove away to Hemel Hempstead General Hospital A&E Department. Meanwhile, I telephoned the Medical Registrar on call and told him that my son was on his way to the A&E Department, with pyrexia and skin rash. Hashi and Aliyya accompanied him.

I returned home to get ready to go to the hospital myself. I had told my wife to phone me from the A&E Department. When she did not, I telephoned A&E and when I spoke to her, she told me that Faisal was seriously ill. I spoke to the Registrar who said that Faisal was in shock and they were trying to resuscitate him. I panicked and did not know who to speak to or what to do. I tried to contact a consultant colleague who had already left for the hospital.

Like a man possessed, I drove to the hospital, praying to Allah all the time. I parked my car and was shown to a room where he was being treated. All the staff and doctors in the room knew me. Faisal was nearly unconscious, his eyes were red and swollen, and he was tossing his head from side to side. I saw the monitor, showing that his blood pressure was low and his pulse was high. I could not bear it, and I burst out to Faisal, "Son, you are going to make it".

These were the last words I spoke to him and I doubt whether he heard them.

I was helpless, going aimlessly from one room to another, trying to clutch at straws. I went to a consultant colleague's room, but he was not there. Back at A&E, I found the consultant in charge and explained to him that my son was in that room. He immediately went in and took over. I never had the courage to go in there myself. Aliyya and my wife were sitting on the floor but they now came out. Meanwhile the hospital was in full swing and all the consultants were aware that my son was desperately ill.

We were given a room to sit where Hashi, Aliyya and I sat and prayed to Allah. Every ten to fifteen minutes, the chest physician, the cardiologist or the A&E consultant would come to tell us that his condition was not getting any better. He was in septicaemic shock and they had given antibiotics and been trying to push fluid through and raise his blood pressure, without any success. The cardiologist's presence was due to the fact that Faisal's heart had stopped and needed a pace maker to be inserted. I knew for a fact that he was not going to pull through and each time somebody came to see us I burst into tears. Hashi remained calm, as if in a dream, not really understanding what was going on. At one point the A&E consultant said – and this was the only voice of consolation so far that morning – that, "his blood pressure has picked up". I was encouraged but only to have my hopes dashed a few minutes later.

I felt helpless, looking for some support from my nearest and dearest. I thought of my elder son Sajal, who had planned to go on holiday that day. He and his fiancée were supposed to go abroad for a week. My hospital colleagues tried to contact him and eventually found him. I spoke to him at about 11 a.m. and told him that Faisal was dangerously ill. In fact, by that time it had come to the point of no return, they were just trying one thing or another to keep his heart beating.

I went and stood outside the corner of the building. There was a light drizzle and people were coming and going as they do every day, while I was standing helplessly in my own hospital waiting for my eldest son to come, so that I could stand with one arm on his shoulder, as if I was lame and unable to bear my own weight.

Sajal and Rachel came within half an hour. We all sat in one room. More consultant colleagues came to see us and there was more bad news. Neither I nor Sajal, who is a surgeon, had the nerve to enter the room where Faisal was lying and where so much torture was going on in his little, slim body.

At around noon or 12.30, a Friday – the most auspicious day in the Muslim calendar more so today because it was the Prophet's birthday – all was over. The A&E consultant colleague wanted our permission to switch off the life support machine, which we gave. Faisal went to eternal sleep at around the time when all pious Muslims were going to the mosque for the weekly Friday Prayer. I am sure his soul joined the others for this Prayer. In life, he had never missed a single prayer. Even on the day he died he said his early morning prayer at 4.30 a.m.

When the final word came, we all burst into a loud cry, except Hashi. She was still stunned. All my consultant colleagues, anaesthetists, chest physicians, cardiologist, and A&E consultants came to console us and they broke down too, but Hashi's eyes were dry. I asked her to cry but no tears came. The scene in that room was indescribable so I am not going to try.

After an hour or so, maybe around 1.30 p.m., Faisal's body was laid in a room which used to be my room when I did the OPD clinic. He was lying with his face upwards, peaceful, calm and solemn. His black beard shone in the glistening July sunshine which was coming through the south-facing window. There were some marks on his face.

I could not stop wailing. His body was still warm. I touched his feet again and again. I remembered those feet, which were so small. I used to steady him when he started walking. I played football with him, the two of us on one side and Sajal on the other. Those lovely brows, similar to mine in my younger days. Only a few days ago he was comparing my youthful photograph with his forehead, and was saying to Aliyya "look my forehead is exactly like my dad's". So many things went through my mind as I looked at his body.

By this time, the news of Faisal's death had spread like wildfire. In the hospital, everybody – from porters to consultants, from clerks to nurses – wanted to say something to us. I hardly realised who was saying what. How the time passed I cannot say. I wanted to stay with Faisal forever. Since the morning, none of us had any food or drink, but we had no desire to do so. I still could not believe it to be true. I thought it to be some sort of dream.

Time wore on. My A&E colleague asked me to take prophylactic antibiotics, which he had brought from the pharmacy. Faisal died of meningococcal septicaemia, so everyone who had come into contact with him must take these antibiotics. We all took it with a sip of water and this was our only drink of the day.

At around 3 p.m. we decided to leave Faisal where he lay and we went home. I did not have the nerve to drive.

We arrived home, empty, dazed and without any human feelings of pain or emotion. As if all of us were numb, walking in space, not on the earth. We all sat on the carpet and cried together.

I thought I must telephone the mosque and let them know. After dialling a few times, I got hold of Seraj Khan who was in charge of Muslim burials. He came immediately. Meanwhile I phoned one or two of my immediate friends.

I will never forget Seraj Khan's contribution. He said "Don't worry about anything – I am going to arrange his funeral and the necessary religious arrangements".

News spread within the community, neighbours, and our homes in

Bangladesh like wild-fire. Even before we reached home, there were colleagues who knocked on the door to pay their sympathies.

At home during the afternoon, evening and at night, there were streams of people from the local community, Hindus, Muslims, and Christians, all of whom wanted to say a few words to us. But of course, we could not speak coherently to anyone. The only sane and rational person at home was Rachel, my son's fiancée, who managed all the telephone calls, received the visitors and answered their queries. A friend's wife brought some soup for us, the only food we consumed.

The night descended, the night when I would have been in a hotel, enjoying my 60th birthday and getting ready to meet my fellow medics from the medical schools.

We passed the night of 18th July awake much of the time. There was no one to console us. There was only me, my wife and Sajal, all of whom craved consolation. We three prayed together in the early morning and I asked Hashi to read from the Quran. But she did not know how to read it – she had not practiced it in a long time, and tried but could not. Sajal and I tried to read from the English translation just to get some peace and consolation somewhere.

Back in Bangladesh, on occasions like this, relatives take over and do all the counselling and religious ceremonies so that the bereaved are left to mourn.

Aliyya was obviously heartbroken, but was consoled by her parents and spent most of the time with them. The way she expressed her grief was different from ours. She was at least able to take consolation from her "deep religious conviction" that Faisal's death was written on that day, even before he was born. I as a Muslim should believe it, but common sense takes over and tries to deny it.

On Saturday, the postbag was full of condolence letters, postcards and there were constant telephone calls and an unending stream of visitors. We felt barely human at the time and were unable to talk to many of the visitors. Most of them were from the Asian community and some from London, the Midlands and other parts of the country.

There was one person who came from London and we were so tired and exhausted that Rachel told them that we were in no position to see them. He was offended, and argued on the doorstep that he had come all the way from London. He probably had a point, but if I were in his position, I would not have minded even if I had to go to his house a hundred times. Was he genuinely sad or had he just come to show us his so-called sympathy? A person with real feeling and sorrow would not have minded at all. I felt that perhaps he came to see us in our worst hour not with a heavy heart, but to see as an onlooker, like people who stop and have a look at the road traffic accident or the air crash.

Saturday was a sunny, pleasant summer's day. Rachel had to put a notice on the door saying "No more visitors please – the family needs rest". That notice brought tears to my eyes. Why, why is it me? Night came and we told ourselves that one day had passed since Faisal's death. This is the way more days, weeks, months and years would pass, but we would never see him or be able to hug him.

Sunday morning was fresh, sunny, with a smell of flowers from the gardens. The birds were still singing in the garden – the same way they had sung the day Faisal got married exactly a year earlier. But what a difference between that song and this one, I thought.

More guests came from far and near and I was getting worried about how to receive Julekha, who was returning that evening from Austria. She was only 17, a close friend of her brother and affectionate towards him. She would arrive after a 24-hour coach journey – how would we break the news to her? Who would do it? How would she react?

Her coach was due to arrive at 6.30 p.m. At 6 p.m. we still had a visitor, a distant relative. We asked her to leave and she did so reluctantly. Oddly, exactly six weeks later, she died too from acute heart failure.

Julekha phoned from Dover that she was well and that the coach would arrive in St. Albans on time, with no idea of what news awaited her. I asked Sajal to go and pick her up because Julekha would be tremendously happy to see him.

She came home but looked tired. Sajal had told her nothing about Faisal. We all sat in the conservatory. Sajal, Rachel, Aliyya, myself and my wife. Outside was calm, still sunny, and the birds were still singing. Julekha sat nearby me. She must have realised that something was amiss because everybody was so silent. Why was nobody smiling or greeting her with open arms and kisses on the cheek as was usually the case? She must have wondered why I had not shaven in three days. She sitting between me and Sajal.

Sajal broke the news to her in simple terms: that after a sudden illness lasting less than twelve hours, Faisal, her dearest brother, had died on Friday morning. She burst into uncontrollable tears and all of us joined her. I cried so much and had so many tears rolling down my cheeks that as a medical man I never thought it was possible. That was how the news was broken to my dearest daughter, Julekha. She now had only one brother. How sad, how pathetic. Who can answer the question why?

Night fell. There was added anxiety when Rachel developed a high temperature. Although all of us who came into contact with Faisal were given prophylactic antibiotics, her temperature worried us. It later turned out her fever was due to a reaction to those antibiotics.

We were in constant touch with my brother-in-law, Kafi, in Bangladesh. He was much younger than us, but a capable man of many parts. On hearing this sad news, he decided to come immediately – for this gesture I will remain ever grateful to him.

On Monday 21st July Kafi arrived at the airport and was met at the airport by our friend Mr Biswas. Kafi arrived at our home around 7 a.m. His presence gave us a lot of confidence and courage. He sat with Hashi and took her hand in his. This touch from one's own flesh and blood is worth much more than any sedatives or counselling. Kafi could not say anything. What could he say? All that was needed was his presence and this alone was a tremendous boost for the morale of the whole family. As the sun rose, and the day progressed, there were further visitors. This time they were received and managed by Kafi. Rachel was now mainly concerned about making food for the family.

Muslim tradition and Islam demand a quick burial, but this could not be done in the UK, because the necessary formalities could not be completed during the weekend.

Saying goodbye

We decided that the burial would take place on Tuesday after midday prayer. Faisal's mortal remains were at the undertakers in St. Albans. In Islamic society the body is surrounded by people reading the Quran until the burial takes place, which is of course not possible here in this country.

At 10 a.m. on Monday 21st July, Sajal, Kafi and I went to the Registrar's Office to collect Faisal's death certificate. Sajal drove and I sat in the back with Kafi. The Registrar, a nice gentleman, already knew me and the tragedy that befallen us. He issued the certificate with no questions asked.

After collecting the certificate, with the help of other local friends I went out to the city centre to buy other necessary articles that would be required for the ceremonial wash at 10 a.m. on the day of the funeral. I remember going to British Home Stores where I found people happy and cheerful on a summer day. I told myself none of the fellow shoppers would have any inkling as to who I was and what was going through my mind. Only three days ago we were as happy as the next person on the road and now I am a wretched father trying to buy things needed for my son's funeral. What a tragedy. This is happening the wrong way round. Faisal should have done this for me, which would have been the natural thing to do. But what I am doing is unnatural, unacceptable and pathetic.

By nightfall, everything was ready for the burial on 22nd July 1997.

It was once again a bright, clear day with pleasant sunshine. We were expecting a lot of people in our house, in the mosque and at the cemetery.

In the morning, Hashi told me to shave, which I hadn't done for four days. I had not looked at my face in the mirror during that time. She insisted we must give our son a "nice farewell". My face was full of white beard and black circles under my eyes, a consequence of incessant weeping, waking at night and lack of nutrition. After shaving I put on a clean Islamic dress with a cap on my head.

Faisal's body was with the undertaker, which was about a mile from our home. The events would start 10 a.m. Faisal's body would be ritually washed in the Islamic tradition. The coffin would lie in state at our house for an hour and a half and then the hearse would go to the local mosque, where prayers would be said, followed by a special funeral prayer called 'Janaza'. From there the hearse would go to the cemetery where the burial was scheduled for 2 p.m.

By 9.30 a.m. on 22nd July the house was full of people from near and far. It was decided that Kafi and Julekha would stay at home and receive the visitors, and Sajal, my wife and I would go to the undertaker where the ritual washing would be done by religious Muslims. In truly Islamic tradition, this is done by males to the males and females to the female. Aliyya, a converted Muslim, still wearing a veil or hijab in public, insisted she would like to be present during the washing. We had no alternative but to agree with her. We reached the undertakers office at 10 a.m, where another five people had already assembled. Two were Faisal's friends and three were from the local mosque and were very well known to us. Sajal, my wife and I did not have enough courage to attend the ritual, so we waited outside. Five men and my daughter-in-law went inside for the washing which we were told would take an hour.

I have seen many such washings as a young boy in my village in Bangladesh. The body is kept on a platform and every part of the body is cleaned with new soap, new towels and warm water. All the orifices are individually cleaned and dried. When the body is thoroughly cleaned and dried, two pieces of white cloth (again new and washed), are wrapped around it (in women three pieces are required). When this is complete, the body is ready for the Janaza Prayer. The body is kept on the platform and the Imam leads a prayer for the soul of the deceased. This prayer can be done in the mosque or near where the person will be buried.

When Faisal's ritual wash was complete, he was taken into another room and we were asked to see him. His whole body was wrapped in a snow-white cloth, only his face was displayed. One of the men who took the leading part in washing said to me: "Look, doctor, how well he looks – ready to travel to the next world!" Faisal's face looked peaceful, as if in a deep sleep, which he liked so much. When alive, he would sleep until midday with the scorching sun beaming through the window and his mother would scold him to get up. Now my Faisal was in a deep sleep – eternal sleep – and no one could wake him. His black beard and wide forehead with slightly curly hair gave an appearance of someone who had fallen a martyr in a holy war. Our eyes were dry and we ourselves felt peace within.

Faisal's coffin was put in a hearse and brought to our house. By the time we arrived, the whole house, including the garden, was full of people. There were some who were genuinely shocked and came to pay their sympathy to us, but we felt there were others who just came as if for a day out and some sort of picnic. Some of them asked very personal questions to Julekha, who was on her own to receive the guests. There were others who were anxious to have their refreshments. I did not have the time or sense to see who had come, but I saw many of my colleagues, such as the Chair of the Staff Committee, Medical Director, representatives from the Trust Board Chairman, and representatives from the Bangladesh Medical Association. Despite our request, there were lots of flowers. True Islamic tradition forbids any flowers for the dead.

Faisal's coffin was displayed in the new dining room, his face turned towards Mecca. We allowed Aliyya to spend some time with Faisal on her own. This was the very room they got married in, in the Islamic way, exactly a year ago, and my speech had then ended "That they be happy forever in this life and beyond!" After Aliyya, we the immediate family members, Sajal, Julekha, my wife and me, gathered around the coffin. We all spent quite some time there. He was so peaceful, so sublime and looked so handsome. I stroked his beard with the back of my hand and joked "Not a single grey hair", which brought a smile on the face of Julekha. We all kissed his forehead – it was ice-cold.

After we moved away, it was the turn of the visitors. There were people from other religions who were told not to touch the coffin for it was in a 'Pure State'. Only Muslims could touch it. There were many Muslims who were continually reciting from the Quran from the corner of the room, when the procession of people entered from one end and came out from the other. Many of those now present has been in this room on Faisal's wedding day a year earlier. The birds were still singing in the trees and there was plenty of food displayed in the garden, mostly brought by friends and relatives. What a contrast between this food and bird song compared with a year ago. Why? I have asked this question many times before and still do, but there is no answer.

The coffin was transferred to the hearse and Faisal's last journey started. In the driveway there were people and more people, women, children, men, Asians, whites and blacks. It was out of the same driveway that he and his newly-wed wife were taken in my car, showered with white petals and confetti, as Sajal and I drove them slowly to Luton airport for their honeymoon only a year ago. What a different procession and what a different atmosphere...

The hearse gradually inched towards the mosque. There are two mosques – one Bangladeshi and another Pakistani. Faisal's coffin was taken to the Bangladeshi mosque where the whole mosque was full of people. There were all of Faisal's friends from university, all young, many of them bearded like Faisal. Normally the mosque is only a tenth full for a mid-day prayer, but for the *Janaza* Prayer there was not a single seat available. There were people standing in the road and their cars blocked the road causing a traffic jam.

After the midday prayer, the *Janaza* Prayer was said, attended by the whole community, Bangladeshis, Pakistanis, Indians, Mauritians, Arabs and Africans. The lid of the coffin was taken off and there was an orderly queue past the coffin to see Faisal's face. When they had all passed, Sajal kissed his forehead and I was the last one to kiss him goodbye, and Sajal and I closed the coffin. It was carried to the hearse that was waiting outside.

I sat near the coffin on one side and Sajal sat on the other. It was an all-male affair. Women are not allowed to go to the mosque or to the cemetery.

The hearse started its slow journey towards the cemetery. There were many cars following us. Those of us inside were silently reciting from the Quran – "Allah is one and Almighty and Prophet Mohammed is His messenger!"

The hearse arrived at a T-junction in the cemetery. There were hundreds of people already gathered there, most of them are unknown to me. It is traditional that the immediate relations carry the coffin on their shoulders, from the hearse to the grave. There were four people carrying, with Sajal and I in front, and there must have been many others following behind. It was hot and sunny and I was carrying my beloved son's body on my shoulder.

It was almost five hundred yards from the hearse to the grave which was quite deep, nearly six feet. The floor was concrete and the walls brick-built, unlike in Bangladesh, where there is no system of brick and cement, and the body is left bare on the soil, only covered with white cloth.

Faisal's coffin was lowered gently into the grave. When the coffin firmly rested on the floor, the lid was once again removed and his face was turned towards Mecca. This was my last glimpse of him. The lid was put back and a concrete slab was put in to secure the grave.

Sajal and I, being the chief mourners, had the privilege of putting soil on the grave first. I did it gently. When Sajal put in some lumps of soil, for some reason a concrete slab broke in half and fell on to the coffin. I managed to retrieve it and secure it firmly. The other people took over and put the soil on to the grave and when finished it looked like a mound. When the last bit of soil had been put in the ceremony was almost over, except that the Imam said the final prayer to Allah for the peace of the departed soul of Faisal and the others who were lying in this cemetery for it to continue until the day of Judgement.

At the cemetery, there were hundreds of people, mostly young and from various universities, most of whom I didn't know. There were Arabs, white Muslims, Asians and Africans. Some of them came to embrace me and console me and I asked them how they had come to know Faisal. To my surprise, most of them said they had never met "Brother Faisal", but knew him through his works, lectures, videos and tapes. This was the first time I learned that Faisal was a popular speaker on Islamic and religious affairs. Apparently, he had been a regular at various Islamic conferences up and down the country, and had undertaken research on Islam, because of his passion for understanding our religion, the fate of Muslims and the after-life. From the many people from various backgrounds who came to his funeral I realised for the first time how popular Faisal had been in Islamic circles. The events and sights on that afternoon at the cemetery, and the young people who came in droves, showed me that Faisal's life had not been in vain. He had achieved so much in his short life that I felt consoled.

Islamic tradition demands that people leave the graveyard as soon as the burial and religious ceremony is over. Once the mourners go more than forty yards beyond the grave, angels descend on the grave to ask questions about the deceased's deeds – good or bad – carried out in this world.

How I got from the graveyard to my house, I do not know. But when I did arrive at the house, I found the house and garden full of people. Some of them were eating, others just roaming in the garden. Some were sad, others showed no emotion. I could not eat much, nor could my wife. Instead we looked after others and listened to what they were saying. Most people were saying "It was all written in his fate". "It was Allah's wish". Who could argue with these sentiments. Certainly I was not in a position to do so, but I kept on asking myself – why me? Why? Why? I said to myself: if a very religious person such as the Grand Mufti or the Imam of the holy mosques of Mecca and Medina were confronted with the same situation, would he accept that it was "written" or "Allah has taken him away", in other words, as God's wish? I just wonder. People's kind words and their condolences did not penetrate me and the same question kept on creeping back: Why? Why me?

One by one most people left and by 7 p.m. almost everybody had left. The house was empty, a quiet vacuum. Only six people were in the house, including Kafi and Rachel. Rachel did wonderfully well. She kept the house going and prepared food for us for the night, which we ate in the conservatory, silently. Night fell. I kept on thinking: my beloved son is in the graveyard. This is his first night there. So many nights will come until the day of Judgement.

The following morning, Wednesday, the postman dropped off more mail, letters, and cards from colleagues, unknown people and many of my patients. Some contained hand written poems in calligraphy. I stayed indoors while Sajal, Kafi and Rachel went shopping.

On Thursday, the day was fine to start with, but clouds gathered. Kafi had to return to Bangladesh. Sajal drove him to the airport and was caught in a terrific thunderstorm, but got there safely. Hashi and I sat in the conservatory and said to ourselves that last Thursday, at this time, our Faisal was alive and with us, and now, a week later, he is so far away that no one can reach him. Sure, all of us will have to join him, but for the moment that is no consolation.

With Kafi gone, the house was only occupied by the immediate family. Aliyya had come and gone. She was upset and being consoled by her parents and others. She was young. Her loss would be filled, but as parents it would never be for us.

A week later, Sajal and Rachel were still with us, but had returned to part-time work. Aliyya would stay with us for one night and then at her parent's home the next.

I had noticed a distinct change in Hashi. She looked angry all the time, and would not speak to me properly but looked at me as if I were a stranger. When she did speak, she was trying to apportion blame.

First, blame on herself, for leaving Faisal at his in-law's house on his own; for not going to see him with me at 10 p.m.; for not telephoning at around midnight before we went to bed to see how he was doing. If she had done some of those things, maybe he would have been saved. That seemed to be her reasoning, anyway.

She blamed me for not diagnosing or appreciating the severity of the situation when I saw him at 7 p.m. and again at 10 p.m. She asked what sort of doctor was I when I could not diagnose such a serious condition. She blamed me for not accompanying him to the hospital when the ambulance was called in the morning.

She blamed Aliyya: why did she take all the responsibility on her own shoulders? What care and attention did she provide between 10 p.m. when I last saw him, and the following morning? Why did she not seek help from us or from the doctors whose telephone number was left at her disposal? She felt angry that this irresponsible young girl did not even give Faisal necessary support during the night. She blamed her for all this and with some justification.

She blamed the GP who did not examine him properly and failed to give him antibiotics. She blamed the hospital for not doing much in the first two hours on that Friday morning.

Unfortunately, some of Hashi's criticisms of Aliyya hit home and the girl became upset, unstable and depressed. Her talk was not coherent. The whole atmosphere of the house, which was already gloomy, was made more so by Aliyya and Hashi's attitudes towards each other. It was an unbearable atmosphere. I was worried that Aliyya might harm herself to seek attention.

One evening, Aliyya packed her bag, wrote a lengthy letter about her life with Faisal, and left. We were relieved that one source of tension had been removed and now we did not have to face her every single moment. Her parents used to come every day. They were understandably appreciative and took their daughter back, still wearing a hijab and apparently still Muslim.

The house was empty, terribly empty. I was still on compassionate leave but what could I do? Who should I speak to? Whatever conversations we had were about Faisal and what we had done wrong. There was so much guilt and no one to turn to. I spoke to a psychiatrist friend of mine, who explained that it was a grieving period and no matter what, one day this phase of guilt would not persist. I tried to support my wife but she was not consolable – she poured out her anger against the world, against me, against Aliyya, and against herself.

I took her to various places locally to get away from the four walls of the house, but wherever we went, we would only discuss Faisal. Faisal had grown up here in this area, so all the parks, playing fields and leisure areas were full of his memories. We would come back home more upset and depressed than we had been before going out. I found some consolation by going to the mosque and praying with other people, but Hashi would not do that, so she remained confined within the house.

One day a man came and knocked on the door. He was about mid-forties and named John. He said that he had heard about us from his friend, Pam. He was from an organisation called 'Compassionate Friends'. He came in and told us how his 18-year-old son died suddenly one evening. Somehow, we felt mentally relieved that there were other fellow sufferers like ourselves. John left lots of literature about the anguish that people feel after the loss of their loved one. We could not read them because it was too traumatic, but in some indefinable way John's visit was quite helpful.

We also contacted the Meningitis Trust, and two women came to see us one day. Both of them were well-dressed and well-mannered. They tried to give us facts and figures about deaths from meningitis and meningococcal septicaemia. We – particularly Hashi – did not find them helpful. They left us some literature, including the names and addresses of fellow sufferers and details of events organised by the Meningitis Trust. Somehow, we did not feel able to contact these people.

Although we were mentally half-dead and both lost weight, I was concerned about my two surviving children. Sajal returned to his work at Whittington Hospital and had to make a decision about his wedding and reception, which had all been finalised before this tragedy took place. However, my main concern was for Julekha, such a tender little flower, who was to sit her 'A' levels and how was she going to cope?

While I was still on leave one evening, Sajal and Rachel came to discuss their wedding. The date had been fixed for the 6th September and the reception two weeks later after their honeymoon. The cards had been printed, guest lists, venue and menu had all been finalised and a deposit had been paid. It would have been the happiest occasion of my life and we as a family had decided what clothes we would wear. Faisal and Aliyya would wear total Islamic dress, Sajal and I would wear made-to-measure lounge suits.

When the disaster struck I did not know what to do. Should we cancel the whole thing? So that evening when we were together, including Rachel, we broached the idea of postponing the wedding for a while. Rachel was very upset and started crying.

According to Muslim rites the mourning period lasts 40 days. The wedding day of 6th September fell just outside 40 days. So I relented.

I took the view that our grief, our loss, our pain, would never diminish even if the wedding took place a year or two later so why delay? I agreed that everything should go ahead as planned – let my pain not be a handicap to others. I think Rachel and Sajal were relieved and we also felt better that a decision had been taken.

A few friends and relations were surprised at our decision, and I had to explain it to them.

During my compassionate leave, I never did any work in the garden, which was over-grown; the vegetable plot was not watered so the plants withered. Whenever I went in the garden, I felt Faisal's touch. This was the place he played cricket, badminton and golf. This is the tree he climbed as a young boy and fell. That apple tree is still there, that ground is still there, but my Faisal is beyond reach.

Two weeks passed. Hundreds of letters, cards and other messages came. They were all piled neatly on the mantelpiece, window sills and other spaces around the room. During the week we also had printed a letter for sending to those hundreds of well-wishers who visited us, sent cards, letters or telephoned us, conveying their condolences. It was a simple letter expressing our gratitude for their kindness.

26

Nothing feels normal

I decided to return to work about two weeks after the events. I was dreading it. It was my hospital – I had worked there for nearly 20 years – I knew every corner of the hospital and some of it had been built before my very eyes. How could I pass the A&E Department, which was so familiar to me? How could I make the journey to the hospital – along the same roads as my son was taken by the ambulance? I was full of foreboding and scared of how to face my colleagues, secretaries, medical, and nursing staff and the patients. I did not feel myself a human being. What was I going to do with the patients, when I could not save my own son? What was the point of treating others? So many questions and queries clouded my already disturbed mind.

Still, I made the decision. and at midday on a Monday, I decided to face whatever lay ahead and started the seven-mile journey to my hospital. The road was quiet; the day was dry and bright. I drove slowly. This was the road I had driven along for so many years. I knew every inch of this road. All the while, I was only thinking of my son, his journey to the hospital in the ambulance, the pain he had and the 'torture' he endured during the resuscitation. I was always thinking about him, and his youthful, bearded face constantly flashed through my mind's eye.

I arrived at the hospital and decided not to park the car in the consultant's car park. Instead I parked it in another car park for the junior medical staff, clerical and other ancillary staff. I stayed in the car for a few more minutes; I could not see any people in the car park. I took my brief case and started walking towards my office through a tunnel which is normally used when it rains or snows. The tunnel comes out very close to my office. I avoided eye contact with whoever came in front of me.

I opened my office door and immediately felt better. The room had been cleaned, tidied and dusted. It looked spacious and lovely. It smelt nice and I noticed a bunch of fresh freesias, very skilfully arranged. I smelt them. They were lovely. For a moment I forgot my pain and suffering. There was a card signed by my secretary, nursing and clerical staff. There were about eight signatures with a simple message of "Welcome back". I sat in my chair at my desk, just sat there simply, and stared into space towards the window and the hospital beyond. Then there was a knock at the door. It was Joy, my secretary. I smiled – she smiled back. I thanked her for the flowers and card.

Monday afternoon clinic was usually my follow-up clinic, which meant that I knew the patients already and they came at two-monthly, three-monthly or six-monthly intervals, depending upon the case. I put on my white coat, took my stethoscope and gradually started walking to the familiar clinic. All the staff – clerical, nursing, and ancillary – were getting on with their work. They might have been thinking about me, or perhaps not. Perhaps they felt sorry for me, maybe saying to themselves or their colleagues "poor fellow".

I went to the clinic room. The nurse was as pleasant as before and did not say much about what had happened.

Facing the patients was another ordeal. I started seeing the patients in the usual way and as soon as the first patient walked in, she sympathised with me. Somehow all the patients knew about this tragedy. Many of them tried to console me. I thanked them but felt it would have been better if they hadn't mentioned it. Some of my patients are elderly, in their seventies and eighties. Some of them said they were better and had much less pain since I last injected them. I kept on asking myself – Is life fair? Here is a woman of 83, still alive and well and I am here to treat her, whereas I lost my own son aged only 23. How can this life be fair? Who decides? Is it Allah? If so, is Allah fair? These questions kept on coming into my mind.

The first day passed and I managed. Setting off for home, I went to my car through the tunnel again, avoiding all eye contact with anybody passing.

I could not avoid a consultant anaesthetist colleague. He was a foreigner like me. He knew Faisal when my wife was in hospital with her gall bladder operation. Also, his son and Faisal were classmates. This colleague was involved in the resuscitation of Faisal during that fatal morning. I stopped and both of us broke down. What could one say? A few words were exchanged and we went on our way.

The following day I went to another hospital in the morning for a private clinic. Once again, all the nurses, clerical and medical staff were very sympathetic and wanted to know how my wife was coping. All the patients knew about it and tried to bring up the subject.

The next day – another hospital, another set of staff, clerical, medical and nursing. The nurse who helped me was herself a mother of children of my son's age. She touched my hand and said "I am sorry". I controlled my tears with great difficulty. Patients came and went, and without exception they all were kind and conveyed their condolences to me. There was one patient who was relatively young, in her mid-forties. I had known her for a long time. I started asking her the usual questions regarding her health. She was the only person who did not bring up the subject. I finished examining her and prescribed the necessary medication. She stood up to go and then came closer, touched my hands and said "I know your feelings, doctor. If it is of any consolation to you, my two sons were killed on the same day in a car accident". I said I was sorry for her and inside I felt here was somebody who was even worse off than me. There was another patient that I had known for 15 years, who was very badly affected with arthritis, but never complained. She was always cheerful and I knew that her eldest son had been killed in a traffic accident a few years back. She said "You know me doctor; you know what happened to me – look forward and get on with life".

All these little comments and advice really worked well for me. They gave me a lot of courage and confidence, but unfortunately no counselling was available where it was needed, for my wife. I saw my GP and asked him. I spoke to my psychiatric friends for professional help, but Hashi was not keen. Instead she got busy collecting photographs of Faisal from his birth until his death and framed them in a very big frame and hung it on the wall. In any conversation, she would only show interest if it concerned Faisal, his memory and the events that led to his death.

She ignored the people around her. I wanted to take her out of the home situation, but she would not budge. I was in a real dilemma as to what to do. Sajal, as a junior doctor, hard pressed, newly married, had to commute to Southend, and he too was at breaking-point. Whenever he came home he would argue with his mother about Faisal's death. Being an educated and intelligent man, he would directly blame her and me for it. There was not a single word from him that let us look forward to building our life without Faisal. Since he was the elder son and an able one, I was looking for support from him, but none came. Instead I just used to get upset hearing these arguments with his mother. His work suffered and his colleagues noticed he was not as effective as before. Some of them recommended counselling, which he thought was useless.

Julekha was even more stressed because of her 'A' level exams and the preparation ahead, in addition to the loss of her dear brother.

This was the situation I was in within a month of Faisal's death.

I started writing the diary again from 7th August. I wrote:

"I thought I would never write the diary again, for all intent and practical purposes I am dead – with the demise of Faisal. Still I felt life must go on, and I took up the pen. My hand trembles, my heart is empty; there is a big gap and wide hole which will never be filled up until my dying day".

8th August – "Great emptiness continues. Hashi wakes up every morning and becomes delirious with self-pity and guilt. I wake up at night several times and feel it unreal and a sort of a dream".

9th August – "Once again Hashi was hysterical in the morning – cried loudly about Faisal and once again took the blame on herself. I had difficulty in controlling and consoling her. I myself am very wounded – when I am on my own, tears roll down my cheeks and I cannot control them, and on top of that I have to console everybody else".

10th August – "Sajal and Rachel have now returned to their flat. Sajal had been here since that fateful day of 18th July. Sajal is deeply hurt – more so because he never gave Faisal brotherly love when he was alive. I do not have the energy to do anything such as cutting the grass and picking fruit".

11ᵗʰ August – "I intended to out go somewhere for a few days – perhaps the New Forest – but neither Hashi nor Julekha were interested. So I am incarcerated within the four walls.

I was thinking that my colleague Alex Benjamin retired on his 60ᵗʰ birthday. I lost my dearest son on my 60ᵗʰ birthday, no holiday, no consolation, no counselling and expected to do a full-time job – so what is my life expectancy? I feel there is nobody who cares for me and my welfare, whereas I do for everyone".

12ᵗʰ August – "I took Hashi to the Wildlife Nature Reserve and also to No-Man's Land in Wheathampstead. Still our conversation was mainly around Faisal, and of course, these places contained a lot of memories of Faisal and Sajal playing football, and cricket on these fields.

13ᵗʰ August – "Life is continuing somehow. There is not a single moment I can forget the situation leading to Faisal's death".

14ᵗʰ August – "Today is the 50ᵗʰ anniversary of India/Pakistan Independence from Britain. I remember that day very well as a 10-year-old boy. I would have thought I did very well in the 50 years, but one night a disaster struck and I consider myself a failure".

15ᵗʰ August – "It was exactly a month ago Faisal passed away. It is still unbelievable and unacceptable. Our wound is too deep to heal at any time. Hashi is still depressed and God knows when she is going to recover".

16ᵗʰ August – "I had another argument with Hashi. She is still in deep depression, not trying to pick herself up. None of us knows how to cope with the situation".

20ᵗʰ August – "Mood is subdued everywhere – who knows how long this is going to continue? Aliyya came with her father. Hashi did not communicate, I don't think she likes her presence, but it's wrong".

22ⁿᵈ August, Friday – "It was exactly five Fridays ago that Faisal departed for heaven. Memories still very vivid and fresh. After Jumma Prayer I went to pay a visit to Faisal's grave."

23rd August – "Sajal and I went to the Muslim graveyard, to attend the burial ceremony of an elderly Pakistan lady. There were very many people present there. Faisal's grave is still fresh and this lady is going to be his neighbour in the graveyard until the day of Judgement. After the burial, we said our 'Magreb' Prayer at the graveyard."

25th August – "Bank Holiday – Carnival at St. Albans. It was raining and I did not mind a bit that the carnival was washed away. There were so many memories of the carnival with Faisal as a young boy. Sitting on the pavement for the floats to pass by. Remember throwing the coins to the float. Remember we got excited when we got some free gift from the float. Hearts bleed. I wish I could do it with Faisal's children – that would have been the fulfilment.

Faisal's death has sparked off the discussion amongst the family as to whether we deviated too much from the path of Islam and hence Allah has punished us. Does it mean that we should be more religious than before? Mind you, we always had been and still are God-fearing individuals. True we have not prayed five times a day, true we do not exactly follow the tenets of Islam, but in our hearts we are still true Muslims and will always be."

26th August – "Conflict is going on in my mind about science and religion. Who is right? Where do I find the answer?"

27th August – "I took the plunge and listened to Faisal's tape of his speech given in January 1996. I am amazed. Never did I realise that he was such a forceful speaker and his conviction towards Islam was so deep. I wished I had heard this before, so that I could argue with him. I only think how much of a learned scholar in Islam he would have been, had he lived!"

28th August – "I did a full day's work, but remained subdued and depressed. While driving to the hospital, I kept thinking that six weeks ago an ambulance took my Faisal to the hospital down this road, but never returned. At home, Hashi is still indirectly accusing me of neglecting Faisal on that fateful evening and feels I could have done more! This is causing me more hurt and frankly I don't know how long my heart can withstand the assault from all sides. Instead of helping each other, we are destroying each other."

29th August, Friday – "Today is the 40th Day. In Islamic culture this is the end of official mourning. We invited a few people from the mosque to have supper with us and pray for Faisal's departed soul."

30th August – "Hashi is still damaged – bordering on a mental breakdown."

31st August – "I woke up with a telephone call from my brother-in-law, Kafi, from Singapore. He gave me the sad news of the death of Princess Diana. I could not believe it and felt it was a dream. However, I came downstairs and switched on the TV which explained everything. It was indeed a tragic loss and I realised how Mr Al-Fayed felt at his son Dodi's death. In a strange sort of way, I felt consoled that Diana, the most beautiful woman in the world, had died. Dodi Fayed – the son of a multi-millionaire has gone – which gave me some comfort and courage."

1st September – "In the morning I went to London to Austin Reed to collect my suit which was ordered before the tragedy, to wear at Sajal's wedding. The shops were deserted – people and the whole nation were in mourning Diana's death. I collected my suit and tried it on – the tailor wanted to know why I had lost so much weight. I did not want to upset him by telling him the true reason."

2nd September – "Julekha, Hashi and I went to Wembley to buy a sari for wearing at Sajal's wedding reception. This is the first time that Hashi has gone out of the house – it made her feel good."

3rd September – "Julekha has returned to school for her new term. She is completely broken at the loss of her brother. Everybody in the school came with new vigour and enthusiasm after the summer break, whereas we all had the worse misery a human being can ever get."

4th September – "I am on two days annual leave – booked long ago – in happier times, for Sajal's wedding. This would have been such an enjoyable time. We had booked a hotel, where our family and the *family of Aliyya would reside during the whole weekend in Leeds. But now we have to do the solitary journey ourselves. Exactly 7 weeks ago this night, Faisal was taken ill – who knows what would have been the outcome had I taken more care that night on 17th July? I cleaned and washed my car today – First since the tragedy."*

5th September – "(Leeds) – Hashi, Julekha and I are here in this hotel in the centre of Leeds – a city which bears so much pain in our hearts. It was to this city that I came five months ago with my new car and my newly-wed son and daughter-in-law. This is a city I don't know much about and today I got lost on our way to the hotel and ended up in the same road in which Aliyya and Faisal had their rented accommodation. All three of us burst into tears as we drove past that house. It was heartrending and unbearable. We have come to Leeds for such a joyful and happy occasion, but our heart is full of pain and agony. I asked myself many times – was it worth it? Should we have continued with this wedding or postponed it? I don't know what Allah had in His mind when He took Faisal away. We all remained depressed all evening. Sajal is supposed to be having a 'stag night' with his friends – he is also traumatised at the loss of his only brother – but he has to go through the motions. Had Faisal been alive today, he would have been so proud to show us around 'his city'."

6th September '97 – "In more than one way it was a remarkable day. This is the day when my elder son Sajal got married to Rachel in Leeds. The wedding went smoothly according to English tradition. The Registrar came to the hotel to conduct the wedding; I became restless, upset and broke down several times, for Faisal. The most traumatising and upsetting time was when the photographer was taking the family portrait. I could not bear it. It was only one and a half months ago that there were five of us and now there are only four. What did we do to deserve this? I have asked this question many times, but who can give me the answer?"

Searching for causes

My suffering and pain became magnified by the behaviour of others. This was my son's marriage: we were not entirely happy with it, but nevertheless agreed to go ahead. We would certainly have taken more time to decide had there been no Aliyya and her marriage to Faisal. Faisal's marriage enhanced our view of Sajal's marriage. We thought there would be two English daughters-in-law. Rachel's parents were dead against this marriage, which we could understand, but they did not have to take it out on us.

Rachel's parents knew how broken we were – and yet still we were going ahead with this. Apart from the fact that Sajal is Asian and Muslim, there was not a better bridegroom they could get for Rachel. But they did not speak a single word of sympathy to us. I thought, the man is a priest, a man of God, but what about his heart? There is no compassion, no mercy in his heart. This behaviour of Rachel's parents added to our misery.

We sat at the same table during the meals, but there was no eye contact and no view exchanged. What a pity. How mean can a human being be? How low could human mentality sink in? A man of God? I will never forget or forgive them.

This day is also remarkable for another reason. This is the day when Diana the Princess of Wales was buried. The whole nation – perhaps half of the world was witnessing the event on the TV. We did witness it from time to time and saw the people throwing flowers at the coffin as it passed through the streets of London and then on to the M1 motorway to Northampton.

After the wedding, Julekha, Hashi and I started out for St. Albans. The journey was smooth, and as we passed Northampton we came across flowers on the motorway and embankments, left over from Diana's procession. We arrived home at 9.35 p.m.

> *7th September – "Sajal and Rachel have left for Zanzibar for their honeymoon. Hashi and I took them to the airport. Pray to Allah for their safe return."*

Earlier, Sajal, Julekha and I went to Faisal's grave and prayed for him. We told ourselves that this day Faisal and Aliyya would have taken them to the airport. What a lovely sight that would have been. Sajal looked unhappy about the behaviour of his parents-in-law yesterday. I wondered if this was the price we would have to pay for staying in a foreign land in the UK. What an enjoyable occasion this would have been, had it been in Bangladesh. In Eastern culture one gets relations and friends through marriage. Lots of disputes between the families are settled through marriage, but here, for no apparent reason and despite our terrible loss, Rachel's parents were unforgiving.

> *9th September – "Still condolence letters keep on coming. Faisal's memory is too vivid. I still keep on asking myself why?"*

> *10th September – "Dr and Mrs Das came to visit us at lunch. They have come to the UK from India for their annual visit. I have known them since 1968. They are our oldest friends. We enjoyed each other's company. We joked, teased and pulled each other's legs but no more! I could not speak freely. Hashi was in tears most of the time."*

> *11th September – "Exactly two months ago – to this day, Faisal was ill at his in-laws house. Who knows what would have happened had he lived with us?"*

> *12th September, Friday – Two months ago, this Friday I lost my dearest son, Faisal. I cannot forget it, I cannot face it. I again went to his grave and prayed for his soul.*

13ᵗʰ September – *"Went to Savacentre with Mr Biswas to buy some drink for Sajal's wedding reception – on the way back stopped to pay homage to Faisal."*

14ᵗʰ September – *"Sajal telephoned from Zanzibar. They arrived there safely."*

15ᵗʰ September – *"At home tried to sort out the guest list and seating arrangements of Sajal's wedding reception, continuing with it as a matter of duty rather than pleasure."*

16ᵗʰ September – *"Went to St. James Court Hotel in London and walked past Buckingham Palace. The whole pavement is covered with flowers. There were hundreds of verses written by hand or typed and pinned to the wrought iron railings of the Palace. There were toys and teddy bears. There was an aura of sweet smells. There were bouquets of flowers – some fresh, some old and scattered everywhere as far as the eye could see. People are still shocked at the loss of Diana. As I walked past, my sorrow and my burden was somewhat eased. I told myself: if Diana and Dodi can lie peacefully in their grave, then I am not worried about my Faisal."*

17ᵗʰ September – *"Once again, I went to St. James Court Hotel in Buckingham Palace Road, for the very final seating arrangements and the menu, with the hotel authority."*

18ᵗʰ September – *"I went to the airport to receive my sister-in-law, Daisy and her husband Zahid. They are both doctors and work in Saudi Arabia. Normally it would have been such a happy meeting – but seeing them did not lift my mood. Daisy, Zahid and their daughter Uki looked well, their first visit to the UK. We are grateful to them that they have taken the time and trouble to come and see us."*

19ᵗʰ September – *"I took Aliyya's maternal aunt to the hospital and injected her knee."*

20ᵗʰ September – *"Got a letter from Ilias, from my village home – They are all shocked at Faisal's demise. Also I have been told that Rahim, my childhood friend has died. So many memories are recalled. Sajal and Rachel have returned from Zanzibar. We went to St. James Court Hotel again; taking the table flower arrangements for tomorrow's wedding reception."*

21st September, Sunday – "This is a memorable day, for this is the day we had the wedding reception for Sajal. It was a successful day which started with the arrival of the guests at noon. The reception was with soft drinks only. Some of my colleagues, friends and relations came. I am grateful to Daisy and Zahid who came all the way from Saudi Arabia. Julekha conducted the whole thing in a magnificent way – everybody praised the way she managed it. Uki was due to speak, and practised it quite a lot, but at that moment she broke down and could not manage it. The whole proceedings started with a recitation from the Holy Quran by the Imam of the local Bangladeshi mosque. We were disappointed with Rachel. She was told by my wife beforehand to cover her head when the Quran was being recited. This is the tradition in Muslim culture and she was told to do so. It would have enhanced her prestige amongst the Muslims, 90% of the guests. But she did not. We felt hurt inside, and let down. There was nothing I could do except to tolerate it. After the loss of Faisal, these things do not mean anything. Perhaps we have to learn to accept this sort of behaviour in future.

I had to give a speech, which I did with great sadness in my mind. I was so happy when I gave a similar speech a year earlier during Faisal's wedding, when I was full of life. In fact, one of the happiest moments of my life was when Sajal and I bade farewell to Faisal and Aliyya at Luton Airport, when they went off to Edinburgh for their honeymoon. But this speech is lifeless, senseless and just going on along the stream without any enthusiasm. My speech has been video-taped and can be seen or heard in full. But I began by saying that the speech which was prepared for this occasion, cannot be delivered for the reason all of you here know. I told them how happy I was but my happiness is subdued by my great loss. I concluded by saying that we pray to the Almighty for the health and happiness of the newly married."

22nd September – "I spoke to Aliyya. It seems she is upset because some are blaming her for Faisal's death. There may be some truth in it, but Faisal will not come back.

23rd September – "Zahid and Daisy went to Cambridge with Sajal. I am still perplexed and dazed at the loss of my son Faisal."

24th September, Wednesday – My poor Faisal – I shudder to think what would have happened today had he been alive!"

This diary entry related to the events that occurred when we invited Aliyya and the whole family to have a meal with us, including her grandfather. Because he dislikes Asian food, a special lamb roast was done for him. The whole idea was for our relations, Zahid and Daisy to meet Aliyya and her family. Everybody back home had seen her picture and video, but not in person.

The big table was full of food of different kinds, some Bangladeshi, some English. Aliyya came with her parents and grandfather. We were surprised and shocked to see her arriving without a hijab. My wife asked why. She replied "It's a long story". I smelt a rat, but could not say anything at the dining table or in front of our guests. As soon as we finished our main meal and before the dessert, I asked Aliyya to come and join me in my study. I asked: how come she had come in front of the guests without her veil, whereas before she would not remove it even in front of my elder son? Her answer was a terrible shock. I could not believe my ears. She told me in a cool and calm voice that she was no longer a Muslim. She had renounced it that morning. What could I say? My worse fear had come true. I always knew that there was something in this girl who was hiding something in her past under the veil of Islam. I had told my wife before that her conversion to Islam was like the many people that go off to India and Nepal as hippies or others who go to become Buddhists or Moonies. She had done the same and we fell into her trap, gave her my son in a wedding and now this.

I asked her why she had renounced Islam. She said she had her doubts when Faisal was alive, but he kept her going. In that study there was no one else except her and me. What could I as an educated person say or do? Had I been devout and not so educated, I might have harmed her physically in that room.

All I said to her was that she came from the gutter, in the name and the disguise of Islam, into a middle-class, educated and happy family. She destroyed it and was now moving back to the gutter. This language was too strong for her. She burst into a loud cry, which people could hear from the other room, and her parents, particularly her mother, must have guessed what had happened anyway. They came rushing in and a commotion started. I told everyone that she had renounced Islam, and of course people were speechless. Meanwhile, her mother though disabled and walking with the help of an elbow crutch, got her strength, collected her like an eagle and stormed out of my house.

Inside the study, her father, my wife, and I continued the sterile discussion of how, what and why? Near midnight they left – with a comment "We are still friends aren't we?" I replied "Of course".

25th September – "Sajal came and we were re-living the experience of last night. Faisal's friend Ali-Ibrahim came and we all talked about this mentally unstable girl who we used to call Faisal's wife. I hope my dearest boy is not watching this from heaven."

Faisal's marriage to Aliyya would not have happened if there not been this Islamic lobby among his friends. All the Muslims convinced us that this girl, whatever may have been her past, was now pure Muslim, wore a hijab, prayed five times a day and followed all the other tenets of Islam, so she was the right person for Faisal. Faisal was only a child, not yet established in his life, and since he could not continue his studies in law we resigned ourselves to the idea that he was not going to be a graduate and must look for a job, and indeed he did get one with British Airways.

But when this beautiful girl, tall, blonde and a student at the local public school came to our house, with a bunch of flowers, and expressed a wish to marry Faisal, and Faisal's friends were all in favour of it, it did not take long for us to accept it. We felt particularly that we had been looking for a nice girl for my elder son Sajal, an Oxford graduate, and still could not find one, and therefore how could we refuse such a girl, who had come begging us for Faisal's hand. We relented and agreed with the marriage, provided her parents agreed.

Her parents, of course, were delighted that they had got an inexperienced boy from a disciplined family for their troublesome daughter. They readily agreed and the marriage took place.

27th September – "Julekha and I went to Faisal's grave and prayed. The wound is so fresh. Still I continue to think how much pain and suffering he had on that night of 17th July."

29th September, Sunday – "We all went to Woburn Zoo. This was the first outing for Hashi. She is still visibly depressed. She cheered up a bit when she saw some of the animals in the wild."

29th September – "Invited a few of Faisal's friends to have a meal with us. Today, a friend of Faisal's came from Blackburn. He is preparing for a year out to go to the Yemen. Faisal would have done the same. How poor I am. I have lost such a fine son. Allah bless him."

4th October – "My brother-in-law, with his family, has now left for Saudi Arabia. Their presence here undoubtedly helped us in this very traumatic time. Their daughter Uki kept us amused and occupied."

5th October – "Human nature and behaviour is so peculiar and unpredictable. Aliyya's father came, no doubt at the instigation of his daughter and wife, and virtually demanded everything Faisal possessed. This really added insult to injury. I know that in English law his daughter is entitled to everything, but the couple were both devout Muslims and according to Islamic Law all the things should be divided amicably.

We had a heated discussion and I frankly told him that whatever Faisal had would be sold and the proceeds would go to establish an Islamic School (Madrassa) in Bangladesh. The man is spineless and does everything he is asked to do."

7th October – "The conversations between my wife and me are still about Faisal and nothing else and I have come to the conclusion that this girl is the root of our misery and damage. She is mentally unstable and will do further damage to very many people in her life time."

(As people sometimes do in the depths of their misery, I was casting around for someone – anyone – to blame for Faisal's death, and in my grief I targeted Aliyya, whose instability had worried us for some time, and who, perhaps, should have called the GP, though whether or not that would have saved Faisal's life at that stage is impossible to answer.)

> 8ᵗʰ October – "Aliyya's father meant to come today with a list of things his daughter wanted, but he didn't. We are getting tense and suspicious that they might go to solicitors, in which case she will get everything. Faisal's death, Aliyya's betrayal of renouncing Islam and now this. How much can one individual tolerate? There is no one who can share our grief and misfortune."

> 9ᵗʰ October – "Ali-Ibrahim and Feracep came with the list of things the evil girl wants. We are prepared to give her everything she wants but were so surprised at the peculiarities of human behaviour."

I feel that Faisal died an honourable death, because this marriage would not have lasted, and the one year it did, was due to total sacrifice on the part of Faisal. I feel Faisal gave life for this girl, who never loved him and had no feelings for him.

> 14ᵗʰ October – "Ali-Ibrahim is doing some negotiating about the division of Faisal's assets between the two families."

> 15ᵗʰ October – "Winter is closing in. Aliyya's father came to give a final physics lesson to Julekha. We told him not to come any more."

> 16ᵗʰ October – "Ali-Ibrahim took some articles to Aliyya's house. They are playing tricks, have not given anything back, and we feel they are up to something."

> 17ᵗʰ October – "Hashi has sorted out Faisal's articles and in fact sold some of them. The proceeds will go to the mosque."

> 19ᵗʰ October – "Sajal came home. We mended Faisal's desk. It is now in a tip-top condition except that the occupant is not here."

> 20ᵗʰ October – "On my way home I paid a visit to Faisal's grave. There was nobody nearby, so I spoke to Faisal loudly."

21st October – "Nearly 30 years have passed in the UK. It had been an uphill struggle to reach where I am now, but it seems all in vain! Faisal has left us forever. We could not protect him. My father protected me and saved me from various serious illnesses in the village – where there were no doctors, no medicines, not even pure water. The conditions were medieval, but he protected us. But I, remaining at the heart of civilisation and being a doctor, could not save him. Sajal got married to an English girl and I can visualise how it is going to go and what future awaits, for I have so many friends who married English girls and who have lost their identity. There are Muslim colleagues who are so anglicised that they have not bothered to circumcise their male children and have given them English names. This total loss of identity is of course bound to happen. I had high hopes for Julekha, but her physical strength is getting low because she has an eating disorder. I am quite sure that whatever may be the underlying cause, she is starving and her future does not look bright. So where do I go? How can I lift myself up?"

22nd October – "As if there is no end of the suffering and agony. We are already still in shock due to Faisal's death and subsequent betrayal of his wife, but this morning we were further shocked and surprised to get a solicitor's letter from Aliyya's parents about returning all the possessions of Faisal! It was really so upsetting. We suspected that something like that might happen, and now indeed it has happened. However, Allah gave some succour, for we were told by friends and neighbours, that we should demand every penny of the funeral expenses. It gave us some hope and courage."

23rd October – "Hashi and I went to see our solicitors with a draft letter from us. It was a good letter – where we have demanded all the funeral expenses, including the refreshments and where we hoped that they would realise that life is not so simple. When they went to their solicitor, they did not realise or think about the funeral expenses."

24th October – "It is one of those days - My Faisal's birthday! He would have been 24 today. What a pain. How cruel is the world? Who knew this time last year that he would not be around for his

24th birthday? We invited a few of Faisal's friends for an evening meal. It gave us some comfort. Earlier I had managed to come home at lunch time and went to Friday Prayer. Later I visited Faisal's grave site."

26th October – "Hashi and I went to London today to attend the Walima (wedding reception) of Mr Mannan's son. This was our first outing to any reception. The main reason for our participation was that this young man is an Islamist and had been a friend of Faisal. He came to attend the funeral of Faisal – though I did not see him or even if I did I never recognised him. At the reception, there was segregation of the sexes – women sat separately in another room and I had traditional Bangladeshi food together with some Bangladeshi friends. I was subdued and came home as soon as the meals were taken. We knew the area well, for we stayed there when we first came to this country, but nothing interests us anymore."

27th October – "On my way home I once again stopped at Faisal's grave and prayed for him. Ali-Ibrahim phoned to say that Aliyya's parents went to his shop following the solicitor's letter and he looked worried. I got some pleasure in hearing that."

28th October – "Took some further photographs for enlarging. They are all Faisal's. Such a nice and easy name – It will remain like music to my ears until I die."

30th October – "Winter setting in. There was a hard frost this morning. Wrote a Press Release about the events that led to Faisal's death. It was all ready to go to the local newspaper, but stopped it at the objection raised by Hashi and Julekha."

31st October – "This was the first time I said Friday Prayers at the Hemel Hempstead mosque. I prayed to Allah for the peace of Faisal. On my way home I visited his grave."

1st November – "Another letter from the solicitors who are refusing any liability for funeral expenses. I do not think they have solid ground to get away from it. I think they have got trapped in their own net."

5th November – "Hashi and I went to Faisal's grave and prayed for him. From there we went to the garden centre to buy some wall-flowers. Julekha and I have written the reply to the solicitor's letter. Where is it going to end?"

6th November – "Faisal left me with one limb, one eye and one arm. I will never recover – Don't know when or where I will get peace. Slight comfort – Julekha got an interview from Manchester University to read Medicine."

11th November – "In the evening a few of Faisal's friends came and spoke about Faisal's work and activities. Difficult to believe he is not with us."

12th November – "My work was not heavy. The days are short and darkness sets in quickly. Hashi and I visited Faisal's grave again today."

13th November – "Emptiness for Faisal prevails. Normal work continues."

14th November – "Busy at the hospital. Could not visit Faisal's grave this Friday."

16th November – "I went jogging on my own and managed 15 minutes. Hashi stayed at home."

19th November – "Went to work with subdued mood and really upset about the whole situation – in particular my life with Hashi – at the aftermath of Faisal's death. After lunch, I went again to the cemetery to attend yet another funeral of a young Bangladeshi man who had died in a road traffic accident."

20th November – "Faisal – such a good name, how long can I withstand his absence?"

21st November – "Not a stressful day. Dr Falkowski gave me a tape to listen to. This is about death. Everybody has different viewpoints about it. I listened to it. It did not give me any comfort. I was surprised that Aliyya's father came to return the remainder of Faisal's clothing. I think the idea was to make friends – as a result of the solicitor's letter. I did not let him in."

26th November – *"Julekha's interview at Manchester. I took her to Watford Junction and bade her farewell and wished here luck. This was her first trip on her own. Went to collect her from the station. She says interview went well."*

28th November – *"We cheered up a bit this morning when Julekha got a letter from Cambridge for an interview. It would be so nice if she could make it there."*

30th November (Sunday) – *"Went out jogging. Hashi took part in it, first time since Faisal's demise. All of us went to Faisal's grave – the sadness is not diminishing a single bit."*

2nd December – *"I feel lonely, insecure. No one to talk to either at work or at home. No one to share my feelings, no one to look at me and say 'you look tired today'. No one says 'you are quiet today'. It's as if I have no one in this world. My wife, the children – I do not get any emotional support. Since Faisal's death I have been comforting all the members of the family but there is no one for me! How long I will survive, I don't know.*

3rd December – *"Bitterly cold weather. I had to go to the BUPA hospital to see an in-patient. There I became emotional. At the end of the corridor there was a chair – which is still there. Faisal was sitting there, overlooking the green field and the aircraft taking off and landing at Luton Airport. Faisal and I sat there in April – when the consultant surgeon did the ward round. I was emotional because that chair is still there – the field is still green with new crops, but my Faisal is far away – so far away that no one can reach him."*

4th December – *"At hospital, the work load is down, both the NHS and private work. Came home via the BUPA hospital. On my way I kept on thinking about the turn of events that led to Faisal's demise. I still cannot believe it. Faisal's friends came – they're all totally devoted to Islam – and they always remind me that it was pre-destined, so I should not feel hurt or aggrieved. But as a father this is not easy to accept."*

5th December – "*Cold weather continues. Attended a lunch-time meeting. On my way I visited Faisal's grave. It was only 4 p.m. but pitch dark at the cemetery. No one was there except me. It was dark, cold and muddy and my son lies there. I looked at the sky – there was a crescent and lone star flickering in the far distance as has done for centuries. Perhaps those stars and moon have seen many tragedies worse than mine, perhaps witnessed many battles over the centuries since human beings started inhabiting this planet. But who cares for individuals feeling like myself?*"

6th December, Saturday – "*Went shopping briefly. It was so very crowded for Xmas. People are naturally happy at this festive season, but nobody knows the fire raging in my heart. After my Isha Prayer – suddenly Faisal appeared in my memory and I could not control myself and burst into tears.*"

8th December – "*In the morning, Hashi and I took Julekha to Hatfield Station for her trip to Cambridge for the interview. The road to Cambridge is so well known to us and we have so many happy memories. We wished Julekha the best of luck for her interview.*"

10th December – "*In the evening, a Jamaican lady paid a visit to us. It was kind of her. Her daughter – also a university student, died suddenly with meningitis. So she knows the pain and we shared one another's grief.*"

12th December – "*Today my Sajal is 30 years old. Pray to Allah for his long-life. I still vividly remember the day he was born. Because of Faisal's absence there is no birthday celebration. We remember fondly two years ago, when Rachel first came to our house – we all went to the K2 Restaurant and had such a lovely time. Who knew that on his 30th birthday, his brother would not be around?*"

14th December – "*I was thinking to myself about my eldest sister, who died of cholera in 1942. It was fifty-five years ago. How many people remember her? Perhaps not more than ten people in our village. So 55 years from now – how many will remember Faisal? Certainly I won't be here. With Allah's blessing, Julekha will be a grandmother at 72! But I will remember Faisal until my dying day and far beyond.*"

15th December – "Yet another drama with regards to Faisal's estate. Aliyya's father came and stirred up the wound. The man has no self-respect and individual guts – and is totally driven by his wife and two daughters. Poor Faisal, he may be watching from heaven what has happened to us, his wife and his in-laws, whom he valued so highly. They have sunk to the bottom of human dignity."

16th December – "Hashi has left for Bangladesh this evening. Hope and pray to Allah that she reaches there safely. Sajal, Julekha and I took her to the airport, in freezing weather and with a heavy heart. All the way to the airport, all our conversation was centred on Faisal. I reminded the children that we last came to the airport in July to see off their cousin – how the cheerful frame of mind that was and now our feelings all so much down that it is difficult to express. Our whole world fell to pieces with the demise of Faisal. It was a good thing that Hashi agreed to go to Bangladesh on her own. She needed to be amongst her own brothers and sisters and other relations away from the site of mental trauma. Julekha has her 'A' level examinations, and it was not possible for her to go and therefore I stayed behind with her. Julekha feels lonely, even more so after her mother left for Bangladesh."

17th December – Last night I had disturbed sleep. Sajal has left for Southend in the freezing cold and snow. Too much strain on him as well. Newly married, should enjoy life, but this tragedy is putting a shadow on everything. Out of the whole sad situation, there was a slight ray of hope of happiness which was that Julekha has been offered a place at Manchester University to study Medicine – provided she can make the grade. I was thinking about Faisal who was lying in that cemetery in the cold and dark."

18th December – "I went to the Pakistani grocers shop for some condiments. There were lots of people. Everyone knew me. Everyone knew the tragedy. I told myself – yes – I am well-known in the town; I was privileged, happy, and well-off, but none among these people are more sad than myself. I would swap my place with anyone, including that butcher cutting the meat, had I got my Faisal back."

19th December, Friday – "I took this day off. After Friday Prayers I went to the graveyard. It is a quagmire – a pathetic place to see someone's near and dear one's lying there."

21st December – "Shortest day. Foggy, cold and miserable. There had been no sunshine for a week. What a contrast to the longest day of the year – particularly the state of affairs of the mind. We had no idea what awaited us. Only 3 weeks after the longest day my Faisal passed away."

24th December – "Xmas Eve – but there is no excitement. We have not even opened many of the Xmas cards. We have not brought down the Xmas tree from the attic. What is the point? Not for a single moment can I forget Faisal. I remember those days, when the children were young, we all brought presents for them – sometimes more than one for each of the children. They would have been scattered around the Xmas tree – and we would open them on Xmas day. Faisal, of course, would have known what was there, for he used to peep into it when no one was watching. Those were the happy days – never to return. When Faisal was much younger and believed in Father Christmas, I scattered the presents around the fire place. In the morning he came down and shouted – 'So there is a Father Christmas after all!' Those childhood words still ring in my ears and will continue to do so until I die."

25th December – "Christmas Day – It was decided that Sajal and Rachel will come to cook Xmas dinner for us. I prepared everything including the turkey, which we brought from a Pakistani shop. We did not have the traditional Xmas lunch; instead we prepared the food for supper. Xmas lunch had always been so exciting – particularly when cutting the cake. We always used to bury a pound coin and the excitement reached its climax whoever found it. By a stroke of luck, Faisal used to win most of the time."

26th December – "Boxing Day – I went for Friday Prayer with Sajal, then we both went to the cemetery to pray for Faisal. I kept thinking was it worth it for me to stay in this country? I have lost a son; his marriage to a local girl was disastrous. Rachel is better, but not what we expect for the eldest daughter-in-law. In this situation

*she is the lynch-pin of the house. But the culture is different. I
can't expect much and we have accepted it as such."*

*29th December – "Stayed at home. Cleaned Hashi's car, which had
not been done since Faisal passed away. I knew this was deliberate
and sentimental. Faisal drove this car. It was his touch and dust
of his feet that Hashi did not want to get rid of. Tomorrow starts
the holy month of Ramadan."*

*31st December – "It is now 12.30 pm. Julekha and I were watching
TV to say goodbye to the year – which brought such havoc to our
lives and welcomed in the New Year of 1998. Some of the Hindu
friends brought food for me and Julekha. I am grateful to them in
those dark days – they were helpful."*

So the year of 1997 came to an end. This was the year that started
with so much hope and expectation. I was dreaming of becoming a
grandfather, I was going to be sixty, and I could retire at any time I liked,
not giving a damn about NHS reorganisation and departmental politics,
which had caused so much anguish in me over the past five years. I
had been much relieved that Faisal was at last on some sort of track
rather than wandering around for the past ten years. He passed his first
year exam and was looking forward to a year of further study in Islamic
Studies in Yemen. Aliyya was going to follow him. My other son Sajal,
was now engaged to Rachel – despite her parents' disapproval and was
due to get married this year. My daughter, Julekha, has got interviews in
Cambridge as well as in Manchester to study medicine and was sure to
get a place somewhere. We remained in good health and the monetary
situation was better, with fewer demands from Bangladesh.

Little did I know that my life would change forever on my 60th birthday
– the 18th July 1997. I hate this date from the bottom of my heart. On
this day, I lost the most precious thing in my life. I lost my second son,
a grown up son, only married for less than a year. His death was so
sudden, so traumatic, that we were never prepared for it. What's more,
as a doctor, I know he died from a curable condition. I have called this
book *Climbing the Tree and Falling* – because in my life it is as if I did
reach the top of the tree and succeeded in getting the desired fruit, then

slipped, lost my foothold and fell down, breaking my limbs and making me disabled. Also I feel like Icarus: I was trying to fly towards the sun, and in the attempt I failed and fell into the sea.

That was my feeling as the dreadful year of 1997 ended, dark, with pinpoints of light from the kindness and sympathy of colleagues, neighbours and many of my patients.

A consultant colleague wrote "if it is of any consolation to you, my son aged 20, died in a road traffic accident 10 years ago". Later I heard of another two of my consultant colleagues who lost their adult sons, one who had a brain tumour and the other was murdered.

I always cherish a poem written by a patient in her own hand writing:

Perhaps, if we could see
the splendour of the land
to which our loved ones
are called from you and me
we'd understand..

Perhaps, if we could hear
the welcome they receive
from old familiar voices
all so dear we would
not grieve..

Perhaps, if we could know
the reason why they went
we'd smile and..
wipe away the tears that flow
and wait content,

With love

PART IV
AFTER THE FALL

28

Home and abroad

998 started as 1997 ended: dull, depressed, dreary, cold and lonely. Our big house felt empty. My son, newly married, had moved away to his place of work. Julekha, my daughter, was at home but I was now getting worried about her. My wife was in Bangladesh. I had urged her to go there, in fact, so that she would be amongst her brothers and sisters, far away from the scene of disaster. I felt strongly that if she did not go to Bangladesh she would have a serious mental breakdown from which she might not recover.

But while she was away, I became more worried about my daughter. Julekha was only seventeen and her 'A' Level exams were approaching. She had been very close to Faisal and when he died she was not at home. Now, with her mother away, there was only me in this big house to console her in the deep winter months. She went off her food, lost weight and remained in her room most of the time. Though grieving myself, I had to continue my work to maintain my livelihood; I'd had to send my wife off to prevent her breakdown, and now my daughter was showing signs and symptoms of anorexia. What could I do? Whom should I approach for help? There was nobody. In desperation, I thought of asking my wife to return to the UK earlier than planned. I asked my brother-in-law, Kafi, to reschedule it for the 19th January. Julekha's spirits lifted a bit with this news, but when it turned out that it was not possible she broke down completely. I became angry and upset and shouted at her, asking her what she wanted me to do? I had tried everything for everybody, but who was doing anything for me? Was I not a human being? Had I not lost my son? Had I not got to work? Who did she think I was, man or machine? She understood, being a very intelligent girl, and somehow kept going until her mother returned a week later.

On her return from Bangladesh, Hashi looked a bit more cheerful. She was talking, even smiling, and I remember as I was driving home from the airport she said, "We will have to rebuild our life". It was an important utterance from her and I deeply appreciated it.

But, like me, she was concerned about Julekha's health. She had lost an awful lot of weight, her periods had stopped, and she looked pale and unwell. Her extremities were always cold, she had low blood pressure and a slow heart rate. All this indicated some serious physical problem developing on top of her mental anguish due to the loss of Faisal. Sajal came from his hospital. Neither he nor his new wife was any help to Julekha. There had been no sympathetic word or support from him. I suppose he, too, was grieving in his own way. I felt the burden would have been much less if we had all sat down as a family and consoled each other. Unfortunately, this did not happen and what's more, the reaction of our son, to whom we looked for support, had the opposite effect. He would argue with his mother and criticise her. What could his poor mother do? If he had at least ever sat near her and put his arm round her shoulders, it would have had a tremendous effect on her.

I felt I must seek some help from a colleague who specialised in this area. He came to my house and agreed with me that Julekha did have a psychological problem - depression - and along with that, anorexia nervosa. Psychotherapy was arranged, which did help her a bit and she started working hard for her 'A' levels.

It was at this time that my brother-in-law, Dr Ahsan, who had been working in Bhutan, decided to visit us. His presence was a godsend. A very nice and friendly man, he had been very close to the boys, so naturally Faisal's death had hurt him as well. He stayed with us for a month. Also, my sister-in-law came from Saudi Arabia, for a health check-up, and my wife felt very much better for seeing a blood-relative.

On the other hand, the solicitor's letters about the distribution of "Faisal's assets" kept on coming and we advised our solicitors to reply and counter-claim for the funeral expenses. It was an uncomfortable situation, which we could have done without. Aliyya and her parents realised that they were not going to win and put out some feelers about compromise. We spoke to our solicitors and we too decided to settle without procrastinating any further. It was calculated that Faisal's estate was worth £650, excluding the funeral expenses. I decided to pay the amount in full with the proviso that Faisal's widow gave up all future claims, including the title deed of Faisal's grave. According to English law, the widow is legally entitled to keep this. They prevaricated for a few days, then signed a document accepting all our terms. This was as it should be, for I believed that she had never loved Faisal, and had only embraced Islam and married Faisal to escape from her horrid past. She knew in her heart that she had been playing for time with all these pretences and that sooner or later she would have left Islam and Faisal. I am sure her parents were also aware that it had been a temporary phase. It was for this reason that her parents never addressed her with her Muslim name of Aliyya, but instead they called her by her English name, Jane, even when she was with us. We were fools and never realised it until Faisal died. I have no doubt that even had Faisal lived, separation and divorce would have come sooner rather than later.

While we were deep in mourning in the New Year of 1998, Jane and her parents not only went to the solicitors for Faisal's estate, but we gathered that Jane was reunited with one of her previous boyfriends, with whom she had split up in order to embrace Islam. She had apparently been on a skiing holiday in the US that winter. How could we tolerate this? In Eastern culture and in Islam such behaviour is not possible, but whenever I spoke to my Caucasian colleagues and friends about this, invariably the answer was, "She's young". So the money from Faisal's estate of £650 must have helped her with her skiing holiday.

I now discovered that during the previous summer holiday Faisal had taken a temporary job with a mobile phone company. We were told that the company life insurance policy was worth fifty thousand pounds. Faisal had declined it, for life insurance is not allowed in Islam. Also, for reasons unknown to us, he gave up the job just a week before he died. If he had had the life insurance and not given up the job, Jane would have been richer by £50,000 in 1997. When the Chief Executive of the phone company learned about Faisal's death, he wrote a glowing tribute to him, which still hangs on the wall of my study.

I strongly believe in providence and I think back and wonder: supposing that pregnancy had survived and I had had a grandchild, and Faisal had then died what would have happened? She would have renounced Islam and gone back to her previous carefree life, and what would have happened to my grandchild? We would not have had any access to the child who would have been brought up in a different way and would still have been entitled to a share of my estate. So it was all for the best.

The first anniversary of Faisal's death was approaching and we were wondering how we would cope. We had been thinking about doing something in memory of Faisal.

We travelled to Leeds one evening and met with Faisal's Islamic friends. I could not control myself and broke down into uncontrollable tears. I told them that Faisal had been happy there in Leeds, and that we wanted to do something in his memory. They were very pleased and suggested a library should be opened in his name. We agreed, but as it happened, they themselves left the university, new students came who did not know Faisal, so the whole project never got off the ground.

Meanwhile, we decided that it would be impossible for us to stay at home during his first death anniversary on the 18th July. Hashi, Julekha and I decided to go to Bangladesh during that time. I was still in full employment and had quite a bit of difficulty in getting one month's leave. However, it was managed and we all left for Bangladesh on Saturday, 4th July. The day before, I went to visit Faisal's grave and found the place was emitting a sweet aroma. Later I gathered that Julekha had been earlier that day and spread some perfume on the grave.

In Bangladesh, we decided to stay in a hotel rather than becoming a burden on any of the relatives. At the hotel, lots of people came to see us, but I neither had the enthusiasm nor the inclination to talk to anybody, particularly my nephews, their young wives and children, for I had found them terribly wanting over the last year, when there had not been a single letter or telephone call to console me or my family in a foreign land.

The only person who came to see us in the UK during those dreadful days was Kafi, and when he returned home, nobody, from my brother downwards, went to see him to enquire how we were coping, though at that time my brother was occupying a top position in political circles and rubbing shoulders with the then Prime Minister. We found no sympathy or kindness towards us; accordingly, I kept almost silent during my stay in Bangladesh.

Normally I feel euphoric on reaching Bangladesh. The trees, green fields, the noise and crowd of the metropolis reminds me of my younger days, when I lived here; but this time I could not get cheerful about anything. It was the summer season, terribly hot and humid, and the only pleasure I had was to watch the birds on the lake in front of our hotel. Friends and relations came in their best attire, but I was not responsive to their presence. I had no peace of mind and I did not know what I could do to get some. My mind was floating all the time, as if looking for Faisal.

My brother-in-law told me about an orphanage in Dhaka. My wife and I went there. It was run by a charity and there were about 150 boys of various ages from 10 to 18. We saw the boys reading in the makeshift school, with one teacher. I was told that these boys had suffered the death of either one or both of their parents. We found some solace there and mixed freely with the boys, perhaps hoping to find Faisal amongst them. I thought to myself that these boys had been through a very rough time: many had been left on the streets without food or shelter before they were brought to this orphanage and yet they were alive and well. My Faisal, by contrast, had been living in the most developed country in the world, yet had died in less than twelve hours of illness. Was it fair?

We met up with the head of the orphanage and offered one day's food for all the children and a cash donation.

My wife and daughter were also very subdued, so to get away from the capital, I decided to take them to Chittagong, the city where I had qualified. I had not been back there since 1964. Julekha, who was intending to study medicine, was keen to see "Dad's medical school". We took the plane to Chittagong and at the request of an old friend, stayed in his house, which was a great mistake. I had not met this friend since our college days. Our situations had changed; we were both married and had families, and he had stayed in Bangladesh while I lived in England. Moreover, I was still in deep shock at the loss of my son, and nobody could understand the pain and suffering I was going through.

Our personalities also had changed after thirty years. We stayed three nights, because I did not wish to offend him by going to a hotel. I took my wife and daughter to my medical school and was totally disappointed. New buildings had cropped up, and the whole area was so congested that we decided to leave. I went to the students' dormitory, to the room that had been mine, and met the current occupants. In the kitchen the old cook was there and he still remembered me after all those years.

On arriving back in Dhaka, we were getting ready to go to Kushtia and then to my village in Dharmadaha so we could be there on the 18th July, the first anniversary. I felt that if I was to get any peace, I would get it in the village where I was born, where my parents were buried, where my brother and nephews were well off enough to look after us for a few days.

Before we started our journey to Kushtia, we decided to buy some clothes for the beggars and poorest people in the village, to be distributed on the first anniversary of Faisal's death. With the help of my brother-in-law, we bought some saris for the women and *lungis*, loin cloths, for the men. Also, we bought some food and sweetmeats for the poor of the village.

When we started our journey on the 14th July we were fully loaded with our luggage, and the extra luggage for the village folk. My daughter had a bad memory of travelling to my home district the last time she had come, some six years earlier, when we had a terrible time at the Goalundo Ghat and at Rajbari due to the derailment of the train.

Whenever I travelled to Bangladesh, there had always been the problem of how to travel from Dhaka to Kushtia and from there to my village, about 150 miles. Transport is unreliable and so crowded that it is impossible to use public transport.

We decided to hire a people-carrier taxi with six seats. One of my relatives accompanied us, so we were four, plus the luggage. The taxi, as always, had a reconditioned engine and had been worked hard on the rough roads and in my view would fail an MOT many times over. But we had no option, for that was the only transport available.

The driver was a young man, maybe twenty-five, and though polite, he was not to my liking. I found out during our journey that he was a Christian in an overwhelmingly Muslim country. As the journey started, he put his tape player on with an old cassette of music to his own taste blaring out at the highest decibels he could manage. I was sitting next to him in the passenger seat and felt that in this hot and humid weather, without any air-conditioning and a journey of nearly eight hours ahead, it was unendurable. I asked him to stop the music, which he did, though he was not happy about it. The roads in Bangladesh are not up to anything like western standards and are almost always single carriageway, and drivers have no traffic sense whatsoever. Accidents are quite common, with head-on collisions and fatalities, but nobody cares. Our driver speeded up. I was afraid that at any time something disastrous would happen. I told him in no uncertain terms that I had hired him for the whole journey and was paying him and his boss a hefty sum by Bangladeshi standards, so he must listen to me and slow down. I was not willing to risk my life and the lives of my wife and daughter. He listened and slowed down a bit. We covered 75 miles and reached a ferry crossing at Aricha Ghat. The ferry carries not only taxis and motor vehicles, but heavily loaded trucks going out to the provinces from the capital. There was a queue of vehicles but this unruly young man must have been used to it because he jumped the queue and went to the front, despite my protestations. I later gathered that he was in such a hurry because he had been instructed by his boss to drop us in Kushtia and return on the same day, covering a distance of 300 miles.

However, soon he was in trouble. He was caught by the traffic warden and was asked to go to the back of the queue, which he was not willing to do and a commotion ensued, which attracted the traffic police. Now, there was a big crowd surrounding our vehicle and people were all staring at us, particularly at the two ladies inside. In the melee, I was more concerned about missing the ferry, for if we did, the next one would not be till six hours later. I was completely at a loss what to do, for this young man was none too bothered and still arguing with the police. It was a desperate situation. I asked my relative to go out and speak to the policeman on my behalf. He must have explained to him that we were from England and only half way through our journey, and keen to get this ferry. In Bangladesh, nothing is impossible, but everything is done by the back door. I was reliably told that if I bribed the policeman 200 Taka, about £2.00, he would let us pass and allow us to stay at the front of the queue. Against my principles, I handed over the money to my relative who discreetly passed it to the policeman. The portly policeman was happy, came to us, saluted me and invited me for a cup of tea. I politely declined and thanked him for his help. We boarded the ferry to cross the Meghna River, swollen with the water of the rainy season.

After the crossing, still only half way through our journey, we asked the driver to stop at a place for lunch. While we were having our food, we offered some to the driver and I noticed very dark clouds behind us. I had been away for a long time, so I wasn't used to seeing such dark clouds, so common in monsoon time in Bangladesh that nobody takes any notice. I thought the cloud was behind us and might not affect us, but I was wrong. I also heard a hissing noise during our lunch break, as if the tyre pressure was going out. Before we resumed our journey, we asked the driver to check the tyres, which I was assured were in good condition.

As soon as we resumed our journey, the pouring rain caught us from behind. The rain drops were so big and constant it felt as though someone was pouring water on the windscreen from a bucket. We proceeded slowly and were afraid that flooding or some other mishap would interrupt our journey. Our fears were justified.

We reached a place with some shops where people were milling around. It was afternoon and the rain had lessened in intensity, but not stopped. The driver suddenly halted because of some trouble with the taxi. He got out in the quagmire. I followed him. It turned out one tyre was flat. There must have been a puncture. The young man reassured me that there was a spare tyre in the boot, but when he opened it, to his and my dismay we found that the spare tyre was also flat. Then I remember the hissing sound I had heard when we were having lunch. We were now in a locality quite unknown to us and it was at a time when nobody would venture out after dark, because it would not be safe.

Since leaving Dhaka we had not had any decent toilet facilities and had been waiting to reach home. Now we were stranded, with no hope of getting the tyres mended, for there were no facilities in this small locality. Inside the car it was hot and humid, and outside it was a muddy quagmire. The situation was desperate, particularly for my daughter and wife. The young relative who was with us was really helpful again. He went to a nearby shop and explained the situation and asked the owner whether we could rest in his shop while the car tyre was mended. The man reluctantly agreed. My daughter and my wife sat on a small bench and I went to find out how the tyre was going to be mended.

It turned out that the driver would have to take the flat tyre to the nearby town, about fifteen miles away. Off he went, not sure how long it would be before he would return. I asked the local people what we should do. There were many suggestions. Since we had already paid the driver half of his total fare and we had done half the journey, we decided it would not be unreasonable to abandon him altogether and get a fresh taxi to our destination. But there was no taxi in that small village. We would have to go to the nearest town, the one where the driver had gone to get the tyre mended, to find a taxi. Everybody agreed that a taxi would definitely be available from that town, Jhenaidah. But how would we get to Jhenaidah, with four people and so much luggage? It was a nightmare. I felt sorry for my daughter, who had experienced similar travel problems on her last visit. Her impression of Bangladesh was not good.

We got hold of a motor scooter, locally called a "baby taxi." Somehow, we transferred the luggage to this "baby taxi". Most of the people were watching our misfortune, but none gave us a hand to load and unload. However, we somehow crammed into the mobile deathtrap. The driver was, as usual, very poor, but gentle. His name indicated he was a Hindu, in an overwhelmingly Muslim country. We were very grateful to him for his careful and cautious driving. We covered the fifteen miles in about an hour. He managed to take us to a taxi stand and found a good four-wheeler. We settled the fare to our destination and were so relieved to get a decent taxi, with the prospect of reaching our destination before night-fall.

We started our journey towards Kushtia, reasonably happy that everything was now going to be fine. About an hour into our journey, there was a tap at the window. It was our former driver.

We stopped. He was upset that we had abandoned his taxi and taken another one. He had apparently managed to have the tyre repaired and fitted, and had caught us up. I explained that he had left us without telling us how long it would take, or what we were supposed to do in that small village. Anyhow, I gave him some money, with which he was satisfied, and he returned to Dhaka. We continued our journey and reached Kushtia just after sunset, some three hours later. The family, both in Kushtia and in Dhaka, were worried stiff as to what had happened to us. At that time there were no mobile phones for us to be able to keep in touch with them.

We reached my father-in-law's house. My mother-in-law was alive, though somewhat disabled following a stroke. At the house, there was loud wailing from the women. This was the first time we had met after our disaster of losing Faisal. We settled for the night and were looked after really well by my brother-in-law and his wife.

The following morning, the 15th July, we woke up somewhat recovered from the ordeal of the journey from Dhaka. I made a courtesy call to my brother's house. The house looked happy, with all the children grown up and most of them employed and earning money. My brother was the president of the local political party who were in power. He now had enormous power over the Government officials. Financially, they were all well off.

I did not find any of them sympathetic to me, and not a kind word was said about our loss. They simply had no idea what I was going through with the first anniversary of my son's death. My sister-in-law, who claimed credit for my upbringing during my schooldays, and my brother, who took all the credit for my medical school expenses, were oblivious to my pain and suffering. I kept unusually quiet, for what could I say? During the past year they had never sent me a letter of condolence or made a telephone call to find out how we were coping. My eldest nephew, who works in Dubai in telecommunications, never even bothered to phone me to ask how we were. So I knew very well that none at that house, including nine children and their wives, had any idea of my pain. What was more, I learned that during our stay in Kushtia, the whole family were preparing to go to Dhaka, to attend the wedding of my second nephew's sister-in-law. I told my wife that this was the situation in that house, which she understood. We were preparing to start for my village of Dharmadaha on that day. While I was at my brother's house, one of my wife's brothers-in-law, a doctor, came to see her. He was a nice young man, very sophisticated and successful. Obviously he was sad at our loss and he said to Hashi:

"Never show your weakness to others; people may shed crocodile tears outside, but many are happy inside at your disaster". I think he was absolutely right.

So we started for our village on a rainy and humid day. We hired a microbus and, though it was the rainy season, the road was clear right to the front door of the house, a situation quite unthinkable when I was a student. It took us only one and a half hours to cover the distance of 36 miles, which in those days would have taken the best part of a day.

At the village, I met my eldest brother and his wife, who were both now very old. I met my nephews, all of them married and with children of their own. It had been my home, but that has now changed. The old house was destroyed in the civil war in 1971. Now only the land remained, but all other landmarks, including the coconut, jackfruit and mango trees had gone. I was virtually a stranger visiting, rather than a relative coming home. All the family and the villagers, men, women and children, flocked around us. The mood was sombre; some women wept behind their veils. My brother, a village headman and a religious man, consoled me that it was Allah's will, it was predestined and there was nothing one could do.

We had some discussion within the family as to what we could do in the village to keep Faisal's memory alive. There was a suggestion that there was no Madrassa – Islamic School – within 10 miles of the village, and it would help the boys and girls of the poor families if they could learn the reading and writing of the Quran, and also other subjects. This suggestion appealed to us and later we agreed to fund a school in the village. At the time of writing, it is a well-established institution in the locality, and has upwards of 400 pupils, boys and girls, from the age of five to eighteen. Pupils have taken the equivalent of GCSE Exams, with brilliant results.

I was glad that I was in my village on the 18th July 1998, the first anniversary of Faisal's death. Though I felt as though a fire was burning inside me, I was extremely busy from early morning, with my nephews and the village folk, to earmark an area for the proposed Madrassa. We located a plot of land adjacent to our dwelling house where my parents are buried. I liked the situation, approachable from the main road. We measured up the land, made a temporary boundary and a signpost was erected: "Proposed site for Faisal Wajed Dhakil Madrassa". It gave all of us a tremendous feeling and our minds were full of the Madrassa and how it would look. What would the future hold? How much money would be required? Who was going to supervise the work? All these questions occupied my mind and that is how the first anniversary of my Faisal's death was passed. During that day, some people came to consult me as a doctor, but I politely declined to see them and they were all too aware of the reason.

It was extremely hot and humid and at night it was almost unbearable. There were mosquitoes, creepy-crawlies and the unbearably humid heat. On top of that, we were still anxious about our personal security. We stayed in the village for three nights and most of them were virtually sleepless for me. My wife and Julekha managed to catch up with some sleep, because they had the only electric fan available in the house.

During those three days, I took my daughter to the bank of the river, which was full to the brim as always happens in the rainy season. I explained to her how, as a child, I used to jump into the swollen river from the cliff and how excited I used to be during this fishing season. It reminded me very much of my childhood, though I was told that the river no longer contained fish as it used to in the past, mainly because of over-fishing. I had binoculars with me, so did some bird-watching. The birds I watched were only known by local names, and there were no bird books available to give me their proper names.

We returned to Kushtia after three days and finalised plans for the Faisal Wajed Madrassa. I did not discuss it with my brother in Kushtia because I did not think it was necessary, as he had not shown any sympathy for my despair. Later, when he heard from other people, he criticised it. By this time I had lost all respect for him and it did not matter whether he was for or against it.

After staying for a few days in Kushtia, we returned to the UK, where my best friend, Mr Biswas, met us at the airport and drove us home in the pleasant sunshine. On our return home, the house felt empty, sad and lifeless. The garden was overgrown.

There were some cards of sympathy on the anniversary of Faisal's death, but what greeted us most was the emptiness. Over the past month in Bangladesh, we had always been surrounded by relations, friends and ordinary village folk, so there had been less time to dwell on our tragedy, but here we were again thinking about nothing but Faisal's absence. My son Sajal was in his flat and was on holiday. I spoke to him on the phone, but he made no attempt to come and see us. I wrote in my diary on 3rd August '98: "This is what is going to happen for the future".

I became busy at work and also looking after the garden, but my wife's depression returned, very much the same as it was before our travel to Bangladesh. I spoke to the GP for any help he could provide. He suggested some psychotherapy at the surgery and she continued with her weekly therapy for a few weeks.

The situation changed for the better when we got our daughter's 'A' level results at the end of August. She had managed to get the required grades for entry to medical school in Manchester. It was the single most uplifting bit of news for the whole family, particularly my wife. We thanked Allah the Almighty for this small mercy.

I continued my daily work routine, counting the days until my retirement. I did not take any interest in the medical politics of the hospital and I avoided my consultant colleagues if I possibly could. Though we were happy with my daughter's entry to medical school we felt very apprehensive about her study. She was still anorexic and looked unwell, as if all the strength had been drawn out of her. At eighteen she should have looked attractive, jubilant and full of life, with nothing to worry about, but her brother's death had crippled her psychologically. The reason she chose Manchester was that her brother had been at Leeds University, also in the north of England. It was a miracle and a great credit to her that she had made the grade.

Manchester was far from home, with no friends or relations nearby and we wondered how she was going to cope. Endless discussions took place between my wife and me, for there was no one we could ask for advice. My son and daughter-in-law were detached from the family and hardly took any interest in family affairs, either before or after the tragedy. In an ideal situation, particularly in eastern culture, the whole family sits down and discusses the situation and the view of the eldest son of the family carries a lot of weight. But in my situation, though I had a well-qualified, well-placed son and now equally well qualified daughter-in-law, I found them wanting in any family discussions or decisions. I tried my best but in the end we gave up. All the major decisions had to be taken by me, in close co-operation with my wife.

I had some money in my research fund, which had to be spent before I retired. So I decided to attend a European Congress in Rheumatology, in Geneva. I thought it would be a good opportunity to visit Switzerland and decided to take my wife and daughter. This would give them a further break from the monotonous and gloomy atmosphere at home.

We landed at Geneva Airport in the afternoon, settled down in our hotel on the edge of Lake Geneva, and went to the lavish reception for the delegates at another nearby hotel.

During my career as a consultant rheumatologist, I had had the opportunity to attend this sort of reception all over the world, but it had never before been possible to take my wife, because of our young family, so this was the first official reception that my wife, and for that matter, my daughter, had attended. The food was plentiful, drinks were in abundance and the whole atmosphere was pleasing. For an entire evening, we forgot our woes. Little did I know what was waiting for us the next day.

The following day, I went to attend the Conference and Hashi and my daughter went out on their own to look around the city and do some shopping. They had lunch out. Julekha had a sandwich with mayonnaise inside, which must have been infected. That night she had incessant diarrhoea and vomiting, and also had a bit of a temperature. She was already weak from the eating disorder, so this severe diarrhoea and vomiting made her very ill and dehydrated. We had been to Bangladesh and the remote village only the month before and remained well, yet here in Switzerland, in the heart of Europe, my daughter had been struck with food poisoning and was seriously ill.

We managed to get a doctor who agreed with me that it was food poisoning, but I found he was not interested in finding out the cause of it, which would have need the stool to be analysed. Instead, he suggested some intake of oral fluid, which she was unable to retain. I was extremely unhappy with her condition. In desperation, I asked for the doctor again that night; a new one came and I explained to him that my daughter was dehydrated, unable to retain any fluid and that frankly she needed to be admitted to hospital for intravenous fluid replacement. The doctor disagreed with me and advised us to leave things as they were.

The following day she was so weak that she was unable to get up from bed without help. Fortunately, her diarrhoea and vomiting had ceased, but the dehydration and weakness persisted. Her temperature abated. At the hotel, I found a Pakistani waiter, who had been very kind and concerned about us. With his help, we managed to get some oral re-hydration fluid, which we encouraged her to drink. The rest of our days we virtually spent within the four walls of our hotel room and the day we left Switzerland, on 10th September, she needed a wheelchair at the airport. She had to start at the university the following week.

In normal circumstances, the journey to the university for her to pursue a medical career, like her brother, would have been a joyful occasion. We parents would have been totally at ease in taking her to the Hall of Residence, for we had now accumulated enough experience with her two older brothers. But this time, instead of being happy, we all felt very sad that our Julekha was leaving home. This sadness was due to the shock of Faisal's death, which was still very fresh in our minds, and also she had not fully recovered from her illness the previous week

Nevertheless, we found the University of Manchester vibrant with young people. We took her to her self-contained room in a hall of residence, with a kitchen to be shared with other girls. Though it was a small and somewhat cramped room for her, with all her books and articles, I told her it was a thousand times better than mine in Bangladesh, which I had to share with at least two other boys. The following morning, with heavy hearts, we left Julekha in Manchester, some 180 miles from home and as we were leaving the university area, my wife started sobbing uncontrollably. Not only were we leaving our daughter behind, but Hashi had spotted a young man of similar age to that of our Faisal, similarly bearded and looking very much like him. He was sitting on the steps of a building, perhaps waiting for his parents. My wife asked me to stop the car, and had another good look at the boy, who did indeed have some similarity to Faisal. We drove past and set off for home.

So my daughter started her life as a medical student at Manchester, a city that would be more familiar to us during the next five years.

We would have lots of happy memories of that city: Julekha's success as a medical student, becoming lead violinist in the university orchestra and qualifying as a doctor.

At home that week in September, I was trimming the laurel hedge in the front garden. It reminded me of the last summer when I was cutting the hedge and Faisal and Aliyya had appeared. I had spotted a wasp nest and all three of us had laughed and joked about it. And now, this summer when I was doing the same, the laurel tree was still there, the wasps were again hovering around, but my Faisal was no more – far away from human reach. In every nook and corner of the house and the garden there was something connected with Faisal, reminding me of him, of his childhood, his teenage brooding years and his happiness with Aliyya.

By autumn 1998, Julekha had been at the University for three months. But she was finding it hard to continue with her studies. Physically she was exhausted by her anorexia, mentally she could not adjust to the loss of her brother and also she had no one from her old school as a friend. So she felt homesick and I was at a loss at what to tell her. I knew as a doctor how hard the medical course is, and that you have to keep up every day rather than "catch-up later". One day in November, when she came home, I put it to her that she had three options: continue to study and be a doctor; take a year off to think it over; or leave medicine and do something else.

Julekha is a very conscientious girl, very bright and has her feet on the ground. She understood what we were talking about. On her return to university, she made a renewed effort, and saw a clinical psychologist about her anorexia. Fortunately, she had a group of friends who were very helpful to her. Though they were not from the area, she struck up a friendship with some of them, which continues today. All of them qualified as doctors and are on their way to establishing themselves in society.

November is a month which is gloomy, becomes dark too quickly and has hardly any sunshine. The leaves are all brown and some trees are bare, and we all wait apprehensively for the coming winter. Though I started my work at the hospital, my mind remained clouded and sad for Faisal.

I decided to clean the roof of the conservatory, where the dirt had accumulated over the past year, to let the meagre sunshine through.

I had nearly finished, but when I came to the last two panels I was hurrying and my mind was not properly on the job. I missed the step of the ladder and fell from a height of six feet on to the concrete slab below. As soon as I hit the ground, I knew something was terribly wrong with me. I had severe backache and an unbearable pain in my right wrist. I was able to stand up and, holding my right wrist with the left hand, shouted for some help to my wife, who was indoors

An ambulance was called and I was taken to the A&E department of my own hospital. It must have been approximately one p.m. and I was supposed to do my clinics there at two. The doctor on call knew me, and immediately gave me a pethidine injection to relieve the acute pain. An x-ray showed a complicated fracture around the right wrist. I was admitted, and a consultant colleague did the internal fixing under general anaesthetic, followed by plaster immobilisation. The following day I was discharged and remained "left-handed" for six weeks. There were complications and whatever could go wrong with this fracture and its aftermath did go wrong. This happens at times even when one is a doctor

I got an invitation to attend a medical seminar in Paris. My right hand was still in plaster, but still I accepted the invitation and my wife accompanied me. We were met at the airport by a young man, driving the latest model of Mercedes-Benz car and we asked him to take us to the hotel, making a detour to visit the place where Princess Diana and Dodi Fayed had been killed. The driver was an ex-Army man and spoke good English. He took us through the underpass and pointed out the site of the accident.

After reaching home from Paris, Hashi remained reasonably well for a few days; then again the gloom returned. I kept myself busy at work, but for her, as the children were gone, she was alone at home, always thinking about our loss.

29

Pilgrimage

We decided things might be better if we made the Pilgrimage to Mecca, which would take us out of our home surroundings with all the memories of Faisal. It would help us spiritually to be at the centre of the Islamic holy places. Our daughter, herself very disturbed in her mind, wanted to accompany us, to spend the Christmas holidays with us in Mecca.

All three of us arrived at Jeddah Airport on the evening of 22ⁿᵈ December '98. My sister-in-law and her husband, both doctors, were working in Saudi Arabia and were waiting for us at the airport, with their daughter, Uki. All of us felt excited at meeting our own relations and being able to be present at the holy places in the holy month of Ramadhan. We stayed for two days in Jeddah, a beautiful city on the edge of the Red Sea. During the month of Ramadan month all the shops, restaurants and bazaars are closed and the place deserted, but it comes to life at sunset and remains vibrant throughout the night until the early morning.

On our first day in Jeddah, though we, the adults, were fasting, the two girls, Julekha and Uki, were not. We could not find any food for them anywhere, as all the outlets for selling food were closed. It would be wrong even to ask shopkeepers for food during the daytime and one might even be penalised. I am not sure how the non-Muslim expatriates cope during the Ramadan month.

On the evening of 23ʳᵈ December we sat, along with thousands of people, at the coast of the Red Sea with a red glow of sunshine as it was setting. All the people were waiting for the siren to indicate the time for breaking the Ramadan fast. It was really very enjoyable. After breaking our fast with a picnic that we had with us, we walked along the coast where there were lots of facilities to entertain children and adults. For the time being, all of us forgot the pain and anguish we had suffered over the past year. My wife was at last her usual self in the company of her sister in a different place. My wrist was still in a supportive bandage and it was still not possible to use it for carrying weight.

The following day, 24th December, we travelled to Mecca by taxi. All Muslims know about the two holy places, Mecca and Medina, and aspire to visit Mecca at least once in their lifetime. This is the holiest of holy places in Islam, for it was here the Prophet Muhammed was born in 570 AD and started preaching a new religion which is now known as Islam, and there are about a billion people who follow this religion, which has spread to all the continents of the globe.

Mecca is about forty miles from the port city of Jeddah, and we went there by taxi. Most of the taxi-drivers are either Afghans or Pakistanis. The journey was pleasant, the road was broad and smooth. Traffic was not too bad. As we approached the Holy City of Mecca I saw the road sign which prominently displayed "MUSLIMS ONLY". Non-Muslims are not allowed to enter the city perimeter at all. If they did, there would be severe punishment. As we proceeded to the city centre there were more signs of "Muslims only". There is a by-pass road for non-Muslims to avoid Mecca.

We arrived at the Holy City and made ourselves comfortable in the hotel. We then started the ritual of 'Umra' which is called the Lesser Pilgrimage. The main Pilgrimage is called Hajj, but the Umra is also a Pilgrimage though not as elaborate a ritual as Hajj, which we performed 10 years later.

There were two unforgettable moments.

Firstly the ritual of Umra requires certain dress codes. For men, this consists of two pieces of long towel, one around the waist, tied with a simple knot and covering the legs to just above the ankles, and the other piece covering the upper part of the body, but exposing the right arm. For women, as for men, the apparel is simple and white in colour. It consists of a long skirt and long blouse covering the whole body, only exposing the fingers and toes. The women also have to wear head-scarves. So when all the men and women assemble at the centre of the mosque, it looks like a white sea of about a million people. This goes up to more than three million during the Hajj Ceremony. This dress code symbolises equality and uniformity in the eyes of Allah. In this vast gathering, everybody is equal, whether a person is a rich millionaire from Saudi Arabia or the United States, a poor wood-cutter from the jungle of Africa, or a landless farmer from Bangladesh: they all are wearing only two pieces of cloth, standing in the scorching sun, seeking forgiveness from the Almighty. The other significance is that when a Muslim dies, he or she would be covered with a simple shroud, no matter how wealthy the person had been in life. Therefore, these two or three pieces of cloth are the only earthly belongings that would accompany you on your death. Indeed, many Muslims preserve these clothes with the intention of wrapping the body in them.

The other ritual is the circumambulation of the Kaaba, the cube-shaped house at the centre. Muslims believe this house was built by Abraham along with his son Ishmael, as ordered by Allah the Almighty. Muslims all over the world face towards this Kaaba, five times a day wherever in the world they are. Every Muslim house possesses a copy of the holy Quran and a picture of a black cube-like structure, the Kaaba. When I first saw this structure from a distance of about two hundred yards, I felt some change in myself and in fact my heart skipped a beat. I was overwhelmed with emotion, not only due to reverence, but also because nearly one billion Muslims scattered all around the globe pray towards this structure and aspire to visit this place at least once in his or her life time. The cube-like structure is surrounded by a large circular courtyard, beyond which there is a huge mosque, built and extended over the centuries. Inside the courtyard, the floor is spotlessly clean, made of white marble. One has to walk round the Kaaba seven times, anti-clockwise. For those who are near the Kaaba, the circumambulation, or *Tawaff* as it is called in Arabic, is shorter in distance than for those who are at the periphery of the circle. Those who are young, healthy and energetic remain close to Kaaba and can even touch it, but as for me, I did the seven times circling from the periphery. After each circle and also during it, one has to recite certain verses from the Quran. In Ramadan time, while fasting, to do those seven circles in the scorching heat was extremely physically demanding. Once this is completed, the next step is to walk between two hills called Saafa and Marwa, a distance of half a mile. Again one has to do it seven times, which symbolises the trouble Hagar, the wife of Abraham, faced, looking for water for her infant son, Ismael. She ran from one hill to the other seven times to find water. The legend says, and Muslims believe, that water was found on the instruction of Allah. This source of water is still there and is called Zam Zam water. All Muslims collect it and take it home at the end of the Pilgrimage, and some keep it to anoint their shrouds when they are buried.

To do the Umra and visit the most sacred places of Islam in Mecca and Medina was an experience never to be forgotten. It did give my wife and me peace of mind at a very vulnerable time. People fall back on religion at difficult times for comfort, and certainly we did get some consolation there, especially since my deceased son was particularly religious.

The visit also gave me a glimpse of Saudi society. Most people who visit the holy places either during the Hajj or the Umra are from rural areas of the world; many are illiterate and this may be the only time they come out of their village environment and experience an entirely different sort of world. For me it was different and I viewed Saudi customs from a different perspective.

Before I visited Saudi Arabia for the Umra, I had eye-witness accounts from two of my colleagues about the rude behaviour of the airport staff at all levels. My colleague, who also practiced medicine in England, became so fed up with unnecessary delays at the airport on his way out of the country – this was before 9/11 – that he went to complain at the desk. His punishment was to be sent to the back of the queue; as a result he missed his plane. He told me that he would rather visit Israel than Saudi Arabia. So I had some inkling of what to expect at the airport, but never did I expect such a negligent and careless attitude to the incoming passengers. At the entry, there was a kiosk where two people were working as entry officers. They both suddenly stopped work and had some tea and cigarettes, while there was a very long queue of tired people. They seemed not to care. At the Customs, the suitcases were opened and everything was scattered all over the place.

It seems "please", "sorry", and "thank you" does not exist in the Saudi vocabulary. My impression of Saudi Arabia is that they have become very rich, very suddenly, and hence the gradual evolution of human decency has not developed. During my stay of two weeks I never found any Saudi nationals who spoke politely, as you might expect in many other countries. The exception to this rule I was told by my brother-in-law, who was working there at the time, was their behaviour towards white people in general and Americans in particular. These people, whether from Europe or from anywhere in the world, got preference and experienced a very different attitude.

Another incident occurred during our stay which highlighted this lack of courtesy and respect.

People who visit Saudi Arabia for Umra or Hajj are given a visa which only allows visits to the holy places of Mecca and Medina. No one is allowed to go beyond the boundaries of these two cities. I think this restriction is justifiable because if there were open access to the whole of the kingdom, there would be thousands of illegal immigrants from the poorer countries. So I appreciate that there has to be a rigid rule about the movements of people who enter Saudi Arabia in order to visit the holy places, but there should perhaps be exceptions if there are valid reasons for seeking to visit other parts of the country.

Our relatives lived in the desert city of Hail, where my sister-in-law was a consultant histopathologist, and her husband, a consultant nephrologist. They came to meet us at Jeddah Airport, about an hour and a half's flight from Hail, and we would have liked to visit them in Hail, but the Saudi Embassy in London declined to grant permission. However, we gathered from our brother-in-law, who is a resident there, that we could visit them if we had a letter from the Governor of Hail, stating that he would be willing to accept us, and another permit from the Governor of Medina, to allow us to leave the boundary of Medina.

My brother-in-law had managed to get permission from the office of the Governor in Hail and he brought the letter with him. Now we needed permission from the office of the Governor in Medina. This was a nightmare.

We had only two days in Medina, during which we had to perform the religious rites, pay homage to the grave of the Prophet and the other two Caliphs buried there, and try to get the permission we needed from the Governor's office.

The Governor's office was a short distance by taxi from where we were staying. On the first day we could make no headway. Nobody wanted to know about us. All the people in the Governor's office had a laid-back attitude and the office itself was closed by mid-afternoon during Ramadan. The first step was to fill in a set of forms, all in Arabic which I couldn't read. My brother-in-law, though fluent in spoken Arabic, could not read or write the language, so we had to find a Saudi national who would act as a guarantor. How and where were we to find this person? The situation seemed hopeless, but the following day, the last day of our stay in Medina, with the help of a Bangladeshi doctor, we managed to get a Saudi national, a very nice and pious man named Ali, to accompany us to the Governor's office and sign the necessary declaration. We thanked him profusely.

The afternoon was drawing to a close and we were nowhere near getting the permission. There were many other people waiting like us and I was told that we needed photographs of myself, my wife and daughter, and that we also had to pay a fee of 100 Saudi Riyals per head, which had to be submitted to the State Bank nearby. We would then get a receipt which we would have to produce to the clerk along with our passports. And this had to be done before the office closed at 3.30 pm, which meant I had only one hour to do all these tasks. Given the attitude of the Government officers, I had no hope whatsoever that this would be possible, and I was thinking of returning to England from Medina, which would have been a great disappointment. Then something unexpected happened. As I was loitering in the long corridor of the Governor's office and thinking about the situation, I noticed a door slightly ajar, and a smart looking young man sitting at his desk in a military uniform, with a Captain's insignia on his epaulette. I knocked on the door and entered his room. He could speak few words of English, but was very well behaved. Without much delay I brought out my British passport and left it in front of him and tried to explain to him that I was a doctor and a consultant physician, holding a British passport, working in England, and that I wanted to visit my sister-in-law in Hail, but was having this uphill struggle. By this time, my brother-in-law, spotted me there and joined in. He spoke excellent Arabic and explained matters in detail to the officer, who listened carefully and pressed a bell. In came the clerk with whom we had been dealing for the past two days. The officer looked at his watch and told the clerk in Arabic that before the office closed in an hour's time he must get the necessary permit ready. The clerk took our passports and got on with the job; no photographs and no fees were required. We sat in the office with the captain, who showed us the insignia of a major, a rank to which he had been promoted, and so he would shortly be leaving that office. We congratulated him and thanked him profusely for the enormous help he had given us. Since my brother-in-law and I were both doctors, he started telling us about his own physical problems, and we listened very sympathetically. While we were still in the office, the clerk came back with a piece of paper with all the signatures and necessary stamps. We had the permission and our passports; once again, we thanked the major and left the office.

My wife and sister-in-law were not aware what was going on and so they had gone out. We now needed to leave for the coach station immediately, to catch the last coach for the six-hour journey. Time for another nightmare. We were waiting in a taxi with all the luggage, and as soon as we spotted the two sisters, we shouted to them to jump in. We arrived at the coach station, just as the last coach was leaving. We stopped it, bought the tickets and hopped in. The coach was nearly empty, with only a few passengers, and we set off towards Hail.

Hail is a desert town some 250 miles north of Medina. At one time, it was all desert with perhaps a few oases of palm groves, but now, with the petrodollars, it is a thriving town with modern hospitals, shopping malls and wide roads. It was in the District General Hospital that my sister-in-law and her husband worked.

On the coach, my impression of Saudi citizens changed favourably. There was a Saudi man sitting next to me in full Arab dress who asked me to offer my hand to him. I could not understand what he was saying. My brother-in-law explained that he wanted to offer some perfume to me. I accepted it and thanked him. It was a friendly gesture and broke the ice for that long journey through the desert. The road was magnificent, the coach was ultra-modern and the driver was an Indian. There were only ten passengers (of which we were six), two of them children.

It was the month of Ramadan and of course, everyone was fasting. The coach stopped at a filling station to break the fast. The place reminded me of Wild West films. There were one-storey prefabricated houses, where stoutly-built, long distance lorry drivers were lying down on wooden beds, waiting for the sun to go down. We passed through the rows of wooden beds, where there were no women and we were given a secluded area designed for families.

The sun was setting in the desert far away, and I had seen a sunset over the sea, but this was a sunset in the desert and was equally beautiful and very peaceful.

After breaking our fast, we boarded the coach again in the dark, and travelled on through the desert. During our journey to Hail, we were stopped at least twice at checkpoints, where we had to show the correct documents which we had had so much trouble getting. We arrived safely in Hail at around 10 p.m. and made ourselves comfortable in our sister-in-law's apartment within the hospital compound.

It was the end of December 1998, though we had never noticed how Christmas came and went. On the 31st December a group of doctors from the hospital arranged a party to which we were invited. There was a lot of Indian food, but no alcoholic drinks. We stayed until after midnight, when the New Year started.

During our stay in Hail, we went into the desert in a four-wheeler jeep, owned by Riad, a Saudi colleague of my sister-in-law's. Our destination was a small village where there is the grave of a sixth century AD Arab poet called Hatem Tai. This name was well known to me, as a boy in rural Bengal, from stories of his generosity. His real name was Hatim al-Tai, a Bedouin from the Tai tribe. He died a few years after the birth of the Prophet, before the revelations of the Quran. Riad told me that quite a lot of people from the Indian sub-continent visit this place. When we reached the place there was virtually nothing to see: an area was cordoned off and his grave was somewhere within that area. In strict Islamic tradition, which Saudi Arabians follow, there should be no markings for a grave, even if the person had been rich and famous

From there we trundled on further into the desert, where there was no road, no markings and the driving was by satellite navigation. Wherever one looked, it was golden sand, which had its own beauty. Within this huge desert we spotted the greenery of some palm groves. I asked Riad to go near the oasis and stop. There was a well and a few goats were wandering about. Riad shouted in Arabic for anyone inside a small hut. A young man came out and from his appearance I immediately guessed he was not a Saudi, nor an Arab, but must be from the Indian sub-continent, probably from Bangladesh. I was right. I could not believe that any human being could live in such an isolated place. It turned out that he had been living there for five years. The land was owned by a Saudi man, and this man's job was to look after the goats and water the date trees and some vegetables. I asked him whether there were any other people nearby. He said a mile from there, there was a similar oasis where all of his relatives live and they often meet. He was from a remote village in Bangladesh, earning some money with which he intended to buy a shop in his village, get married and start a family. We wished him luck and left.

On our way back to our house, we stopped at a crossroads where I found two desert wolves had been shot and hung with a rope. Riad explained that the wolves are a real menace to the farmers; so sometimes they shoot them and keep them hanging to deter the other wolves. Because of the dry desert conditions, the corpse does not decompose and remains mummified for quite a long time.

We left Hail by air on a short internal flight to Jeddah on 4th January 1999, and flew home early the following day

So the New Year of 1999 started. Julekha resumed her study in Manchester. I went back to work, with very little contact with colleagues, friends or relations. Over the past eighteen months we had come to realise that in this world you are on your own feet. True, there might be one or two people who would stop and enquire after you, perhaps sympathise, but in the main you have to pick up the pieces yourself and move on, so that is what I did, and started looking forward to my retirement.

Faisal in 1997

Epilogue

T wenty long years have passed since I lost my son, Faisal. With his death I fell from the top of the tree, like the title of this book.

Faisal died on my 60th birthday and now I am well over 80 years, a ripe old age in any culture. Twenty years is a long time, and the wound may have healed but the deep scar remains which hurts me in every waking hour of my life. I consider myself like a man with the loss of one leg, hobbling towards the finishing line of the race of life.

Over the past twenty years, lots of water has passed down the River Thames, and I have lost so many relatives and friends but there have been additions to the family as well.

I was due to retire in 2003, but the Hospital Trust wanted me to continue for another year while they reorganised the post. I complied and stayed until 2004.

In July 2004, my secretary Joy Jones who had been with me for twenty years and shared the same birth date also retired at the same time. She, along with other staff in the department organised a farewell party, attended by the nurses, physiotherapists, clinical and other ancillary workers. A consultant surgeon colleague gave a speech and I was presented with a two-seater wooden garden bench and an album containing many photographs from my days when I started twenty-four years earlier until my retirement. They were such moving photographs and I never even realised they existed. Those presents are still in my proud possession.

I left the hospital with a heavy heart. Though I have been happy at my work and have rendered satisfactory services to the community, the death of my son at the same hospital overshadowed everything else. Overwhelming sadness and grief surpassed all other emotions.

Four months after my retirement, a consultant colleague organised a black-tie dinner. My wife Hasina and I were the chief guests.

After the dinner, the Chairman of the Medical Staff Committee, in his speech, paid handsome tribute to my work at the hospital for the past twenty-four years. He also mentioned that tragic event in July 1997 saying that the "whole Trust was stunned and stopped for a while on that fateful day".

In reply, I thanked everyone for organising the dinner and revealed that a secondary school had been established in my son's name in my village in rural Bangladesh. Everybody was pleased and appreciative of the news and even twenty years later some of my colleagues not only enquire about the welfare of the school, but make modest contributions to the 'Faisal Wajed Memorial Trust' - a registered charity both in the UK and in Bangladesh, which has tried to benefit my childhood home area in a number of ways.

In Bangladesh, we have established a secondary school in my native village of Dharmadaha. It has more than three hundred pupils, mainly from poor backgrounds. Girls outnumber the boys. The first batch did their GCSE's in 2004. It is situated over an acre of land with a two-story 'U' shaped building with 18 teachers and other ancillary staff.

The results from the school are outstanding. Many pupils from the school have been to university to study economics, engineering, medicine and other subjects. Many school leavers, mainly girls, have joined the thriving garment industry in the capital Dhaka, while others have joined the armed forces.

We visit the school, which is known locally as the Madrassa, every year. It gives us comfort that Faisal is remembered through the school. In one of these visits, my wife asked a small boy who was going to the school clutching some books where he was going. He answered he was going to "Faisal Wajed Madrassa". It made her happy. The little boy never knew who we were and who Faisal was.

We have recently built a further extension to the existing building and have applied for permission for a Vocational Training Centre. If it is approved by the Government, there will be further opportunities for the village girls in enhancing their technical skills.

At the request of the villagers, the Trust procured an acre of land on the banks of Mathabhanga River and built a wall for a cemetery for the poor and landless people of the village. There is a small prayer room within the cemetery and a number of commemorative benches along the banks of the river where people can sit and relax. It is really a very worthwhile place for the villagers to visit.

There are also scholarships for the poor and needy students who go on for higher studies. Some funds are provided for buying books, clothes and transportation to travel to other parts of the country.

We also make donations to the Deaf, Dumb and Blind Society as and when asked for.

In England, regular sums of money are donated every year on Faisal's birthday to a local primary school where Faisal studied and was very happy. With this money, needy students are financed for school outings where the parents are unable to contribute. Also, a corner of the school library has been named after him with a plaque in his name.

In Verulamium Park, St. Albans, a commemorative metal bench has been installed on a prime location, under a 150-year-old oak tree, close to the Roman wall, with the inscription 'Dedicated to the loving memory of Faisal, (1973-97) who played in these fields as a child; From his parents Dr and Mrs Wajed'.

I feel happy when I see a mother sitting on the bench and the children playing nearby. It gives me immense peace of mind. A wooden plaque in Faisal's name has been installed in the wall of the recently opened museum, at the St. Albans City Centre.

I visit Faisal's grave every Friday, whatever the weather. His is one of the best kept graves in the Muslim section of the local cemetery. The headstone is kept neat and tidy. On the anniversary of his death, I put white roses, one for every year since his death and put an advert in the national newspaper 'In memoriam' column.

Sometimes in good weather I sit there on my own and think about him and how he would have looked now, had he been alive. I kept imagining that probably he would have receding hair and a few streaks of grey in his black beard. I talk to him and ask his forgiveness for not being pro-active and not being able to keep him, although I am a doctor.

Over the past 20 years I have lost my eldest brother Mohammed Rafiz Uddin in my native village. He died in very old age, about mid 90's. He was the main breadwinner for the family, a very pious and God-fearing man. Also, I lost my eldest sister-in-law Sakina Begum, wife of my eldest brother. She also died of old age and was a mother figure to me.

I lost my parents-in-law, Mohammed Habibur Rahman and Mrs Rabia Rahman, who were responsible for looking after my wife and new-born son, when I left for England.

My elder brother, Ibrahim Hossain who was primarily responsible for the guidance in my upbringing, and encouraged me to study medicine, died not long ago, due to age-related illness. My sister-in-law, Mrs Hazera Begum, also died of pancreatic cancer. During her illness, as well as my brother's illness, I have contributed whatever monetary assistance needed. May their souls rest in peace. I also lost my sister Zarina Begum. I had three sisters, the eldest of whom died of cholera in 1942 when I was five years old. Now I have only one surviving sibling well over 90 years old.

Also in Bangladesh, my brother-in-law, holding the position of Chief Engineer in the Government of Bangladesh, died at a young age. His name was Abdul Quader. We remain grateful to him for building the Eastern wing of the school, in Faisal's memory.

Here in England, I have lost many of my friends and acquaintances over the past twenty years. Notable among them is my secretary Joy Jones, who became a family friend and who started to transcribe this manuscript.

Also I mention the name of Sunil Biswas, who was known to us since we moved to St. Albans in 1979. He was always there when we needed him. He is the one who received my brother-in-law Kafi at the airport during those dark days. When he heard the news of Faisal's death, he just cried like a child. I tried my best to repay his debt when he was ill with pancreatic cancer.

There is a special mention of another friend, Amal Majumder OBE. During the days immediately after Faisal's death, he was always with me, encouraging me to talk, accompanying me wherever I went. I tried my best to help him during the last days of his life. His family asked me to give a eulogy at his funeral, which I did and I still have that speech. His widow, Mrs Chandrima Majumder remains a close family friend and has generously donated £10,000 to the Faisal Wajed Memorial Trust which we have used to make a first-floor extension to the school and named it 'Majumder Hall'.

My son, Shajehan Wajed, a Fellow of the Royal College of Surgeons of England and now established as consultant surgeon in a hospital in the south-west of England is happily married to Rachel, a physician specialising in paediatric oncology.

We are blessed with five grandchildren. My son's children, Rebekah, Adam and Daniel, are now teenagers. Rebekah was ten years old when she visited her ancestral home in the district of Kushtia in Bangladesh, and saw the school where Dada (Bangladesh name for paternal grandfather) went. She thoroughly enjoyed her stay in the village. Though she could not speak the local language, she mixed with the relatives, girls and boys of her age.

Julekha gets her MRCP in 2009.

My daughter Julekha Wajed, who was so traumatised after her brother's death, against all the odds made the grades to get into medical school and graduated from the Manchester School of Medicine. She is now a Fellow of the Royal College of Physicians of London and well established as consultant rheumatologist in a renowned hospital in Surrey. She is happily married to Mr Ashar Wadoodi, a Fellow of the Royal College of Surgeons of England. Ashar is a transplant surgeon in a teaching hospital in London.

Julekha has given us two grandchildren. Rafi is now four years old, and he keeps me amused with his interesting and inquisitive questions. He helps me in the garden in the same way my Faisal did. Rafi has a sister Ishaal, who is 18 months old.

All the grandchildren live quite far away from us, but we try to visit as and when possible. We enjoy their company.

In my personal life, I have maintained the Licence to Practise as required by the General Medicine Council. I still do part-time consultancy work, when the opportunity arises, which allows me to go out of the house, and enjoy treating the patients, and keep in touch with the latest developments in my speciality.

By the Grace of Almighty I am still physically active enough to look after my garden and do DIY tasks around the household.

Though I am not in tune with modern technology, I still manage the basics with a computer.

Though twenty years have passed since we lost Faisal, it seems we can never get over it; this is something the sufferer only can appreciate.

When I see the tragic deaths of young people and their parents' grief on the TV, I truly realise the agony they are going through.

In writing this book, at least I have been able to offload some of my mental anguish.

Acknowledgments

In writing this book, I pay tribute to my wife Hasina Wajed, who came to this country at a very young age with limited knowledge in English, having no relations and friends. While I was busy with my post graduate study and surviving on pittance from a government scholarship, she raised three children, catering for all their needs. As young mother she did it with courage, conviction, enthusiasm and common sense. It was when the children left home that we lost our middle son, which prompted me to write this memoir. To this day, she remains the anchor for the family, advising the grown-up children and grandchildren. I am grateful to her for not enquiring too much about what I am writing, and trusting that after 51 years of marriage I have nothing but love and respect for her.

The draft of the manuscript of this book was completed 20 years ago. I have been hesitant to get it published. Even when it was submitted to the publisher I sought the advice of my son Shahjehan Wajed, whose answer was typical of a surgeon "You have a story to tell, Dad, so get it published and be damned". My daughter Julekha Wajed enquired from time to time "How is the autobiography coming on, Dad?"

In Bangladesh, my brother-in-law A.H. Kafi, a highly intelligent and successful man, had always been a great help in every situation, and along with his wife Jesmine Jahan (Daisy) he will be delighted to see this book published, for we have discussed it with them many times in the past.

My friend Brigadier M. Salim who has kindly written the foreword for this book, was my roommate and class friend in the first year in medical school. We still meet from time to time. He himself is a published author of professional books and has always encouraged me to publish my memoir. At one time, he even offered to get it published in Pakistan.

Dr Ali Akbar, another brother-in-law of mine, an agricultural scientist resident of Canada offered his expertise to get it published online . I remain grateful for the offer.

In England, I am most grateful to Janet Beazley for typing and re-typing the manuscript and submitting it to the publisher. I have lost count as how many times I have visited her home in Hatfield.

My thanks are due to Raymond Canham, the photographer who took the family portrait in happier times, for his help with the photographs used in the book. I am also grateful Subbir Hussain (Abir) from Bangladesh, for the work he has done in supplying the maps of India.

My sincere thanks to John Chandler for the cover design.

Finally, this book would never have seen the light of the day without the direct assistance and guidance from Karl Sabbagh. I knew Karl from his writing in various journals, periodicals and books but only recently I found out that he is also the managing director of Skyscraper Publications. I remain extremely grateful to Karl and his wife Sue for editing the original manuscript, correcting the grammatical mistakes and advising me as how the book should be presentable to readers worldwide. My appreciation and thanks to Sue Sabbagh for the hospitality extended whenever we have visited them.